SHAKESPEARE IN PRODUCTION

THE MERCHANT OF VENICE

For over four hundred years, in every country where Shakespeare's plays have been performed, *The Merchant of Venice* has aroused controversy and excitement.

This edition is the first to offer a comprehensive account of the *Merchant* in performance. Charles Edelman's introduction challenges many of the myths and preconceptions associated with the play, and shows how historical events and cultural attitudes have shaped actors' interpretations and audience responses. The commentary, printed alongside the text, describes how different actors, directors and designers have approached each character and episode on stage, film and television, from the first performances in the 1590s down to the present day.

The extraordinary variety of *The Merchant of Venice* in production, from England to the United States, from Germany to Israel, from Canada to Australia to China, presented here in a clear and original way, will give every reader new and different insights into one of Shakespeare's most powerful but troubling plays.

SHAKESPEARE IN PRODUCTION

SERIES EDITORS: J. S. BRATTON AND JULIE HANKEY

This series offers students and researchers the fullest possible staging of individual Shakespearean texts. In each volume a substantial introduction presents a conceptual overview of the play, marking out the major stages of its representation and reception. The commentary, presented alongside the New Cambridge edition of the text itself, offers detailed, line-by-line evidence for the overview presented in the introduction, making the volume a flexible tool for further research. The editors have selected interesting and vivid evocations of settings, acting and stage presentation and range widely in time and space.

ALREADY PUBLISHED

A Midsummer Night's Dream, edited by Trevor R. Griffiths
Much Ado About Nothing, edited by John F. Cox
Antony and Cleopatra, edited by Richard Madelaine
Hamlet, edited by Robert Hapgood
The Tempest, edited by Christine Dymkowski
King Henry V, edited by Emma Smith
Romeo and Juliet, edited by James N. Loehlin
The Taming of the Shrew, edited by Elizabeth Schafer

FORTHCOMING VOLUMES

Macbeth, edited by John Wilders
Twelfth Night, edited by Elizabeth Schafer
Troilus and Cressida, edited by Frances Shirley

THE MERCHANT OF VENICE

EDITED BY
CHARLES EDELMAN
Edith Cowan University, Australia

PUBLISHED BY THE PRESS SYNDICATE OF THE UNIVERSITY OF CAMBRIDGE
The Pitt Building, Trumpington Street, Cambridge CB2 IRP, United Kingdom

CAMBRIDGE UNIVERSITY PRESS
The Edinburgh Building, Cambridge CB2 2RU, UK
40 West 20th Street, New York, NY 10011-4211, USA
477 Williamstown Road, Port Melbourne, VIC 3207, Australia
Ruiz de Alarcón 13, 28014 Madrid, Spain
Dock House, The Waterfront, Cape Town 8001, South Africa

http://www.cambridge.org

First published 2002

Printed in the United Kingdom at the University Press, Cambridge
Typeset in Monotype Ehrhardt 10/12.5pt, in QuarkXPress™ [SE]
A catalogue record for this book is available from the British Library

ISBN 0 521 77338 5 hardback
ISBN 0 521 77429 2 paperback

Some portions of this book have appeared, in different form,
in *Shakespeare Survey* and *Theatre Notebook*.

For Stratford's Gang of Three

CONTENTS

ILLUSTRATIONS

SERIES EDITORS' PREFACE

It is no longer necessary to stress that the text of a play is only its starting-point, and that only in production is its potential realised and capable of being appreciated fully. Since the coming-of-age of Theatre Studies as an academic discipline, we now understand that even Shakespeare is only one collaborator in the creation and infinite recreation of his play upon the stage. And just as we now agree that no play is complete until it is produced, so we have become interested in the way in which plays often produced – and pre-eminently the plays of the national Bard, William Shakespeare – acquire a life history of their own, after they leave the hands of their first maker.

Since the eighteenth century Shakespeare has become a cultural con-struct: sometimes the guarantor of nationhood, heritage and the status quo, sometimes seized and transformed to be its critic and antidote. This latter role has been particularly evident in countries where Shakespeare has to be translated. The irony is that while his status as national icon grows in the English-speaking world, his language is both lost and renewed, so that for good or ill, Shakespeare can be made to seem more urgently 'relevant' than in England or America, and may become the one dissenting voice that the censors mistake as harmless.

'Shakespeare in Production' gives the reader, the student and the scholar a comprehensive dossier of materials – eye-witness accounts, contemporary criticism, promptbook marginalia, stage business, cuts, additions and rewrit-ings – from which to construct an understanding of the many meanings that the plays have carried down the ages and across the world. These materials are organised alongside the New Cambridge Shakespeare text of the play, line by line and scene by scene, while a substantial introduction in each volume offers a guide to their interpretation. One may trace an argument about, for example, the many ways of playing Queen Gertrude, or the politi-cal transmutations of the text of *Henry V*; or take a scene, an act or a whole play, and work out how it has succeeded or failed in presentation over four hundred years.

For, despite our insistence that the plays are endlessly made and remade by history, Shakespeare is not a blank, scribbled upon by the age. Theatre history charts changes, but also registers something in spite of those changes. Some productions work and others do not. Two interpretations may be entirely different, and yet both will bring the play to life. Why? Without setting out to give absolute answers, the history of a play in the theatre can often show where the energy and shape of it lie, what has made it tick, through many permutations. In this way theatre history can find common ground with literary criticism. Both will find suggestive directions in the introductions to these volumes, while the commentaries provide raw material for readers to recreate the living experience of theatre, and become their own eye-witnesses.

J. S. Bratton
Julie Hankey

This series was originated by Jeremy Treglown and published by Junction Books, and later by Bristol Classical Press, as 'Plays in Performance'. Four titles were published; all are now out of print.

ACKNOWLEDGMENTS

Without the advice and encouragement of many, this book could never have begun, no less been completed.

Werner Habicht offers proof, if proof is necessary, that the most distinguished Shakespeareans are invariably the most generous with their time and knowledge. If readers find this book worthwhile, much of the credit belongs to him, and to Jonathan Bate, Julia Briggs, Alan Brissenden, Alan Dessen, John Drakakis, Alison Findlay, Penny Gay, Andrew Gurr, Michael Hamburger, Michael Hattaway, Dennis Kennedy, Ton Hoenselaars, Wilhelm Hortmann, Rosalind King, Alexander Leggatt, Avraham Oz, Carol Chillington Rutter, Kate Shaw, R. S. White and to other friends, colleagues and students.

Two editors of other volumes in this series, Richard Madelaine and John Wilders, offered much valuable advice. The fine actor, Gordon Gould, and equally fine director, Jack O'Brien, also have my thanks for their willingness to share their reminiscences with me.

I must thank my colleague Wolfgang Frick for his expert work in translating documents from the German; I have also imposed upon Peter Bedford, Dragana Zivancevic, Bill Leadbetter and Fr. David Watt for their knowledge of Hebrew, Spanish, Latin and matters historical.

I could not have done without the assistance of my very professional colleagues at the Edith Cowan University Library, the Scholars Centre at the University of Western Australia Library and the staff at the many libraries, museums and theatres around the world. In England, I benefited from the expertise and courtesy to be found at the Shakespeare Centre and Shakespeare Institute at Stratford, and at the London Theatre Museum. Louise Ray at the Royal National Theatre was extraordinarily helpful.

In the United States and Canada, those at the Folger Shakespeare Library, the Theatre Collection of the New York Public Library and the Harvard University Theatre Collection helped me through a maze of potential problems, as did Ellen Charendoff and Jane Edmonds at the Stratford Ontario archives, Jim Taylor at the Washington Area Performing Arts Video Archive, and Robert Orchard, Katalin Mitchell and others at the American Repertory Theatre. Thanks also to the Columbia University Library, and to Tom Leowe of the University of Michigan's Theatre Department.

Part of my research was done while I had the privilege of being a member of the Common Room at Wolfson College, Oxford – my appreciation to Professor Jon Stallworthy and his colleagues for their kindness and hospitality. My thanks to the School of International, Cultural and Community Studies of Edith Cowan University for awarding me a travel grant.

Finally, I am grateful to the general editors of the 'Shakespeare in Production' series, J. S. Bratton and Julie Hankey, and to Sarah Stanton of Cambridge University Press, for inviting me to do this edition, and for providing such expert guidance. As usual, Lesley, Jacob and David Edelman offered support and assistance.

EDITOR'S NOTE

My first experience of the *Merchant* in performance was in 1962, when CBS TV broadcast the New York Shakespeare Festival's production from Central Park. Since then, especially in the past few years, I have seen a good many other productions – some in person, others by the archival videotapes now held in increasing numbers by theatre companies and libraries. When the practice of recording productions first began, these tapes were hardly watchable, but now the quality can be so high that one is able to gain a genuine impression of the performance.

Obviously, almost all of the commentary in this book is taken from reviews, biographies and other printed sources, but where no reference is given for an observation on a more recent performance, the reader may assume that it is my own.

THE SALADS, LANCELOT, ARRAGON

The text of the play given here is identical to M. M. Mahood's 1987 edition for Cambridge University Press, which serves up three 'Salads', as they are usually called: Solanio, Salarino and Salerio. But some editions, and nearly all productions, combine Salarino and Salerio into one character, and give him the latter's name.

In my introduction and commentary, where the distinction is unimportant, I silently change Salerio to Salarino, but when commenting on an actor's interpretation, I have been forced to adopt the somewhat clumsy, but I hope clear, Salerio/Salarino. When discussing Solanio and his friend together, I take the coward's way out and use 'the Salads', although I quite like the great theatrical diarist Gordon Crosse's 'Sallies'.

Lancelot is often spelled Launcelot, and Arragon is often Aragon. Except in quotations, I have adopted Mahood's spelling.

ABBREVIATIONS

Amer. I	Shattuck, *Shakespeare On the American Stage*, vol. I
Amer. II	Shattuck, *Shakespeare On the American Stage*, vol. II
Annals. I	Odell, *Annals of the New York Stage*, vol. I
Annals. II	Odell, *Annals of the New York Stage*, vol. II
APA	Association of Producing Artists
ART	American Repertory Theatre
BDET	*Boston Daily Evening Traveler*
BET	*Boston Evening Transcript*
BG	*Boston Globe*
ctd	cited
CR	*Chicago Review*
CSM	*Christian Science Monitor*
CT	*Chicago Tribune*
CW	*Catholic World*
DM	*Daily Mail*, London
DT	*Daily Telegraph*, London
Enc	*Encounter*
ETJ	*Educational Theatre Journal*
FT	*Financial Times*, London
GCA	*Globe and Commercial Advertiser*, New York
Gdn	*Guardian*, London
GM	*Globe and Mail*, Toronto
HR	*Hudson Review*
IHT	*International Herald Tribune*
Ind	*Independent*, London
IO	*Inter Ocean*, Chicago
Irv.Amer	*Mr Henry Irving and Miss Ellen Terry in America*
JC	*Jewish Chronicle*, London
JE	*Jewish Exponent*, New York
JP	*Jerusalem Post*
LD	*Literary Digest*, New York
Lst	*The Listener*
Macl	*Macleans*
NQ	*Notes and Queries*
NR	*New Republic*

NS	*New Statesman*
NYDN	*New York Daily News*
NYP	*New York Post*
NYPL	New York Public Library
NYRB	*New York Review of Books*
NYT	*New York Times*
Obs	*Observer*, London
PAC	*Performing Arts in Canada*
pmt	promptbook
PP	*Plays and Players*
qtd	quoted
RSC	Royal Shakespeare Company
SB	*Shakespeare Bulletin*
Shak. I	Odell, *Shakespeare from Betterton to Irving*, vol. I
Shak. II	Odell, *Shakespeare from Betterton to Irving*, vol. II
SN	*Shakespeare Newsletter*
SQ	*Shakespeare Quarterly*
SR	*Saturday Review*
SS	*Shakespeare Survey*
ST	*Sunday Times*, London
TA	*Theatre Arts*
TES	*Times Educational Supplement*
TJ	*Theatre Journal*
TLS	*Times Literary Supplement*
TW	*Theatre World*
VV	*Village Voice*, New York
WSJ	*Wall Street Journal*
WP	*Washington Post*

Note

Journal references appear in an abbreviated form in the text, but can be found in full in the Bibliography.

PRODUCTIONS

This list provides a guide to productions mentioned in the text. For earlier productions, the year indicates the first, or most significant performance of a particular actor or by a particular company – throughout the eighteenth and nineteenth centuries, English, American and German actors worked at many theatres in the course of their careers, so a complete and detailed chronology is not possible here.

Unless otherwise noted, English theatres are located in London, but even in the age of the patent duopoly, the luminaries of Drury Lane and Covent Garden frequently performed in Ireland and in other cities in England. American productions that had their main run in New York often toured elsewhere. Productions at Stratford, with the exception of John Barton's in 1978, were in the Shakespeare Memorial Theatre, later renamed the Royal Shakespeare Theatre.

In early productions especially, Portia was played by any number of actresses. Only the main ones, where they are known, are given here.

Year	Manager/ Director	Company/ Theatre	Shylock	Portia
*c.*1596	W. Shakespeare (author)	Lord Chamberlain's		
1605	Shakespeare	King's Men		
1701	George Granville (author)	Lincoln's Inn Fields	Thomas Doggett	Anne Bracegirdle
1741	Charles Macklin	Drury Lane	Macklin	Kitty Clive
1752	Lewis Hallam	Williamsburg	Patrick Malone	Beatrice Hallam
1767	Charles Macklin	Covent Garden	Macklin	Maria Macklin Elizabeth Younge [Mrs Pope]
1777	F. L. Schröder	National, Hamburg	Schröder	Dorothea Ackermann
1783	A. W. Iffland	National, Mannheim	Iffland	Karoline Renschübb
1784	J. P. Kemble	Drury Lane	Kemble	Elizabeth Kemble
1786	J. P. Kemble	Drury Lane	Tom King	Sarah Siddons

Year	Manager/ Director	Company/ Theatre	Shylock	Portia
1797	Ferdinand Fleck	National, Berlin	Fleck	
1800	G. F. Cooke	Covent Garden	Cooke	Harriet Murray
1803	J. P. Kemble	Covent Garden	Cooke	Sarah Siddons
1814	Edmund Kean	Drury Lane	Kean	Miss Smith
*c.*1815	Ludwig Devrient	National, Berlin	Devrient	
*c.*1835	Karl Seydelmann	National, Berlin	Seydelmann	
1836	Charles Kemble	Covent Garden	Kemble	Helen Faucit
1837	Benjamin Webster	Haymarket	Samuel Phelps	Polly Huddart [Mrs Warner]
1839	William Macready	Haymarket	Macready	Helen Faucit
1841	William Macready	Drury Lane	Macready	Mary Warner
1852	Karl Quanter	Hoftheater, Dresden	B. Dawison	
1853	Catherine Sinclair	San Francisco Theatre	Edwin Booth	Sinclair
1854	Edwin Booth/ Laura Keene	Royal Victoria, Sydney	Booth	Keene
1858	Charles Kean	Princess's	Kean	Ellen Tree [Mrs Kean]
1861	Edwin Booth	Winter Garden, NY	Booth	Jane Eliza Thomson [Mrs Charles Young]
1867	Edwin Booth	Winter Garden/ Haymarket	Booth	Marie Methua Scheller
1875	Augustin Daly	USA tour	E. L. Davenport	Carlotta Leclercq
1875	Squire Bancroft/ Marie Bancroft	Prince of Wales	Charles Coghlan	Ellen Terry
1875	F. von Dingelstedt	Burgtheater, Vienna	F. Mitterwurzer	
1879	Henry Irving	Lyceum	Irving	Ellen Terry
1886	Lawrence Barrett	USA tour	Barrett	Minna Gale
1887	F. R. Benson	Stratford	Benson	Ethel Johnson
1889	Barrett/Booth	USA tour	Booth	Helena Modjeska Minna Gale
1893	F. R. Benson	Stratford	Lyall Swete	Constance Benson
1893	Richard Mansfield	USA tour	Mansfield	Beatrice Cameron
1894	F. R. Benson	New Theatre, Oxford	Benson	Constance Benson

Year	Manager/ Director	Company/ Theatre	Shylock	Portia
1897	Ben Greet	Olympic	Nutcombe Gould	Lily Hanbury
1897 ff.	F. R. Benson	Stratford/touring	Benson	Constance Benson Marion Terry Margaret Halstan Eleanor Calhoun
1898	Augustin Daly	Daly's, NY	Sidney Herbert	Ada Rehan
1898	William Poel	St George's Hall	Poel	Eleanor Calhoun
1901	Jacob Adler	People's, NY	Adler	Sara Adler
1903	Jacob Adler/ Arthur Hopkins	58th Street, NY	Adler	Meta Meynard
1905	Max Reinhardt	Deutsches, Berlin	R. Schildkraut	Else Heims Agnes Sorma
1905	Arthur Bourchier	Garrick	Bourchier	Violet Vanbrugh
1905	E. H. Sothern/ Julia Marlowe	USA tour	Sothern	Marlowe
1907	Ermete Novelli	USA tour	Novelli	Olga Giannini Novelli
1907	F. R. Benson	Stratford	Arthur Bourchier	Violet Vanbrugh
1906–7	Robert Mantell	USA tour	Mantell	Marie Russell
1908	Herbert Beerbohm Tree	His Majesty's	Tree	Alexandra Carlisle
1910	Gerolamo Lo Salvio	Film d'arte Italiana	Novelli	Olga Giannini Novelli
1910	Oscar Asche	Australian tour	Asche	Lily Brayton
1911	Boris Thomashevsky/ Rudolf Schildkraut	People's, NY	Schildkraut	Sara Adler
1913	J. Forbes-Robertson	Drury Lane	Forbes-Robertson	Gertrude Elliot
1913	John Drinkwater	Birmingham Rep.	Ivor Barnard	Margaret Chatwin
1913	Max Reinhardt	Deutsches, Berlin	Albert Basserman	Else Heims
1915	Henry Jewett	Boston Opera House	Lark Taylor	Cynthia Latham

Year	Manager/ Director	Company/ Theatre	Shylock	Portia
1915–18	Ben Greet	Old Vic	Greet	Beatrice Wilson Sybil Thorndike Margaret Halstan Hutin Britton
1916	Herbert Beerbohm Tree	New Amsterdam, NY	Tree	Elsie Ferguson
1918	George Foss	Old Vic	Russell Thorndike Ernest Milton	Florence Saunders
1918	Max Reinhardt	Deutsches, Berlin	Alexander Moissi	Else Heims
1919	J. B. Fagan	Court	M. Moscovitch L. Bouwmeester	Mary Grey Muriel Pratt
1921	W. Bridges-Adams	Stratford	L. Bouwmeester	Dorothy Green
1921	Walter Hampden	Broadhurst, NY	Hampden	Mary Hall
1921	Max Reinhardt	Schauspielhaus, Berlin	Werner Krauss	Agnes Straub
1922	Robert Atkins	Old Vic	Ernest Milton	Florence Buckton Sybil Thorndike
1922	David Belasco	Lyceum, NY	David Warfield	Mary Servoss
1923	Robert Atkins	Old Vic	Atkins	Florence Buckton
1924	Robert Atkins	Old Vic	Hay Petrie	Florence Saunders
1924	Max Reinhardt	Josefstadt, Vienna	Fritz Kortner	
1925	Andrew Leigh	Old Vic	Balliol Holloway	Edith Evans
1925	Walter Hampden	Hampden's, NY	Hampden	Ethel Barrymore
1927	Jürgen Fehling	Staatliche, Berlin	Fritz Kortner	Elisabeth Bergner
1927	Andrew Leigh	Lyric, Hammersmith	Lewis Casson	Sybil Thorndike
1928	Winthrop Ames	Broadhurst, NY	George Arliss	Peggy Wood
1928	Ben Greet	England tour	Greet	Margaret Webster
1928	F. R. Benson	King's, Hammersmith	Benson	Madge Compton
1929	Harcourt Williams	Old Vic	Brember Wills	Martita Hunt
1930	Andrew Leigh	USA tour	M. Moscovitch	Selena Royle
1930	Maurice Schwartz (excerpts)	RKO Vaudeville	Schwartz	
1932	John Gielgud	Old Vic	Malcolm Keen	Peggy Ashcroft
1932	T. Komisarjevsky	Stratford	Randle Ayrton	Fabia Drake

Year	Manager/ Director	Company/ Theatre	Shylock	Portia
1932	Ernest Milton	St. James's	Milton	Mary Newcomb
1934	Max Reinhardt	Campo San Trovaso, Venice	Memo Benassi	Marta Abba
1934	Stanley Bell/ Oswald Stoll	Alhambra	Franklin Dyall	Marie Ney
1935	Arthur Phillips	Lyric, Hammersmith	Phillips	Rosemary Scott
1936	Leopold Jessner	Habimah, Tel Aviv	Aharon Meskin Shim'on Finkel	Hanna Rovina
1938	John Gielgud/ Glen Byam Shaw	Queen's	Gielgud	Peggy Ashcroft
1938	Orson Welles	Columbia Records	Welles	Brenda Forbes
1938	Donald Wolfit	People's Palace	Wolfit	Rosalinde Fuller
1943	Lothar Müthel	Burgtheater, Vienna	Werner Krauss	
1943	Esmé Church	British tour	Frederick Valk	Kay Bannerman
1948	Michael Benthall	Stratford	Robert Helpmann	Diana Wynyard
1953	Albert Marre	NY City Center	Luther Adler	Margaret Phillips
1953	Hugh Hunt	Old Vic	Paul Rogers	Irene Worth
1953	Dennis Carey	Stratford	Michael Redgrave	Peggy Ashcroft
1954–5	Michael Benthall	Australian tour	Robert Helpmann	Katharine Hepburn
1955	Tyrone Guthrie	Stratford, Ontario	Frederick Valk	Frances Hyland
1956	Michael Benthall	Old Vic	Robert Helpmann	Diana Wynyard
1956	Margaret Webster	Stratford	Emlyn Williams	Margaret Johnston
1957	Jack Landau	Stratford, CT	Morris Carnovsky	Katharine Hepburn
1959	Tyrone Guthrie	Habimah, Tel Aviv	Aharon Meskin Shim'on Finkel	Shoshana Ravid
1960	Michael Langham	Stratford	Peter O'Toole	Dorothy Tutin
1962	Joseph Papp/ Gladys Vaughan	Delacorte, NY	George C. Scott	Nan Martin
1962	Allen Fletcher	Globe, San Diego	Morris Carnovsky	Jacqueline Brooks
1963	Erwin Piscator	Freie Volksbühne, Berlin	Ernst Deutsch	Hilde Krahl

Year	Manager/ Director	Company/ Theatre	Shylock	Portia
1963	Richard Baldridge	APA, Ann Arbor	Paul Sparer	Rosemary Harris
1965	Clifford Williams	RSC, Stratford	Eric Porter	Janet Suzman
1966	George Tabori	Stockbridge, MA	Alvin Epstein	Viveca Lindfors
1969	Otto Schenk	Austrian/W. German TV	Fritz Kortner	Sabine Sinjen
1969	Orson Welles	unfinished film	Welles	
1970	Jean Gascon	Stratford, Ontario	Donald Davis	Maureen O'Brien
1970	Jonathan Miller	National, Old Vic	Laurence Olivier	Joan Plowright
1971	Terry Hands	RSC, Stratford	Emrys James	Judi Dench Susan Fleetwood
1972	Yossi Yzraeli	Cameri, Tel Aviv	Avner Hyskiahu	Germaine Unikovsky
1972	Cedric Messina	BBC TV	Frank Finlay	Maggie Smith
1972	Peter Zadek	Schauspielhaus, Bochum	Hans Mahnke	Rosel Zech
1973	Jonathan Miller	BBC TV	Laurence Olivier	Joan Plowright
1973	Ellis Rabb	Lincoln Center, NY	Sydney Walker	Rosemary Harris
1976	Bill Glassco	Stratford, Ontario	Hume Cronyn	Jackie Burroughs
1978	John Barton	RSC, Stratford	Patrick Stewart	Marjorie Bland Lisa Harrow
1980	Jack Gold	BBC TV	Warren Mitchell	Gemma Jones
1980	Barry Kyle	Cameri, Tel Aviv	Avner Hyskiahu	Gita Munte
1980	Zhang Qi-hong	Chinese Youth Theatre	Jiang Shui	
1981	John Barton	RSC, Stratford	David Suchet	Sinead Cusack
1984	John Caird	RSC, Stratford	Ian McDiarmid	Frances Tomelty
1984	Mark Lamos	Stratford, Ontario	John Neville	Domini Blythe
1985	Thomas Langhoff	Deutsches, Berlin	Fred Düren	Dagmar Manzel
1987	Bill Alexander	RSC, Stratford	Antony Sher	Deborah Findlay
1988	Michael Langham	Washington, DC	Brian Bedford	Kelly McGillis
1988	Peter Zadek	Vienna Burgtheater	Gert Voss	Eva Mattes
1989	Michael Langham	Stratford, Ontario	Brian Bedford	Seana McKenna
1989	Peter Hall	Phoenix/46th Street, NY	Dustin Hoffman	Geraldine James

Year	Manager/ Director	Company/ Theatre	Shylock	Portia
1991	Tim Luscombe	English Shakespeare Company, Lyric, Hammersmith	John Woodvine	Lois Harvey
1992	José Carlos Plaza	Teatro María Guerrero, Madrid	José P. Carrión	Ana Belin
1993	C. T. Gonzaga	Limite: 151, Brasilia	Edney Giovenazzi	Gláucia Rodrigues
1993	David Thacker	RSC, Stratford	David Calder	Penny Downie
1993	Mark Lamos	Hartford Stage Co., Hartford, CT	Mike Nussbaum	Joan McCurtrey
1994	Peter Sellars	Goodman, Chicago	Paul Butler	Elaine Tse
1994	Jude Kelly	West Yorkshire Playhouse, Leeds	Gary Waldhorn	Nichola McAuliffe
1994	Kang Ansheng	Children's Art Theatre Shanghai	Xia Zhiqing	Cai Jinping
1995	Peter Zadek	Berliner Ensemble	Gert Voss	Eva Mattes
1995	Barry Edelstein	NY Shakespeare Festival	Ron Leibman	Laila Robins
1996	Alan Horrox	Thames Television	Bob Peck	Haydn Gwynne
1996	Marti Maraden	Stratford, Ontario	Douglas Rain	Susan Coyne
1997	Gregory Doran	RSC, Stratford	Philip Voss	Helen Schlesinger
1998	Richard Olivier	Shakespeare's Globe	Norbert Kentrup	Kathryn Pogson
1998	Andrei Serban	ART, Cambridge, MA	Will LeBow	Kristin Flanders
1999	Michael Kahn	Washington, DC	Hal Holbrook	Enid Graham
1999	Trevor Nunn	Royal National	Henry Goodman	Derbhle Crotty

INTRODUCTION

Mark Twain is thought to have said that Shakespeare was not really the author of the plays, 'they were written by someone else of the same name'. Although the comment appears nowhere in Mark Twain's works, and has been attributed to others in relation to Homer, not Shakespeare, it still serves as the most sensible solution to the perennial authorship question. Similarly, this introduction, especially when looking at the play as it was first performed, is not about Shakespeare's *Merchant of Venice*, but about another play, also by Shakespeare, of the same name.

In fact, it is very possible that our play was not originally known as *The Merchant of Venice*: on 22 July 1598, perhaps a year or two after the first performance, 'a booke of the Merchaunt of Venyce otherwise called the Jewe of Venyce' was entered for printing at the London Stationers' Register. This is both revealing and reassuring, since *The Jew of Venice* is a more appropriate title – when printed in 1600, *The Merchant of Venice* may have been preferred only to avoid confusion with Marlowe's *The Jew of Malta*.

Critics are fond of pointing out that Shylock is not the 'Merchant of Venice', and that his is not an especially long role, appearing in only five scenes. But amongst the male characters, Shylock has the largest part, with nearly *twice* as many lines as Antonio – no less than *Hamlet*, this is a play with a central star role, one so famous that like Cervantes's Quixote and Dickens's Scrooge, he has become a common word, a distinction not even Hamlet can claim; today, in our age of 'director's theatre', *Merchant* performances are, like *Hamlet* performances, usually identified by the name of the main actor, not the director.

There is one enormous difference, however, between Shylock and Hamlet or any other great Shakespearean character: *The Merchant of Venice* is unique in that we are told that a performance in Shakespeare's time, and the audience's appreciation of it, would have been entirely different from what we experience today.

THE MERCHANT OF VENICE IN THE 1590S

In his review of Peter Hall's 1989 production, Jack Kroll of *Newsweek* (1 January 1990) makes what has been a standard observation in *Merchant* criticism for over two hundred years, that 'Shakespeare's first audience would have been amazed' by a sympathetic portrayal of a Jew. Although Kroll finds Dustin Hoffman's 'painfully real' Shylock impressive, he qualifies his approval by quoting Harold Bloom's opinion, ' "an honest production of the play, sensitive to its values, would now be intolerable in any Western country" '.

Indeed, in *Shakespeare: The Invention of the Human*, Bloom proves an eloquent spokesman for this most enduring of Shakespearean myths:

> One would have to be blind, deaf, and dumb not to recognize that Shakespeare's grand, equivocal comedy *The Merchant of Venice* is nevertheless a profoundly anti-Semitic work . . . The unfortunate Dr Lopez, Queen Elizabeth's physician, was hanged, drawn, and quartered (possibly with Shakespeare among the mob looking on), having been more or less framed by the Earl of Essex and so perhaps falsely accused of a plot to poison the Queen. A Portuguese *converso* [converted Jew] whom Shakespeare may have known, poor Lopez lives on as a shadowy provocation to the highly successful revival of Marlowe's *The Jew of Malta* in 1593–4, and presumably Shakespeare's eventual overcoming of Marlowe in *The Merchant of Venice*, perhaps in 1596–7.[1]

However, like the famous non-barking dog in the Sherlock Holmes story, the curious thing about the evidence connecting Lopez to Marlowe and Shakespeare is its non-existence. Marlowe's play was always a money-spinner; Henslowe records that it took in thirty-five shillings when acted in February of 1593, and the following year it played to good houses *before* Lopez's execution.[2] There is no good reason to think that things would have been different had Lopez never existed, for Lopez's being, or having been, a Jew was hardly mentioned at his trial. So far as can be found from prosecutor Sir Edward Coke's notes, neither he nor anyone else said, or even implied, that being a Jew was an indicator of treacherous intention – Coke was trying to establish a Catholic, not a Jewish assassination plot.[3] Whether or not Lopez was guilty (current scholarship indicates that he was)[4] is beside the point – if he was railroaded, his having been Jewish had nothing to do with it. From the time of Lopez's indictment and trial to his execution on 7 June 1594, there is no record of victimisation of other Jews in London, or of any call to expel Jews or *conversos* residing there.

Obviously, one may still argue that even without the inspiration of Lopez, the original Shylock conformed to an anti-Semitic stereotype, but no such theatrical tradition existed. The only Jew to appear in extant Elizabethan

1 Bloom, *Shakespeare*, pp. 171–2.
2 Foakes and Rickert, *Henslowe's Diary*, p. 255.
3 *Calendar of State Papers*, pp. 90–6, 453–62.
4 Berek, 'The Jew as Renaissance Man', pp. 149–53; D. Katz, *Jews*, pp. 90–6.

drama before Marlowe's Barabas is the moneylender Gerontus in Robert Wilson's *The Three Ladies of London* (1584) – he is the most honourable character in the play, the most contemptible being Mercadore, an Italian merchant. Still, John Gross writes, 'to an Elizabethan audience, the fiery red wig that [Shylock] almost certainly wore spelled out his ancestry even more insistently than anything that was actually said. It was the same kind of wig that had been worn by Marlowe's Barabas, and before that by both Judas and Satan in the old mystery plays.'[5]

This 'fiery red wig', which will reappear in our story, has a rather strange history. There is no mention of Barabas's hair colour in Marlowe's play, neither is there any real connection between Barabas and Judas; even if there were, while 'it is an old and familiar tradition that Judas Iscariot had red hair, the actual evidence is rather scattered and not very abundant'.[6] In 1846, the noted scholar John Payne Collier discovered and published a poem written on the occasion of Richard Burbage's funeral, which reads, in part,

Heart-broken Philaster, and Amintas too
Are lost forever, with the red-hair'd Jew.[7]

Like most of Collier's 'discoveries', this was a forgery – he claimed to have seen and copied it from an original in the library of the antiquarian Richard Heber (conveniently Heber had died in 1833, and his entire collection was auctioned off). Why Collier decided to give Shylock red hair is hard to say; perhaps he was influenced by Thomas Jordan's crude ballad, 'The Forfeiture', published in 1664. Sung to the tune of 'Dear, let me now this evening dye', it starts

You that do look with Christian hue
Attend unto my Sonnet
I'le tell you of as vilde a Jew
As ever wore a Bonnet

and goes on to tell a twisted version of the *Merchant* in which Jessica, not Portia, dresses up as a lawyer and tricks her father, who

. . . by usury and trade
Did much exceed in riches:
His beard was red, his face was made
Not much unlike a Witches.

---

5 Gross, *Shylock*, pp. 16–17. For a more detailed argument denying that Shylock conformed to a stereotype, see Edelman, 'Which is the Jew'.

6 Baum, 'Judas's Red Hair', p. 520.

7 Collier, *Memoirs of the Principal Actors*, p. 53.

To think this doggerel could have anything to do with *The Merchant of Venice* as it was performed more than sixty years previously is positively ludicrous, yet E. E. Stoll, in his often-cited argument for the 'traditional' Shylock, accepts the work of the 'old actor' (Jordan had worked as an actor at the end of the Caroline era) as proof of Shylock's appearance.[8]

If we assume that all Elizabethans hated Jews, then we can easily assume that it was fine for Antonio to call Shylock a dog, to spit at him and then demand that he become a Christian. But we might also assume that Shakespeare and many others at a London playhouse knew a good deal about Venice, and would therefore know that a 'real' Antonio would have earned little approval. Although Venice segregated Jews into the world's first Ghetto, established in 1516, it guaranteed them the right to go about their business, and to practise their religion, free from interference or molesta-tion,[9] and while Jews were always regarded as candidates for conversion, any attempt to force them to convert was forbidden by law.[10] It is often argued that Shakespeare's audience would have approved of Antonio's version of 'mercy', because baptism would save Shylock's soul, with or without his permission, but Shylock has been placed in a position similar to that of the Jews of Spain one hundred years earlier: convert, or make their living else-where. To many, Shylock's forced baptism would have been associated with the Spaniards, who had just tried to murder the Queen, and with the Papacy, which had excommunicated her in 1570.

Even if Shylock's religion, in itself, is not enough to make him a villain to the original audience, there is still the matter of Shylock as usurer to be con-sidered. People making their way to the playhouse to see *The Merchant of Venice* in 1597 could stop at a bookstall and buy Miles Mosse's moral tract condemning the charging of any interest, *The Arraignment and Conviction of Usurie*, but they could also buy a book containing tables of interest rates.[11] No economy can exist without the availability of credit, and except for an extremely conservative faction, it was accepted that usury was the charging of *excessive* interest. In the absence of loan banks, ordinary citizens borrowed money from an acquaintance, or found an acquaintance to act as broker to negotiate the loan with someone else. One prosperous Englishman who

---

8 Stoll, *Shakespeare Studies*, p. 255.

9 Chambers and Pullan, *Venice*, pp. 338–49. In a 1977 article, Brian Pullan finds little trace of popular resentment against Jews in Renaissance Venice, and where it did exist, it seems to have been amongst Greeks or other minorities, not Italians (Pullan, 'A Ship with Two Rudders', p. 54).

10 Roth, *Venice*, p. 116.

11 Jones, *God and the Moneylenders*, pp. 78, 144 ff.

loaned large sums at interest, sued when he was not repaid and also acted as a broker, was William Shakespeare of Stratford.[12]

The latter parts of this Introduction will show that it in recent times, few productions of the *Merchant* can take place without public discussion over whether it should be performed at all, or at the very least, without school packs or other material justifying its presentation, explaining that the original audience held different attitudes than we do today. Ironically, this can have an effect opposite to what is intended: the natural response to *The Merchant of Venice*, from those rare persons with no 'knowledge' of it before entering the theatre, is likely to be similar to that of the spectator once observed by Heinrich Heine: 'When I saw this play at Drury Lane, there stood behind me in the box a pale, fair Briton, who at the end of the Fourth Act, fell to weeping passionately, several times exclaiming, "The poor man is wronged."'[13] 'Passionate weeping' is not required, nor are we expected to think of Shylock as a person free of serious faults (obviously, he is not), yet the entire history of our play, everywhere in the world, shows that it has been most successful when Shylock was *not* acted as a villain, or thought to be one. For us to fully understand the history of Shakespeare's *Merchant of Venice* in production, we must replace it with that 'other' Shakespeare play of the same title.

That play was a success: the title page of the 1600 Quarto notes that it was acted 'divers times'; the first recorded performance was at court on 10 February 1605, followed by a second performance two days later. Since Shylock is the largest and best male part, it is likely that Burbage was the first to play him, but no genuine contemporary document confirms this, and any speculation about casting is only that. Whoever the actors may have been, the *Merchant*'s place in the King's Men's repertoire nine or ten years after it was written argues for its popularity, but there is no further record of the play being shown, in any form, until George Granville's adaptation, *The Jew of Venice*, opened in 1701.

GRANVILLE'S *JEW OF VENICE*

Jewish presence in England increased markedly during the 1600s: as W. D. Rubinstein notes, the Commonwealth had an underlying culture of philo-Semitism, the Puritans seeing themselves in many respects as the

---

12 Honigmann, 'World Elsewhere', pp. 41–5; Honigmann, *Shakespeare's Impact*, pp. 8–14.

13 Furness, *A New Variorum Edition*, p. 449.

re-embodiment of Old Testament Judaism.[14] In 1656, Cromwell gave the Jews permission to remain in England and to open their first synagogue in Creechurch Lane.

During the Restoration, Jewish economic power and status rose further. It was still a tiny community, and nearly all Portuguese or Spanish *Sephardim*: in 1677 a London directory had forty-eight Portuguese, and two German (in Hebrew, *Ashkenazi*) names.[15] As the Glorious Revolution approached, Anglo-Jews were officially residents – politically, they were essentially the English branch of Holland's Jewish community, something much to their advantage, for the Revolution could not have succeeded without the financial support of the Dutch-Jewish company of Machado and Pereira.[16] Although this point is disputed by historians, Rubinstein and David S. Katz argue persuasively that from the Glorious Revolution until late Victorian times, the status of England's Jews was little different from that of the Quakers or other dissenters, and in many respects was better than that of English Catholics.[17] On 23 June 1700, William III knighted Solomon de Medina, a rich London Jew who was in partnership with Machado and Pereira; six months later *The Jew of Venice* opened at Lincoln's Inn Fields.

Granville retains much of Shakespeare's text, but many passages are shortened, altered or transposed,[18] and Morocco, Arragon, the Gobbos, Solanio, Salarino and Salerio (the 'Salads') are omitted. Taking the place of the missing scenes is a banquet at the end of Act II, when Shylock, Bassanio and Antonio celebrate the 'merry bond' by offering toasts to wealth, and then witness an elaborate masque, 'Peleus and Thetis'.

The prologue, spoken by the ghosts of Shakespeare and Dryden, is perhaps of greater interest than anything in the play proper. 'Shakespeare' announces,

> To day we punish a Stock-jobbing Jew.
> A piece of Justice, terrible and strange;
> Which, if persu'd, would make a thin Exchange.

---

14 Rubinstein, *History of the Jews*, pp. 44–5.

15 *Ibid.*, p. 62.

16 D. Katz, *Jews*, p. 157.

17 In the 1680s *Ashkenazi* immigration to England increased, and by 1690 enough German Jews lived in London for them to form their own independent community. The first *Ashkenazi* synagogue, later known as the Great Synagogue, was founded in Duke's Place in 1690. In 1695 the London census showed 853 Jewish names, 255 (30 per cent) of them *Ashkenazi* (Rubinstein, *History of the Jews*, p. 61).

18 See Halio, *Merchant*, pp. 61–2.

The late 1690s and early 1700s saw a major shift in economic power 'from countryside to town, and from landowner to businessman, profoundly unsettling the traditional order'.[19] Particularly notorious were the 'stock-jobbers', busily amassing wealth through speculative dealings in joint-stock ventures: their excesses led to an Act of 1697, restricting their number in London to one hundred, with twelve places reserved for Jews and twelve for other 'aliens'. So Shylock, once a Venetian moneylender, has become a London dealer in investment schemes, despised by arch-Tories such as Granville.

Thomas Betterton was a sixty-six-year-old Bassanio, and Anne Bracegirdle played Portia. Thomas Doggett, who played Shylock, was one of the most popular comic actors of his day: according to Colley Cibber, who admired Doggett greatly, Congreve wrote the characters of Ben in *Love for Love* and Fondlewife in *The Old Bachelor* expressly for him.[20] Records of London's 1700–1 theatre season are scanty, and we do not know how often *The Jew of Venice* was performed, but in any event it is difficult to agree with Gross's view that *The Jew of Venice* 'held the stage for forty years',[21] for it was hardly ever seen after 1701. There is record of one performance in May 1703, three in the 1721–2 season and two in 1722–3, but none at all for the ensuing three years, and less than one a year after that – with just one recorded performance between 1736 and 1741. Given these circumstances, it is fair to say that Granville's adaptation, while interesting in and of itself, plays little part in the performance history of *The Merchant of Venice*. No tradition existed in the interpretation of Shylock, or of any other role, when Charles Macklin took the stage on 12 February 1741, and no expectation on the part of the Drury Lane audience had to be confirmed or denied. *The Merchant of Venice* was a new play.

'THE JEW THAT SHAKESPEARE DREW'

Born in Ireland in 1699, Charles Macklin was a popular favourite in a variety of roles amongst provincial audiences of the early 1730s. John Fleetwood, the patent holder of Drury Lane, engaged him to play small parts for the 1733–4 season, but that season fell into disarray when a dispute between Fleetwood and the actors, led by Theophilus Cibber, led to the defection of Cibber's group to the Haymarket. Macklin remained loyal to Fleetwood, though, and his importance at Drury Lane grew.

Several factors contributed to Drury Lane's decision to mount *The Merchant of Venice* in 1741: the renewal and strengthening of the Stage Licensing

---

19 Hoppit, *Land of Liberty*, p. 4.   20 *Biographical Dictionary*.
21 Gross, *Shylock*, pp. 91–2.

Act in 1737 placed the Lord Chamberlain in charge of theatrical censorship, establishing 'a much more rigorous system of state surveillance, which would endure until 1968', over the theatre.[22] The inherent difficulties in getting a play approved encouraged managements to rely on Shakespeare and others whose plays were already part of the repertoire, and not subject to new scrutiny. Furthermore, there was no need to set the takings of the third performance aside, as was customary, for an 'author's benefit'.[23] Since the *Merchant*, in its original text, had not been performed within living memory, it would have brought with it the excitement of a famous play being seen for the first time by everyone present, the perfect vehicle for a popular actor in his first starring role.

Descriptions of Macklin's Shylock are consistent in giving us a fierce and malevolent figure, driven by his hatred of Antonio. Francis Gentleman was only thirteen in 1741, and his *Dramatic Censor* was published in 1770, so he presumably saw Macklin in the 1760s:

> in the level scenes his voice is most happily suited to that sententious gloominess of expression the author intended; which, with a sullen solemnity of deportment, marks the character strongly; in his malevolence, there is forcible and terrifying ferocity; in the third act scene, where alternate passions reign, he breaks the tones of utterance, and varies his countenance admirably; in the dumb action of the trial scene, he is amazingly descriptive; and through the whole displays such unequalled merit, as justly entitles him to that very comprehensive, though concise compliment paid him many years ago, 'This is the Jew that Shakespeare drew.'[24]

The famous 'concise compliment' is attributed to Alexander Pope, supposedly paid when he and Macklin met after a performance.

Portia was played by Kitty Clive, a delightful comedienne who received more unfavourable criticism for this performance than for any in her long career.[25] Gentleman calls it 'a ludicrous burlesque on the character . . . in the spirited scene she was clumsy . . . in the grave part – sure never was such a female put into breeches before! – she was awkwardly dissonant'. In the trial, 'as if conscious she could not get through without the aid of trick, [she] flew to the pitiful resource of taking off the peculiarity of some judge, or noted lawyer; from which wise stroke, she created laughter in a scene where the deepest attention should be preserved'.[26]

---

22 Dobson, 'Improving on the Original', p. 64.   23 *London Stage*, pt. 3, p. cx.

24 Gentleman, *Dramatic Censor*, p. 292.   25 *Biographical Dictionary*.

26 Gentleman, *Dramatic Censor*, p. 297.

Macklin's text for the 1740–1 season, although probably abbreviated, would have been very close to the Quarto text of 1600. There is no record of any interpolation, and all characters, including Morocco and Arragon, were present – Arragon fell out of the play during the first season, and was not seen again until Charles Kean's revival of 1858, but 'Morochius' appeared in some, although not all, London performances of the *Merchant* until 1757: the 1773 Bell edition, without either of Portia's unsuccessful suitors, is probably close to the play that Macklin performed later in his career.[27]

On 7 May 1789, Macklin, at the age of ninety, began a performance, but found himself unable to continue past the first scene, and retired from the stage. For nearly fifty years, he had defined the role of Shylock.

GERMANY: SCHRÖDER, IFFLAND, FLECK

As the Macklin era was drawing to a close, the history of *The Merchant of Venice* in modern Germany began. Friedrich Ludwig Schröder was chiefly responsible for introducing Shakespeare to the German theatre; in 1771 he took over the management of the Hamburg National Theatre from his step-father Konrad Ackermann, and brought *Hamlet* to the stage in 1776, followed by *Othello* and *The Merchant of Venice* in 1777.

Using the translation of Christoph Martin Wieland, Schröder cut nearly all of the fifth act. Not much has been written about his Shylock – he is thought to have played him much as Macklin did, harsh and vindictive, while retaining some of the audience's sympathy.[28] More important, perhaps, than Schröder's own performances is the influence he had as guest director in Vienna, Mannheim and elsewhere – one of his associates in Mannheim was the playwright-actor August Wilhelm Iffland.[29]

Schiller admired Iffland as an actor but did not think much of his plays,[30] perhaps because at the time they were more popular than Schiller's. During the 1780s the Mannheim National Theatre developed strongly under Iffland's leadership, and upon transferring to the National Theatre of Berlin, Iffland mounted several visually spectacular productions of Shakespeare.[31] As the Jew, he presented a comical figure – indeed he may have been the first actor to play Shylock this way – speaking with a foreign accent, and regarded as 'irksome' and 'impish' rather than seriously threatening.[32] He wore a 'blue

---

27 *Shak.11*, p. 15.
28 Williams, *Shakespeare on the German Stage*, p. 133. I am very much indebted to Williams's magisterial study.
29 Bruford, *Theatre Drama*, p. 34.   30 *Ibid.*, pp. 255, 302.
31 Banham, *Cambridge Guide*, p. 470.   32 Häublein, 'Ein Stück', p. 37.

coat with fur trimming, a caftan and red stockings. His performance was an aggregation of small mannerisms, commonly accepted as typical of the Jews. He pattered across the stage with mincing footsteps, he walked in circles when worried, he crumpled his cap in distress during the trial scene.'[33]

Ferdinand Fleck had his first success as Gloucester, opposite Schröder's Lear; he played Shylock in 1797, only four years before his death at the age of forty-one. His was a different Jew than Iffland presented: the poet, critic and Shakespeare translator Ludwig Tieck thought Fleck 'horrible and ghostlike, but . . . always noble'.[34]

ENTER KEMBLE

The 1788–9 season that saw Macklin's final exit from the English stage was also John Philip Kemble's first as manager of Drury Lane – the *Merchant* was performed once, on 17 January 1789, with Kemble as Shylock and his sister, Sarah Siddons, as Portia.[35] The handsome and dignified Kemble never considered himself suited to the role, however, and when he later staged the *Merchant*, it was usually with Tom King, the original Sir Peter Teazle and a much-loved actor, but no Shylock: the best that Gentleman could say about him was that his performance 'is by no means so deficient as many principal parts' then being acted in London.[36]

Kemble published his own edition of the *Merchant* 'as first acted at the Theatre Royal in Covent Garden', in 1810. Taken together with Elizabeth Inchbald's 1808 edition, also 'as Performed at the Theatre Royal', these versions give us a reliable record of the play as it was presented at this time. As in the Bell edition, both Morocco and Arragon are missing, but the Kemble and Inchbald texts make some sense of the casket theme by rewriting Bassanio's choosing speech in 3.2.[37] Songs for Lorenzo and Jessica are interpolated, and except for the Shylock scenes, huge chunks of the play are deleted. Overall, though, Kemble retained more of the Quarto text than did Macklin, and the order of the scenes is not altered – that 'improvement' was yet to come.

While Kemble's work in preparing a relatively coherent text is to be admired, we should remember that his production was rarely seen – in the 1790s, aside from a few summer performances at the Haymarket, Londoners had the opportunity to see the *Merchant* only once every two years. But this

---

33 Williams, *Shakespeare on the German Stage*, p. 135.

34 Devrient, *Geschichte*, vol. I, p. 525.

35 This was not Kemble's first attempt at the part – he did it at Smock Alley, Dublin, and for his London debut in January, 1784.

36 Gentleman, *Dramatic Censor*, p. 293.   37 See Appendix 1.

changed when Thomas Harris and W. T. 'Gentleman' Lewis engaged George Frederick Cooke for the 1800–1 season at Covent Garden,[38] and London audiences learned what those in the provinces had known for years: the new Macklin had arrived. However, he did not stay long.

GEORGE FREDERICK COOKE, EDMUND KEAN

Cooke was forty-four years old when he made his debut at Covent Garden.[39] An actor of immense power, he would have had a long and distinguished career, but frequent non-appearances due to drunkenness made employing him a risky proposition: at the time, Covent Garden had no one to compare with Drury Lane's Kemble, so the risk was worth taking.

Like David Garrick, Cooke chose *Richard III* for his debut. His Shylock, first seen 10 November 1800, earned qualified praise from the *Porcupine*: 'His acting was uncommonly striking, his knowledge of the author complete, but his declamation jars upon the ear, as he is accustomed to give a whole line on one unvaried harsh note . . . In every scene there was much, very much, to commend; in the great scene with Tubal, everything. The audience seemed electrified by his excellence in it.'[40]

The 1800–1 season was the high point of Cooke's career; over the rest of the decade, non-appearances due to 'indisposition', and appearances that *should* have been non-appearances, grew too frequent for managements and audiences to tolerate. In 1810 he embarked on an American tour, and for the first time Americans could experience the full power of *The Merchant of Venice*. 'Thespis' of the New York *Columbian* writes that Cooke's performance was

> more than acting, it was nature improved and refined by the most
> consummate art. Mr Cooke, beyond all other players that have appeared on
> the American boards, adheres with more critical accuracy and studied
> uniformity to the text and spirit of his author. He is less solicitous to
> attract admiration by polished gestures and striking attitudes . . . The
> great points of playing are, consequently, at times in some measure lost.
> No actor appears less inclined to gain applause, at the sacrifice of nature
> and propriety.[41]

Less than two years later Cooke died, virtually destitute, in New York. He was buried in the Strangers' Vault of St Paul's Church, and in 1820, another

38 Hare, *George Frederick Cooke*, p. 113.
39 He had appeared in London before, at the Little Theatre, Haymarket, in 1778.
40 Hare, *George Frederick Cooke*, p. 119.   41 *Annals.II*, pp. 359–60.

famous Shylock, Edmund Kean, had the remains moved to the churchyard and commissioned a monument to his great predecessor.

It may seem odd to place Edmund Kean near the end of a section, rather than the beginning, but contrary to what is generally believed, Kean did not bring any radically new conception to Shylock. The legend of his first appearance at Drury Lane has been recounted many times, and to say that it has been 'embellished' is to put it charitably.

An article in *New Monthly Magazine* of May 1834 relates that when Kean turned up at the theatre, an unnamed actor said, 'I say! he's got a black wig and beard! Did you ever see Shylock in a black wig?'.[42] This fanciful account, written after Kean's death, was accepted by Frederick William Hawkins, whose 1883 biography of Kean reveals that he took 'a little *black* wig from his little bundle . . . heedless of or inattentive to the astonishment on the faces of his companions'.[43]

But there is no compelling reason to believe that *any* Shylock wore a red wig before William Poel in 1898: Johann Zoffany's portrait of Macklin as Shylock shows him with dark brown hair, and a coloured engraving of Kemble's Shylock, issued in 1809, reveals him to be black-haired and bearded.[44] The notion that Kean would harbour a 'secret' Shylock, and play him differently than he had done so successfully in the provinces, is not only absurd, but is inconsistent with the one opening-night story that does have an air of truth about it: Kean's friend, Joseph Drury, former headmaster of Harrow, was in the house and is said to have murmured 'he is safe!' when the audience applauded Shylock's first line. Drury was living in retirement near Exeter, and had seen Kean perform there; should the actor have presented some new and different interpretation, Drury surely would have commented on it.

Playing before the same type of stock scenery Kemble would have had twenty years earlier, and using the same text, Kean's performance was well within the boundaries defined by his two most important predecessors. When 'Mr Kean from Exeter' stunned Drury Lane on 26 January 1814, it was as a new and brilliant actor, not a new and brilliant Shylock – had Kean emulated Garrick and Cooke, and chosen *Richard III* for his debut, the result would have been the same.

Coleridge's famous remark about Kean, 'To see him act, is like reading Shakespeare by flashes of lightning',[45] is not merely general praise, he is

42 *qtd* Cornwall, *Life of Edmund Kean*, p. 219.
43 Hawkins, *Life of Edmund Kean*, vol. I, p. 126.
44 Lelyveld, *Shylock on the Stage*, p. 42.
45 *qtd* Bate, *The Romantics on Shakespeare*, p. 160.

describing the most important element in Kean's approach to the art of acting. As Charles Shattuck notes, 'Kean's forte was naturalism – the vivid realisation of exactly what emotional state, vocal tone, and bit of behavior was to be called up at every instant in the stage life of a character.'[46] Coleridge was not the only great poet to notice this: to Keats, 'other actors are constantly thinking about their sum-total effect throughout a play. Kean delivers himself up to the instant feeling, without a shadow of a thought about anything else.'[47] These perceptions serve as reminder that whatever the 'sum-total effect' of Kean's Shylock, it did not derive from a considered interpretation of the role as an organic whole.

Kean impressed William Hazlitt, though Hazlitt correctly predicted in the *Morning Chronicle* of 27 January 1814 that the young actor would be 'a greater favourite in other parts'. To Hazlitt, Kean did not sufficiently show the 'the morose, sullen, inward, inveterate, inflexible malignancy of Shylock', but

> in giving effect to the conflict of passions arising out of the contrasts of situation, in varied vehemence of declamation, in keenness of sarcasm, in the rapidity of his transitions from one tone and feeling to another, in propriety and novelty of action, presenting a succession of striking pictures, and giving perpetually fresh shocks of delight and surprise, it would be difficult to single out a competitor.[48]

Two years later, Hazlitt gave an even more favourable opinion, noting 'Mr Kean's manner is much nearer the mark',[49] and returned to the subject again in 1817, with a well-known, and most misleading, comment:

> When we first went to see Mr Kean as Shylock, we expected to see, what we had been used to see, a decrepid old man, bent with age and ugly with mental deformity, grinning with deadly malice, with the venom of his heart congealed in the expression of his countenance, sullen, morose, gloomy, inflexible, brooding over one idea, that of his hatred, and fixed on one unalterable purpose, that of his revenge . . . so rooted was our habitual impression of the part from seeing it caricatured in the representation, that it was only from a careful perusal of the play itself that we saw our error . . .[50]

Hazlitt's description of these other Shylocks has been accepted as 'a composite portrait as actors since Macklin had presented him',[51] but who were

46 *Amer.1*, p. 50.   47 *qtd* Bate, *The Romantics on Shakespeare*, p. 201.
48 Hazlitt, *View of the English Stage*, p. 179.   49 *Ibid.*, p. 296.
50 *Ibid.*, pp. 323–4.   51 Gross, *Shylock*, p. 107.

these 'decrepid old' Shylocks, and when did Hazlitt see them? Hazlitt joined the *Morning Chronicle* as parliamentary and theatrical correspondent in 1812, and he is unlikely to have been a regular theatregoer before that. After his wedding in 1808, he resided at Winterslow in a cottage belonging to his wife – he may have seen Kemble or Cooke in the provinces, or in London, but what we know of these Shylocks hardly puts them into the 'bent with age' category. After Cooke, the *Merchant* was seldom seen in London: a more likely explanation is that Hazlitt's other Shylocks existed only in his imagination, and that he had rarely, if ever, seen *The Merchant of Venice* before January of 1814; Hazlitt would not have been the first newcomer to theatre criticism to claim more playgoing experience than he actually had.

This is not to say that Kean's Shylock was not in some respects more sympathetic than Macklin's or Cooke's. Shylock is an 'outsider', and as Jonathan Bate notes, Kean, with his illegitimate birth and poverty-stricken youth, was an outsider himself, who specialised in outsider parts. Such an actor would have special appeal to the radical Hazlitt, and to the Whig-dominated audience at Drury Lane, a theatre that served as a home 'for Opposition politics, and a reading of Shakespeare as a friend of the people against the autocracy of government'.[52] There is also the intriguing matter of Kean's own Jewish ancestry – his father had brothers named Aaron and Moses.[53] That this could have been a factor, even a major factor, in Kean's portrayal of Shylock is undeniable, but it is also undeniable that another of Kean's triumphs was Barabas in *The Jew of Malta*.

LUDWIG DEVRIENT, KARL SEYDELMANN

Just as Edmund Kean was the greatest of English Romantic actors, Ludwig Devrient held that status in Germany, and his Shylock commanded the German stage over the same period that Kean's did the English and American – they were nearly exact contemporaries. As Simon Williams notes, Devrient's Shylock seemed to have spent his life 'building up resentment against the hated Christians; in fact, this hatred was the dominant concern of his life, making his demand for Antonio's flesh an act of desperate rebellion, a necessary consummation, yet a triumphant culmination of years of bitterness, suffering and martyrdom'.[54]

Complicating any discussion of Devrient's characterisation is the fact that he often changed it, this inconsistency exacerbated by a serious drinking problem. He played Shylock

---

52 Bate, 'Romantic Stage', p. 107.   53 *Ibid.*, p. 108.
54 Williams, *Shakespeare on the German Stage*, p. 137.

either with a distinctly dark skin or speaking in a recognisably Jewish accent, dressed as a Venetian Jew, or as a Polish or Hungarian Jew. But he always took care that the character's nobility – a quality which audiences constantly associated with European culture – was persistently to the fore . . . perhaps no German actor so completely embodied the tragic dimensions of the role.[55]

Only a few years younger than Kean and Devrient, and also going to an early grave, was Karl Seydelmann. Born in Silesia, he made his way to the German stage via Prague, and came to be regarded as Devrient's successor in Berlin in the 1830s;[56] Mephistopheles, Iago and Shylock were some of his best roles. As the Jew, he 'was the incorporation of a persecuted nation's accumulated wrath. Even in his outbursts of fiendish rejoicing over Antonio's ruin, in his sanguinary yearnings to take the life of his arch-enemy, in his tremulous exaltation whilst anticipating his revenge, he compelled his audience to feel that there was some justification for all those manifestations of extravagant excitement.'[57]

WILLIAM CHARLES MACREADY

Yet another contemporary of Edmund Kean was William Charles Macready; he lived so much longer that he is easily mistaken for someone of a later era, but he was only five years younger, and after his London debut in 1816, he became Kean's rival for the unofficial title of England's leading actor. Macready first played Shylock at Covent Garden in 1823, when he was thirty, but only sporadically after that – he never considered it a good part for him, and given his triumphs as Hamlet, Lear, Macbeth and Claude Melnotte in *The Lady of Lyons*, there was little reason to persist. He did perform the *Merchant* somewhat more frequently in the late 1830s and early 1840s; he appears to have anticipated Irving in lending Shylock an unusual air of refinement. The *Spectator* (12 October 1839) said,

> Mr Macready has endeavoured to give personal dignity to the Jew, and to soften down the ugly features of the character by assuming an erect port and a frank and cordial manner, that are quite inconsistent with the persecution and insults to which the whole tribe are subject; he makes us wonder that a man of his appearance should belong to a despised race, much more that he should be accustomed to such indignities as Shylock reminds Antonio of putting on him.

55 *Ibid.*, pp. 137–8.   56 Williams, *German Actors*, p. 85.
57 Beatty-Kingston, 'Shylock in Germany', p. 87.

Macready's Portia at this time was Helen Faucit. She 'became the gravity of the learned doctor better than the gayety of Portia; her sprightly sallies at the expense of her suitors were forced, and her modest sweetness was not wholly free from the approach of affectation'.[58] The *Spectator* closes by remarking, 'we ought not to pass by the two scenes of Venice without praise, but they made others look shabby by comparison'.

The comparative quality of Macready's Venice and Belmont sets is not important; that the scenery should be mentioned at all is. The 1820s saw the introduction of gas and calcium lighting, i.e. 'limelight', to London's theatres, innovations that demanded greater attention to the quality of what was being illuminated, and Macready's tenure at Drury Lane marks the gradual transition from the 'stock' *Merchant* to one with scenery expressly designed for the play. In contrast to 1839, when only the Venice scenes were worthy of a brief comment, the December 1841 production drew this reaction from *The Times*:

> The scenery is in the best possible taste, very beautiful, and yet nicely discriminated, so as not to overbalance the drama. The effect of the tribunal, with the forty, was most imposing, reminding us of that produced by the Roman Senate in Mr Macready's revival of *Coriolanus*. The moonlit garden in the fifth act is particularly beautiful, sparkling with soft light, and melting away into a poetic indistinctness at the back.[59]

THE SOCIAL CONTEXT

From the time of Macklin through to the late nineteenth century, reviews of English productions make little mention of Shylock as a representative character of the Jewish race. One can only speculate why this was so: while not disregarding such phenomena as the debate over the Jew Bill of 1753, or the barriers that kept Nathan Rothschild, elected four times, from taking his seat in Parliament, it appears that the rights of England's Jewish population, always comparatively small, were not a major factor in English political life.[60]

A progression of other Jewish characters made its way to the London stage. Ironically, the first was created by Charles Macklin in 1769, the Italian

---

58 Faucit's Portia is discussed further, p. 22.   59 *Shak.*II, p. 227.

60 In *Shakespeare and the Jews*, Shapiro questions the conclusions of Katz and other historians (see above, p. 6), who regard this time as one of improvement for England's Jews, as 'wishful thinking' (p. 193). But Shapiro's own use of incidents such as the Jew Bill of 1753 as proof of pervasive anti-Semitism is equally questionable.

Jew Beau Mordecai, a minor figure in his enormously successful farce, *Love à la Mode*, where not only Mordecai, but the Scottish Sir Archibald Macsarcasm (the role Macklin wrote for himself), and the Irish Sir Callaghan O'Brallaghan are satirised. In 1772 Richard Cumberland wrote Napthali, a Jewish stockbroker and moneylender (a small part and one of the less likeable characters) into his comedy *The Fashionable Lover*; in the same year the broker Moses had a four-line role in Samuel Foote's *The Nabob*, followed two years later by the friendly Moses Manasses in Foote's *The Cozeners*. Sheridan gave the English theatre the 'honest Israelite' Moses in *The School for Scandal* (1776), and other kindly Jews followed: Sheva in Cumberland's *The Jew* (1794), Nadab in his comic opera *The Jew of Mogadore* (1808) and the warm-hearted central roles in two plays by Thomas Dibdin, Abednego in *The Jew and the Doctor* (1798), and Ephraim in *The School for Prejudice* (1801). Some of these plays were popular for a long time, and one, *The School for Scandal*, is a major work: except for Nadab, the Jewish characters are taken from contemporary English life, and that they are mostly sympathetic means that we have travelled some distance from Granville's 'stock-jobbing Jew'.

Of infinitely greater importance was a brilliantly drawn character, taken not from the Exchange, but from London's underworld: with the publication of *Oliver Twist* in 1838, and its subsequent stage adaptations, Fagin, virtually overnight, replaced Shylock as the most important fictive Jew in English culture. Although Jews were never a large proportion of London's poor East End neighbourhoods, their increasing numbers during the nineteenth century inevitably meant that some would turn to crime: 'Fagin was probably untypical of the run of London criminals of the time, but the portrait of him offered by Dickens was not an inaccurate depiction of the common view of the Anglo-Jewish malefactor.'[61] As is well known, Dickens encountered protests about his depiction of Fagin, and later tried to make amends with the kindly Riah in *Our Mutual Friend*.

CHARLES KEAN

Macready's production, with its attention to details of staging, began a new phase in the *Merchant*'s history, and it marked the close of another. The exclusive right of London's two patent theatres to perform spoken plays ended in 1843, and so the names Drury Lane and Covent Garden disappear from our story – they were devoted more and more to opera, while the newly licensed smaller houses such as the Haymarket (now allowed to operate

---

61 Rubinstein, *History of the Jews*, p. 69.

throughout the year), the Princess's and the Lyceum became the focus of Shakespearean production in London.

The link between Macready and Charles Kean is direct, for the younger Kean used Macready's promptbooks, copied for him by the stage manager and prompter George Ellis, in preparing his own productions. His skills as an actor never approached those of his father, but as a director and *The-atrical* manager his influence on Shakespeare in the English theatre was greater and more lasting. When he assumed control of the Princess's in 1851, Kean embarked on a series of Shakespearean productions, of which *The Merchant of Venice*, opening on 12 June 1858, was the most spectacular ever seen until that time. John William Cole provides this description of the opening scene:

> The curtain draws up and we discover ourselves in Venice, the famed Queen of the Adriatic, 'throned on her hundred Isles' . . . we see the actual square of St Mark with the campanile and clocktower, the cathedral, and the three standards, painted from drawings taken on the spot; restored, as in 1600, when Shakespeare wrote the play, and the incidents he has so skilfully interwoven are supposed to take place. Throngs of picturesquely-contrasted occupants gradually fill the area, passing and re-passing in their ordinary avocations. Nobles, citizens, inquisitors, foreigners, traders, water-carriers, and flower-girls are there; a flourish of trumpets announces the approach of the Doge, who issues in state procession, on his way to some public ceremony.[62]

Kean's text was also very different from anything seen before. Although their parts were much reduced, Morocco and Arragon were restored, *The Times* (14 June 1858) noting,

> whereas the story of Portia and her caskets has hitherto seemed only subordinate to that part of the action in which Shylock and Antonio are chief figures, full justice is now done to the whole of the plot as designed by the author, and thus a play that has hitherto been attractive solely on account of certain isolated scenes is now interesting from beginning to end.

While the spectacle at the Princess's warranted the attention it received from the critics, the performances were unexciting: *The Times* did note that 'Mr Charles Kean is seldom seen to more advantage than as Shylock', but clearly the fire of his father, or even of Macready, was not lit. For developments in the acting of the *Merchant*, we must look to Germany and America.

---

62 Cole, *Life of Charles Kean*, pp. 264–5. One of the flower-girls was the ten-year-old Ellen Terry.

DAWISON, BOOTH, MITTERWURZER

Bohumil Dawison made his acting debut at the age of nineteen in his native Warsaw; after establishing himself in Hamburg, he went on to important roles in Vienna and Dresden.[63] Known for his Hamlet, Othello Lear and Richard III, he was the first Jewish actor to play Shylock in Europe, and he also toured to the United States. William Winter of the New York *Tribune*, as bigoted and vindictive a critic as the American theatre has ever known,[64] was usually suspicious of foreign actors, but he had some good things to say about Dawison's performance at New York's Stadt Theatre in September of 1866:

> The chief merits of it were authority and executive skill. The chief defect of it was an indefinable yet clearly perceptible pettiness in the quality, fibre, or essence of the character. Whatever else Shylock may not be, he is terrible. Dawison's embodiment evinced duplicity, greed, and implacable malignity, but, notwithstanding his uncommon advantages of physical stature and intellectual force, it was not terrific . . . the dress was skilfully fashioned to accentuate the height and leanness of the figure; the elocution was exact, fluent, and consistent, marked by a slight accent, intended to denote that Shylock is a foreigner in Venice, and that accent was intensified in moments of vehement utterance.[65]

In the spring of 1853, during the days of the California gold rush, the actress Catherine Sinclair, who had achieved some notoriety due to her recent divorce from Edwin Forrest, engaged a nineteen-year-old actor for a season at the San Francisco Theatre. The *Placer Times and Transcript* (9 September 1853) duly noted:

> Last evening Mr Edwin Booth had a full house at this theatre on the occasion of his benefit. He performed for the second time the part of Shylock, in Shakespeare's play the *Merchant of Venice*. He was highly successful in this difficult delineation of character, giving promise of great future excellence in it. As Portia, Mrs Sinclair acquitted herself with much credit, her performances in the court scene being in our opinion, the most judicious and excellent piece of acting she has rendered on the San Francisco boards.

Booth went on to achieve an unchallenged pre-eminence amongst American actors; as with Edmund Kean, Shylock did not rank with Hamlet, Othello or Iago as one of his great roles, but he played the part often, especially as he grew older. His Jew was very much in the tradition established by Macklin –

---

63 Ewbank, 'European Cross Currents', p. 133.   64 Atkinson, *Broadway*, p. 91.
65 Winter, *Shakespeare on the Stage*, pp. 163–4.

hard, cruel and single-minded in his pursuit of revenge – John Ranken Towse, one of the major critics of the day, writes 'his portrayal was a most harmonious blend of racial prejudice and hate, insatiate avarice, dignity, craft, revengeful passion, and abject defeat. He made no pretence of elevating it with any touch of patriarchal or romantic nobility.'[66]

For all of his fame, Booth cannot be seen as part of a move towards a greater naturalism that was later to distinguish Shakespearean acting in America, but in Germany this movement had begun. The actor Joseph Schildkraut says of Friedrich Mitterwurzer, 'in a period when the German stage was dominated by the romantic and declamatory school of acting, [he] was one of the few exponents of the nascent era of realism'.[67] Known for his interpretation of Hjalmar Ekdal in *The Wild Duck* and other Ibsen characters, Mitterwurzer showed Shylock to be driven by malice, 'the common moneypeddling Jew, rich beyond all measure, greedy and mendacious',[68] a strange mix of the traditional German clown Hanswurst, and the intense realism he brought to Ibsen.[69]

FROM THE BANCROFTS TO IRVING

Squire and Marie Bancroft were having great success with the genteel comedies of Tom Robertson at their small Prince of Wales Theatre on Tottenham Street,[70] so their decision to offer *The Merchant of Venice* in 1875 represented a new direction.

Charles Kean cut the *Merchant* drastically, but he did not alter the order of the scenes. The Bancrofts, hampered by a tiny stage, were forced to take a radical approach to the text: as Squire Bancroft recalls: 'I took upon myself the great responsibility of rearranging the text of the Play, so as to avoid change of scene in sight of the audience, and to adapt the work, so far as possible, to its miniature frame.'[71] He delayed 1.2 until after the first interval, and combined 1.1 and 1.3 into one scene, setting it 'under the arches of the Doge's Palace . . . [with] a lovely view of Santa Salute'. The necessary passage of time between 1.1 and 1.3 was established 'by carefully arranged processions and appropriate pantomimic action from the crowd of merchants, sailors, beggars, Jews, who were throughout passing and repassing'.[72] Clement Scott mentions one important detail missing from

---

66 Towse, *Sixty Years*, p. 189.   67 Schildkraut, *My Father*, pp. 40–1.
68 *qtd* Williams, *German Actors*, p. 132.
69 Williams, *Shakespeare on the German Stage*, pp. 145–6.
70 Jackson, 'Actor-Managers', p. 115.   71 Bancroft, *Bancrofts*, p. 226.
72 *Ibid.*, p. 227.

Bancroft's list – gondolas – one seemed 'to hear the ripple of water as [they] glide on'.[73]

Bancroft's invention, born of the necessity to economise on set changes, became standard practice – while different actor-managers adopted different sequences, they always grouped the Venice and Belmont scenes, the journey from one to the other taking place during an interval. Beerbohm Tree, recalling the Bancroft *Merchant* years later, remarks that it was 'the first production in which the modern spirit of stage management asserted itself, transporting us as it did into the atmosphere of Venice, into the rarefied realms of Shakespearian comedy'.[74]

The production was not a success, due mostly to Charles Coghlan's decision to underplay Shylock in a style more suited to the modern comedies in which he had excelled, 'a moody, sulky, and uninteresting person'.[75] Obviously, one cannot have a good *Merchant* without a good Shylock, but the Bancrofts came close, for as Tree remembers, 'it was here that Ellen Terry first shed the sunlight of her buoyant and radiant personality on the character of Portia'.[76]

ENTER PORTIA

Portia is by far the largest part in the play, but some aspects of the character place her out of the first rank of Shakespeare's comic heroines. Although a transvestite role, it is not one of the 'breeches' parts so loved in the Restoration theatre:[77] instead of dressing up like Rosalind, 'in all points like a man / A gallant curtle-ax upon [her] thigh', she wears a legal gown, possibly reverting to civilian dress for the very brief 4.2. Unlike Rosalind, Viola, Julia or Imogen, she does not don male attire to escape danger or find her true love, but only to participate in a legal proceeding – unlike the other heroines, she gets her man in the middle of the play, and no resourcefulness or bravery is required until she decides to help her new husband's friend out of trouble; until then, her role is entirely passive. Hence we can understand why Sarah Siddons thought her 'a character in which it was not likely that I should excite any great sensation', while Fanny Kemble noted that Portia 'is not a part that is generally much liked by actresses, or that excited much enthusiasm in the public'.[78]

Apart from being comparatively unexciting, there is also the fact that Portia is, in some respects, less than admirable. She is the chief agent of

73 Scott, *Drama of Yesterday and Today*, p. 583.   74 Tree, *Thoughts*, p. 44.
75 Scott, *Drama of Yesterday and Today*, p. 188.   76 Tree, *Thoughts*, p. 44.
77 See Hankey, 'Victorian Portias', p. 433.   78 *qtd ibid.*, p. 434.

Shylock's downfall – after invalidating the bond through the 'no jot of blood' quibble, she unnecessarily (or so it seems) engages in a prosecution that quickly becomes a persecution: indeed, Ellen Terry notes, 'whatever view one takes of it, it is impossible to admire it, although it may be defended on the ground that the end justifies the means'.[79]

Before Terry, no actress advanced her career, or even made a lasting impression, as Portia. The great Shylocks who preceded Irving – Macklin, Cooke, Kean – played opposite any number of Portias, depending on when and where they happened to be doing the play, while Terry had the advantage of long-term employment in the Lyceum company. Also, the extent to which the text was cut in the eighteenth and nineteenth centuries turned Portia into a relatively minor role: without Morocco and Arragon three scenes are gone, and gone along with them is any coherent treatment of the riddle of gold, silver and lead. Bassanio's casket scene was always much abbreviated, as was Act v, if Act v was played at all.

Helen Faucit's performance has probably received more attention than it deserves because of the notoriously negative review of the Irving production that appeared in *Blackwood's* (December 1879) – that the author was *Blackwood's* publisher Sir Theodore Martin, Faucit's husband, was an open secret. Martin deplored all the qualities Terry brought to the role in an implied, and at one point explicit, comparison with his now retired wife:[80] reading this review, one might think that Portia was an important part for Faucit, but Faucit spent only a few seasons with Macready, and Macready did not do the *Merchant* that often; most of her later career was in minor provincial companies. In 1867 she appeared in Manchester, and the *North British Daily Mail* was unimpressed, saying that the casket scene was 'painful . . . bordering on the ridiculous', adding that 'Portia was never one of Miss Faucit's best characters, and she is now more than ever past looking the part'.[81]

Terry came to Portia with the advantage of being relatively young, twenty-eight, with a slim figure and great physical beauty. James Spedding (known primarily as an authority on Sir Francis Bacon) writes of her performance for the Bancrofts, 'everything that she had to do seemed to come equally easy to her, and was done equally well; and the critic who would undertake to define the limits within which her power lies must be either very sagacious or very blind and deaf'.[82]

Some of the cuts and rearrangements the Bancrofts made to the text would have been a help, not a hindrance, to Terry – indeed, Spedding

---

79 Terry, *Four Lectures*, p. 121.   80 See pp. 25, 192, 234.
81 *qtd* Carlisle, *Helen Faucit*, pp. 218–19.
82 Spedding, *Reviews and Discussions*, p. 361.

observes that 'the part of Portia is not a long one'. In this version, instead of first being 'aweary of this great world', Portia was thrust into the tension of Morocco's choice of caskets. Spedding admired 'the reserved and stately courtesy with which she received the Prince of Morocco, and explained to him the conditions of his venture; her momentary flutter of alarm as he went to make his choice; her sudden relief, mixed with amusement, when he began by dismissing the leaden casket with contempt'.[83]

Terry's brilliance was wasted opposite the quiet Shylock of Coghlan, but Henry Irving was looking for an Ophelia in 1878, and acting on the advice of his friends Sir Frederick and Lady Pollock, he engaged Terry. After her success in that part, and as Pauline in Lytton's ever-popular *Lady of Lyons*, Irving cast her as Portia, and the result was, in terms of longevity and audience approval, the most successful production ever of *The Merchant of Venice*.

So much has been written about the Lyceum *Merchant*, which opened on 1 November 1879, that only a few main points can be dealt with here – Irving's stage business is well recorded in reviews, biographies and other historical literature, and key moments, such as his famous 'return' to an empty house after Jessica's elopement, are described in the textual commentary.

Lyceum productions were highly regarded for the quality of their scenery, but the *Merchant* of 1879 was not particularly lavish, its total cost being only £1,200. As Irving's biographer August Brereton notes, the production was 'a revelation, but it was made so by the intelligence and admirable acting, not, as some people seem to think . . . by the scenery'.[84] The story of how Irving decided to play Shylock after observing Levantine merchants while on a Mediterranean cruise is well known; it is also said that he went for a more dignified Jew because he knew how limited an actor he was, without the physical or vocal power of a Macklin or a Kemble. In a remarkably well-written review, the *Spectator* (8 November 1879) describes the qualities Irving brought to Shylock, and the social attitudes that articulate spectators brought to, and derived from, the performance:

> Probably, to every mind, except that of Shakespeare himself – in which all potential interpretations of his Shylock, as all potential interpretations of his Hamlet, must have had a place – the complex image which Mr Irving, presented to a crowd more or less impressed with notions of their own concerning the Jew whom Shakespeare drew, was entirely novel and unexpected; for here is a man whom none can despise, who can raise emotions both of pity and of fear, and make us Christians thrill with a retrospective sense of shame. Here is an usurer indeed, but no more like the

83 *Ibid.*   84 Brereton, *Life of Henry Irving*, vol. II, p. 301.

Henry Irving as Shylock.

customary modern rendering of that extortionate lender of whom Bassanio borrowed 'monies', than the merchants dei Medici were like pawnbrokers down Whitechapel way; an usurer, indeed, and full of 'thrift', which is rather the protest of his disdain and disgust for the sensuality and frivolity of the ribald crew out of whom he makes his 'Christian ducats', than of his own sordidness . . . a Jew, in intellectual faculties, in spiritual discipline, far in advance of the time and the country in which he lives, shaken with strong passion sometimes, but for the most part fixed in a deep and weary disdain.

This Shylock is not from the world of Whitechapel pawnbrokers – in mentioning contemporary Jewish life, the critic instantly dismisses it as being of no relevance to the play. Irving is opposed to another Shylock, the presumed Shylock of two centuries ago, and it is in comparison with this Shylock that Irving can 'make us Christians thrill with a *retrospective* sense of shame'.

While Irving played a fuller text than was customary at that time (he included Morocco but not Arragon), Portia's part was still heavily cut. What most endeared Terry to the audience, and offended the more conservative critics, was her beauty, her gaiety and the frankness with which she portrayed her sexual desire for Bassanio. *Blackwood's* was especially disapproving of how Terry held Bassanio

> caressingly by the hand, nay, almost in an embrace, with all the unrestrained fondness which is conceivable only after he had actually won her . . . There is, altogether, a great deal too much of what Rosalind calls 'a coming-on disposition'[85] in Miss Terry's bearing towards her lover. It is a general fault with her, but in Portia it is painfully out of place.

Terry's forwardness was also more than Henry James could cope with. To this 'miserable little snob',[86] as Theodore Roosevelt once called him, Terry

> giggles too much, plays too much with her fingers, is too free and familiar, too osculatory, in her relations with Bassanio. The mistress of Belmont was a great lady, as well as a tender and clever woman; but this side of the part quite eludes the actress, whose deportment is not such as we should expect in the splendid spinster who has princes for wooers. When Bassanio has chosen the casket which contains the key of her heart, she approaches him, and begins to pat and stroke him. This seems to us an appallingly false note, 'Good heavens, she's touching him!' a person sitting next to us exclaimed – a person whose judgment in such matters is always unerring.

James's 'unerring' judge was the former Portia, Fanny Kemble.[87]

AFTER IRVING

The Lyceum production marks a major turning point in the history of the *Merchant*: Irving joined Macklin, Cooke and Kean as a Shylock against

---

85 *As You Like It*, 4.1.112–13.
86 *qtd* Cunliffe, *Literature of the United States*, p. 258.
87 James, *Scenic Art*, pp. xviii, 143.

whom future performers would be measured, and for the first time Portia attracted considerable notice. This was as true in the United States as it was in England, since Irving's company made no less than six American tours between 1883 and 1903.

One nearly immediate effect of Irving's success was that the play would no longer be acceptable without Act v. When Lawrence Barrett staged the *Merchant* in 1886, using his friend Edwin Booth's text, *Shakespeariana's* critic complained, 'The charming fifth act, which so ideally and joyously rounds out the comedy, is altogether cut, and only a ragged here and there, and a consciousness of inconsequence, in scenes not wholly dedicated to the Jew, remain vaguely to remind us of the perfect whole we miss.'[88]

Booth and Barrett jointly mounted a new *Merchant* in the following season, and 5.1 was restored, the newly executed set revealing, as described in the Philadelphia *Item*, Jessica and Lorenzo in a 'dreamy Italian garden by moonlight, with rose-colored lamps and twinkling stars'.[89] They went to great lengths to ensure that the other sets, too, would outdo anything yet seen in America: Act i showed 'the Piazzetta of St Mark along the south side of the Palace of the Doges, whose columned facade filled the side of the stage to the audience's right', and for Act ii Shylock's house stood beside a bridge spanning a canal, high enough so that a gondola could pass underneath with its gondolier standing.[90] The beautiful Polish actress Helena Modjeska, who had great success as Ophelia, was their Portia. Her performance was distinguished by the quiet earnestness with which she delivered the 'mercy' speech.[91]

As noted, Booth's Shylock was a much darker character than Irving's, and some of the stage business in his promptbooks is reminiscent of Victorian melodrama. He was not unaware that his performance might be seen as a libel against the Jewish people, but like many an actor after him, he believed that to play Shylock essentially as a villain was to remain faithful to Shakespeare's intention, however problematic that might be to modern sentiments. He once wrote to Richard Mansfield, another notable Shylock, 'it is not easy to estimate how much the antipathies to the Jewish race have been sharpened by those portrayals of the wolf-like ferocity of the one great figure that typifies the spirit of usury'.[92]

Mansfield, an accomplished musician as well as a versatile actor, played only a few Shakespearean leads in a career cut short by an early death; his great successes were as Jekyll/Hyde in a stage adaptation of Stevenson's tale, and as Cyrano de Bergerac. The story of Mansfield's *Merchant* is a strange

---

88 'The Drama', pp. 523, 524.   89 *qtd Amer.II*, pp. 48–9.
90 *Ibid.*, p. 48.   91 See p. 223.   92 *Amer.II*, p. 50.

one:[93] while on his third American tour of 1887–8, Henry Irving saw Mansfield perform, and was so impressed that he invited him to appear for a season at the Lyceum, a season that unfortunately did not prove to be a success. Mansfield ended up owing Irving a large amount of money, and subsequently developed an irrational and obsessive hatred of his erstwhile friend – when he came to play Shylock in 1893, opposite his wife Beatrice Cameron as Portia, Mansfield most wanted to better Irving, about to embark on another American tour, by returning to the 'true' Shylock of Shakespeare. He wrote to William Winter, 'I shall make Shylock what Shakespeare evidently intended: a hotblooded, revengeful & rapacious Oriental Jew.' Winter then praised Mansfield's interpretation for having 'brought into the strongest relief the craft and wickedness of his motives, the malignity of his hatred, and the deadly determination of his passion for revenge', but the production played to poor houses in Chicago, where Irving had been a short time previously. Mansfield blamed Winter: 'Damn your criticisms! . . . I had a deuce of a time getting our only patrons, the Jews, to come and see *The Merchant*, because *you* made me out a fiend and a vulture.'[94]

More successful in post-Irving America was Augustin Daly, one of the most powerful managers of the century, known especially for bringing elaborate spectacle to his productions of Shakespeare. Daly's first encounter with the *Merchant* was in 1875, and he followed the (by then) traditional pattern of a rearranged text to allow for scenic tableaux. Towse thought that the 'the rich dressing and picturesque setting' made 'small amends for the irreverent and often incapable treatment of the text',[95] but he admired the Shylock of E. L. Davenport:

> He surpassed Edwin Booth in range, though inferior to him in subtlety and electrical tragic inspiration. His Jew was a forceful and consistent study, masterful, keen, with a note of menace in its sarcastic self-control. He was intense rather than tempestuous, and tore no passion to tatters . . . the concentrated, cool, and deadly purpose of his acting in the court scene was appalling, and his final collapse a tragic picture of blank and irremediable despair.[96]

Twenty-three years later Daly chose *The Merchant of Venice* for what was to be his last and most sumptuous Shakespearean production. Unlike his previous effort, this was after Irving's American tours and the Booth/Barrett revival, and Daly was determined to surpass them. Venice was prettified – Shylock's house, 'mouldy and crumbling' in Booth and Barrett's production,

93 For a fuller account see *ibid.*, pp. 211–25.   94 *Ibid.*, pp. 217–18.
95 Towse, *Sixty Years*, p. 130.   96 *Ibid.*, p. 131.

Augustin Daly's staging of the carnival following the elopement of Jessica and Lorenzo.

was gaily painted and covered with roses, and there were more extras providing atmosphere than had ever been seen in the *Merchant*.[97] Apart from the scenery, Daly's leading lady, Ada Rehan, was the only real attraction – Sidney Herbert was too limited and inexperienced an actor to succeed Davenport, and Daly's last production was not one of his triumphs.[98]

The Shylock of Scottish-born Robert Mantell, an audience favourite in a variety of heroic roles, would have been more important had he been able to play New York in his prime, but he had to remain outside the state because of a pending arrest warrant for failing to meet alimony payments. His Hamlet and Othello were a hit with the public, but received only guarded approval from the critics, due to his tendency to over-act in the more passionate scenes. One would expect that these excesses would be even worse as Shylock, but to Mantell's credit, he gave a controlled performance, moving William Edgett to write in the *Boston Evening Transcript*, 'so perfect is his command of himself that he is able to give a quiet and downright restrained earnestness to the single phrase, "I am a Jew", in the midst of a long speech that is aflame with uninterrupted passion and pathos'.[99]

Even when allowing for the varying perceptions of individual critics, around the turn of the century we see a definite pattern emerging in American attitudes to the way Shylock should be played. Irving still cast a long shadow over his successors, who found themselves hard-pressed to place their own stamp on the role: Mansfield and Sothern, in presenting a physically unpleasant and undignified Shylock, received little approval for their efforts, while Mantell earned respect for his restraint.

JACOB ADLER AND THE YIDDISH THEATRE

In 1901, the founder of one of America's great theatrical families, Jacob Adler, became the first actor to play Shylock in Yiddish, at the People's Theatre on New York's Lower East Side. A refugee from the pogroms of Czarist Russia,[100] Adler saw Irving when he was resident in London, and his own characterisation earned favourable comparisons.[101] The poet Morris Vintshevski wrote in the Yiddish newspaper *Forverts*,

97 *Amer.II*, pp. 92–3.

98 Photographs of Augustin Daly's sets for his last great Shakespearean revival of 1898 are in *ibid*.

99 7 March 1907, *qtd ibid*., p. 239.   100 See below, pp. 41–3.

101 Adler's career, and the history of the *Merchant*, was affected by the fire at London's Hebrew Dramatic Club in 1887, in which seventeen people died. This shut the Yiddish theatre of London down for some time, and Adler was forced to move to New York.

as hard as Henry Irving's task was to depict a human Jew while remaining true to the words of the great Englishman's play, it is all the more remarkable when a Jew undertakes to perform Shakespeare's words before a Jewish audience . . . Mr Adler's Shylock will forever stand even higher than Irving's, for however great the latter may be, he can never sufficiently understand the Venetian Jewish merchant's pride.[102]

Two years later, Adler did Shylock again, still speaking in Yiddish, but this time with an English-speaking supporting cast that included Meta Maynard as Portia. The company toured the major cities of the north-east, and finished with a week on Broadway; before the opening, Adler spoke of his interpretation in an interview with the New York *Evening Telegram*: 'He is a patriarch, a higher being. A certain grandeur, the triumph of long patience, intellect, and character has been imparted to him by the sufferings and traditions that have been his teachers.'[103] Adler believed that Shylock, 'a good man of a persecuted race', never intended to exact Antonio's pound of flesh, but brought the case to court 'to show the world that his despised ducats have actually bought and paid for it. His whetting the knife on his sole is a hyperbolical menace: his sardonic smile, accompanying this action, is the only sharp edge that shall cut the self-humiliated Merchant.'[104]

For this revival, the producers hired the scenery and costumes from Augustin Daly's 1898 *Merchant*, giving Adler production qualities he could hardly have dreamt of when acting downtown at the People's. The reaction of the Yiddish press was expectedly enthusiastic, and reviews in the English-language papers ranged from respectful to very favourable: the *New York Times* (26 May 1903) said that Adler 'fell, as it were, between two stools . . . the grim austerity of Irving and the malignancy of Mansfield were alike absent'; to the *Theatre* (18 November 1903), Adler

> is indeed avaricious and vindictive, but above all, he is the passionate, proud, and scornful vindicator of Israel as against the despiteful usage of the Christian merchant and his friends . . . Despoiled by the court in which he has asked for justice, he casts one look of ineffable contempt upon his persecutors, then walks off in superb, silent dignity, a martyr-type of his nation.

This production was successful enough to warrant a revival on Broadway two years later, and at the same time as Adler was recreating his Shylock at the 58th Street Theatre, another Jewish actor, Rudolf Schildkraut – soon to be Adler's friend and rival – was making his mark in Max Reinhardt's production at Berlin's Deutsches Schauspielhaus.

102 28 December 1901, *qtd* Berkowitz, 'A True Jewish Jew', pp. 80–1.
103 28 May 1903, *qtd* Alter, 'When the Audience', p. 151.
104 *qtd* Berkowitz, 'A True Jewish Jew', p. 80.

Jacob Adler as Shylock and Meta Maynard as Portia, Broadway production of 1903.

RUDOLF SCHILDKRAUT AND MAX REINHARDT

Max Reinhardt's film of *A Midsummer Night's Dream* (1935) gives us an idea of what his Berlin *Merchant* must have been like – the sets were as opulent and colourful as any ever designed and executed for a Shakespeare play. In the *Berliner Volks-Zeitung*'s description:

> The Renaissance – it glowed everywhere in rich colours, in the fullness of life and happiness: Renaissance in the magnificent, cheery halls of Belmont Castle, where the rich, graceful, brilliant Portia[105] holds court surrounded by pleasure and games, and is hotly pursued by princes from all the nations in the world! Renaissance in the secluded corners of the lagoon city. Richly dressed Venetian youths warm themselves on sun-drenched piazzas . . . the night throbs to the tempting sounds of the guitar, serenades sing out, carnevalesque and masked figures flit over jetties and bridges to the flickering light of torches . . . then another moonlit night full of celestial poetry, full of love and music; a tender, warm haze in the air; a few stars looking down furtively from the dusky violet sky; the all-pervading scent of blossoms and the soft tones of a flute from behind the greenery . . .[106]

Another keynote was the liveliness and rapid movement of the performance, to Heinrich Hart, 'a racing, romping, wriggling, storming from beginning to end'.[107]

The Romanian-born Schildkraut joined a touring troupe of German actors while in his teens. He soon became a favourite in comedies and operettas in Vienna, where the opportunity to study with Friedrich Mitterwurzer turned him into a major classical actor. Hermann Sinsheimer remembers Schildkraut's Shylock:

> a full-blooded actor and a conscious Jew, he entered into the feelings of a hunted, tormented and therefore unbalanced being, through whom generations of Jews voiced their shrill protest against their persecutors of all times. At the same time, Schildkraut imbued the character with an unspeakable melancholy, which was elemental compared with the ennui of Antonio. Injustice was round him like a shroud.[108]

The liberal German journals praised Reinhardt for presenting 'not a roaring predator, but instead a human individual against the background of an entire national history', while the nationalist critic Friedrich Diesel attacked the production and Schildkraut in particular for 'branding this

---

105 Else Heims, according to Helene Richter in *Shakespeare Jahrbuch* (1907), 'portrayed Portia vividly and with natural charm'. Agnes Sorma also played Portia in that production.
106 10 November 1905, *qtd* Fischer-Lichte, 'Theatre as Festive Play', pp. 172–3.
107 *Der Tag* (11 November 1905), *qtd ibid.*, p. 174.
108 Sinsheimer, *Shylock*, p. 142.

malicious, insidious, vindictive haggling Jew as a martyr, as a prosaic defender of trampled human rights'.[109]

In 1911 Schildkraut went to New York and joined Boris Thomashevsky's Yiddish company, playing first Lear and then Shylock. While the Yiddish critics were proud of a Jewish actor having achieved such great success on the classical German stage, some felt that it got in the way of a truly 'authentic' performance: to Joel Entin of *Di Tsukunft*, 'when someone has since child-hood kept his distance from the Yiddish masses . . . it is difficult to rejoin them'.[110] When Schildkraut returned to New York in 1920, the *New York Times* (12 November 1920) saw 'a remarkable and memorable Shylock . . . it stands forth as a daringly modernized portrait in the spirit which a latter-day realism enjoins upon the stage', and David Belasco, soon to venture forth with his own production of the *Merchant*, said of Schildkraut, '[he was] the most natural Shylock I have ever seen, and I have seen all of the best Shylocks for a generation'.[111]

Unlike Adler, Schildkraut never performed with an English-speaking cast, but taken together their influence extended well beyond the confines of the Yiddish theatre, as they were seen by the major newspaper critics, and by a wide cross-section of American theatre people. Henceforth, the key quality to be demanded of a Shylock in America was to be 'latter-day realism' and understatement (this is ironic coming from a theatrical tradition known for its excesses). However dark a characterisation of Shylock might be, an underlying nobility would be expected.

NOVELLI, SOTHERN AND MARLOWE

Another foreign actor to make an impression in America was the Italian star, Ermete Novelli, who brought his company to the United States in 1907, with himself as Shylock and his wife, Olga Giannini, as Portia. Novelli was con-sidered at the time to be the successor to Tommaso Salvini as Italy's premier actor; Benjamin de Caseres wrote in *Theatre Magazine* (March 1907), that his Shylock was 'a creature whose vengeful wickedness, unmerited suffer-ings and demoniacal furiousness leave their tracks in the memory from act to act and long after the final curtain'.

Winter, though, deplored everything that Novelli did, saying 'his ideal of the character was seen to be simply ignominious, his Shylock being nothing

---

109 Engel, *Berliner Tageblatt* (13 November 1905), Diesel, *Deutsche Zeitung* (11 November
      1905), *qtd* Fischer-Lichte, 'Theatre as Festive Play', p. 171.
110 October 1911, *qtd* Berkowitz, 'A True Jewish Jew', p. 83.
111 *Ibid.*, p. 86.

Ermete Novelli as Shylock.

more than a trivial Jew pawnbroker . . . a trivial trickster, a sly contriver of mischief, a commonplace creature of low cunning and petty spite'.[112] It is indeed likely that Novelli appeared overly flamboyant only a few years after Irving's final tour, but Winter's condemnation seems excessive: some of

112 Winter, *Shakespeare on the Stage*, pp. 164–5.

Novelli's stage business was remembered and recorded with approval (presumably by the stage manager) in the promptbook of Winthrop Ames's Broadway production of 1928.[113] Several years later, Novelli made a film of the *Merchant*, of which some fascinating fragments remain.[114]

Although none ever acted Shylock in English, Adler, Schildkraut and Novelli would have made America in the early twentieth century an exciting place to be for anyone interested in *The Merchant of Venice*. To their work we must add that of E. H. Sothern and Julia Marlowe, who maintained and extended the pictorial Shakespeare tradition.

Sothern was a competent but unexceptional actor, and the main draw cards of his productions were Marlowe's acting and the brilliant settings. H. T. Parker of the Boston *Transcript* (15 December 1905) describes Sothern's Act I scene:

> Our eyes traversed the Venice of romance – not the hackneyed square of
> the lion and St Mark's and the doges' palace. They wandered down long
> irregular canals in the blazing sunshine of a Venetian noon. They left the
> gray cool of Venetian walls misty in the soft starlit, lamplit night. Here was
> the striped mooring for a gondola, there a waterside shrine, and there again
> the great dome of Santa Maria della Salute.[115]

As for Marlowe, the *New York Times* (5 November 1905) notes that her 'loveliness seems never so potent, her art never so satisfying as through the medium of Shakespeare', her Portia 'wholly a delight to listen to, by reason of the flawlessness of her wonderful diction and the resonance and music of her voice'.

But the same reviewer delivers a harsh attack against Sothern, showing once again that American critics expect a Shylock who, if not totally sympathetic, at least shows a measure of dignity:

> The one element of this latest Shylock which impresses itself with
> unpleasantest force is the fact that in its externals it is the filthiest figure that
> has yet appeared to typify the great poetic creation, and no sort of argument
> can justify it . . . it is inconceivable that the elegant Venetians would transact
> affairs with so unprepossessing, so menial a man as Mr Sothern shows us.

ENGLAND AT THE TURN OF THE CENTURY

Three figures loom large in the history of English Shakespearean production from the last decade of the nineteenth century until the post-World War I

---

113 Examples cited below, in the text and commentary.   114 See p. 86.
115 15 December 1905, *qtd Amer.II*, p. 273.

years, but as none brought anything new to *The Merchant of Venice*, we must pass over them quickly here.

F. R. Benson, whose 'Bensonians' toured Britain year after year, provided employment and training for several generations of actors who would later go on to great things. Gordon Crosse, the London barrister whose thirty-one volumes of theatrical diaries provide an incomparable view of Shakespeare in England from 1890 to 1953, first saw Benson's Shylock in 1894: 'he made a good deal of whetting of the knife, and tapping with it the seal on his bond in answer to the taunts of Gratiano . . . but Shylock did not seem to me to be among his best parts'.[116]

Ben Greet, Benson's near-exact contemporary, specialised in outdoor productions of Shakespeare during the summer months, and went over to schools tours in the winter; he also barnstormed America for many years. In a rare London engagement, he staged the *Merchant* at the Olympic Theatre in May of 1897; William Archer objected to a slavish imitation of Irving's style:

> One might have imagined that Mr Ben Greet, being, by the very nature of his enterprise, dispensed from the obligation of scenic display, would revel in his freedom and seize the opportunity to let Shakespeare tell his own story after his own fashion. But not a bit of it! We must have all the drawbacks of a spectacular Lyceum setting without its beauties.[117]

Few people command more respect in the history of Shakespearean performance than William Poel. As the founder of the Elizabethan Stage Society, he made it his life's work to remove Shakespeare from the nineteenth-century pictorial theatre, and return him to the style of Elizabethan times. Although his theories, radical at the time, have by now been almost universally accepted, as a director and actor he was such an eccentric that the productions themselves must be regarded as no more than oddities.

Poel's *Merchant*, performed in December of 1898 at London's St George's Hall, was one of his last experiments. Crosse, as did nearly everyone who saw a Poel production, agreed that 'the absence of scenery was surprisingly little felt', but the quality of the acting was another matter: Poel, assuming that the Elizabethan Shylock was a low-comic role, 'played the part in a red wig, shabby clothes, and with the avowed intention of giving the Elizabethan view of the character as a grotesque & unsympathetic villain . . . he was a serio-comic, screaming Shylock with a shuffling gait and a querulous manner, but there was little or no dramatic fire behind his shrieking and jerking'.[118]

116 Crosse, *Diaries* vol. I, p. 54.
117 Archer, *Theatrical World*, pp. 151–2.   118 Crosse, *Diaries* vol. II, p. 70.

Given that 'scenic Shakespeare had reached such extremes' by the end of the nineteenth century that it probably would have come to an end even without Poel,[119] his *Merchant* must be seen as a step backward, since it perpetuated the idea of Shakespeare's Shylock as a comic villain – as noted, in attempting to recreate what he *thought* was the original Shylock, he may have been the first to play him in the fabled red wig.

BEERBOHM TREE

English productions of the *Merchant* in the post-Irving era generated little excitement, but in 1908, Herbert Beerbohm Tree, who could legitimately claim to be Irving's successor as England's leading actor, joined the fray.

Shylock was Tree's third big Jewish role – in 1895 he was a huge success as Svengali in a stage adaptation of Du Maurier's *Trilby*, and in 1905 he played Fagin in yet another version of *Oliver Twist*. *The Times* (6 April 1908) felt that these two characters, flamboyant villains both, informed the third: he was 'perhaps unable to forget previous stages of existence in which [Tree] was Svengali or Fagin'. When Tree took the play to New York, Montrose Moses, an important local critic, made the same observation: 'when the evening was over, in memory we did not conjure up the "Jew that Shakespeare drew", but rather Mr Tree's Svengali and Fagin'.[120]

The costume was necessarily different, but Tree's nose, beard and hair for Shylock were very similar to what he wore in *Oliver Twist* – the New York *American*'s description of his appearance evokes more of Dickens than Shakespeare: 'In his brown gabardine and golden yellow headgear as he first appeared he was most picturesque. His hook nose, with his gray and tangled beard, lent him a dangerous look, yet did not exclude dignity or intellect. His gestures were throughout Semitic.'[121] After Svengali, Tree would be always known, in the words of *The Times* critic, for going 'into fits . . . [which] never fails to delight his public', and he seized every opportunity that Shylock affords for them. These patented 'violent paroxysms' left reviewers cold in both London and New York: to Towse in the *Nation* (18 May 1916), Tree was 'commonplace, tricky, melodramatic, and unimpressive'.

Two other Tree trademarks were grandiose scenery (as usual, the text was rearranged to group the Venice and Belmont scenes), and a stage full of extras. Robert Atkins, who would later play Shylock himself, was Tree's Duke. He recalls:

119 Moore, 'William Poel', p. 21.
120 *qtd Amer.11*, p. 197.   121 9 May 1916, *qtd ibid*.

The scenes were massive and magnificent to look at, and all Jewry seemed to be in the cast . . . my entrance on the Rialto to open the play broke into a host of Jews, magnificent specimens hired from the East End, haggling over the sale of their wares to Gentiles, and many a Yiddish expression floated into the auditorium. The articles for sale were theatrical props, but after a few nights they were found trying to sell genuine watches, rings and necklaces and if successful picking up the money at the end of the performance.[122]

As something of a publicity stunt, Tree cast the American Elsie Ferguson as Portia for his New York production of 1916. Ferguson, a beautiful young actress with a large following, had done only modern light comedies, and was thrust into this major Shakespearean role with no real preparation. The New York critics, with admirable generosity, found all that they could to praise in her performance, the *New York Times* (9 May 1916) noting 'the complete charm of her Portia in those portions of the play that lie at Belmont . . . the princess whose fate lies in one of the three inscrutable caskets has beauty and intelligence and a captivating humor'. But even Ferguson's most ardent admirers had to agree with this critic that her voice was 'monotonous in tone, a voice trained too long, perhaps, in the contemporary drama', and with Towse, who said that this Portia, while 'very fair to look upon, was the work of a Shakespearean novice, utterly undistinguished in manner and diction' (*Nation* 18 May 1916).

Had Ferguson's charm and talent been given a chance to mature with a longer period of training under such an experienced manager as Tree, she might have proved a great success in parts such as Rosalind and Viola, but after her failure as Portia, she never attempted Shakespeare again.

ASCHE AND BRAYTON, FORBES-ROBERTSON, BASSERMAN

The Australian actor Oscar Asche brought an English company to the country of his birth in 1910 for a tour that included the *Merchant*, with his wife, Lily Brayton, as Portia. In speech as well as appearance, Asche's Shylock was the modern equivalent of the supposed Elizabethan stage Jew – he was probably the first actor to give Shylock a Whitechapel-Yiddish accent. This innovation, if it was indeed Asche's, is significant, as it further defines an English Shylock's 'Jewishness' by its similarity to the East European Jews of London's East End.[123] Local critics praised Asche for breaking with what

---

122 Atkins, *Robert Atkins*, p. 64.

123 E. H. Sothern tried what purported to be a Yiddish accent for a time, but one can only guess what it sounded like. The *Boston Transcript* mentions 'lisping sibilants, catarrhal gutturals, and strange nasal tones' (*qtd Amer.II*, p. 273).

appears to have become, since Irving, the orthodox approach. The *Sydney Mail* (2 March 1910) comments:

> The generally accepted interpretation regards the Jew as one entitled to a good deal of sympathy – the representative of a despised and cruelly treated race, a father who has been deserted and robbed by the daughter he loves – but Mr Asche recognises no room for sentiment in his pourtrayal [*sic*] of the part. In his view Shylock is a grasping, vindictive miser, whose whole mind is concentrated upon the accumulation of wealth and bitter hatred of the Christians who so openly show their contempt for him and his people.[124]

Like Laurence Olivier, Sir Johnstone Forbes-Robertson was considered one of the great Hamlets, and, like Olivier, he did not attempt Shylock until late in his career – he waited until his farewell season of 1913. To Crosse, Forbes-Robertson was second only to Irving: not nearly 'so grand and sympathetic . . . but more like a Jew of the 16th century, though withal a Jew of impressive and dominant personality. He played with grim intensity and a touch of grotesqueness that was quite appropriate to [Shakespeare's] conception.'[125]

When Forbes-Robertson took the production to New York, the *New York Times* (22 November 1913) placed more emphasis on the negative or villainous elements of the portrayal. Shylock was 'a wolfish creature who in his general attitude towards the Christians realizes exactly what one expects from the physical presentment . . . one gets from it absolutely no sense of extenuating qualities of mind or heart or devotedness to religion or race'.

At the same time as Forbes-Robertson was in New York, Albert Basserman, whom Sinsheimer believed to be 'the greatest German actor of [his] time . . . the heroic figure of the German stage',[126] replaced Schildkraut in Max Reinhardt's Berlin production, opposite Else Heims as Portia.[127] Siegfried Jacobsohn describes him as a 'giant with a large hook nose, scruffy hair, untidy grey beard and threateningly pointed eyebrows . . . uttering noises like a wild beast',[128] and the *Shakespeare Jahrbuch* reviewer calls him 'ugly, eerie, malignant, almost grotesque'.[129] Like so many German actors, Jewish and gentile,[130] Basserman fled Germany when Hitler came to power.

---

124 For the *Merchant*'s colourful history in Australia, see especially Gay, *Merchant*, pp. 49–66; Golder and Madelaine, *O Brave New World*.

125 Crosse, *Diaries* vol. v, p. 151.   126 Sinsheimer, *Shylock*, p. 141.

127 Else Basserman was also in the production, probably as Nerissa.

128 *qtd* Sehrt, 'Der Shylock', p. 82.

129 Kahane, 'Max Reinhardt's' Shakespearezyklus, p. 118.

130 Sinsheimer notes that Basserman was a 'full-blooded Aryan', *Shylock*, p. 142.

Ending up in Hollywood, he appeared in many films; his last performance was as the avuncular Sergei Ratov in Michael Powell's *The Red Shoes* (1948).

THE OLD VIC, ENGLAND AT WAR

London's Old Vic Theatre, already established as an opera house under the management of Lilian Baylis, embarked on its initial Shakespeare season in 1914. The first productions were rather nondescript affairs, but this changed radically when Ben Greet offered to take over the Shakespearean part of the operation; from the beginning of World War I until well after World War II, Old Vic Shakespeare was a London institution, although the continued opera programme and the effect of German bombs meant that the company often had to perform in other theatres.

With so many called to war service, the *Merchant*, having one of the smallest casts of any Shakespeare play, was a popular choice. But the acting was always to be competent at best: they had one exceptional actress, Sybil Thorndike, whose early training was on Greet's American tours – she played Portia a number of times opposite different Shylocks from 1915 to 1928. Crosse rated her second only to Ellen Terry:

> Her silent acting in the three casket scenes was worth going far to see; the varying emotions showing themselves but kept under control by serene power. In the Trial Scene she was quieter than most Portias, there was no staginess; but when she begs the ring she rightly showed the rather hysterical excitement of reaction after a great strain.[131]

Thorndike notes in her delightful memoir of Lilian Baylis that the company often played in Bethnal Green, East London, as the theatre was given over to the more profitable opera on Saturday nights: 'A converted swimming bath made a fine theatre, and a large audience, mostly Jews, filled it week after week. I think it was the most vivid and intelligent audience I've ever played to – it was only then I realized what the Jewish race does for our theatre.'

Baylis's comment was,

> I do like to see the Jews coming, don't you dear? . . . Even if they aren't Christians, it must do them good, but I wish we didn't have to give them *The Merchant of Venice*, the Christians all behave so badly. Of course, I sometimes wonder how they get the money to come to the best seats, when they look so poor. Still, they do laugh in the right places, and I don't suppose they steal stamps, because they're so clever at getting money. I wish we had that sort of cleverness for getting money for the Vic![132]

131 Crosse, *Fifty Years*, p. 63.   132 Thorndike, *Lilian Baylis*, p. 73.

Such remarks are just silly, not pernicious, but they epitomise the lack of significance the English theatre had given to the *Merchant* since the days of Irving: strikingly absent from published comment is consideration of the play's relevance to the contemporary world, a world in which European Jews were being subjected to horrific privation.

The great wave of Jewish immigration to the Western democracies started in 1880; between 1881 and 1914 over 3,000,000 Jews fled from the renewed and violent anti-Semitism in Russia and Poland, a relatively small number, perhaps 100,000 to 150,000, settling in England. These new-comers swamped London's existing Jewish community – approximately 60,000 in 1880 – and by 1901, the East End/Whitechapel area had about 42,000 Russian-born Jews,[133] visible enough to provoke anti-Semitic sentiments in the less tolerant portions of British society, and anti-Semitic statements in the British press. Amongst the worst of these was in the same journal that attacked Irving's *Merchant*. *Blackwood's* (February 1901) complained,

> every European country except our own has the Hebrew it deserves, but we get them all in turn. The Jewish aristocracy, the Sephardim of Portugal and Spain, who gave us Disraeli in the third generation, have ceased to arrive. The Dutch Jews, with their long pedigree, are stationary. Even the more plebeian German Jews are fast giving place to the outcasts of Russia and Poland – the wild, hunted-looking creatures, with fur caps and baggy, greasy clothes, who may be seen gaping about them most days at the London Docks. It is a proverb that the nearer the East a Jew dwells, the more degraded he is.

But in clear contrast to the situation in the United States,[134] the Jewish population of England was relatively small, and had little influence on mainstream English culture: Shylock could be a Dickensian Whitechapel Jew without arousing any protest. Undoubtedly, actors who performed Shylock in this way did so in the sincere belief that this was how Shakespeare expected the character to be played; what becomes more and more astonishing as we proceed through the twentieth century is that English critics and audiences, albeit with some notable exceptions, continued to accept and approve of it.

Within this context, the work of Maurice Moscovitch is a most interesting phenomenon. According to the New York *Literary Digest* (13 December 1919), Moscovitch, born in Odessa in 1871, 'went upon the stage at fourteen;

133 Rubinstein, *History of the Jews*, pp. 95–6.
134 See below, p. 44.

when he was twenty-three he came to America and for over twenty years played in the Yiddish theaters of New York's East Side and in other Northern cities'. Trying his luck in London, he became a popular figure amongst Jewish audiences at the Pavilion in Whitechapel, and in 1919 the promoter J. B. Fagan hired him to play Shylock for a new production that opened at the Court Theatre in London, after a brief season in Manchester.

Moscovitch knew Jacob Adler, had worked with him and almost certainly would have seen his Shylock, but his interpretation of the part was quite different – clearly not the 'higher being' of whom Adler spoke. Although he was billed as a Russian or a Russian-Jewish actor, after a long residency in the United States Moscovitch spoke English, but with a slight accent that most found apt: Crosse said that it was 'of use in helping to set Shylock apart from the others'. He considered Moscovitch to be 'in the realistic vein, not the great tragic figure of the Kean tradition; grotesque rather than tragic, but grimly natural more than anything else'.[135]

Desmond McCarthy was perhaps more impressed than he should have been, since he believed Moscovitch was acting in an unfamiliar language: 'he has survived triumphantly the drawback of acting in a foreign tongue; proving himself the best elocutionist in the cast, only keeping a slight accent such as an actor might assume to stress the differences between Shylock and the Venetians'. To McCarthy, this was 'a realistic Shylock, and being himself a Jew, instinct prompts him to all those gestures and movements which an actor of another race can only acquire by painstaking mimicry'.[136]

These observers' use of words such as 'natural' and 'realistic' show that to play Shylock as someone from the East End, which is what Moscovitch himself was in their somewhat mistaken view, was to be faithful to the text. Hence we read in the *Illustrated London News* that 'the sweeping dignity which Irving gave this Jew, the romantic nobility a Forbes-Robertson suggested, the colour Tree threw upon him, are all swept clean away by Mr Moscovitch's realism, and with him *it is a case of going back to Shakespeare*'.[137] Whether it was from Moscovitch's carrying the part too far in one direction, or from *The Times* critic's lack of understanding of what he saw, one can only be troubled by his description of this Shylock as 'rather greasy, snuffling, with a strong sense of humour and not a shred of dignity', and then stunned by the closing comment: 'We do not excuse, but begin to understand, pogroms' (10 October 1919).

What this critic began to understand was reported in his own newspaper two months previously:

135 Crosse, *Diaries* vol. VII, p. 12.
136 McCarthy, *Drama*, p. 14.
137 *qtd LD* 13 December 1919, emphasis added.

ONE ENORMOUS POGROM: 'KILL THE JEWS AND SAVE RUSSIA'

> Terrible stories are reaching Warsaw of the state of anarchy beyond the
> Polish lines in Volhynia. Atrocities are taking place there which equal the
> worst of the Reign of Terror in Moscow and Petrograd . . . men carry
> badges with the inscription 'Kill the Jews and Save Russia' . . . Unexampled
> massacres of the Jews have been taking place . . . Sometimes they have been
> rounded up in the main street of the town and fire opened with machine-
> guns from one end; sometimes they have been burnt alive. (*The Times* 5
> August 1919)

Fagan's production ran until late March of 1920; Moscovitch left the
company a week before it closed,[138] in order to allow the famous Dutch actor,
Louis Bouwmeester, to realise a long-held ambition to play Shylock for an
English audience (*The Times* 22 March 1920). Reginald Denham, then at
the start of his career, played Solanio, and describes Bouwmeester's
performance:

> He couldn't speak English and played the part in Dutch. We, of course, *did*
> play in English: his bilingual son stood in the wings and waved a handker-
> chief whenever we had to speak . . . his interpretation of Shylock did not
> follow the pattern of Irving, who sentimentalized and humanized the
> character, or of Moscovitch, who emotionalized it. Bouwmeester made the
> Jew a fiend incarnate straight up from the nether regions. His 'business' in
> the trial scene, when he goes to cut the pound of flesh from Antonio's bosom
> . . . was unadulterated horror.[139]

AMERICA, ENGLAND AND GERMANY IN THE 1920S

Brooklyn-born Walter Hampden got his early training as a Bensonian in
England, and soon after his return to the United States in 1907, he was
successful in both classic and modern roles, eventually forming his own
company. His production of *The Merchant of Venice* opened in New York in
May of 1921, and from the critics' response we are able to see some of the
differences between American and English ideas of the play at that time.

Hampden's interpretation was little different from that of Oscar Asche
or E. H. Sothern: he was, in the words of Alexander Woollcott, 'a senile,
dirty, and singularly malignant Shylock . . . without a single one of the

---

138 Moscovitch went on to play a variety of roles in two very successful tours of
     Australia. American audiences were to see his Shylock in a different production in
     1930 (see below, p. 48).

139 Denham, *Stars*, p. 92. Two years later, Bouwmeester did Shylock again at Stratford
     in a special Saturday matinée.

traditional appeals for sympathy which have accumulated through the generations in the gradual process of "civilizing" *The Merchant of Venice*.[140] To O. W. Firkins, writing in the *Weekly Review* (28 May 1921), Hampden's Shylock

> is squalid; it is aged, it is (in parts) unbalanced or hysterical. The text does not to require Shylock to be any or all of these things: it does not forbid him to be any or all of the three. There is not the smallest improbability in the supposition that all three of these traits were gratifying to an Elizabethan audience. There is grave doubt whether any one of them recommends the play to an audience of our time.

Significantly, Heywood Broun noted 'it is the sort of Shylock Henry Ford would enjoy' (*LD* 4 June 1921).

Broun's reference to the powerful industrialist, whose notorious anti-Semitism was expressed in articles in his own *Dearborn Independent*, and later in his active support of Hitler, shows that an American performance of the *Merchant* could not be isolated from contemporary political questions, questions that were of the greatest importance to millions of Americans. Well over 2,000,000 Jews emigrated from Eastern Europe to America in the late nineteenth and early twentieth centuries, forming the huge Jewish communities that existed, and still exist, in New York and other major cities: by 1929, New York alone was home to over 2,500,000 Jews, fifteen times as many as London, a city of the same size. They had, it is fair to say, fifteen times the impact on business, the arts and intellectual life in general, and their presence was central to the manner in which the *Merchant* was to be performed.

The great showman David Belasco, whose *Merchant* opened in December of 1922, seized upon every opportunity for scenic effects, making the usual rearrangements of the text in order to allow them. Ludwig Lewisohn wrote in the *Nation* (3 January 1923):

> He gives us the Italy of the sixteenth century; he gives us Venice, the Venice of Titian and Veronese, even to the russet hair, the formal gardens, the tang of Oriental gravity and glow. The scenes and costumes are at once correct

---

140 With the acerbic wit for which he is famous, Woollcott later adds:
> At the end of the trial scene last night Mr Hampden responded with a graceful curtain speech to the genuine and hearty applause. Thereafter his representative sped the reviewers on their way with the assurance that, whereas the final scene would be given, as a matter of principle, Mr Hampden would not act in it. This quickly allayed any suspicion that Shylock would do a dance in the moonlight. (*NYT* 14 May 1921)

and splendid. To deny that or to seek to belittle it would be mere captiousness. Nor are the pictures mere pictures. In the best Meiningen-Reinhardt tradition there is at every moment the stir and movement of life.

It is tempting to dismiss this as empty-headed extravagance, but Stanislavski, who saw the production while in New York with the touring Moscow Art Theatre, expressed his admiration: 'Belasco's production of *The Merchant of Venice* exceeds in sheer lavishness anything I ever saw, and for its technical achievements, the Maly Theatre could envy them.' Indeed, in piling on the realistic detail, Belasco took the same serious approach to Shakespeare that Stanislavski took to Chekhov (driving Chekhov to distraction),[141] and Stanislavski went beyond the scenic atmosphere to say, 'such an actor as David Warfield, whom I saw in the part of Shylock, we have not got'.[142]

Warfield started out with comic Jewish characters for Weber and Fields's burlesque troupe, and went on to a distinguished career on the Broadway stage. In 1922 he decided to retire, but not until he tackled the one role he had always wanted to play.[143] Stark Young finds the performance moving, but misconceived: 'an East Side father, an old, tired man, pathetic, pious, hopeless but not stupid, bitter, suffering. Mr Warfield's impersonation of Shylock lacks power and lacks variety and range, but it has humanity and infinite, patient pathos.' But,

> however well meant, [it is] more distressing than that of the more traditional Shylock that he avoids . . . Mr Warfield substitutes for the elemental forces a tamer range of values; mild ideas of right and wrong, of justice and conduct, the middle-class necessity for approval. This Jew of his has only pathos, solitude, life driven inward, poisoned, suffering.[144]

Several weeks after Belasco's production opened in New York, the Old Vic, in the third of five seasons under Robert Atkins, continued with its series of *Merchant*s, first with Atkins himself as Shylock, then with Hay Petrie, known heretofore as a comic actor. Atkins was less overtly villainous than his recent predecessors – *The Times* (17 January 1923) was surprised by his first appearance, 'a quiet, sly old man, bored rather than angry or resentful, and awakening slowly to his opportunity'. But Petrie, as Crosse notes in his diary,

---

141 See Stanislavski's promptbook entry for the start of *The Sea Gull*, *qtd* Braun, *Director*, p. 63; Marker offers an interesting discussion of Belasco's production, *David Belasco*, pp. 178–202.

142 Magarshack, *Stanislavski*, p. 366.

143 Bordman, *Oxford Companion*, pp. 699–70.

144 Young, *Immortal Shadows*, p. 41.

returned to the 'dirty, shabby little Hebrew', although he still managed 'to make this insignificant creature tragic. He did not overwhelm us by great moments but he was acting all the time, driving home the character by word and look and gesture. The slightly foreign accent which he adopted helped, though not much.'[145]

Florence Saunders, an adored actress who died in 1926 at the age of thirty-five, was Portia. Crosse found her 'beautiful, gracious, strong, and humorous – all that Portia should be . . . she was more anxious over Morocco's choice than Arragon's [and] there was much fear of *his* choosing right'.[146]

Two other admired actresses were to play Portia over the next few years. When Walter Hampden returned to New York in 1925, Brooks Atkinson, then at the start of his long tenure as theatre critic of the *New York Times*, did not discuss Hampden at all, but was enthusiastic about the 'iridescent Portia' of Ethel Barrymore: 'It is a Portia lovely in the florid bowers of Belmont, and forceful as the learned upright judge in the court of justice. If these two contradictory aspects of the part sometime bespeak the license of a dramatic poet, they are sufficiently plausible in Miss Barrymore's acting.'[147]

Along with bearing the same initials, Elisabeth Bergner was Barrymore's equal in both talent and beauty. Alexander Woollcott considered her 'the ablest actress living today',[148] but when she played Portia for Jürgen Fehling at the Staatliche Schauspielhaus of Berlin in 1927, her performance was overshadowed by the Shylock of Fritz Kortner.

Kortner had already played Shylock for Berthold Viertels in 1923 and for Max Reinhardt in 1924 – he did not see the character as a noble victim, but as one driven to violent hatred by persecution. As he explains in his memoirs:

> Fehling wanted to see Shylock presented in a more humane fashion than his true character allowed. In this respect, Reinhardt, under whom I had played the role in Vienna, was somewhat similar. I could not comprehend his perception of the role and he hated mine – perhaps Fehling had the very laudable intention of not feeding the anti-Semitism which was all around us by then. I, however, wanted to be that Shylock who had been treated inhumanly by Christianity, and so became inhuman himself.[149]

As he did in Otto Schenk's television production over forty years later,[150] Kortner spoke his lines at a very slow, measured pace, and the other actors

145 Crosse, *Diaries* vol. VIII, p. 137.   146 *Ibid.*
147 *NYT* 28 January 1925; see p. 223 for Barrymore's delivery of the 'mercy' speech.
148 E. Katz, *International Film Encyclopedia*, p. 111.
149 *qtd* Sehrt, 'Der Shylock', pp. 79–80.   150 See p. 87.

had to adjust to it – C. Hooper Trask wrote in the *New York Times* (1 April 1928) that the production's tempo 'dragged . . . to an inexcusable degree', and that Bergner 'did not come off with any particular halo'.

This was to be the last major production of *The Merchant of Venice* in Germany for more than thirty years. At the same time, with the savagery of anti-Semitic attacks in Hungary and Austria intensifying, Lewis Casson revived it for the Old Vic company, with himself as Shylock and his wife Sybil Thorndike as Portia. Casson 'spoke in the accent of the Jews of the modern East London ghetto – he pronounced "well" as "vell" and "was" as "vas" '[151] – and he rivalled Sothern as the most physically repulsive Shylock ever, unkempt, dirty, with hooked nose, scraggly hair and beard, a caricature of a caricature. St John Ervine likened Casson to 'an old clo'man from the Palestine Road in Manchester . . . a good and well-considered performance that was by far the best in the production, but lacked the magnificence of baffled rage and the courageous abandonment of a man whose life is filled with despair'. Thorndike was impressive in the trial, but 'not temperamentally suited . . . to any of the witty, gay women, the Rosalinds, the Beatrices, and the Portias' (*Obs* 23 October 1927).

The following year, New York saw a Shylock as different from Casson's as could be imagined, when George Arliss appeared in Winthrop Ames's production. Atkinson describes how, in Arliss's 'well-bred interpretation, Shylock becomes a gentleman himself; even in his misery there is a suggestion of instinctive elegance' (*NYT* 17 January 1928).

This performance proved to be profoundly influential in a unique way. Arliss's greatest film role was as Benjamin Disraeli, first in a 1921 silent, and then in a sound version made soon after he played Shylock for Ames: at the time Shylocks in the English theatre were consistently becoming more ugly and villainous, Arliss redefined him as the distinguished Victorian prime minister of Italian-Jewish heritage – so convincing was his portrayal that many assumed, incorrectly, that Arliss himself was Jewish. Laurence Olivier writes in his memoirs, 'I must admit to having been so impressed by the interpretation of Disraeli by Mr George Arliss in an exceptionally good talkie made in 1929 that, to be honest, I lifted it ("pinched" is such a common word) for my playing of Shylock.'[152] Of course, in 'lifting' Arliss's Disraeli, Olivier was also lifting his Shylock.

Along with a distinctly original Shylock, Ames had Peggy Wood as Portia, who had 'all the personal charm, quick wit, and effulgent beauty associated with this poetic figure, and she moves about the stage with lightness and grace . . . enduring with gentleness the Prince of Morocco's impetuous suit,

151 Casson, *Lewis & Sybil*, p. 142.   152 Olivier, *Confessions*, p. 236.

she is the romantic maiden of the play; but she is most lustrous, perhaps, when Bassanio is selecting his casket' (Atkinson, *NYT*).

THE 1930S

We have already recorded the last important German production of the *Merchant* before World War II. 1930 marked this occasion in the United States, with Maurice Moscovitch's return to the American stage after his years in England and Australia, in a new version directed by Andrew Leigh.

Just as Adler borrowed Daly's settings, Leigh used those of Winthrop Ames, but as Richard Dana Skinner notes, Moscovitch had 'none of the sardonic malice and aristocratic contempt of George Arliss' (*Commonweal* 31 December 1930). It is difficult to know how much Moscovitch might have changed his interpretation from the days with Fagan, since different reviewers' perceptions may account for different descriptions: to H. T. Parker,

> the actor did not embody the sufferings and the defeats of his race as Irving's Shylock was said to do. He reared no superhuman figure as Mansfield did. He rioted in no oriental temperament after the manner of Novelli. Observe him in the bargaining with Antonio and Bassanio, all alert of hands, face and body, persuading and agreeing, wheedling, demurring, consenting again. Then, left alone, tense with remembered affronts and ingrained aversion.

Parker thought that 'the Portia of Selena Royle was pleasurable to look at, and pleasant to hear, but never really emerged from the cool sphere of an acted part . . . always a bit too arch and a bit too preoccupied with the effect of gesture and expression'.[153]

Maurice Moscovitch went on to Hollywood, where he took part in some major films, including a splendid performance as Mr Jaeckel in Charlie Chaplin's *The Great Dictator*.

The Merchant of Venice now disappears from the American stage for close to twenty years, but throughout the pre-war period, and during the war itself, English audiences had ample opportunity to see it. July of 1932 saw the opening of the new Shakespeare Memorial Theatre at Stratford, and to mark the occasion the governors invited the Russian director Theodore Komisarjevsky to do the *Merchant*. Known for innovative productions of Chekhov and other European dramatists, Komisarjevsky had never directed a Shakespeare play in England, 'and his arrival in Stratford was tantamount

153 Parker, *qtd NYT* 16 November 1930.

to an invasion'.[154] As Dennis Kennedy notes in *Looking at Shakespeare*, Komisarjevsky, like Reinhardt, treated the play as carnival: the set was a skewed Rialto with tilting buildings, which split down the centre to reveal a Belmont that rose on a hydraulic lift, 'a jester's cartoon world, and the performance style was in key with the scenography'. The action started with a *commedia dell'arte* sequence of dancing Pierrots, forced off the stage by an Arlecchino later revealed to be Lancelot Gobbo.[155]

The production was hastily put together with only five rehearsals, but it was an audience favourite – neither performers, critics nor spectators seemed overly concerned with the social implications of turning the play into a burlesque (in the true Italian sense of *burlesco*). As *The Times* (26 July 1932) observes,

> It is possible that an Elizabethan finding himself in the Memorial Theatre tonight would have recognized in Mr Randle Ayrton's Shylock the Jew he had been accustomed to see played at the Globe. If he retained his taste for a little Jew-baiting he might have laughed uproariously at the despairing rage of the crafty alien usurer hoist with his own petard. Moral sensibility does not lend itself to such laughter, but we may confess that the hardening process so skilfully applied by the actors to our hearts is good for the play.

The Times adds that 'Miss Fabia Drake played Portia with strength and charm, though she would be well advised to drop her comic make-up in the court scene.'

Five months after Komisarjevsky opened at Stratford, John Gielgud directed a new *Merchant* for the Old Vic. With a nod towards William Poel's methods, Gielgud used a single unit set; his Shylock was Malcolm Keen, whom Crosse found 'like Petrie and Casson . . . just an ordinary Jew who can rise to tragic emotion when his situation demands it', and his Portia was Peggy Ashcroft. Crosse regards Ashcroft's Portia as 'miles better than her Rosalind', although he places her in the second rank, behind Terry, Thorndike and Saunders: 'she not only acted with charm and beauty in the Belmont scenes, especially in [3.2] which was beautifully played all round – but in spite of her slight physique she had a fine dignity in the trial, and dominated the scene as Portia should'.[156] Peter Fleming of the *Spectator* (6 December 1932) thought the production was 'very good theatrical entertainment'.

154 Mennen, 'Theodore Komisarjevsky's Production', p. 388.
155 Kennedy, *Looking at Shakespeare*, pp. 127–9.
156 Crosse, *Diaries* vol. XIII, p. 137; vol. XV, p. 110.

On 30 January 1933, Adolf Hitler was sworn in as Chancellor of Germany. Although Shakespeare performances were an important part of propaganda minister Joseph Goebbels's cultural programme, they were hampered by many of Germany's finest theatre people having left the country: one such exile was Max Reinhardt, who took his talents to the United States, but in 1934 was invited to Italy to direct the *Merchant* as part of Venice's *Biennale*. The production, done outdoors at the Campo San Trovaso, featured the renowned Pirandello actress Marta Abba as Portia, and Memo Benassi, who added Shylock to his list of important roles that already included Ibsen's John Gabriel Borkman. Reinhardt made complete use of the environment – his dramatic adviser Heinz Herald noted that the play 'actually takes place amongst palaces from the age of the Venetian Dukes, on night-black canals, slender and graceful bridges'.[157] For the Belmont of Act v, 'a garden was improvised on the steps of the bridge, so that it seemed as if all the characters, as they stepped out of their gondolas, were disembarking at Belmont from the Brenta'.[158]

Another exile from Nazism was Leopold Jessner, a major figure of the Berlin theatre of the 1920s, who served as director of the both the Staatstheater and the Schiller Theatre,[159] and who directed the Habimah Theatre of Tel Aviv's first *Merchant of Venice*, performed in Hebrew, in 1936. Needless to say, the decision to do the *Merchant* in Palestine was a controversial one: as Avraham Oz notes in his essay on the *Merchant* in Israel, Jessner made a series of public statements, explaining how the play was to

> remain a legend, though one in which the legendary harmony was upset by the special weight of Shylock's role. His was not to be a patient Shylock, accepting his tragic lot quietly; rather he would be a long-struggling Shylock, who eventually falls victim to the treacheries of his adversaries. Not just one Shylock who was beaten in his battle with Christian society: he was to be The Jew.[160]

Portia was played by Hanna Rovina, whose performance in *The Dybbuk* had established her as the company's leading actress. Two actors, Aharon Meskin and Shim'on Finkel, alternated as Shylock: 'Meskin was an heroic figure, making use of his commanding physical stature and resounding voice; Finkel emphasized Shylock's spiteful bitterness.'[161] Jessner was famous in Germany for using a stairway to connect various levels of the stage, enhancing meaning through comparative positioning of the characters; it featured

157 qtd. Fischer-Lichte, 'Theatre as Festive Play', pp. 176–7.
158 Speaight, *Shakespeare on the Stage*, p. 208.
159 Oz, 'Transformations', pp. 60–1.   160 *Ibid.*, p. 61.
161 *Ibid.*, p. 64.

in the trial, as Shylock, 'ridiculed by the entire court, his yellow badge attached to the back of his Jewish gabardine, stood upright on a higher level than the judge, who sat below, speaking his lines in a thundering voice while everybody froze as if suddenly hypnotized'.[162]

Despite Jessner's intention, most critics, and much of the public, saw the play as irretrievably anti-Semitic. A series of protest meetings culminated in a public mock-trial, with Shakespeare and the Habimah as co-defendants; 'its verdict was that neither Shakespeare nor Jessner could be accused of anti-Semitism, since Shylock was given many positive traits to balance his negative side, and that the Habimah deserved praise for bringing to light the difficult issues the play contains'.[163]

Having directed the *Merchant* at the Old Vic six years previously, John Gielgud chose to mount a new production, with himself as Shylock, for his Queen's repertory season in May of 1938. Influenced by Granville-Barker's perception of the play as a 'fairy tale', Gielgud and his co-director Glen Byam Shaw had the famous design team known only as 'Motley' provide 'a pastel, semi-permanent setting, and costumes which suggested all the colour, luxury, and romantic exuberance of Venice'.[164] Peggy Ashcroft was an ideal Portia for such a production: Crosse writes, 'Miss Ashcroft now seemed more at home with the lighter side of Portia than when I saw her in 1932. Her surrender and mercy speeches were well, not strikingly well: her silent pause during Morocco's choice really beautiful.'[165]

Audrey Williamson describes Gielgud's Shylock as 'a dingy, rancorous, fawning creature of the ghetto, greyly redolent of the slum and the usurer's attic'.[166] Employing what Crosse thought to be 'an unnecessary amount of foreign accent',[167] he emulated Casson in ugliness, the *New Statesman* (7 May 1938) noting his 'gummy, blinking eyes, that suggested some nasty creature of the dark', and adding, 'at a time when Jews are being driven to mass-suicide by unsurpassed brutalities, the spectacle of his baiting becomes almost unbearable'.

This critic is referring to reports such as this one, published in the *New York Times* of 28 June 1938:

WAVE OF SUICIDES RENEWED IN VIENNA

A renewed wave of suicides among Jews is sweeping Vienna as the result of Nazi orders that Jewish employees be released by both 'Aryan' and Jewish

162 Review in *Bamah*, qtd ibid., pp. 61–2.   163 Levy, *Habima*, pp. 125, 126.
164 Williamson, *Theatre of Two Decades*, p. 60.
165 Crosse, *Diaries* vol. XVI, p. 151.
166 Williamson, *Theatre of Two Decades*, pp. 60–61.
167 Crosse, *Diaries* vol. XVI, p. 151.

firms. The employers are forbidden to give severance pay . . . Today the writer saw an elderly Jewish woman, who was sitting in a park, roughly treated by a Hitler Youth group while many spectators applauded.

The *New Statesman* is unique in even mentioning these 'unsurpassed brutalities', but their importance seems to be that they made certain parts of the play very unpleasant to watch. Many years later, Gielgud agreed with Kenneth Tynan's description of Shylock 'as a comic monster . . . I would have liked to have been more comic myself'.[168]

In October, Donald Wolfit brought his *Merchant* to London's huge People's Palace. Playwright Ronald Harwood, in his biography of Wolfit, describes his Shylock 'as a villain full of venom and hatred, spitting on the Christians at the end of the trial', noting that his former employer conceived Shylock 'as a young patriarch, in keeping with the requirements of Talmudic law that enjoins Jews to marry young'.[169]

FREDERICK VALK

On 19 June 1938, between Gielgud's and Wolfit's appearances, Lord Beaverbrook's *Sunday Express* ran an editorial decrying the 'big influx of foreign Jews into Britain. They are overrunning the country. They are trying to enter the medical profession in great numbers. They wish to practise as dentists. Worst of all, many of them are holding themselves out to the public as psychoanalysts.' One such Jewish refugee was not a dentist or a psychoanalyst, but the actor Frederick Valk, the Tubal of Fehling's 1927 production. Although usually referred to as a Czech, he was born in Hamburg, and took out Czech citizenship after becoming a star of Prague's German theatre – having a Czech passport saved his life, since there was no visa restriction between Czechoslovakia and Britain when Valk was forced to flee in 1939.[170]

Tyrone Guthrie engaged Valk to play Othello for the Old Vic in 1942, and the following year cast him as Shylock, a role he had done often in Prague, for Esmé Church's touring production. It was, in the words of Diana Valk, 'Shakespeare at the Coal-Face', as the Old Vic toured throughout northern England and Scotland; her husband's Shylock was 'a retiring man [with] a touch of the religious fanatic as he stalked black-robed across the narrow stages of miners' halls and community centres. He was neither extravagant nor ostentatious, a rich man preferring not to seem so lest he inflame the envy of his fellow-Venetians.'[171]

168 Gielgud, *Acting Shakespeare*, p. 62.   169 Harwood, *Sir Donald Wolfit*, p. 155.
170 Valk, *Shylock for a Summer*, pp. 35, 23–8.   171 *Ibid.*, pp. 35–6

In Scotland, the theatre would sometimes be filled with Polish airmen, and Valk 'took it for granted that the Poles would be hostile to the last man to Shylock and perhaps to himself, but . . . they were an exemplary audience'. One evening a Polish Colonel entered Valk's dressing room, made a formal speech of which Valk did not understand a word, kissed the bemused actor, and left.[172]

In March of 1943, the production had a short season at the New Theatre in London. Crosse thought that Valk's 'fine voice and his power of passion made him an excellent Shylock in the vigorous style. A curious feature was that throughout [1.3] he was quiet, friendly, laughing. Except for the "fawning publican" speech, no one not knowing the story would have guessed he was hostile to Antonio.' Kay Bannerman, though, was too young and immature for Portia: 'her shrinking horror at the thought of having to marry a drunken German was a good touch, and her seeming to tell the Duke secretly her plan for outwitting Shylock in the Trial a bad one'.[173]

THE THIRD REICH

Another persistent myth about *The Merchant of Venice* is that it was the Nazis' favourite play, but as Hortmann notes, although *unser Shakespeare* continued to be performed throughout the Third Reich, after 1933 the number of productions of the *Merchant* dropped to less than a third of what it had been before Hitler came to power, and Berlin saw only one production during the entire era.[174] A play with such speeches as 'Hath not a Jew eyes', and with a young Christian falling in love with a Jewish girl, would not necessarily appeal to the Nazis; all of the cutting and rewriting needed to turn the *Merchant* into a completely anti-Jewish tract would have led most directors, party members or not, to other plays.

One notorious exception was Lothar Müthel, whose production opened at the Vienna Burgtheater on 15 May 1943. The text was adapted so that Jessica became the result of an adulterous affair between Shylock's wife and a gentile, making her acceptable under the Nurenberg laws,[175] and Werner Krauss was selected to play Shylock. Krauss, who had done the role for Reinhardt in 1921,[176] had just completed the violently anti-Semitic film version of Lion Feuchtwanger's novel *Jud Süss*, directed by Viet Harlan, in which he played the main role and five other Jewish characters.

172 *Ibid.*, p. 22.
173 Crosse, *Diaries* vol. XVIII, p. 71.
174 Hortmann, *Shakespeare on the German Stage*, pp. 134–5.
175 Grunberger, *Social History*, p. 371.   176 Verch, 'The Merchant', p. 85.

Harlan and Krauss were also planning a film of the *Merchant*, and at a press conference Krauss said that his Shylock would be such 'that no one in the world will ever again accept a slice of bread from a Jew'.[177] The film was never made, but Krauss, like his director Müthel a member of the Nazi party, earned the praise of the Nazi *Völkischer Beobachter* for his stage performance:

> Every fiber of his body seems impregnated with Jewish blood; he mumbles, slavers, gurgles, grunts, and squawks with alarming authenticity, scurries back and forth like a rat, though he does so the hard way – knock-kneed; one literally smells his bad breath, feels the itching under his caftan and senses the nausea that overcomes him at the end of the court scene.[178]

After the war Krauss and Müthel made the absurd claim that they had no anti-Semitic intention, and were ordered to do the play by the Nazi governor of Vienna – Krauss always thought his long-term ban from the German stage to be an injustice.[179]

THE POST-WAR PERIOD

New York had not seen a professional production of the *Merchant* since 1930. In February of 1947, the Shubert organisation engaged Donald Wolfit's company for a season, but upon learning that the plays were to be *King Lear*, *As You Like It* and *The Merchant of Venice*, Lee Shubert asked Wolfit to drop the *Merchant*. Ironically, the *New York Times* (15 February 1947) reported, 'several outstanding Jewish leaders . . . may intercede for "The Merchant" on the grounds that its barring would constitute a form of censorship, something against which the theatre is now fighting'.

While relatively few within the American Jewish community wanted the play banned from performance, or even from study in the public schools, most expected, given the way the play had usually been performed before the war, that Shylock would be acted within the Irving, or even the Adler, tradition, even if such an interpretation was not truly 'Shakespearean'. This attitude informs Atkinson's review of Wolfit's performance, which went ahead without incident; to the end of his career, Atkinson remained steadfast in his belief that Shakespeare wrote Shylock as a comic villain, but he was disappointed with Wolfit: 'Mr Wolfit's Shylock, which is incidentally cursed with a grotesque make-up – lacks stature. When Shylock

177 Rentschler, *Ministry of Illusion*, p. 158.
178 *qtd* Elwood, 'Werner Krauss', p. 96.
179 Hortmann, *Shakespeare on the German Stage*, p. 135.

is played as a man of dignity and character, his experience is more than a tabloid sensation, it is a tragedy. *In the twentieth century perhaps we know better than Shakespeare did* how painful a tragedy it is' (*NYT* 24 February 1947 [emphasis added]).

The stories of Allied soldiers' horror and amazement as they entered the concentration camps are too numerous and well known to need recounting here, and it might be expected that after 1945, no production of the *Merchant* could go on anywhere without at least some recognition, such as Atkinson offered about Wolfit, of its contemporary significance. Yet many British artists, in their undoubtedly genuine belief that they were being faithful to a great literary classic, saw nothing wrong with presenting anti-Semitic stereotypes: that David Lean could choose to make *Oliver Twist* in 1947, and then be surprised when no American distributor would release the film, is truly dumbfounding.[180]

A few months before Lean's film opened in Britain, Michael Benthall's production of the *Merchant* began its Stratford season, with Diana Wynyard, 'more Juno than Proserpina', as Portia (*Gdn* 21 April 1948), and the Australian dancer-actor Robert Helpmann as Shylock. Helpmann's make-up and vocal mannerisms were similar to those Alec Guinness used as Fagin for Lean: the *Guardian* called him 'abundantly Jewish', and what 'abundantly Jewish' meant is shown in a later review of Helpmann's performance: 'his curled and greasy locks, his great prune-coloured eyes, jutting lower lip and hawk-like nose were complete transformations of his own natural appearance'.[181]

Michael Redgrave went to the Amsterdam Ghetto to study Jewish culture in preparing to play Shylock for Dennis Carey at Stratford in 1953.[182] Tynan saw the result as 'highly intelligent – a major prophet with a German [*sic*] accent', but he was less than happy with the great amount of effort the portrayal seemed to require: 'his performance is a prolonged wrestling match with Shylock, each speech being floored with a tremendous, vein-bursting thump; the process also involves his making a noise like a death-rattle whenever he inhales, and spitting visibly whenever he strikes a "p" or a "b"'.[183]

Physically, Redgrave was slightly less unprepossessing than Helpmann: the hooked nose, long black hair and beard were still there, but in a less

180 Brownlow, *David Lean*, pp. 233, 237.

181 Clarke, *Shakespeare at the Old Vic* (not paginated). Benthall's production was revived, basically unchanged in style, for the Old Vic's 1954–5 tour of Australia, with Katharine Hepburn as Portia, and for a 1956–7 season in London.

182 Billington, *Peggy Ashcroft*, p. 144.

183 Tynan, *A View of the English Stage*, p. 130.

angular fashion, without Helpmann's curled ringlets across the forehead. Peggy Ashcroft spoke her lines, according to Tynan,

> with the air of a woman who would never commit the social gaffe of reciting in public, with the result that the lines flow out newly minted, as unstrained as the quality of mercy itself. Her handling of the tiresome princelings who come to woo her is an object lesson in wit and good manners; later, in the court-room, we wept at her compassion; and the last act, invariably an anti-climax, bloomed golden at her touch.[184]

Also in 1953, New York was at last able to see an American production of the *Merchant*, when Albert Marre directed the play for the New York City Center, with Luther Adler realising a long-held ambition to follow 'in his father's footsteps as Shylock',[185] alongside Margaret Phillips as Portia. Adler was the opposite of Helpmann or Redgrave in appearance and behaviour: 'his Shylock was intelligent, cultivated, and mature. He cut a handsome figure indeed, dressed neither raggedly nor garishly, according to either of the more usual conventions, but in sombre and dignified elegance'.[186]

In general, critical response to the production was one of mild disappointment. Adler impressed everyone, but the reviewers felt duty-bound to make a distinction between what they believed the play meant once, and what it meant in 1953 – almost all of Harold Clurman's article in the *Nation* (21 March 1953) is on this topic, and the performance is hardly discussed – indeed neither Clurman nor Thomas Barbour even mentions Margaret Phillips.

TYRONE GUTHRIE

Having arrived at the year 1955, we might observe that it had been a long time since any production sent the play off in a major new direction, but this situation changed profoundly when Tyrone Guthrie, after two years of trying, persuaded the Stratford Festival of Canada to present *The Merchant of Venice*.

The Festival Board's reluctance seemed justified when the editorial pages of Canada's newspapers followed with sharp exchanges over the propriety of the decision, and Guthrie himself did not help matters by remarking that his Jessica was going to be 'strikingly pretty in a Jewish sort of a way'.[187] But his bringing Frederick Valk to Canada was a public relations and artistic masterstroke: not only was Shylock to be played by a Jewish refugee, but by a Jewish refugee who was a fine actor.

184 *Ibid.*, p. 131.   185 Barbour, 'Theatre Chronicle', p. 283.
186 *Ibid.*   187 Edinborough, 'Shakespeare Confirmed', p. 438.

Guthrie's interpretation of *The Merchant of Venice* was the most important since Irving's: it established entirely new perspectives from which the
play has been considered ever since. Guthrie was the first to show something
we have now come to expect when seeing the *Merchant*, a homosexual relationship between Antonio and Bassanio. At the time, reviewers were tenta-
tive about even discussing this point: Atkinson (*NYT* 1 July 1955) does not
mention it at all, although it seems inconceivable that he failed to notice it,
while Alice Griffin writes, 'as effectively played by Robert Goodier, Antonio
was an older man, deeply attached to young Bassanio, hurt at the youth's suit
for the hand of Portia, but generously agreeing to finance it. At the trial,
though fearful, he was almost eager to die for Bassanio' (*TA* September
1955). Walter Kerr notes that 'Antonio and Bassanio were latent homo-
sexuals'[188] (there was nothing latent about it); Henry Hewes was more
explicit: 'By acknowledging the physical love between Bassanio and Antonio
(who is, after all, the title character) Mr Guthrie lends the play a logical base.
Antonio is established as a man ready to make any sacrifice for the boy he
loves . . . Donald Harron catches the ambiguity of Bassanio's position
beautifully' (*SR* 23 July 1955).

Hewes's comment is noteworthy – the homosexual theme is not imposed
on the play, but makes it 'logical'. Guthrie added no lines to the text; if
Goodier and Harron were able to make the character relationship clear, it was
by doing what every actor does, using gestures, facial expressions and physical attitudes, while speaking and listening. Now, over forty years later, it is the
rare director who does *not* make the sexuality of the male characters an inte-
gral part of a production; this could never have happened if doing so were
only in response to some current fad. Guthrie notes,

> the relationship between Antonio and Bassanio is not meant to suggest that
> of uncle and nephew, or just two friends, but that Antonio is in love with the
> younger man . . . it is obvious that the idea is expressed between the lines,
> not baldly and explicitly. In epochs when conventional respectability was of
> great importance – the nineteenth century, for example – the hint of an
> 'irregular' relationship will have been studiously ignored. Thus the theme
> will have been omitted from the play and the character of Antonio will
> therefore have been rendered more simple. He just becomes an entirely
> uninteresting 'good' man.[189]

Far from being 'good' men in this production, Antonio and his fellow
Christians 'are not only fools and prodigals: they are also heartless, arrogant,
vindictive, and cruel' (Atkinson, *NYT*); at the end of the trial scene, 'as the

188 Kerr, *Thirty Plays*, p. 170.   189 Guthrie, *In Various Directions*, p. 98.

physically and mentally stunned money lender is led away, the assembled Venetians gloatingly taunt and boo and spit on him' (Beaufort, *CSM* 2 July 1955). As for Valk, he was 'brilliant as Shylock. He had spite and venom without losing our sympathy. He was noble and just when compared with the shoddy Christians with whom he dealt.'[190]

To these two production concepts, the male characters' sexuality and the Venetians as persecutors – the first not seen before and the second given great prominence – Guthrie added a third in 1959. Invited to Israel to direct a new Habimah production, he set the play in contemporary Venice.

Although not all previous productions of the play in the post-Macklin era were done in one version or another of Renaissance costume, no professional production in the twentieth century had ever been set in the contemporary world – Guthrie's Habimah production was thirty-four years after the Birmingham Repertory's famous 'plus-fours' *Hamlet*.[191] In 'a busy Venice', Guthrie provided 'a lively and rapid succession of entrances and exits, with Salerio and Solanio portrayed as a pair of American businessmen holding their umbrellas in the rain while passing comments on city affairs, with Gratiano constantly on the move in a dancing step, humming merry jazz tunes'.[192] His Shylocks were the same two actors, Shim'on Finkel and Aharon Meskin, who had performed the role for Jessner. Meskin commented during rehearsals,

> when I first played Shylock, I stressed mainly the national, pathetic element. This time I shall endeavor to portray a more human Shylock: he has got a measure of fanaticism but he has his weaknesses as well. Guthrie has told me that at the beginning of the play Shylock is a thriving merchant, a kind of Rothschild. This has given me much help. I have even obtained a picture of Rothschild.[193]

Avraham Oz notes that Meskin 'did indeed physically resemble "a kind of Rothschild"',[194] giving the part resonances that would not have been apparent in a period setting.

THE OTHER STRATFORD

The influence of Guthrie's new reading of the play, and his style of direction in general, made itself felt in England when Michael Langham, who had worked closely with Guthrie in Ontario, staged the *Merchant* at the 'other'

---

190 Edinborough, 'Shakespeare Confirmed', p. 438.
191 The Croydon Repertory Theatre did a modern-dress *Merchant* in 1935.
192 Oz, 'Transformations', p. 64.   193 *Ibid.*   194 *Ibid.*

Stratford, in Warwickshire. Langham updated the period to the eighteenth century; Gareth Lloyd Evans noted that placing the story in the Age of Reason made it 'less of a terrible tussle between comedy and tragedy than a swift clean exercise in that witty irony by which the proud cupidity of Shylock's world and the self-indulgent opulence of Belmont become consanguineous'.[195]

The most significant thing about Langham's production is that it marked a definite step away from the English Shylock-from-Whitechapel tradition, in place since the turn of the century, by virtue of Peter O'Toole's commanding performance as the Jew. O'Toole had never seen the play done,[196] and came to the role unencumbered by tradition – he was as handsome and distinguished as Casson was repulsive. He did add to his nose, although not as much as his predecessors, but gone were the long beard and curly wig of Helpmann, replaced by the actor's own elegantly cut beard and hair, 'just touched with grey'.[197] John Russell Brown notes that making Shylock's costume 'more dignified than usual' meant 'that when he returned after his daughter's flight, with his gown torn and muddied, the audience was at once aware of a great reversal . . . his rapaciousness was not evident, for he was dressed too well for a miser'. Redgrave's crouch was also discarded: O'Toole 'walked too upright to suggest cunning or unbridled hatred'.[198]

To A. Alvarez in the *New Statesman* (23 April 1960), 'O'Toole imposes on the audience a pressure of emotion and dignity which transforms Shylock from an ambiguous figure hovering somewhere between caricature and melodrama into a major tragic hero', while Dorothy Tutin as Portia

> wisely did not try to compete . . . Her talent is all of the surface: a matter of delicacy and prettiness and a sensitive voice so finely tuned as to sound almost piping. She was bright and easy in the comic scenes, lightly romantic where romance was needed; in the trial scene what she lacked in strength she made up in cleverness.

O'Toole was blessed with extraordinary support. Along with Tutin, the cast included Denholm Elliott as Bassanio, Ian Holm as Lorenzo, Jack MacGowran as Old Gobbo, Patrick Wymark as Gratiano, 'the club bore who runs on like a river while all around him throw up their hands', and Ian Richardson as Arragon, 'washed-out and black-suited, with mother and

195 Evans, 'Shakespeare Memorial Theatre', p. 162.
196 Wapshott, *Peter O'Toole*, p. 57.
197 Roberts, *PP* 1960. The hair and beard remained his own until he required a haircut and shave for a *Lawrence of Arabia* screen test; he used a wig and false beard after that (Wapshott, *Peter O'Toole*, p. 71).
198 Brown, 'Three Directors', p. 136.

Peter O'Toole as Shylock in Michael Langham's production, Stratford, 1960.

tutor to match, [he] turns his choice of caskets into a ceremonial parody of bloodless nobility' (Alvarez, *NS*).

CENTRAL PARK, THE APA

Just as Michael Langham had England's most brilliant young actor for his Shylock, Joseph Papp and his co-director Gladys Vaughan chose the American claimant to that title, George C. Scott, for their 1962 production, which opened the New York Shakespeare Festival's Delacorte Theatre in Central Park (where all performances were, and still are, free). Papp encountered the strong opposition of New York's Board of Rabbis, the situation exacerbated by CBS TV's decision to televise the performance; in a letter to the *New York Times* (15 June 1962), the Board's president denounced the play as 'an amalgam of vindictiveness, cruelty, and avarice'. Raised in an orthodox Jewish family, Papp had little time for the Board, whom he considered 'establishment Jews' similar to those who looked down on his working-class father,[199] and both the production and the CBS broadcast went ahead as scheduled.

Papp's combativeness was incorporated into the advice he gave to Scott: 'Never turn the other cheek . . . you want to hurt these people who have hurt you. Don't softsell it. People will understand your anger.'[200] If an angry, vengeful Shylock was wanted, no actor in the world was as capable of providing it as this one: Arthur Gelb of the *New York Times* (22 June 1962), considered Scott's Jew 'a multi-dimensional human being, turned almost psychotically villainous through accumulated persecution, both real and imagined'. Robert Hatch saw him as 'a proud, powerful man, deeply committed to his traditions and driven to the point of insanity by the hostility and (worse) contempt of the proper Venetians' (*Nation* 14 July 1962), and Jack Kroll of *Newsweek* (1 September 1990), writing years later, remembers Scott as 'one of the great modern Shylocks . . . eyes flashing with hatred, voice rasping with irony and indignation, his Shylock swooped down on Antonio in righteous fury'. Unfortunately, no videotape of the CBS broadcast survives, but more than a hint of Scott's Shylock can be seen in the film *The Hustler*, made the previous year: his portrayal of the gambler Bert Gordon had the same, inimitable vocal quality, described as 'rasping' in no less than three reviews of the *Merchant*.[201]

Although Guthrie's Habimah *Merchant* was the first modern production set in its own time, the relative obscurity of the company, performing in Hebrew, limited its influence; of greater moment was the first English-language contemporary-dress production, directed by Richard Baldridge for the Association of Producing Arts (the APA) when that company was resident at the University of Michigan in 1963. Perhaps it is surprising to attach such importance to a performance given in a college town, but the cast included many who already were, or would one day be, major figures in the American theatre;[202] they would take Baldridge's concept with them, affect-

199 Epstein, *Joe Papp*, p. 175.   200 *Ibid.*

201 Griffin, 'New York Season', p. 554; *Time* (29 June 1962); *Variety* (27 June 1962).

202 Rosemary Harris played Portia, Paul Sparer was Shylock, and Will Geer was Old Gobbo/Tubal. Jack O'Brien, later Artistic Director of the Old Globe Theatre of San Diego, was also in the cast.

ing how Shakespeare, not just the *Merchant*, was to be performed in future years. Furthermore, Ellis Rabb, then the company's Artistic Director, restaged this production in San Francisco in 1970 and at Lincoln Center in New York in 1973 (without public acknowledgment that Baldridge, who died in 1964, was its original creator), so what Baldridge began ultimately reached a wide audience.

Baldridge placed the action in the Venice of Federico Fellini, opening brilliantly with movie credits flashed on a screen, followed by photographs of Venice, as Antonio and his companions sat at an outdoor café, listening to the sound of modern jazz. Edwin Wilson describes the Lincoln Center version as 'a *dolce vita* world where women wear silk jump suits and men drape white raincoats over their shoulders, and everyone wears sunglasses . . . drinking Cinzano in a lush, indolent, atmosphere' (*WSJ* 13 March 1973). Shylock moved through this world dressed in a 'dark suit, homburg, grey gloves – the moneyman in a society that needs him and rejects him' (Kroll, *Newsweek* 19 March 1973), while a languid Portia avoided the advances of a white-suited Morocco and an elderly Arragon in a wheelchair.

ERWIN PISCATOR, GEORG TABORI

For obvious reasons, no country found it as difficult to deal with *The Merchant of Venice* in the post-war period as did Germany. Early attempts to produce it seized on the liberal critic Alfred Kerr's view of Shylock as 'the only man of honour in this play',[203] but such performances earned the customary response that the intention may be admirable, but this was simply not Shakespeare's play. Ernst Deutsch, one of the finest German actors of his time, did Shylock for Karlheinz Stroux in Dusseldorf in 1957, and approached the role as one from Greek tragedy – although not guiltless, Shylock was doomed to act as he did by forces he could not control.[204] In 1963, Deutsch had the opportunity to adapt his interpretation to the demands of the 'anti-tragic' Epic Theatre, when Erwin Piscator cast him as Shylock for the Freie Volksbühne of West Berlin, opposite the Portia of Hilde Krahl (later a distinguished Mother Courage).

Hans-Ulrich Schmückle's set of bridges and *palazzi* was created through black and white photographic projections, while gondolas rested on a canal made of polished mirrors, and the audience was kept informed of the necessary historical dimension by projected titles such as 'the Jewish residents of Venice were excluded from commercial shipping activity', or statistical tables

---

203 *qtd* Verch, '*The Merchant*', p. 87.   204 *Ibid.*

to show the extent of Venice's commercial empire, with Shylock's 'anguished face' comprising the Belmont sky of 5.1.[205]

In this environment, Deutsch was 'a profoundly human Shylock, driven into his thirst for revenge by circumstances and in spite of himself': he 'inspired the compassion demanded in the reception of tragedy when he finally broke down . . . [and] uttered his "I am content" with a trembling voice'.[206] Like Moscovitch and Basserman, Deutsch was a noted film actor; in 1949 he was Baron Kurtz in Carol Reed's *The Third Man* – perhaps there is a hint of Shylock's interview with Bassanio in 1.3, as he sits with Joseph Cotten at a café table, trying to persuade him to abandon his inquiries into Holly Martin's death.

The Hungarian-born playwright, novelist and director Georg Tabori lost most of his family at Auschwitz. In 1966, as director of the new Berkshire Festival in Massachusetts, Tabori presented the first American production of the *Merchant* to explicitly confront the Holocaust, *The Merchant of Venice as Performed at Theresienstadt*, Theresienstadt being the supposedly 'model' concentration camp that had a cultural programme, including plays. At the start,

> a trapdoor opens and an emaciated being crawls out, then collapses. Men and women prisoners gather obediently, silently, onstage as the war hit 'Lili Marlene' is heard. Nazi officers storm in and take their seats in the front row of the auditorium as prisoners carry the sagging body away . . . inmates enter with pails of water and scrub the floor, slowly approaching the audience . . .[207]

Alvin Epstein, as the inmate forced to play Shylock, wore the 'traditional' long nose and red beard, 'but the role was conceived with a double edge': Epstein was both 'a craven caricature of the Jew as comic villain' and 'a hostile inmate of a prison camp desperately seeking revenge'. Viveca Lindfors was a Portia drained of emotion by the sexual abuse she had received at the hands of her captors; 'she merely recited her lines in a leaden way that complemented the vacant look in her eyes; occasionally, she showed a weary smile that tried to be enticing to one of the guards'.[208]

The trial scene was

> acted throughout with imaginary props, [but] Shylock is suddenly discovered to have a real knife in his hands as he makes ready to take his

205 Kennedy, *Looking at Shakespeare*, pp. 201–2.
206 Verch, '*The Merchant*', p. 87.
207 Feinberg, *Embodied Memory*, pp. 212–13.
208 D. Isaac, 'What's Happening with Drama', p. 465.

pound of flesh. Assaulting a guard after all his fellow actors have drawn back in terror, the actor playing Shylock is himself stabbed to death in the ensuing struggle. An improvised potato-sack curtain was then hand-pulled across the stage. End of play. No fifth act filled with moonlight – no curtain call.[209]

Many audience members left the theatre disturbed and angry, but others reacted with 'deep empathy',[210] affected by Tabori's desire 'to highlight the potential Holocaust lurking at the heart of the play'.[211]

THE 1970S: FROM MILLER TO ZADEK

Jonathan Miller's National Theatre production opened at the Old Vic on 28 April 1970; the television version, broadcast in 1973, is so widely available on video that little detailed description of the performance is required here, and many of its strikingly original moments are discussed in the textual commentary. Laurence Olivier's fascinating Victorian financier Shylock has given the production the status of a 'classic', but at the time, Miller was justly criticised for an incoherent concept that bordered on parody.

Informing Miller's production was that genteel but nasty anti-Semitism of late Victorian England – rarely have the Venetians been such an unattractive lot. While this concept placed the Shylock–Antonio plot in a revealing and provocative light, it turned the rest of the play into a sorry mess; Joan Plowright's Portia was 'a new rich, snobby spinster who, apart from a determination to buy a husband (preferably with a lower income than herself) was utterly indifferent to the events taking place around her' (Ansorge, *PP* 1970). In one of the most perceptive reviews of his long career, Harold Hobson remarks on this and other aspects of the production:

> Mr Miller is, rather sadly, the talented Peter Pan of our stage. Whilst his companions in 'Beyond the Fringe' have matured, he remains the Perpetual Undergraduate . . . his treatment of Portia and the suitors is typical of a weakness that is fatal to his production. The Prince of Morocco is a grinning, conceited idiot . . . Arragon a senile dodderer; and Bassanio a cad on the make. In themselves these are good, isolated jokes; but they ought to have made Mr Miller consider what sort of woman is she who attracts exclusively such admirers . . . Now new interpretations of old plays are precisely what distinguish the liveliness of the British from the fossilisation of the classic French stage. But a new interpretation is precisely what Mr Miller does not in this instance give us. He has not thought beyond the

209 *Ibid.*, p. 464.   210 Feinberg, *Embodied Memory*, p. 211.
211 M. Shapiro, 'Shylock', p. 7.

immediate joke . . . One of the unhappiest consequences of this attitude is that, the romantic scenes having been sent up, and the others merely modernised, it is impossible even to take seriously what is seriously given.

Of Olivier, Hobson adds, 'Sir Laurence will not be remembered for his Shylock. Or if he is, he will be singularly unlucky' (*ST* 3 May 1970).

The year 1972 brought new developments in the long process by which Israeli and German theatre practitioners, and their audiences, have come to terms with the post-Holocaust *Merchant*. Yossi Yzraeli's production for the Cameri Theatre of Tel Aviv began with a Passion Play procession; Avraham Oz, who prepared the Hebrew translation, notes that 'everything was far removed from realism', the most telling example being 'the constant presence of a puppet theatre peering over the white back wall, reflecting, reverberating, and multiplying the action underneath by means of puppets in the likeness of the actual characters on stage'.[212]

Avner Hyskiahu, a short stocky actor known for his comic roles, played Shylock; his portrayal was the deliberate antithesis of what Meskin and Finkel had brought to the Habimah.[213] He was 'a shrewd old Jew, his posture, his gait, his manner of speaking reflecting a life spent making shrewd, furtive money deals, a man accustomed to abuse. He delivers . . . "Hath not a Jew eyes?" snarling at the two *goyim*, practically spitting in their faces. He is a worm turned, but still a worm' (Kohansky, *JP* 24 March 1972).

At the Bochum Schauspielhaus in December 1972, Peter Zadek made it his aim to confront Germany's guilt directly through a 'purgational process',[214] by presenting a Shylock, played by Hans Mahnke, as much like the notorious Werner Krauss as possible: he 'skipped, shuffled and slurched; rubbed hands, spread arms and raised shoulders in the typical manner associated with a bartering Eastern Jew, he glared and grimaced, leered and fawned, switched in a trice from submissive self-abasement to snarling anger and triumphant hooting'.[215] Zadek, like Yzraeli, gave the production an anti-realistic frame: Rosel Zech played Portia as three separate characters, 'the Belmont doll, the romantic bride, the farcical judge', and Ulrich Wildgruber, for reasons unexplained, made Lancelot Gobbo a dialect part by giving him a Swabian accent.[216]

However honourable the intention, provoking an audience (which is not hard to do) often yields contrary and unexpected results: 'Only a few critics believed in Zadek's cryptic catharsis. Most of them thought the production to be in bad taste and politically grossly insensitive. The Jewish community were deeply offended, and many spectators were profoundly

---

212 Oz, 'Transformations', p. 67.   213 Shaked, 'The Play', p. 22.
214 Hortmann, *Shakespeare on the German Stage*, p. 257.
215 *Ibid.*   216 Verch, 'The Merchant', p. 89.

disturbed even though (and partially because) they had enjoyed themselves. Post-Auschwitz *Merchant*s were not supposed to be a laughing matter.'[217] In the ensuing years, Zadek continued to experiment with the play, and as we will see, a different concept occasioned one of the most engaging productions of the 1980s.

JOHN BARTON

At Stratford in 1978, John Barton took the *Merchant* into The Other Place – this was the first major production of the play in a small and intimate theatre, and several reviewers commented on its increased immediacy. Roger Warren describes Christopher Morley's design as 'rather Chekovian in feel, especially the *Three Sisters*-like severe black mourning dresses for Portia [Marjorie Bland] and Nerissa [Diana Berriman], with buttoned-up necks and mutton-chop sleeves'.[218] The Venetians were 'on the whole, a spoiled, boorish bunch, much given to throwing bread-rolls, shooting off cap pistols, and other types of horseplay; and the shock provoked by their deep, instinctive prejudice is the shock of recognition, because they wear the suits that some of our generation's grandfathers wore at public school or Oxbridge' (Nightingale, *NS* 4 May 1979).

We are able to learn a good deal of how Barton, Patrick Stewart and Barton's 1981 Shylock, David Suchet, approached the play from the television series, *Playing Shakespeare*, and from Stewart's essay in *Players of Shakespeare*. Stewart explains,

> I decided . . . that I should avoid the easily recognisable symbolic elements of Jewishness, the ringlets, the gown, the nose and so on. I should add, though, that I had a very large bushy beard and a lot of long, dirty, tangly hair. I wore a shabby, dirty broken-down frock-coat, because I think that the most important thing for Shylock in the play is money, possessions and finance. I thought that if he was obsessed with money he would not waste it on how he appeared.[219]

That this Shylock cared most about 'money, possessions and finance' informed the crisis point of the play, when he 'prostrated himself before his judges, groveling in obsequious acceptance of his enforced baptism'.[220]

Stewart's intelligence as an actor always commands respect, but his portrayal raises difficult questions that derive, I believe, from his own stated

217 Hortmann, *Shakespeare on the German Stage*, pp. 257–8.
218 Warren, 'A Year of Comedies', p. 204.
219 Barton, *Playing Shakespeare*, pp. 171–2.   220 Cook, '*The Merchant*', p. 159.

Patrick Stewart as Shylock and Avril Carson as Jessica in John Barton's production, Stratford, 1978.

intention. In dispensing with 'the ringlets, the gown, the nose and so on', Stewart was not avoiding 'the easily recognisable symbolic elements of Jewishness', he was avoiding the recognisable elements of a *theatrical carica-ture* of Jewishness – even without the standard physical trappings, this was still a Shylock whose insistence on his bond was 'cold-blooded', and who 'couldn't convert fast enough'.[221]

Hilton McRae, equipped with Charlie Chaplin's flap shoes, Harpo Marx's wig and rubber-bulb horn, and a variety of other musical instruments, turned Lancelot Gobbo's part into a series of vaudeville turns, eliciting a range of reactions. Ned Chaillet enjoyed the transformation into 'something more than a laughable servant' (*The Times* 13 May 1978); Bernard Levin was less than amused by McRae's 'dire horseplay', but acknowledged that he 'incidentally establishes some kind of record by being obliged to make music with three different instruments . . . without actually being able to play any of them' (*ST* 21 May 1978).

221 Barton, *Playing Shakespeare*, p. 177; M. Shapiro, 'Shylock', p. 7.

The RSC revived Barton's production in 1981, but a transfer from The Other Place to the Royal Shakespeare Theatre, and cast changes, led to a different emphasis. Roger Warren, who reviewed both productions, points to some of the differences between Stewart and David Suchet:

> In 1978, Shylock had been a shabby Dickensian usurer who even preserved the stubs of his home-rolled cigarettes in a tin, contrasted with Tubal, a well-dressed businessman who smoked cigars. Here, both were visibly wealthy, contrasted not in appearance but by symmetrical positioning, set against one another across a centrally placed table, Shylock bent on revenge, Tubal attempting to dissuade him, both wreathed in cigar smoke . . . Somewhat in the old tradition of humorous Shylocks, Mr Suchet was a loud, coarse joker, who could still make the menace beneath the 'merry bond' unmistakable.[222]

Portia was also a different character in 1981. In 1978–9, neither Marjorie Bland nor her London replacement, Lisa Harrow, was prominent in reviews, but everyone was affected by Barton's third Portia, Sinead Cusack. Cusack comments,

> we played the suitor scenes for their grim, rather than their comic, qualities. I sat in a chair with the caskets in front of me, Nerissa and Betty[223] on either side, while Morocco and Arragon circled us like animals getting ready to pounce, one might say, upon their pound of flesh. Again, this way of playing the scene underscored the pathos of Portia's predicament.[224]

Barton's taking the Morocco and Arragon sequences seriously helped Cusack and her Bassanio, Jonathan Hyde, derive full value from their first scene together, and Bassanio's discovery of 'fair Portia's counterfeit' was a moment of liberation, as Portia hurled the caskets across the stage. This liberation continued in the court scene, 'where Miss Cusack's lawyer [was] less an impersonation than a revelation of her true crop-haired self' (Coveney, *FT* 22 April 1981).

THE TWO STRATFORDS: 1984

Since 1981, the *Merchant* has been a 'main stage' regular for the RSC, with a new production every three to four years: the need to fill the big theatre with a mostly tourist audience has relegated the less familiar plays, if they are done at all, to the Swan or The Other Place. As a result, when it is the *Merchant*'s turn again, each new director and designer must strive, in the words of the

222 Warren, 'Interpretations', p. 141.
223 Balthazar was played as a female servant, hence 'Betty Balthazar' to the cast.
224 Cusack, 'Portia', p. 34.

Monty Python troupe, 'for something completely different'. John Caird's 1984 production was definitely that: to Michael Billington,

> an air of faintly perverse eccentricity hangs over [this] production . . . It stems less from his reading of the play, which views Shylock as a man whose revenge has total emotional justification, than from [David] Ultz's designs which are bizarre and outlandish without having any firm geographical base. As one enters the theatre, one is greeted by two towering baroque organs suggestive less of the Adriatic than of *20,000 Leagues Under The Sea*. The stage, meanwhile, is surrounded by sumptuous plum red patterned curtains and the floor festooned with cushions indicating the bedding department of an Istanbul emporium. And when we get to Belmont the caskets swing through the air on the end of vast prehensile cranes, like movie microphone booms. (*Gdn* 11 April 1984).

Clearly, any Shylock would be 'up against it', but as usual, Irving Wardle managed to see past the excesses and offer some sharp insights, praising Ian McDiarmid's willingness to tackle 'Shylock head on as an unsympathetic figure' (*The Times* 11 April 1984). Billington admired Frances Tomelty's 'unusually vehement and strong willed' Portia, but Martin Hoyle thought her 'intense, hard-driven quality . . . [made] her playfulness a trifle heavy handed' (*FT* 11 April 1984).

Whatever the defects or virtues of this effort, all attention in the 1984 Stratford season was directed to Antony Sher's sensational performance as Richard III. We cannot know if the RSC management read Mel Gussow's comment that were 'Sher to attempt the role, one would look forward to another Shylock' (*NYT* 12 August 1984), but in 1987, when the Royal Shakespeare Theatre was due for another *Merchant*, Gussow's request was granted.

Sher expressed his ideas about his part in Bill Alexander's production in an interview:

> There have been a lot of productions set in the turn of the century – or in the last century – where he's dressed in a frock coat like everybody else and is an assimilated Jew. To me, that is nonsense, because clearly he sticks out like a sore thumb in society . . . We chose to make him a Turkish Jew using a Turkish accent. What we were doing with that was trying to extend the racism and by just making him a very unassimilated foreigner, very foreign, rather than very Jewish, we hoped to slightly broaden the theme of racism. We also wanted to make the racism as explicit and as brutal as described in the text, but never normally done. You don't normally see Christians spitting at him or kicking him or doing all the things that he says they do.[225]

225 *qtd* Raymond, *Theater Week*, 5 September 1988.

Sher's 'blazingly important achievement', to Michael Coveney, was 'the re-appropriation of Shylock as a sympathetic stranger . . . exhilaratingly thickly accented, long-haired and colourfully Semitic, rescued from caricature by tumultuous passion and a devastating force of expression' (*FT* 30 April 1987). This 'stranger' status was emphasised further by the Venetians being more openly and viciously hostile than in any production previously seen at Stratford: 'it seems that the whole of Venice is baiting Shylock and baying for *his* flesh with chants of "Jew, Jew, Jew" ' (Edwards, *Spectator* 9 May 1987). Jessica was also subjected to more prejudice than was usual, snubbed by Portia, ignored by Lorenzo once her fortune was his, and left alone with Antonio at the end of the play.

Alexander also foregrounded the homosexual relationships to a greater extent than in any previous RSC *Merchant*, not only for Antonio and Bassanio, but, as James C. Bulman notes in his thoughtful analysis of the production, for the Salads as well:

> By mirroring this unrequited love of an older man for a youth, the relationship between Salerio and Solanio suggested that homosexuality makes the whole world kin . . . Salerio [Salarino], a middle-aged courtier more fashionably dressed than Antonio, hungers for Solanio, his effete young protégé who sports a plumed hat and is rather heavily made-up. Together, they embody the values of a jaded Venetian culture.[226]

All this created a different context for Deborah Findlay than previous, Portias would have encountered. To Billington, she was 'a tart, astringent figure constantly boxing people's ears, and guilty, to put it mildly, of tactlessness in dismissing Morocco with "Let all of his complexion choose me so" in front of her own black servant' (*Gdn* 1 May 1987).[227]

Also in 1984, Mark Lamos set the first Stratford, Ontario, *Merchant* for eight years in the midst of an early eighteenth-century *carnevale*, with *commedia* masquers who not only participated in Jessica's elopement, but made their often-threatening presence felt at other points in the play. The period was interesting, but the production commonplace for Ontario, with elaborate costumes, quick pace and Morocco and Arragon as buffoons – one very unusual performance was that of Jack Medley as Tubal, in the rich brocade and long periwig of a Goldoni (or even a Congreve) character. Sadly, at a schools matinée, some children began throwing pennies at a group of Jewish

---

226 Bulman, *Shakespeare in Performance*, pp. 127–8. Of course, 'Salerio' is the Salarino of this text.
227 See Findlay's own discussion, 'Portia', pp. 54 ff.

students sitting nearby, an incident that was to have repercussions for years to come (Bemrose, *Macl* 10 July 1989).

ZADEK, LANGHAM, HALL

Peter Zadek returned to the *Merchant* with a strikingly new interpretation that opened at the Vienna Burgtheater in December of 1988. Billington provides a clear description:

> Zadek's *Merchant* was certainly bold and radical in that it subordinated questions of anti-Semitism to an examination of capitalist morality. He set the action in contemporary Wall Street and cast as Shylock a blond, indisputably Aryan actor, Gert Voss, who could, as Zadek said, play Siegfried or an SS officer. This led to a totally assimilated Shylock whose hatred of Antonio was financial rather than racial.[228]

The Venetian scenes, set in Wilfried Minks's steel and glass office tower, dominated the production, and Eva Mattes's Portia got little attention from the critics. Paul Taylor paid her an interesting compliment by describing her as 'one of the least neurotic Portias' he had seen (*Ind* 31 August 1995), but John Peter thought her 'smug' (*ST* 3 September 1995).

The Stratford Festival of Canada's announcement that it was to present *The Merchant of Venice* in 1989, directed by Michael Langham, aroused fears that a repetition of the 1984 penny-throwing incident or something similar might occur. There were immediate protests, and the Canadian Jewish Congress proposed that seminars for student audiences be organised to introduce the play's themes. Then, just before the production opened, 'there was public outcry over what proved to be erroneous reports that the CJC was pressuring the festival to censor the play' (*Macl* 27 June 1996). In fact, even if the CJC wanted the play to be changed, which is most unlikely, it did not need to exert any pressure: Langham had already 'censored' it for Washington's Shakespeare Company the year before.

Brian Bedford played Shylock in both productions; the designers and other actors were different, but the concept was the same. Bedford was 'a Shylock dressed in a glorious blue brocaded robe, as Judaic as an illumination from an old Bible . . . a Shylock who, though rich, for some reason sports a wild shock of unkempt hair and a filthy ragged beard'. The Christians

---

228 Billington, *One Night Stands*, pp. 358. With the same actors in the major roles, this
  production continued for a number of years, and reached a wide European audience
  – in Paris, Berlin, and in 1995 as part of a Berliner Ensemble tour to Edinburgh.

however, came from another era, 'dressed in natty Edwardian suits' (Conlogue, *GM* 2 June 1989).

Langham took the radical step of deleting 'that for this favour / He presently become a Christian'. He insisted this was an artistic decision, not affected by outside pressure, his reason being that Elizabethans would have seen forced baptism as an act of mercy, while it no longer has that meaning today.[229] I have argued that this is a very questionable assertion;[230] be that as it may, Langham's decision was less than consistent, since 'there seems little point in cutting out phrases deemed to be offensive and then have people in the courtroom scene spitting on Shylock' (Ashley, *Stratford Beacon Herald* 1 June 1989).

Indeed, removing the conversion, controversial as it was, was less significant than Langham's other alterations to the text. The promptbook shows that he changed at least forty lines, in what can only be called an extraordinary 'dumbing-down' of the play. A few examples: magnificoes 'of greatest port' became ones 'of highest rank' (3.2.280), Portia's 'true conceit / Of godlike amity' became her 'true concept / Of manly friendship' (3.4.2–3), and in a complete perversion of a vital passage's meaning, 'the commodity that strangers have' is changed to 'the privilege that aliens have / With us in Venice' (3.3.27–8). Two things about this are both astonishing and worrying: first, that Langham would rewrite the play in this manner, and second, that not a single reviewer appears to have noticed it.

Overall, the 1980s saw the *Merchant* move off into several interesting new directions, but the decade ended on a disappointing note with Peter Hall's production, featuring Dustin Hoffman as Shylock, which opened in London and then, with some cast changes, moved on to Washington and New York. Hall enjoys a reputation for careful attention to the intricacies of Shakespeare's verse structure, but in this production English and American actors alike raced through long passages, with a startling lack of inflection or nuance.

Referring to Hoffman's recent success in *Death of a Salesman*, Robert Brustein describes him as more Willy Loman than Shylock: 'he leaves no signature on the role . . . [having] curiously chosen to give an elocutionary performance . . . his youthful Shylock is without size, edge, power, or point of view' (*NR* 12 February 1990). These comments are particularly apt for Hoffman's first scene, written all in verse, when he seemed to be speaking, not acting, his part, but in the prose passages he displayed his 'particular and priceless capacity for expressing the secrets of a man's mind through low-key unguarded utterance' (Wardle, *The Times* 2 June 1989).

229 *ctd* Ward, *SB* 1989.   230 See above, p. 4.

Dustin Hoffman as Shylock in Peter Hall's production, 1989.

Apart from Hoffman's performance, critics on both sides of the Atlantic found little to interest them. To Michael Feingold, Hall 'toys with the *Merchant*'s contradictions, limply, making it clear that he's aware of their presence. Yet he doesn't seem to have made much effort to resolve, or even express them' (*VV* 26 December 1989). Wardle, in commenting on Geraldine James's Portia, compares her with one of Hoffman's great screen roles, regretting 'that it was not possible to bring "Tootsie" on as Portia . . . James plays her in the likeness of a splendid young headmistress, on her dignity even with Abigail McKern's Nerissa, and regally aloof from the suitors'. He admires James's 'high-speed and unfailingly lucid delivery . . . [but] what she lacks is the slightest trace of humour; so that the ring episode changes from a mischievous game into a test of marital status, conducted in arrogant discourtesy to the embarrassed Antonio'.

Brustein's assessment, that 'even critics who have praised [Hall's] version concede that it fails to provide new insight into a play that shrieks for reinterpretation', might serve as introduction to the 1990s: his call would be repeatedly answered in what was to be the best decade in the play's history.

ENGLAND: 1990–1994

Directing the *Merchant* for the English Shakespeare Company, Tim Luscombe sought to depict a violently anti-Semitic society by setting the action in Mussolini's Italy. In what Billington describes as a 'dark and sombre world', John Woodvine's Shylock was 'a wholly credible Homburg-hatted, sober-suited businessman quietly nursing a "lodged hate". He neither rails nor storms but he has a lean intensity that makes people back away nervously in cafés when he mercilessly exposes the fatal flaw of racial persecution: "The villainy you teach me I will execute" ' (*Gdn* 9 February 1991).

The concept is undeniably clever, but perhaps too precise in its historical setting. In an unfavourable review, Peter Holland finds the trial scene rendered incredible by putting it in a fascist courtroom, with the Duke made up to look like *Il Duce*: 'It is difficult to believe that the rule of law was still strong enough in this version of Venice in 1938 for Shylock to have any hope of justice, or that these black-uniformed guards would willingly hold Antonio down for Shylock rather than taking Shylock out and killing him' (*TLS* 22 February 1991). Billington, although agreeing that 'awkward questions' are raised, argues that 'Luscombe's updating gives an over-familiar play urgency, passion, and a high-level theatricality' (*Gdn*).

Such defamiliarising 'high-level theatricality' was even more prominent in David Thacker's 1993 production at Stratford. The setting, as historically specific as Luscombe's, was very similar to what Zadek created in 1988:[231]

---

231 When Zadek's production was shown at the Edinburgh Festival in 1995, it seemed old-hat to some reviewers who saw Thacker's version first.

the financial world of London's 'City', where 'news came from the Rialto by telephone, fax, and computer network, and Shylock could assure himself that Antonio was "sufficient" by referring to the laptop on his desk'.[232] Even more than Olivier, David Calder began as a completely assimilated Jew, 'genial, shrewd and totally lacking in Hebraic trademarks . . . indistinguishable from any other Western businessman' (Wardle, *Ind* 6 June 1993), a Shylock who, 'though wary of Antonio and his retinue, is tired of old battles, and at first sees their unconventional bond as a bit of useful bridge-building' (Nightingale, *The Times* 12 April 1994).

At the start, Calder was less an outsider than Clifford Rose's Antonio, 'tight-lipped and precise, a man whose hidden sexual habits were probably very nasty indeed',[233] ageing and increasingly isolated from the lives of Bassanio and his 'yuppie' friends. But with the loss of Jessica, Calder changed into the Jew of his persecutors' imagination, the Savile Row suit replaced by a black Jewish gaberdine. Russell Jackson saw Penny Downie's Portia 'as a woman who takes her own oath with a determination comparable to that of Shylock, and the unfolding of the truth about the caskets in the scenes with Morocco and Aragon was given its fullest weight';[234] Billington applauded her 'growing intelligence . . . a decent woman visibly upset by Shylock's forced conversion to Christianity' (*Gdn* 5 June 1993).

As good as Calder, Rose and Downie were, they came close to being upstaged by Christopher Luscombe, who demonstrated 'amazing proof that Lancelot Gobbo, long thought the least funny of Shakespeare's clowns, can be deliriously funny'.[235] Luscombe transformed Shylock's servant into an office boy: attired, in his own description, in a 'Debenhams blazer', he made his opening monologue a chat with the audience during a coffee-break. Later, at Belmont 'he was able to move into weekend casuals: polo shirt, checked chinos and sandals (with socks of course)'.[236]

Nearly all reviewers commented favourably on Shelagh Keegan's two-tiered set, 'recalling the steel tubes and walkways of the Lloyds building in the City of London, and filled with the goings-on and equipment of the money market'.[237] Indeed, Keegan deserves as much credit as anyone for the production's success – it is unusual to see a multi-level construction at

232 Jackson, 'Shakespeare Performed . . . 1993–4', p. 340.
233 Holland, *English Shakespeares*, p. 165.
234 Jackson, 'Shakespeare Performed . . . 1993–4', p. 340.
235 Holland, 'Shakespeare Performed', p. 199.
236 Luscombe, 'Launcelot Gobbo', pp. 24, 25.
237 Jackson, 'Shakespeare Performed . . . 1993–4', p. 340.

Stratford, since removing it for another play and then remounting it is both difficult and expensive – Keegan's tubular steel let the action of this *Merchant* move with exciting rapidity from locale to locale through light changes, often without actors leaving or re-entering the stage.

Of all *Merchant* productions in recent times, Jude Kelly's at the West Yorkshire Playhouse in Leeds in 1994 came closest to making Portia the central character. Working within an early twentieth-century period, Nichola McAuliffe acted her 'with overtones of Hedda Gabler, an angry prisoner to her father's will who practised pistol shooting in her home, put bullets into a portrait of her father and played Russian Roulette'.[238] Michael Cashman's Antonio, 'a daringly unsympathetic reading' (Macaulay, *FT* 26 March 1994) also provoked a literary association, that of Aschenbach in *Death in Venice*, 'wearing steel-rimmed glasses, loitering in an art gallery at the opening; elegant and decadent and slightly gone to seed'.[239] In a production where Antonio, Bassanio and the Salads 'inhabit a closety, men-only milieu in Venice', not only Shylock but Portia becomes Antonio's antagonist: 'even after trumping Shylock with her superior command of the law, [Portia] still urges him "Prepare thee to cut off the flesh", not without a spasm of malice against Antonio' (Macaulay, *FT*). Standing apart from this triangle, Gary Waldhorn's Shylock and Jane Arden's Jessica were victims of pervasive racism: Jessica was pointedly ignored at Belmont and then spat at by Bassanio when she told of her father's plans to exact his bond, and in the trial scene, Beerbohm Tree's crowd of Jewish spectators was revived, who became increasingly dismayed at what they saw. Searching for Shylock's house to deliver the deed of gift, and 'pelted with stones by women and children in the ghetto, Portia shows a saddened comprehension of their resentment'.[240]

SELLARS, EDELSTEIN, MARADEN

Later in 1994, yet another radical reinterpretation arrived with Peter Sellars's production, first at Chicago's Goodman Theatre, and then on tour to England, Germany and France. Sellars transplanted the *Merchant* 'from the teeming, multicultural world of 15th century Venice, Italy, to the teeming, multicultural world of 1994 Venice Beach, California' (Zoglin, *Time* 31 October 1994). By casting African-Americans as Shylock, Jessica and Tubal, Asian-Americans as Portia and the other Belmont characters, and Latinos as the Venetians, he hoped 'to touch the texture of life in contemporary America; the metaphor and the reality of anti-Semitism . . . extended to

238 Schafer, *Ms-Directing Shakespeare*, p. 123.
239 *Ibid.*, p. 120.   240 Hopkins, *SB* 1994.

include parallel struggles and their related issues'.[241] As W. B. Worthen notes, 'while the Chicago papers were divided over whether Sellars' exploration of American culture and of Shakespeare was profound or pretentious, Goodman audiences voted with their feet: most evenings saw the audience depleted by as much as 60 per cent after the intermission'.[242]

Neither relocating the play to California nor cross-racial casting was any more 'profound or pretentious' than Thacker's use of contemporary London: the difference was in the execution. Thacker imported the quick pace of the City into his production, but Sellars's *Merchant* moved at subglacial speed for over four hours, much of it presented via television monitors placed on stage and in the auditorium. The monitors showed either the action taking place on stage, relayed through hand-held cameras, or supposedly relevant images, such as the beating of Rodney King and the violence in Los Angeles that followed it. For the trial, Shylock 'had his back to the audience while the TV image of his face got equal, simultaneous treatment as the images of contemporary racism'; Portia's plea for mercy was undercut by a Presidential press conference.[243]

Perhaps the most unfortunate thing about such excesses is that they negated the performance of Paul Butler, who played Shylock 'with basso-profundo self-assurance . . . a hardhearted ghetto businessman who, even when he is humiliated at the end, never loses his cool or stoops for pity' (Zoglin, *Time*), a Shylock able to communicate 'the awful endlessness of someone being expected to turn the other cheek to blow after blow after blow' (Nightingale, *The Times* 18 November 1994).

We have seen how some reviewers of both Beerbohm Tree's and Dustin Hoffman's Shylock saw resonances of earlier Jewish roles. In 1995, Ron Leibman brought much of his extraordinary performance as the notorious lawyer Roy Cohn, in Tony Kushner's *Angels in America*, to Barry Edelstein's *Merchant* for the New York Shakespeare Festival. Edelstein offered what was expected by the mid 1990s: gay relationships and rampant anti-Semitism with a good deal of spitting, but no one could have expected what Leibman brought to Shylock – in some respects similar to Antony Sher, and no less original or confronting. With the same 'hostile, spittling, staccato delivery' he used as Cohn, Leibman gave a performance variously described as 'harrowing, fierce', 'galvanic, fearless' or 'electrifying'.[244]

---

241 Sellars, *qtd* Worthen, *Shakespeare*, p. 77.
242 Worthen, *Shakespeare*, p. 77.
243 King, 'Texture of Contemporary Life', p. 43.
244 Winer, *New York Newsday* 6 February 1995; Brustein, *NR* 3 April 1995; Gerard, *Variety* 7 February 1995.

Ron Leibman as Shylock and Byron Jennings as Antonio in Barry Edelstein's production,
New York Shakespeare Festival, 1995.

With astonishing technical virtuosity, Leibman delivered long speeches in a sustained rage without any loss of clarity; the ferocity of the performance seemed to have taken critics by surprise, for they offered little comment on how it was counterpoised with moments of vulnerability. He rendered 'O father Abram, what these Christians are . . .' (1.3.153–60) as a furious diatribe, stopping suddenly and saying 'To buy this favour, I extend this friendship', with quiet sincerity. Brustein captures the essential quality of Leibman's performance in the observation that as both Cohn and Shylock, he acted 'with an equal disregard for audience sympathy, which may be why he wins it' (*NR* 3 April 1995).

Stratford, Ontario, had a major *Merchant* in 1955, but since then, as we have seen, the play had not fared well. Alexander Leggatt notes that Marti Maraden's 1996 production 'was surrounded by tactical moves to prepare the ground: consultation with leading Jewish groups, lectures, seminars, a background kit for school parties'.[245] This *Merchant* was Ontario's first to be placed in relatively recent times; as did Luscombe in 1991, Maraden chose fascist Italy, but used it more selectively, setting the action in the early 1930s, before Mussolini was drawn into an alliance with Germany.

As Baldridge's Venice of 1963 might have been filmed by Fellini, Maraden's cold and wintry city evoked Bernardo Bertolucci.[246] John Pennoyer costumed the men in 'overcoats, hats, and scarfs to enhance the atmosphere of frigidity'; by contrast, 'Belmont seemed warm and light, with lovely female attendants sketching by a pool, while Portia and Nerissa chatted under graceful Renaissance arches'.[247] Elegantly attired in a pin-striped suit, a homburg covering his yarmulke, Douglas Rain was as quiet and refined a Shylock as Leibman was loud and confronting, but in one aspect their performances were strikingly similar: 'there was not a single moment when he asked for the audience's sympathy'.[248]

Unusually for the 1990s, no homosexual relationship between Bassanio and Antonio was foregrounded, so Susan Coyne as Portia did not need to compete with Antonio for Bassanio's affections in the way that Nichola McAuliffe did. But this was still a woman unhappy about her father's will, nervously smoking cigarette after cigarette, whose racist joke about her black suitor was not softened. Like McAuliffe, she learned a great deal from her excursion to Venice, and she was visibly upset after the trial when some blackshirts recognised and applauded her. Maraden's was easily the best Ontario *Merchant* since Guthrie's, over forty years before.

---

245 *SB* 1997.   246 Newell, *SB* 1997.
247 Hornby, 'Other Stratford', p. 472.   248 Leggatt, *SB* 1997.

Douglas Rain as Shylock in Marti Maraden's production, Stratford Festival of
Canada, 1996.

STRATFORD AND LONDON, 1997–8

Superficially, Gregory Doran's 1997 production for the RSC was similar to Alexander's and Edelstein's: costumed in Renaissance fashion, it had a major actor, Philip Voss, as Shylock, and showed both endemic anti-Semitism in Venice (Voss entered for 3.1 cut and bleeding) and gay or bi-sexual relationships, although much more subtly. But unlike Alexander's production (in which Doran played Solanio) or Edelstein's, this *Merchant*, however 'strong, handsome, and accomplished . . . did not offer any remarkable novelty of insight into the play or (more significantly) contact with our time's preoccupations'.[249]

Doran's *Merchant* opened late in 1997 and continued throughout the summer of 1998, when it was joined by Richard Olivier's production, with the German actor Norbert Kentrup as Shylock, at Shakespeare's Globe in Southwark. As this was only the Globe's second season, less attention was given to the play itself than to the novelty of the theatre and the ways in which it was used, or meant to be used, by both performers and audience – no Globe production suffered as badly as this one did from the appalling misconception that theatregoers of Shakespeare's time, especially the groundlings, would spend their hard-earned pennies in order *not* to listen attentively to a play such as *The Merchant of Venice*. Instead, it seems, they acted like infants, and in the name of authenticity, their modern counterparts should do likewise: in a stinging rebuke, Benedict Nightingale wrote in *The Times* (3 August 1998) that today's spectators 'are being simultaneously asked to pretend they are Elizabethans, and encouraged to behave as if Red Riding Hood and the Big Bad Wolf were on stage'.

The antics began as the audience assembled: 'an Italian madrigal group could be heard performing in the musicians' gallery, while down on the forestage a masked carnival character (Marcello Magni) was teaching the audience a ribald popular song. Eventually the madrigal group descended to perform on the stage level, only to be confronted by Magni's rival group encouraging the audience to join in its aggressive raucousness.'[250] Many happily joined in, but others, myself included, would agree with Dominic Cavendish, who likened Magni to 'a warm-up act on heat' (*Ind* 1 June 1998). During the interval, he invaded the yard and fondled women near the stage, on one occasion earning a punch in the face from an irate husband.

Kentrup learned English especially to play Shylock. At times his accent got in the way of clear understanding, but this was unimportant given that

249 Jackson, 'Shakespeare Performed . . . 1996–8', p. 195.
250 Potter, 'Shakespeare Performed', p. 75.

the goings-on around him left no opportunity to build his performance in any serious way. To John Peter,

> he seems to have no discernible relationship with his daughter and only the sketchiest with the Venetians: the result is that he emotes in a vacuum. The effect is deeply old-fashioned and ponderous. It also means that Shylock, deprived of a network of relationships, becomes more isolated and therefore more of the villain of the piece, solitary and melodramatic. (*The Times* 7 June 1998).

No one seemed to care, though, in the never-ending quest for cheap laughs: for all of the Globe's claims of authenticity, it was still seen as appropriate to have Lorenzo and his friends arrive to carry Jessica off dressed in bunny suits.

AN EXCITING FINISH: SERBAN, NUNN

The Globe *Merchant* was hardly what Brustein had in mind when he called for reinterpretation, but in December of 1998, Brustein's own company, the American Repertory Theatre of Cambridge, Massachusetts, presented a daringly original *Merchant* from guest director Andrei Serban, with Will LeBow as Shylock. LeBow, as provocative as Sher or Leibman, was a Shylock in the mode of comedian Lenny Bruce – nothing escaped the mockery that served to mask the pain he suffered: 'water rats, water thieves, and land thieves . . .' (1.3.19–22) was a song-and-dance routine; he made snorting noises when talking about pork, and he made the sign of the cross at 'nor pray with you' (1.3.30). And so it went throughout the play – even 'hath not a Jew eyes' was done 'while popping up and down behind a miniature screen, a smile painted on his face and revenge burning in his eyes' (Hartigan, *BG* 19 December 1998).

LeBow was surrounded by a fine company, with Kristin Flanders, an 'intense' Portia, living in a Belmont of 'Van Gogh colors on a Rothko-esque canvas' (Hartigan, *BG*), and Jonathan Epstein as a

> humorless, coy, touch-me-not Antonio . . . at the beginning of the play, he walked a fashion ramp forward to sit alone, daintily crossed his legs swingingly, and went through expertly every mannerism that stereotypes precious homosexuality: the flick of head and pasted cowlick, the fussy fingering of face and clothes, the flap of hanky and slap of gloves, and so on. He invited contact only to push away when it approached or brushed against him.[251]

251 Dorothy and Wayne Cook, *SB* 1999.

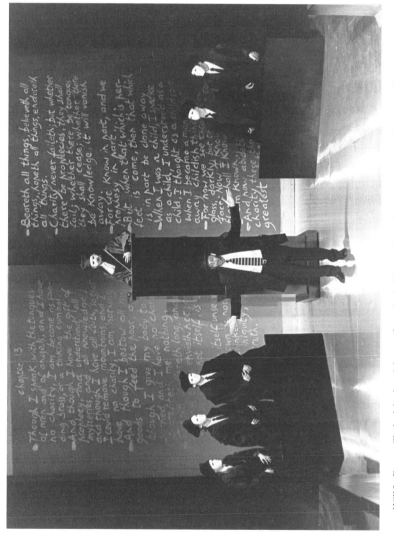

Will LeBow as Shylock in the trial scene from Andrei Serban's production, American Repertory Theatre, 1998.

But this 'privileged, young, gay, merchant' learned, by the end of the play 'both that prejudice might someday come his way and that, in compelling the Jew to become Christian, he might have created a real, if ironically attractive, monster'.[252] Some were offended by LeBow's 'shtick-comedian' Shylock, but others found that Serban's coherent vision and strong cast made this a memorable production.

Trevor Nunn's production for the Royal National Theatre, opening in June of 1999, was one of the rare *Merchant*s, even though it had a remarkable Shylock in Henry Goodman, that must be labelled with its director's name. Its greatest strengths were in the quality of the ensemble, and in the decision to use the National's intimate Cottesloe Theatre, arranged in traverse mode, with the audience on two sides.[253]

Hildegard Bechtler's design brought us into the 1930s, less Venice than the Berlin of Christopher Isherwood's stories. The Venetian scenes were mostly in the centre of the traverse, 'elegant café tables on a black and white chequered floor, much drinking of champagne, the noisy young men of the Christian community in an impressive range of well-cut suits and blacks such as Lancelot Gobbo doing the menial jobs'.[254]

Goodman, his conservative suit not completely covering a prayer-shawl worn underneath, was friendly towards Bassanio, but wary of Antonio, in his first scene. In a very moving 2.5, he and Gabrielle Jourdan as Jessica showed the deep love underlying their troubled relationship, highlighted by their singing, in Hebrew, the traditional prayer *Eshet Chayil*, 'A Woman of Virtue'.[255]

David Bamber's Manchester-accented Antonio was 'a brooding, middle-aged depressive who had long sublimated his secret love for Bassanio into being a self-absorbed businessman' (Peter, *ST* 27 June 1999), his 'dull, centre-parted hair [and] behind-the-fashion suit contrasted splendidly with the dashing playboy elegance of Alexander Hanson's beautifully coiffured Bassanio'.[256] Since there was no cynical hinting at the leaden casket, one felt that Hanson knew the correct answer to the riddle because he had carefully thought about it.

The uniform quality of Nunn's production was most apparent in that the Belmont scenes were as interesting as those in Venice. Derbhle Crotty was the ideal Portia for the 1930s, 'tall, tense and elegant, with a wary, prickly sense of humour' (Peter, *ST*). In a complete reversal of how the Morocco

252 *Ibid.*
253 The production later moved to the large Olivier Theatre, where it lost some of its force.
254 Smallwood, 'Shakespeare Performances', pp. 267–8.
255 See Appendix 2.
256 Smallwood, 'Shakespeare Performances', p. 268.

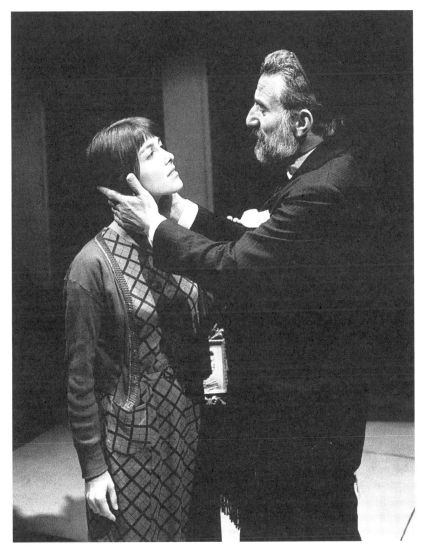

Gabrielle Jourdan as Jessica and Henry Goodman as Shylock in Trevor Nunn's
production, Royal National Theatre, 1999.

scenes are usually played, Portia 'found herself surprisingly wrong-footed
by the exotic poetic earnestness of Chu Omambala's splendid Morocco',[257] a
dashing prince who had Portia desperately hoping he would choose the right
casket, and becoming tearful when he did not.[258]

257 *Ibid.*   258 See pp. 158, 159, 161.

The Gobbo scenes were also part of the production's success, rather than something to be overlooked. Played by black actors Oscar James and Andrew French, father and son invested their parts with genuine humour and uncommon dignity. By following the first and last rule of comic acting, 'don't try to be funny', French was very funny indeed, delivering some of his 2.2 soliloquy as a night-club routine,[259] and in quieter moments, showing a touching affection for Jessica.

To some reviewers, this production was too much of a good thing: although many lines were deleted, the amount of stage business inserted led to a performance over three hours in length. Whether or not this criticism is justified, there can be little doubt that Nunn's *Merchant* brought spectators into the play as deeply as in any production since 1741, when Macklin first gave us 'The Jew that Shakespeare drew'.

THE *MERCHANT* ON FILM

There has never been a major feature film of *The Merchant of Venice*, and given the sensitivity of the play's subject matter, it is very unlikely that one will ever be made. In the silent era, though, it was a popular choice.[260]

Il Mercante di Venezia (1910), one of several Shakespeare films directed by Gerolamo Lo Salvio, survives in a nine-minute fragment in the video *Silent Shakespeare*. Printed in hand-tinted colour, it features Ermete Novelli as Shylock, Olga Giannini Novelli as Portia, and the beautiful Francesca Bertini, at the beginning of her long and brilliant career, as Jessica.[261] There is no indication that the complete film had either the casket or ring sequences; the action is limited to the Jessica–Lorenzo and bond plots, finishing with the courtroom scene.[262] The longest scene, at nearly four minutes, is the combined signing of the bond and Jessica's elopement, all in broad daylight. When the film was released in England, the *Kinematograph and Lantern Weekly* noted, 'The difficult task of putting forward a kinematograph adaptation of *The Merchant of Venice*, has been well undertaken in the present instance; the various scenes are fully played out, and the advantages afforded by the natural background of Venice must be obvious to all.'[263]

---

259   See p. 150.

260   Rothwell, *Shakespeare on Screen*, pp. 175–82, has a complete listing of *Merchant* films and television productions from 1902 to 1986.

261   She is the subject of Bernardo Bertolucci's *The Last Diva* (1982).

262   Ball, *Shakespeare on Silent Film*, pp. 123–5.   263   *qtd ibid.*, p. 122.

THE *MERCHANT* ON TELEVISION

I have noted that Fehling's 1927 production, with Fritz Kortner as Shylock, was Germany's last major *Merchant* before World War II. In 1969, having returned to Germany after a long exile in the United States, the seventy-one-year-old Kortner played Shylock for the last time in Otto Schenk's production for German–Austrian television, with the young Sabine Sinjen as Portia.

Kortner completely dominated proceedings throughout: 'taking advantage of the specific opportunities the screen medium offers, [he] acted with a breathtaking precision and attention to minute detail, presenting a Shylock who, having been treated cruelly by Christian society, in return becomes cruel himself'. With his fringe of white hair and wispy beard, he was 'slow and reflective in his gestures and speech, and as profoundly religious as trusting in his right to justice. It is when thwarted in this right that he develops his cruel thirst for revenge against Antonio, the Christian, a revenge that he thinks to undertake according to God's will.'[264]

The production benefited from the very high standards given to television drama in Germany. Although shot completely indoors (in black and white), a set large enough to allow tracking shots from room to room and a functional canal placed the action in Venice, not a television studio. Within the first fifty lines we saw Antonio in his study, framed in his doorway while conversing with Solanio and Salarino, and then walking through a populated outdoor marketplace before being seated at a table beside an inn – sound mixing created the noises of a busy Venice behind them.

Schenk's vision of the play was a particularly dark one; indeed, a more cynical and unprepossessing group of Christian characters could hardly be imagined. Sinjen was more obvious in instructing Bassanio to choose the leaden casket than any Portia I have seen, Klaus Höring as Lorenzo obviously cared only for Jessica's money, and Max Eckard's Antonio fainted before Portia said 'Tarry a little.'

While many would account this production as uncompromisingly one-sided, and be troubled by Kortner's very slow delivery of his lines (which affected everyone in the cast), its overall quality makes it the best television *Merchant*, a significant attempt to reinterpret the play in light of twentieth-century history.

Cedric Messina's production for the BBC in 1972, with Frank Finlay as Shylock and Maggie Smith as Portia, was as unlike Schenk's as could be. Messina and his cast seemed to be consciously avoiding any hint of engagement with the *Merchant*'s difficult themes, exemplified by the extraordinary

264 Verch, '*The Merchant*', p. 88.

direction of the trial scene, where Shylock's reaction to being forced to convert is never shown on camera.

British television had a more interesting *Merchant* the following year, with the broadcast of Jonathan Miller's 1970 National Theatre production. There were some cast changes, the part of Lancelot Gobbo, already truncated in the stage version, was here (thankfully) reduced to almost nothing, and Old Gobbo did not appear at all. The Victorian interiors were well suited to television, but the age of the cast, with a forty-year-old Bassanio wooing (not very enthusiastically) a forty-four-year-old Portia, was more obvious in close-up than it would have been at the Old Vic.

The BBC production of 1980, produced by Miller and directed by Jack Gold, is perhaps the version seen by most school students, which is unfortunate, since it is a prime example of the dullness which bedevilled the BBC Shakespeare series from its inception to its conclusion. Television being the most realistic of all performance media, Gold fell victim to all its drawbacks while realising none of its potential, and the production values that made Schenk's *Merchant* so worthwhile were absent from the BBC studios. The opening in Miller's TV version works well, because Antonio is indoors, but in Gold's first scene, he is revealed in a brightly lit exterior of Renaissance arches and columns, a deserted Venice without citizens or the ambient sounds they make – to Mervyn Jones, the characters 'were camping out in the ruins of a Roman forum' (*Lst* 18/25 December 1980). Other choices were available, but unfortunately they cost money: the prospect of taping outdoors was obviously never entertained, and as a result, the locale for the entire play, as it was for every BBC Shakespeare, was 'a studio', where no breeze ever blows, Gratiano's instruction, 'let no dog bark' is taken literally and no interior set ever has a ceiling.

Warren Mitchell as Shylock revived the 'stage Yid', not seen for a long time, 'an Eastern European Jew with Yiddish accent, wagging head and exaggerated hand movements familiar from music hall revues, vaudeville skits, and radio comedy programs',[265] a Shylock who actually used the absurd nineteenth-century business of plucking a hair from his beard to test the sharpness of his knife.[266] Gemma Jones, so successful in the television series *The Duchess of Duke Street*, could hardly have found a role to which she was less suited than Portia: as is all too customary, at thirty-seven she was too old for the part, and Gold and Miller did her no favours by making the fatal mistake of having a Nerissa, the lovely Susan Jameson, who was much better-looking than her mistress.

A glimpse of what the television medium might one day do with the *Merchant* was provided in Alan Horrox's film, made for Thames Television

265 M. Shapiro, 'Shylock', p. 7.   266 See p. 219.

in 1996. The key word is 'film', not videotape: David Higgs's cinem-atography, accenting reds and dark browns, included a good deal of exterior location work, and from its opening in a busy Venice street, as Antonio watched a group of red-robed choir boys file past, Horrox's produc-tion beautifully captured the atmosphere of Renaissance Venice, however romanticised.

Bob Peck, in one of the last performances of his sadly short career, was an unusually genial Shylock; like Dustin Hoffman, he showed little passion in the early scenes, and some of the long speeches in 3.1 were rushed, but on the positive side, he and Haydn Gwynne as Portia capitalised upon the intimacy of cinema sound to give fully nuanced readings of their key speeches, without having to raise their voices above a whisper. Gwynne showed real tension with Morocco and Arragon, who were played with dignity, and gave every appearance of being able to choose the correct casket. In a very nice touch, Paul McGann as Bassanio contemplated the riddle of the caskets with only Portia present; Nerissa and Gratiano announced their wedding plans at a celebration feast afterwards.

Unfortunately, the text was so truncated (the film runs only seventy-five minutes) that the production's potential could not come close to being realised – it was more a case of excerpts from the play than the play itself. Given the overall excellence of the acting, including Victoria Hamilton as Nerissa and John Woodvine as the Duke, this was an opportunity wasted.

THE SHYLOCK WHO NEVER WAS

Orson Welles had always wanted to play Shylock, but the closest he ever came was a recording he did with his Mercury Theatre players for Columbia Records in 1938. Whether derived from instinct or careful study, Welles's unparalleled sensitivity to the structure and rhythms of Shakespeare's language is evident in every line, and we can only wonder what a Mercury Theatre *Merchant* would have been like had it ever found its way to the stage.

In the late 1960s, Welles began filming scenes from the *Merchant*. As he did with his monumental *Othello*, he worked with whatever actors he had, wherever he happened to be. The director Peter Bogdanovich was with Welles in Rome as he was editing some footage:

> I have just seen the bell tower on one of the moviola screens, Orson as . . .
> Shylock standing in front of it. The reverse angle of the scene was on the
> second moviola. This was shot in Venice. Another angle of the same scene,
> on the third moviola, was shot in Yugoslavia. Why Yugoslavia? Because the
> Venetian weather had closed in early this year and Orson had gone south to
> the Dalmatian coast, which, he says, having once been part of the Venetian

empire, is full of the right sort of architecture. Orson's closeup in front of the Roman church had been a retake due to scratches on the negative.[267]

Shortly afterwards, the negative disappeared; after Welles died, a four-minute fragment was found in Los Angeles, and was included in the documentary film, *Orson Welles: One Man Band*.

Welles intended to set the action in eighteenth-century Venice, and it remains unclear how much of the play he intended to film, perhaps a short piece for television, with only the Shylock scenes. It is clear, though, that the scenes included were to be reordered: Welles says to Irina Maleva, 'Look to my house', and walks through the streets, past foreboding masked revellers, to Antonio's *palazzo*, where some of 1.3 is acted. Welles confronts Charles Gray with a bitter 'Signior Antonio, many a time and oft / In the Rialto' and that is all we have of Welles's *Merchant of Venice*.

SOME ADAPTATIONS

It was probably in 1903, the year Jacob Adler played Shylock on Broadway, that a fourteen-year-old Jewish immigrant from the Ukraine named Avrom Moyshe Schwartz arrived in New York; as Maurice Schwartz, he would succeed Adler as the Yiddish theatre's leading actor and director. Although he always wanted to play Shylock, Schwartz had no real opportunity to do so until Adler retired, and it was not until 1930 that he got his chance – not in a full production of the play, but in excerpts performed in Yiddish as part of the RKO vaudeville circuit 'playing on the same bill with Ben Blue, or Ike Rose's Midgets, or Rin-tin-tin'.[268]

The *New York Times* (21 April 1930) notes:

> He begins quietly with the dread bargaining between Shylock and Antonio and Bassanio, moves into the parting scene with Jessica and later with the two scornful young men of Venice, and concludes with the apostrophe to old Tubal. It is a passionate, furious portrait that he creates, but precise and controlled in diction and held closely to the rhythm of the verse. It leaves no doubt on the part of Mr Schwartz as to the tragic implications of the character. The 'Hath not a Jew eyes?' speech is delivered in a sort of frenzy, full of despair and a near madness, and the quieter scene with Tubal is likewise replete with revenge and a dark foreboding . . . this Shylock has an undeniable stature, the more remarkable for its swift and sure creation in the heart of a vaudeville bill.

---

267 *qtd* Welles and Bogdanovich, *This is Orson Welles*, pp. 29–30.
268 Berkowitz, 'A True Jewish Jew', p. 153.

Of course, the boundary between an adaptation and an unconventional production cannot be clearly defined: I have set it at the point where there is a substantial, or even complete, rewriting of the play. Hence Tabori's *The Merchant of Venice as Performed at Theresienstadt*, which used Shakespeare's text, is included in the survey of productions, while discussion of Charles Marowitz's *Variations on The Merchant of Venice* and Arnold Wesker's *The Merchant* will be limited to a few comments here.

Marowitz's *Variations*, first performed in England in 1976, is set in British Palestine, 1946; it begins with a news report of the blowing up of the King David Hotel. The Venetians are British – army officers and civilians – and Shylock, in Marowitz's own description, 'is, on the surface, a Jewish money-lender, but covertly, a supporter of the independence movement and a man who finances guerrilla (terrorist) activities'. Many of Shakespeare's lines are used, often reassigned or placed in another context, and many lines from *The Jew of Malta* are imported and given to Shakespeare's characters. As Marowitz himself states, 'it is not easy to integrate styles as different as Marlowe's and Shakespeare's'.[269]

But it is more than a matter of style – both *The Merchant of Venice* and *The Jew of Malta* might have a Jew as their central character, but other-wise they are different in every respect. As a result, Marowitz's play is no more a version of Shakespeare's play than it is of Marlowe's; while interesting in its own right, it does not take us more deeply into *The Merchant of Venice*.

The same must be said of Arnold Wesker's *The Merchant*: an entirely new play rather than an adaptation. In 1993, on the occasion of Thacker's production, Wesker wrote a piece for the *Sunday Times* denouncing Shakespeare's play: 'I seethe at his portrait of the stereotype Jew, unable to pretend that this is simply another Shakespearian character through whom he is exploring greed, bonds, the "quality of mercy", or whatever other portentous themes theatre aficionados plough into this soiled play' (6 June 1993).

Wesker's *Merchant*, written in 1977, is, as Clive Barnes noted in his review,

> his reply to Shakespeare, and his exploration of his Shakespeare's anti-Semitism . . . Wesker sees Shylock and the merchant Antonio – Jew and Christian – as close friends, indeed loving friends, who would literally do anything for each other. It is a friendship strengthened by the prevailing anti-Semitism in Venice, a fact of their lives which both recognize, but ignore. (*The Times* 3 December 1977)

269 Marowitz, *PP* 1977.

Wesker's Shylock insists on lending his friend money without any bond, 'but Antonio insists on it to uphold Venetian law, which requires a bond when a Jew lends money to a Christian' (Eder, *NYT* 17 November 1973).

The play is full of literate and amusing dialogue, but its main difficulty lies in its premise as a 'reply'. If *The Merchant of Venice* is indeed a 'soiled play', Wesker's reworking of the story would carry more weight; but if one is prepared to question seriously the views of Harold Bloom, quoted at the beginning of this introduction, and those of Arnold Wesker, quoted at its end, then no reply to Shakespeare is likely to succeed, for no reply is necessary.

THE MERCHANT OF VENICE

LIST OF CHARACTERS

THE DUKE OF VENICE
THE PRINCE OF MOROCCO, *a suitor to Portia*
THE PRINCE OF ARRAGON, *suitor also to Portia*
BASSANIO, *an Italian lord, suitor likewise to Portia*
ANTONIO, *a merchant of Venice*
SOLANIO,
SALARINO,
GRATIANO,   } *gentlemen of Venice, and companions with Bassanio*
LORENZO,
SHYLOCK, *the rich Jew, and father of Jessica*
TUBAL, *a Jew, Shylock's friend*
PORTIA, *the rich Italian lady*
NERISSA, *her waiting-gentlewoman*
JESSICA, *daughter to Shylock*
GOBBO, *an old man, father to Lancelot*
LANCELOT GOBBO, *the Clown*
STEPHANO, *a messenger*
JAILER
SALERIO, *a messenger from Venice*
LEONARDO, *one of Bassanio's servants*
BALTHAZAR,
SERVINGMAN,   } *members of Portia's household*
MESSENGER,
A SERVINGMAN *employed by Antonio*
ATTENDANTS
MAGNIFICOES OF VENICE
COURT OFFICIALS

THE MERCHANT OF VENICE

ACT I, SCENE I

I.[I] *Enter* ANTONIO, SALARINO, *and* SOLANIO

ANTONIO In sooth I know not why I am so sad.
　　　　It wearies me, you say it wearies you;
　　　　But how I caught it, found it, or came by it,

Three characters in quiet conversation is a low-key opening, and gives the lie to the idea that the Elizabethan playhouse was a rowdy place where the groundlings' attention would have to be gained by a loud or active beginning. As the locale is not given in the dialogue, the action is just 'on the stage' – once painted scenery came into use, a Venetian street became the setting. The stock scenery of Macklin or Kemble would have been of little visual interest; Charles Kean was the first to provide an elaborate opening tableau of Venetian street life, a practice that continued well into the twentieth century, with Max Reinhardt and David Belasco (see pp. 32, 44–5).

For the modern-dress productions of more recent times, a variety of locations, mostly public places, are used. Richard Baldridge and Marti Maraden placed Antonio and his friends at an outdoor café, Jonathan Miller moved them indoors into Florian's and Trevor Nunn had a cabaret 'the morning after'. Jude Kelly started in a 1930s Venetian art gallery, 'with pricey looking bronzes standing about, and a portrait reminiscent of something by Jean Cocteau' (Wilcocks, *PP* 1994); David Thacker's 'City' showed Antonio and the Salads, 'all in white and tan modern business suits, talking in a high-tech two-tiered office complex' (Geckle, *SB* 1994).

Except for Bassanio, Gratiano and Lorenzo entering unannounced, there is no reason why Antonio cannot be at home, but Gordon Crosse, seeing Arthur Phillips's production in 1935, 'had a shock when the curtain rose on "A Room in Antonio's House" and saw the Sallies and afterwards Bassanio and the rest paying morning calls' (*Diaries*, vol. xv, p. 83). Michael Kahn's Antonio was already at dinner (disregarding lines 70–1) before a wall tapestry, with the Salads 'seated at the table, fawning shamelessly over Antonio at its head' (Mahon, *SN* 1999).

1　Tim Luscombe's *Merchant* began with a young couple dancing. Antonio spoke of his sadness after a 'yearning look after the nameless young man' (Biggs, *SB* 1991).

What stuff 'tis made of, whereof it is born,
I am to learn.   5
And such a want-wit sadness makes of me,
That I have much ado to know myself.
SALARINO Your mind is tossing on the ocean,
There where your argosies with portly sail
Like signors and rich burghers on the flood,   10
Or as it were the pageants of the sea,
Do overpeer the petty traffickers
That curtsey to them, do them reverence,
As they fly by them with their woven wings.
SOLANIO Believe me, sir, had I such venture forth,   15
The better part of my affections would
Be with my hopes abroad. I should be still
Plucking the grass to know where sits the wind,
Piring in maps for ports, and piers, and roads;
And every object that might make me fear   20
Misfortune to my ventures, out of doubt
Would make me sad.
SALARINO   My wind cooling my broth
Would blow me to an ague when I thought
What harm a wind too great might do at sea.
I should not see the sandy hourglass run   25
But I should think of shallows and of flats,
And see my wealthy Andrew docked in sand,
Vailing her high top lower than her ribs
To kiss her burial. Should I go to church
And see the holy edifice of stone   30
And not bethink me straight of dangerous rocks,
Which touching but my gentle vessel's side
Would scatter all her spices on the stream,
Enrobe the roaring waters with my silks,
And (in a word) but even now worth this,   35
And now worth nothing? Shall I have the thought
To think on this, and shall I lack the thought

8 Robert Brustein said of Peter Hall's production, 'the only thing that kept me sentient during this tiresome evening was admiring how English actors could add so many syllables to a simple word like "o-c-e-an" ' (*NR* 12 1990).

29b–36a Although included in the 1774 Bell edition, these lines were omitted by actor-managers from Edmund Kean through to Henry Irving.

That such a thing bechanced would make me sad?
But tell not me: I know Antonio
Is sad to think upon his merchandise.   40
ANTONIO Believe me, no. I thank my fortune for it,
My ventures are not in one bottom trusted,
Nor to one place; nor is my whole estate
Upon the fortune of this present year:
Therefore my merchandise makes me not sad.   45
SOLANIO Why then, you are in love.
ANTONIO   Fie, fie!
SOLANIO Not in love neither? Then let us say you are sad
Because you are not merry; and 'twere as easy
For you to laugh and leap, and say you are merry
Because you are not sad. Now by two-headed Janus,   50
Nature hath framed strange fellows in her time:
Some that will evermore peep through their eyes,
And laugh like parrots at a bagpiper;
And other of such vinegar aspèct,
That they'll not show their teeth in way of smile   55
Though Nestor swear the jest be laughable.

       Enter BASSANIO, LORENZO, *and* GRATIANO

Here comes Bassanio, your most noble kinsman,
Gratiano, and Lorenzo. Fare ye well;
We leave you now with better company.
SALARINO I would have stayed till I had made you merry,   60
If worthier friends had not prevented me.
ANTONIO Your worth is very dear in my regard.
I take it your own business calls on you,
And you embrace th'occasion to depart.
SALARINO Good morrow, my good lords.   65
BASSANIO Good signors both, when shall we laugh? Say, when?
You grow exceeding strange; must it be so?
SALARINO We'll make our leisures to attend on yours.
                          Exeunt Salarino and Solanio

50b–6 Cut by Macready, Charles Kean.

   57 Hall pointed to Bassanio's penury by having him enter with a clearly visible rent in his hose
      (Kliman, *SB* 1990); Scott Handy, in Doran's production, ran in, arriving 'late and half-drunk
      for an important meeting' (Smallwood, *SS* 1999).

   58 Gold had Solanio call out 'Gratiano and Lorenzo!' as a loud, and very incongruous, greeting.

LORENZO My Lord Bassanio, since you have found Antonio
> We two will leave you, but at dinner time   70
> I pray you have in mind where we must meet.
BASSANIO I will not fail you.
GRATIANO You look not well, Signor Antonio.
> You have too much respect upon the world:
> They lose it that do buy it with much care.   75
> Believe me, you are marvellously changed.
ANTONIO I hold the world but as the world, Gratiano:
> A stage where every man must play a part,
> And mine a sad one.
GRATIANO   Let me play the Fool.
> With mirth and laughter let old wrinkles come,   80
> And let my liver rather heat with wine
> Than my heart cool with mortifying groans.
> Why should a man whose blood is warm within
> Sit like his grandsire cut in alabaster?
> Sleep when he wakes? And creep into the jaundice   85
> By being peevish? I tell thee what, Antonio –
> I love thee, and it is my love that speaks –
> There are a sort of men whose visages
> Do cream and mantle like a standing pond,
> And do a wilful stillness entertain,   90
> With purpose to be dressed in an opinion
> Of wisdom, gravity, profound conceit,
> As who should say, 'I am Sir Oracle,
> And when I ope my lips, let no dog bark!'
> O my Antonio, I do know of these   95
> That therefore only are reputed wise
> For saying nothing; when I am very sure
> If they should speak, would almost damn those ears
> Which, hearing them, would call their brothers fools.
> I'll tell thee more of this another time.   100
> But fish not with this melancholy bait
> For this fool gudgeon, this opinion.
> Come, good Lorenzo. Fare ye well awhile;
> I'll end my exhortation after dinner.

79b Nunn's Gratiano, Richard Henders, very drunk from a night of carousing, said 'Let me play
the Fool' into the cabaret microphone, as if to say, 'let me be a stand-up comic'. This tied in
nicely with Lancelot's routine at the start of 2.6 (see p. 150).

LORENZO Well, we will leave you then till dinner time.   105
     I must be one of these same dumb wise men,
     For Gratiano never lets me speak.
GRATIANO Well, keep me company but two years moe,
     Thou shalt not know the sound of thine own tongue.
ANTONIO Farewell; I'll grow a talker for this gear.   110
GRATIANO Thanks, i'faith, for silence is only commendable
     In a neat's tongue dried, and a maid not vendible.
               Exeunt [Gratiano and Lorenzo]
ANTONIO It is that anything now.
BASSANIO Gratiano speaks an infinite deal of nothing, more than
   any man in all Venice. His reasons are as two grains of wheat hid   115
   in two bushels of chaff: you shall seek all day ere you find them,
   and when you have them they are not worth the search.
ANTONIO Well, tell me now what lady is the same
     To whom you swore a secret pilgrimage
     That you today promised to tell me of.   120
BASSANIO 'Tis not unknown to you, Antonio,
     How much I have disabled mine estate
     By something showing a more swelling port
     Than my faint means would grant continuance.
     Nor do I now make moan to be abridged   125
     From such a noble rate, but my chief care
     Is to come fairly off from the great debts
     Wherein my time, something too prodigal,
     Hath left me gaged. To you, Antonio,
     I owe the most in money and in love,   130
     And from your love I have a warranty
     To unburden all my plots and purposes
     How to get clear of all the debts I owe.
ANTONIO I pray you, good Bassanio, let me know it,
     And if it stand as you yourself still do   135
     Within the eye of honour, be assured

---

112 Miller's Gratiano, as he was leaving Florian's, intercepted the waiter and took a glass of wine
    from his tray. He then looked at the bill, gasped in dismay and exited.

118–20 Jonathan Epstein, Serban's Antonio, enquired about his friend's 'secret pilgrimage' as if
    struggling to control his disappointment. In Alexander's production, John Carlisle, speaking
    'with distaste', turned his back on Bassanio – Antonio and Bassanio were constantly placing
    their hands on one another in this sequence (Bulman, *Shakespeare in Performance*, p. 126).

My purse, my person, my extremest means
Lie all unlocked to your occasions.
BASSANIO In my schooldays, when I had lost one shaft,
I shot his fellow of the selfsame flight   140
The selfsame way, with more advisèd watch
To find the other forth; and by adventuring both
I oft found both. I urge this childhood proof
Because what follows is pure innocence.
I owe you much, and like a wilful youth   145
That which I owe is lost; but if you please
To shoot another arrow that self way
Which you did shoot the first, I do not doubt,
As I will watch the aim, or to find both
Or bring your latter hazard back again   150
And thankfully rest debtor for the first.
ANTONIO You know me well, and herein spend but time
To wind about my love with circumstance;
And out of doubt you do me now more wrong
In making question of my uttermost   155
Than if you had made waste of all I have.
Then do but say to me what I should do
That in your knowledge may by me be done,
And I am prest unto it: therefore speak.
BASSANIO In Belmont is a lady richly left,   160

138 Sothern instructs that 'occasions' be 'pronounced with four syllables' (*pmt* Sothern[1]).

140 For Barton in 1978, Antonio and Bassanio 'laughingly completed together the aphoristic line about finding your lost arrow by means of another' (Velz, '*The Merchant*', p. 101).

160–75 Schenk's Bassanio, Folker Bohnet, rubbed his fingers together at the words 'richly left'. For Miller, Anthony Nicholls as Antonio took the information about Portia's wealth seriously, 'the gravity with which he listens to Bassanio's proposal for making a coup in the marriage market is as much due to absorption in money-making as to friendship' (Hobson, *ST* 3 May 1970).

Some directors have revealed Portia at this moment. Komisarjevsky had music play while 'the Venice set, on two sliding stages, split in the middle and moved into the wings. Then, as the lighting on the cyclorama changed from apple green to deep pink, a lift carrying Belmont rose to stage level with Portia and Nerissa poised like Dresden china figures – a theatrical reinforcement of Bassanio's description of Portia's virtues' (Mennen, 'Theodore Komisarjevsky's Production', p. 90).

And she is fair, and – fairer than that word –
Of wondrous virtues. Sometimes from her eyes
I did receive fair speechless messages.
Her name is Portia, nothing undervalued
To Cato's daughter, Brutus' Portia.   165
Nor is the wide world ignorant of her worth;
For the four winds blow in from every coast
Renownèd suitors, and her sunny locks
Hang on her temples like a golden fleece,
Which makes her seat of Belmont Colchos' strand,   170
And many Jasons come in quest of her.
O my Antonio, had I but the means
To hold a rival place with one of them,
I have a mind presages me such thrift
That I should questionless be fortunate.   175
ANTONIO Thou know'st that all my fortunes are at sea;
Neither have I money nor commodity
To raise a present sum; therefore go forth,
Try what my credit can in Venice do,
That shall be racked even to the uttermost   180
To furnish thee to Belmont to fair Portia.
Go presently enquire, and so will I,
Where money is, and I no question make
To have it of my trust or for my sake.

Exeunt

Margaret Webster sought a similar effect, in a very different style of production, with 'the figure of Portia (Margaret Johnston) in a poetic attitude . . . dimly shadowed through the gauze – it lifts and we are happy in Belmont' (Matthews, *TW* 1956). For José Carlos Plaza in 1992, a canal bridge descended and upstage walls opened 'to illuminate Belmont's lady, as though she were being seen in his mind's eye' (Fischer, *SB* 1995).

181 Alexander's and Serban's Antonios made their sexual jealousy of Portia clear: Carlisle said 'fair Portia' as if spitting out bad wine (Bulman, *Shakespeare in Performance*, p. 127), while Epstein picked up the empty wallet Bassanio had previously left on a bench, and angrily thrust it back at him.

183b–4 Nunn had Antonio speak the last line and a half as soliloquy – Bassanio having already departed, he was forced to pay everyone's bill at the cabaret; Antonio was also left 'to pick up the tab' in Barton's 1978 production (Wardle, *Times* 22 April 1981). Miller had Antonio leave first, and 'when the waiter who brings Bassanio his gloves extends his hand for a tip, Bassanio slaps the waiter's hand with his gloves and laughs nastily, then follows Antonio through the door' (Perret, 'Shakespeare and Anti-Semitism', p. 148).

ACT 1, SCENE 2

[1.2] *Enter* PORTIA *with her waiting–woman* NERISSA

PORTIA By my troth, Nerissa, my little body is aweary of this great
world.

Ellen Terry and Helena Modjeska were typical of nineteenth-century Portias by starting the scene lounging on a couch (Sprague, *Shakespeare and the Actors*, p. 19). Julia Marlowe was also reclining, 'holding a book which she has been reading', while a 'blackamoor page' fanned her, and Nerissa 'played' a lute to the accompaniment of an off-stage flute (*pmt* Sothern[1]). Hilde Krahl, in Piscator's production, was another reclining Portia, but her Belmont was one of erotic images projected on scenic panels (Kennedy, *Looking at Shakespeare*, p. 202), most unlike Joan Plowright's Victorian interior, crowded with furniture in the television version.

Tim Luscombe evoked the 1930s, with Lois Harvey 'a Jean Harlow look-alike, listening to blues on a wind-up gramophone and munching her way through a heart-shaped box of chocolates' (Holland, *TLS* 22 February 1991). Trevor Nunn's Portia, in essentially the same era, also had blues on her gramophone, but the champagne-drinking Derbhle Crotty, with her long dark hair, was very unlike Jean Harlow.

Some productions place Portia outdoors: Barrett and Booth's set offered a view from the house overlooking a terrace, and in more recent times, Ellis Rabb had Rosemary Harris on her private beach, her yacht moored nearby, along with 'near-nude loungers and strollers; she, barefoot like the rest, is in a floppy, poncho-like robe, her head wrapped in a beach towel' (Watt, *NYDN* 5 March 1973). Both Schenk and Gold placed their television Portias on an outdoor terrace, but the effect in each was different: Sabine Sinjen, unkempt and pouting, sat with her feet in a garden fountain while birds chirped; Gemma Jones was elegantly dressed as she moved about her garden, where all bird life had been exterminated.

Margaret Webster would have heard many bird calls in this scene when she played Portia for Ben Greet in 1928, on 'what was laughingly known as a "pastoral tour" ', performing

NERISSA You would be, sweet madam, if your miseries were in the
same abundance as your good fortunes are; and yet for aught I
see, they are as sick that surfeit with too much as they that starve   5
with nothing. It is no mean happiness, therefore, to be seated in
the mean – superfluity comes sooner by white hairs, but
competency lives longer.
PORTIA Good sentences, and well pronounced.
NERISSA They would be better if well followed.   10
PORTIA If to do were as easy as to know what were good to do, chapels
had been churches, and poor men's cottages princes' palaces. It is a
good divine that follows his own instructions; I can easier teach
twenty what were good to be done, than be one of the twenty to
follow mine own teaching. The brain may devise laws for the   15

out of doors, adapting ourselves to whatever local conditions existed . . . B. G. was
never very specific about what went on where, [but] . . . in *The Merchant of Venice*,
Venice and Belmont had to be geographically separated. It was usual for Nerissa and
me to have our first scene interrupted by B. G.'s piercing growl from behind a hedge,
proclaiming: 'Ye're in Venice, y'fool, y'ought to be in Belmont' (Webster, *The Same
Only Different*, pp. 321, 322–3).

1 Portia, just as Antonio does in 1.1, begins the scene with a reference to her own sadness.
Sinead Cusack remarks that she wanted to play the opening lines 'not in the bored voice of a
child who has too much of everything, but as a cry of anguish from one who finds the whole
business of the caskets very painful' (Cusack, 'Portia', p. 33); so 'world weary' was Nichola
McAuliffe in Kelly's production, 'so tired and angry at the fetters placed upon her by the
conditions of her father's will, that she is swigging wine and firing an unloaded gun into
her own mouth' (Macaulay, *FT* 26 March 1994).

3 The Folio text identifies Nerissa as a 'waiting woman', but modern-dress productions
sometimes imply a different social position. Maraden's promptbook has 'waiting woman'
crossed out and replaced by 'best friend', although this is hardly consistent with the
subservient role Nerissa has throughout the play, given such lines as Gratiano's 'You saw the
mistress, I beheld the maid' (3.2.198). In Miller's Victorian milieu, Anna Carteret's simple
grey dress and her attending to Portia's mail established her as more of a lady's companion
and secretary, as was common in that era. She still had to carry Portia's valises in 5.1,
however.

15a At 'mine own teaching', Nunn had 'noises off' of carousing, and Portia's butler exited to
see to the matter (he returned at 99 with the news of the suitors' departure).

15b–18a The sentence starting 'The brain' was always omitted in the eighteenth and nineteenth
centuries.

blood, but a hot temper leaps o'er a cold decree – such a hare is
madness the youth, to skip o'er the meshes of good counsel the
cripple. But this reasoning is not in the fashion to choose me a
husband. O me, the word 'choose'! I may neither choose who I
would, nor refuse who I dislike, so is the will of a living daughter   20
curbed by the will of a dead father. Is it not hard, Nerissa, that I
cannot choose one, nor refuse none?

NERISSA Your father was ever virtuous; and holy men at their death
have good inspirations. Therefore the lottery that he hath
devised in these three chests of gold, silver, and lead, whereof   25
who chooses his meaning chooses you, will no doubt never be
chosen by any rightly but one who you shall rightly love. But
what warmth is there in your affection towards any of these
princely suitors that are already come?

PORTIA I pray thee over-name them, and as thou namest them I will   30
describe them – and according to my description, level at my
affection.

NERISSA First, there is the Neapolitan prince.

PORTIA Ay, that's a colt indeed, for he doth nothing but talk of his
horse; and he makes it a great appropriation to his own good   35
parts that he can shoe him himself. I am much afeared my lady
his mother played false with a smith.

30–81 Portia's lengthy description of her suitors is often seen as tiresome, or to quote one
Portia, 'interminable' (Cusack, 'Portia', p. 30). In Brazil, Claudio Torres Gonzaga had one
actor play both Morocco and Arragon; the same actor also mimed, from an upstage
platform, each suitor's eccentricity as Portia described it (De Sousa, '*The Merchant*',
p. 471).

While not going to Gonzaga's extreme, other directors have added some interesting stage
business to the sequence. Michael Benthall placed a chess board on stage, 'and both
mistress and maid used chessmen as stand-ins for the unwelcome suitors' (Clarke,
Shakespeare at the Old Vic, np); Doran and his designer Robert Jones placed elaborate
suitors' gifts about the stage – Portia inspected 'an ornate stuffed peacock, a turquoise and
gold vase, a mounted ship, and a gilded frame' as she discussed the attributes of each
sender (Fischer, *SB* 1999). In keeping with Miller's late Victorian setting, Joan Plowright
viewed a picture of each suitor through a stereoscope, thus she could comment literally on
Falconbridge as 'a proper man's picture' (59). Nunn's suitors were shown on a home movie.

36–7 The indelicate reference to the Neapolitan's mother is retained in the Bell and Inchbald
texts, but was cut by Kemble, Charles Kean, Booth and Irving.

NERISSA Then is there the County Palatine.

PORTIA He doth nothing but frown, as who should say, 'And you will
not have me, choose.' He hears merry tales and smiles not; I fear   40
he will prove the weeping philosopher when he grows old, being
so full of unmannerly sadness in his youth. I had rather be
married to a death's head with a bone in his mouth than to either
of these. God defend me from these two!

NERISSA How say you by the French lord, Monsieur Le Bon?   45

PORTIA God made him, and therefore let him pass for a man. In
truth I know it is a sin to be a mocker, but he! – why, he hath
a horse better than the Neapolitan's, a better bad habit of
frowning than the Count Palatine: he is every man in no man. If
a throstle sing, he falls straight a-capering; he will fence with his   50
own shadow. If I should marry him, I should marry twenty
husbands. If he would despise me, I would forgive him; for if he
love me to madness, I shall never requite him.

NERISSA What say you then to Falconbridge, the young baron of
England?   55

PORTIA You know I say nothing to him, for he understands not me,
nor I him: he hath neither Latin, French, nor Italian, and you
will come into the court and swear that I have a poor penny-
worth in the English. He is a proper man's picture, but alas who
can converse with a dumbshow? How oddly he is suited! I think   60
he bought his doublet in Italy, his round hose in France, his
bonnet in Germany, and his behaviour everywhere.

NERISSA What think you of the Scottish lord his neighbour?

PORTIA That he hath a neighbourly charity in him, for he borrowed
a box of the ear of the Englishman and swore he would pay him   65
again when he was able. I think the Frenchman became his
surety and sealed under for another.

---

44 'God' was changed to 'Heaven' in the eighteenth and nineteenth centuries, here and at
l. 46.

46–53 All except the first sentence of Portia's comments on Le Bon were usually omitted during
the eighteenth and nineteenth centuries; Komisarjevsky followed this earlier practice.

54–67 The editor of the 1774 Bell text, Francis Gentleman, sets apart the description of the English
and Scottish suitors in italics, noting 'this whole scene is pleasing, both in action and
perusal, and should not be curtailed; though the theatres judge otherwise'. Managers
continued to 'judge otherwise' throughout the nineteenth century, with Kemble, Charles
Kean, Booth and Irving all deleting it.

NERISSA How like you the young German, the Duke of Saxony's
nephew?

PORTIA Very vilely in the morning when he is sober, and most vilely   70
in the afternoon when he is drunk. When he is best he is a little
worse than a man, and when he is worst he is little better than a
beast. And the worst fall that ever fell, I hope I shall make shift
to go without him.

NERISSA If he should offer to choose, and choose the right casket,   75
you should refuse to perform your father's will if you should
refuse to accept him.

PORTIA Therefore, for fear of the worst, I pray thee set a deep glass
of Rhenish wine on the contrary casket, for if the devil be
within, and that temptation without, I know he will choose it. I   80
will do anything, Nerissa, ere I will be married to a sponge.

NERISSA You need not fear, lady, the having any of these lords. They
have acquainted me with their determinations, which is indeed
to return to their home, and to trouble you with no more suit
unless you may be won by some other sort than your father's   85
imposition, depending on the caskets.

PORTIA If I live to be as old as Sibylla, I will die as chaste as Diana
unless I be obtained by the manner of my father's will. I am glad
this parcel of wooers are so reasonable, for there is not one
among them but I dote on his very absence; and I pray God   90
grant them a fair departure.

NERISSA Do you not remember, lady, in your father's time, a
Venetian, a scholar and a soldier, that came hither in company of
the Marquis of Montferrat?

PORTIA Yes, yes, it was Bassanio! – as I think so was he called.   95

70–4 Serban punctuated the description of each suitor with music in the style of his country,
composed by Elizabeth Swados. Here Kristin Flanders had to shout to be heard above
'Bavarian oompah' music (Cook, *SB* 1999).

75–7 Spoken with quiet seriousness by Robin Mosely in Kahn's production, nicely pointing to the
real threat of Portia's having to accept a completely unsuitable husband should he make a
lucky choice.

80b–1 The 'sponge' line was often omitted in the nineteenth century.

95 Ellen Terry was probably the first Portia to say 'Yes, yes, it was Bassanio' very excitedly,
and then catch herself, hiding her enthusiasm with 'as I think so he was called' (Kleb,
'Shakespeare in Tottenham Street', p. 114). This tradition was maintained by Ada Rehan,
Julia Marlowe, Maggie Smith and Geraldine James.

NERISSA True, madam; he of all the men that ever my foolish eyes
    looked upon was the best deserving a fair lady.

PORTIA I remember him well, and I remember him worthy of thy
    praise.

Enter a SERVINGMAN

How now, what news?   100

SERVINGMAN The four strangers seek for you, madam, to take their
    leave; and there is a forerunner come from a fifth, the Prince of
    Morocco, who brings word the prince his master will be here
    tonight.

PORTIA If I could bid the fifth welcome with so good heart as I can   105
    bid the other four farewell, I should be glad of his approach. If
    he have the condition of a saint, and the complexion of a devil, I
    had rather he should shrive me than wive me.

    Come, Nerissa; sirrah, go before:
    Whiles we shut the gate upon one wooer, another knocks at   110
    the door.

Exeunt

99sd This 'servingman' is usually the 'Balthazar' of 3.4, and is so identified in most editions used
    by nineteenth-century actor-managers.

101–2 Gordon Crosse was unimpressed with Beerbohm Tree's idea that the suitors 'needs must
    pass over the stage and take their leave in dumb show. It is Mr Tree's way to leave as little as
    possible to the intelligence and imagination of the audience, and he should know best what
    class of audience he is catering for' (*Diaries*, vol. IV, p. 100).

103–4 Sothern brought on Morocco's page here, and Portia's own 'Blackamoor page' laughed at
    him; Morocco himself followed (*pmt* Sothern[1]).

106b–8 The last sentence is in the Bell edition, but was always omitted in the nineteenth century.

ACT 1, SCENE 3

[1.3] *Enter* BASSANIO *with* SHYLOCK *the Jew*

SHYLOCK Three thousand ducats, well.
BASSANIO Ay, sir, for three months.

'What news on the Rialto' is the only hint the text gives in placing this scene; Charles Kean's
setting was 'in the square of the Rialto, the exchange of Venice; here was the real resort of
merchants, and not the bridge, as some have erroneously supposed' (Cole, *Life of Charles
Kean*, p. 265). From the Bancrofts on, with 1.3 following 1.1 (see pp. 20–1), there was no
scene change, and to separate the two episodes, aside from lowering and raising the
curtain, extensive stage business was added. Sothern began with the 'discovery' of 'a
gondola by the landing draped with flowers and garlands, in the gondola a flower woman'.
Also present were a woman fruit-seller sitting on the edge of the well and a 'citizen' lying 'on
his stomach, feet upstage'. These supernumeraries would then move off, and the gondola
would be 'steered' to the exit by the gondolier (*pmt* Sothern[1]); alternative instructions are
given for performances without gondolas.

Crosse records that in Benson's version 'all the Venice scenes were played as one –
Bassanio, on leaving Antonio [and] going in to Shylock's house, fetching him out, and
beginning [1.3] without a break'. Beerbohm Tree had Tubal as a bystander in 1.1; he and
Bassanio went off together, and returned momentarily with Shylock (*Diaries*, vol. II, p. 147;
vol. IV, p. 98). Novelli brought the action to Shylock's neighbourhood, appearing 'on the
balcony of his house, in response to a call from Bassanio: he then descended and came into
the street to discuss the business of the loan' (Winter, *Shakespeare on the Stage*, p. 165).

The director who worked the hardest to create a complete Ghetto environment for 1.3
was David Belasco in 1922:

> The synagogue stands at the centre of the Ghetto: worshipers pass in and out and you
> hear the immemorial chants of Israel . . . on Shylock's door-post is fastened the little
> metal capsule holding a tiny scroll of the law which must be saluted by all who pass
> the threshold . . . nothing is left undone to present Shylock against a background of

108

sanctity, tradition, beauty on the one hand, of jeers, injustice, servitude on the other. (Lewisohn, *Nation* 3 January 1923)

Plaza and Kahn also brought the scene into the Ghetto, Plaza with Hebraic music and a backdrop of rugs suspended from the tenements (Fischer, *SB* 1995), Kahn with a group of four elderly Jews (one of whom later turned out to be Tubal), an orange-seller, and two children.

    Since Guthrie's Habimah production, modern-dress versions have relied on properties and stage business to situate the characters – nowadays one expects Bassanio and Antonio to be having coffee at an outdoor café. Miller and Thacker placed the action in Shylock's business office; Horrox, in his visually sumptuous television film, brought Bassanio to Shylock's house, while the fragment of Orson Welles's film shows him, in a series of magnificently framed shots, leaving the Ghetto and walking to Antonio's house, past groups of sinister-looking masked carnival-goers, some played by live actors and some by wooden mannequins.

osd Whether Shylock and Bassanio walk on to the stage, as they would have done in the 1590s, or are 'discovered' by raising the curtain or bringing up the lights, Shylock's dress and demeanour can create a strong impression of his character even before he speaks. George Lichtenberg, a German visitor to London in 1775, describes Macklin:

> Picture a rather stout man with a coarse yellow face and a nose generously fashioned in all three dimensions, a long double chin and a mouth so carved by nature that the knife appears to have slit him right up to the ears, on one side at least, I thought. He wears a long black gown, long wide trousers and a red tricorne, after the fashion of Italian Jews, I suppose. (*Visits*, p. 40)

In imagining a nineteenth-century performance, we should keep in mind that a leading player, or an actor making his debut, would first need to acknowledge the audience's applause upon his first entrance. John Doran, describing Kean on the night of 26 January 1814, notes, 'all that Edmund Kean ever did was gracefully done; and the bow which he made in return to the welcoming applause was eminently graceful'. Only then, with the audience looking on, could Kean take on Shylock's persona, as he 'leant over his crutched stick with both hands', and spoke his first words (Furness, *A New Variorum Edition*, p. 376).

    Upon his debut at the Haymarket in 1837, Samuel Phelps 'promised a treat, his walk and wig corresponding to stamp him about fifty years old; but still had he continued walking through the street with the speed at which he entered, Bassanio would have hard work to keep pace with him' (Rice, *The London Theatre*, p. 64). Phelps is typical of the earlier 1800s in walking on to the stage,

> but Booth began the scene with a picture: Shylock was 'discovered' standing, midway, on a short, broad, flight of steps, where he had at that moment paused, at the mention

of the sum of money which Bassanio wished him to lend to Antonio, and Bassanio was visible, in the act of turning away, as if impatient at the Jew's hesitation. (Winter, *Shakespeare on the Stage*, p. 157)

Booth's friend and sometime colleague, Lawrence Barrett, was

tall, moving with slow strength across the boards . . . standing in a quietude almost statuesque in its pose, robed in his black Jewish gaberdine bordered with red, and marked with a red cross on the elbow, a black and yellow cap on his grey, bent head, the richly jewelled hands betraying the nervous eagerness of his nature as they clutch and twine upon his long knotted staff. ('The Drama', p. 524)

Irving's initial appearance does not appear to have differed greatly from Booth's or Barrett's:

pale and lean visaged, his wisp of grey beard threaded with streaks of black, he leaned upon a stick, his head slightly bowed, so that normally his glance was upwards and askance. His dress was sober and picturesque; under a dark-brown cloak or gaberdine edged with fur he wore a tunic which reached to his ankles. The sleeves of the tunic were full to the elbow, but tightly fitting over the lower arm, with white cuffs turned back above the wrists. The rusty effect of these garments was offset by a wide sash striped with earthy reds and yellows from which hung a tasselled leather pouch. (Irving, *Henry Irving*, p. 339)

Antony Sher's Levantine Shylock was 'discovered in a day bed, flicking at an abacus, surrounded by scales and books' (Coveney, *FT* 30 April 1987). Ron Leibman was 'in his counting house, with beam and balance scale, exhibiting beard, gaberdine, yarmulke, yellow circle, and attributes of the orthodox – a collective gasp from the audience signified its shock' (Ranald, *SB* 1995).

In Bill Glassco's 'world of frock-coats and waistcoats', Hume Cronyn's gaberdine 'marked him as the alien, the stranger whose refusal to conform confirmed the worst suspicions of those who would not have accepted him even if he had conformed' (B. Jackson, 'Stratford Festival', pp. 202–3); Olivier's Victorian coat and stiff collar were identical to those worn by Antonio and the Duke, but as we first see Shylock in his office, busily signing papers, we also notice his yarmulke, and the one worn by his secretary. David Calder, in David Thacker's 'City' of the 1990s, was expensively and stylishly suited, but he pointedly did not wear a yarmulke, setting him apart from business associate Tubal, present during the scene, who did (Jackson, *SQ* 1994).

Patrick Stewart, in contrast to wealthy financiers such as Olivier and Calder, 'was grubby, shabbily dressed in threadbare clothes, smoked hand-rolled cigarettes down to stubs which he saved in a little metal can, and swiped change left for tips on café tables' (M. Shapiro, *Shofar* 1986). In 1981, David Suchet was 'more obviously wealthy and refined' (Greenwald, *Directions by Indirections*, p. 237).

SHYLOCK For three months, well.
BASSANIO For the which, as I told you, Antonio shall be bound.
SHYLOCK Antonio shall become bound, well.   5

Henry Goodman's first moments as Shylock in the Nunn production provide a perfect example of what can be communicated by the careful selection of a simple prop, as he took his tea East European fashion, in a glass rather than a cup, while he and Bassanio talked business at a Jewish café.

1 To Lichtenberg, Macklin's first words were

> slowly and impressively spoken: 'Three thousand ducats'. The double 'th' and the two sibilants, especially the second after the 't', which Macklin lisps as lickerishly as if he were savouring the ducats and all that they would buy, make so deep an impression in the man's favour that nothing can destroy it. Three such words uttered thus at the outset give the keynote of his whole character. (*Visits*, p. 40)

Kean was 'looking askance at Bassanio' (Doran *qtd* Furness *A New Variorum Edition*, p. 376) as he spoke, while Irving gave the opening line 'half turned away from Bassanio – his head slightly bent to one side, his eyes looking forward on the ground. He spoke in an even monotone; his voice was subdued and meditative' (Irving, *Henry Irving*, p. 339). Others noted Irving's 'rubbing thumb and fingers together' (*Amer. II*, p. 163).

Ellen Terry recalls how a blind person once told Irving that he heard 'no sound of the usurer' in his first words, 'it is said with the reflective air of a man to whom money means very little'. Irving immediately 'revised his reading not only of the first line, but of many other lines in which he saw now that he had not been enough of the money-lender' (Terry, *Story*, p. 187).

Fritz Kortner, in Schenk's production, took a long pause before each 'well' (*gut*) in lines 1–5, saying each as a long *g-u-u-t* (Sehrt, 'Der Shylock', p. 83); in his Columbia recording, Orson Welles spoke 'well' as a question, i.e., 'have you anything to add?'.

Will LeBow munched peanuts from a paper bag he carried with him throughout the play. Douglas Rain fed the pigeons – this 'was an ordinary man, narrow in his experience, narrow in his thought, but with an ordinary man's ability to relax and a daily routine that included one small, simple pleasure' (Leggatt, *SB* 1997). Rain's calm approach could not have been more different from Leibman's, 'impatiently tapping a plate on . . . "three thousand ducats" as if he were counting them' (Brustein, *NR* 3 April 1995).

5 Booth: 'Here a longer pause than before, with a curious glance at Bassanio' (Furness, *A New Variorum Edition*, p. 33). Irving had 'a sudden look of intelligence [flash] across his face; the possibility of extracting vengeance on his enemy out of this loan has just occurred to him' (Crosse, *Diaries*, vol. I, p. 172); David Suchet acted as if 'laughter – mocking himself and everybody else – is Shylock's line of defence. The amount that Mr Suchet conveys through

BASSANIO May you stead me? Will you pleasure me? Shall I know
  your answer?
SHYLOCK Three thousand ducats for three months, and Antonio
  bound.
BASSANIO Your answer to that?   10
SHYLOCK Antonio is a good man –
BASSANIO Have you heard any imputation to the contrary?
SHYLOCK Ho no, no, no, no: my meaning in saying he is a good man
  is to have you understand me that he is sufficient. Yet his means
  are in supposition: he hath an argosy bound to Tripolis, another   15
  to the Indies; I understand moreover upon the Rialto he hath a
  third at Mexico, a fourth for England, and other ventures he
  hath squandered abroad. But ships are but boards, sailors but
  men; there be land rats, and water rats, water thieves and land
  thieves – I mean pirates – and then there is the peril of waters,   20
  winds and rocks. The man is notwithstanding sufficient. Three
  thousand ducats: I think I may take his bond.

the one word "well" – repeated at the end of his first three lines – is extraordinary'
(Cushman, *Obs* 26 April 1981).

11 Sothern: 'Shylock strokes his beard with his fingers, Bassanio steps down angrily toward
   Shylock, Shylock cringes' (*pmt* Sothern[1]). Olivier emitted 'a dangerous chuckle' (Billington,
   The Modern Actor, p. 84).

14 Frank Finlay rubbed his thumb and fingers together at 'sufficient'; Antony Sher pronounced
   it as 'suffeesent' (Bulman, *Shakespeare in Performance*, p. 121). Henry Goodman, cordial to
   Bassanio throughout the scene, gestured at this point, inviting him to sit down at his café
   table.

15–18 Olivier looked for the status of Antonio's ships in *Il Tempo*; Calder got the same information
   from his computer. Kortner gave a clear forewarning that Antonio might have over-
   extended himself by naming, with strong emphasis, each of the far-flung ports to which
   Antonio's ships were bound.

17 Olivier superbly evoked the language of the *Sephardi* Jew with his correct Spanish
   pronunciation of the 'x' in Mexico: *Mekhico*.

19–20a Warren Mitchell did not pun on 'pirates' and 'pie-rats'; Olivier and Goodman laughed before
   punning, and both Bassanios laughed weakly in response. Sher gave 'an uncouth snort'
   (Bulman, *Shakespeare in Performance*, p. 121); Dustin Hoffman 'crosses his eyes in despair
   when Bassanio misses his joke about the water-rats and the pirates' (Billington, *Gdn* 2 June
   1989); Messina's Bassanio, Christopher Gable, raised his eyes heavenward in irritation.

21–2 Leibman seemed to take great personal pleasure in saying 'threeee thooowsand ducats!';
   Brian Bedford tossed off the matter as unimportant by speaking offhandedly while reading
   a message given to him by a runner from the Stock Exchange.

BASSANIO Be assured you may.

SHYLOCK I will be assured I may; and that I may be assured, I will
    bethink me – may I speak with Antonio?   25

BASSANIO If it please you to dine with us –

SHYLOCK Yes, to smell pork, to eat of the habitation which your
    prophet the Nazarite conjured the devil into. I will buy with
    you, sell with you, talk with you, walk with you, and so
    following; but I will not eat with you, drink with you, nor pray   30
    with you. What news on the Rialto? Who is he comes here?

Enter ANTONIO

BASSANIO This is Signor Antonio.

SHYLOCK [*Aside*] How like a fawning publican he looks!

---

24 Crosse notes that this is 'almost the only point which raises a laugh' in Irving's performance
    (*Diaries*, vol. I, p. 171).

27–31 Booth surmises that 'Doggett, doubtless, made a strong "point" here, but be very careful
    that you do not: a too strong emphasis or expression of disgust might cause a laugh; the
    whole speech must be spoken impressively' (Furness, *A New Variorum Edition*, p. 36).
    Patrick Stewart agrees, noting 'this speech is often played as hostile and aggressive, but
    why risk antagonizing Bassanio when there are so many intriguing possibilities behind this
    encounter?' (Stewart, 'Shylock', p. 8). Calder was more wary than offended, 'disturbed not
    so much by the prospect of an affront to his religion's dietary laws, as by the threat to his
    self-respect in accepting an invitation to eat where he could not yet be sure he was
    respected' (Jackson, *SQ* 1994). Olivier, another Shylock who enjoyed tacit acceptance in the
    gentile world, laughed through the lines, while Goodman interpolated an 'Oh' at the start
    of the speech, apparently surprised that Bassanio would make such a suggestion.
        Irving displayed a rare moment of anger: the invitation 'acted like a goad and seemed to
    stimulate his hatred for the particular Christian with whom he was dealing' (Irving, *Henry
    Irving*, p. 340). Two celebrated German Shylocks took the same approach, Basserman
    delivering a 'ferocious outburst', and Kortner showing 'Shylock's indignation and superior
    attitude' (Sehrt, 'Der Shylock', p. 83). Sher and Leibman were vitriolic; LeBow, as he often
    did, made a deliberately crude joke, with snorting noises on 'to smell pork', and making
    the sign of the cross while singing 'nor pray with you' as if he were a priest.

28 Orson Welles pronounced 'Nazarite' as 'Nazarete'.

31 Henry Goodman spoke as he perused a Yiddish newspaper.

33–44a It is sometimes assumed that to have a Shylock who is more victim than villain, it is
    necessary to remove these lines, but none of the noted 'sympathetic' Shylocks of the
    past did so. In recent times Jonathan Miller's is the only significant production to cut the

speech entirely, although individual lines are occasionally omitted or relocated in others.

Nineteenth-century audiences would usually see Bassanio exit and greet Antonio off-stage – Shylock spoke while alone. No record survives of how Kean delivered the speech; Macklin did not receive the customary applause when he first entered as Shylock, but when 'he had finished the speech in which Shylock declares his motives of antipathy to Antonio, the audience suddenly burst out into a thunder of applause, which continued louder and louder until the end of the play' (Genest, *Some Account*, vol. III, p. 627). Cooke, according to 'Thespis' of the New York *Columbian*, showed his 'inveterate hatred' of Antonio (*Annals. II*, p. 359), and in giving his impressions of Irving, Crosse uses similar words: 'his venomous hatred to Antonio appears interwoven with the patriarchal semi-sacred aspect of his character in the reference to "our sacred nation" ' (*Diaries*, vol. I, p. 172).

Patrick Stewart, whose view of Shylock is that he is 'an outsider who happens to be a Jew' (Barton, *Playing Shakespeare*, p. 169), notes 'here are no games, no jokes, but bitterness and resentment . . . Shakespeare permits the audience to taste Shylock's real feelings so that they will see through the playacting that is to follow' (Stewart, 'Shylock', p. 20). Stewart played Shylock 'in the round' at The Other Place, a theatre very hospitable to an introspective approach, but on the Stratford 'main stage', Shylock must come forward – addressing the audience in this mode can have overtones of the villain in nineteenth-century melodrama. Ian McDiarmid, in Caird's production, went 'downstage, in true villainous style, to inform the listeners of his revengeful intentions. Thereafter, you are obliged to view all his giggling courtesies, Rabbinical eloquence, and legal precision as a hypocritical ruse' (Wardle, *Times* 11 April 1984). Alexander and Doran mitigated this effect by having their Shylocks speak to the audience without changing position: Sher, intent on confronting his audience, said in 'an intimate sing-song, "I hate him for he is a *Kleestiun*" ' (Bulman, *Shakespeare in Performance*, p. 121), and Philip Voss 'spat out curses in an impassioned eruption of hatred, only to turn innocently back to the merchant in an attempt to creep into his affections' (Smith, 'The Merchant', p. 119).

Thacker used a lighting change, putting David Calder in a single spot for the speech. Although the change itself was somewhat clumsy (judging from the archival video), it did help Calder to underplay the speech. To Russell Jackson, Calder's words 'clearly came from some level of his subconscious' (*SQ* 1994).

On film or television, a clear choice must be made – is Shylock to speak to himself, to the camera or on voice-over? Schenk cut 34–9, with Kortner speaking 40–4 bitterly to himself; Messina also had Frank Finlay think aloud, but Gold showed Warren Mitchell speak directly to the viewers, in a matter-of-fact tone.

As noted, Beerbohm Tree played all of 1.3 with a mute Tubal beside him. To Crosse, this 'was characteristic of Tree's acting methods . . . at variance with the spirit of the scene and the intention of Shakespeare, who was quite capable of supplying Shylock with a foil if he

I hate him for he is a Christian;
But more, for that in low simplicity   35
He lends out money gratis, and brings down
The rate of usance here with us in Venice.
If I can catch him once upon the hip,
I will feed fat the ancient grudge I bear him.
He hates our sacred nation, and he rails   40
Even there where merchants most do congregate
On me, my bargains, and my well-won thrift
Which he calls interest. Cursed be my tribe
If I forgive him!

BASSANIO   Shylock, do you hear?

SHYLOCK I am debating of my present store,   45
And by the near guess of my memory
I cannot instantly raise up the gross
Of full three thousand ducats. What of that?

had meant him to have one, and not to stand alone against the Christians' (*Diaries*, vol. IV,
p. 98). Crosse was no more amenable in 1934, when the business was revived in Oswald
Stoll's production, but he did approve of Komisarjevsky's inclusion of the 'Sallies' in the
scene: 'their presence helped to carry off the pound of flesh proposals as a joke, and
so was good and useful as Tree's Jews backing Shylock in the same scene were not'
(vol. XIV, p. 20).

38–9 George Joseph Bell notes that 'Kean's look in this was most diabolical' (*pmt* E. Kean).
Booth's 'hand clutches, rigidly as a claw, at the word *catch*, and dashes its prey toward a
devouring maw as the idea of *feeding fat* upon it glances into the expression' (Porter, 'The
Drama', p. 122). Thacker cut both lines; Nunn moved 38 and 43–4a to the end of 3.1. 'I will
feed fat . . .' was the only line omitted.

40 Kemble's promptbook has Bassanio and Antonio enter here – obviously they are not meant
to hear what Shylock says.

43a Douglas Rain said 'in-ter-est' slowly and forcefully.

43b–4 In Clifford Williams's 1965 production, Eric Porter was 'subdued . . . a satirical comment
made for his own pleasure' (Brown, *SS* 1966).

44b Charles Kean's edition has 'Re-enter Bassanio and Antonio' here.

45–51 Olivier's verbal mannerism of dropping the final 'g' on verbs was clearly heard with
'debatin' of my present store' (Billington, *The Modern Actor*, p. 84); Warren Mitchell
purposely ignored Antonio for these six lines. Calder did calculations on his computer –
Antonio and Bassanio got tired of waiting and were about to leave when he called out
'rest you fair'.

Tubal, a wealthy Hebrew of my tribe,
Will furnish me. But soft, how many months   50
Do you desire? [*To Antonio*] Rest you fair, good signor!
Your worship was the last man in our mouths.
ANTONIO Shylock, albeit I neither lend nor borrow
By taking nor by giving of excess,
Yet to supply the ripe wants of my friend   55
I'll break a custom. [*To Bassanio*] Is he yet possessed
How much ye would?
SHYLOCK   Ay, ay, three thousand ducats.
ANTONIO And for three months.
SHYLOCK I had forgot, three months; [*To Bassanio*] you told me so.

49 Leon M. Lion played Tubal for Tree in 1908, and in his autobiography he quotes Tree's
instructions:

> Well, whenever I come on the scene, you will be with me, but hidden. You see? A
> repulsive creature – in a ragged gabardine – skimpy, red beard, toothless, gruesome!
> And, when I say to Antonio, 'Tubal, a wealthy Hebrew of my tribe, shall furnish me' – I let
> fall the end of my cloak, *you* peer out – see? – Tubal – and flash a gangrened tooth at
> them. (Lion, *Surprise of My Life*, p. 63)

Thacker used Tubal in a somewhat more subtle fashion: depicted as Shylock's business
associate, he was present during negotiations, and whispered his offer to 'furnish' Shylock
with the needed three thousand ducats.

51b Macready 'saluted Antonio with such well-dissembled courtesy that the audience were
not let into the secret of hypocrisy; and so profound was his simulation of generosity
throughout, that any one who had not heard the opening soliloquy, would have been as
unsuspicious as Antonio of any sinister purpose' (*Spectator* 12 October 1839). Mansfield,
when he first played Shylock, spat to show his hatred of Antonio, though later in his career
he abandoned the business (Sprague, *Shakespeare and the Actors*, p. 20). Forbes-
Robertson 'gave this greeting with pretend surprise at seeing Antonio, and this coupled with
the fact that Bassanio had *told* him that he *was* Antonio, and that he had just been speaking
of him, brought out something of the duplicity in Shylock's character' (*pmt* Ames[2]). Dustin
Hoffman was a 'most genial Shylock . . . he may vow implacable enmity to Antonio in a first
act aside, but you would never guess it from his welcoming smiles and open embraces'
(Wardle, *Times* 2 June 1989).

57b Leibman showed Antonio the ledger where he had written the sum down.

59 Goodman transposed 'I had forgot' and 'three months'; he invited Antonio to take the chair
next to his at the café; Antonio pointedly took one further away.

Well then, your bond; and let me see – but hear you,   60
Methoughts you said you neither lend nor borrow
Upon advantage.
ANTONIO   I do never use it.
SHYLOCK When Jacob grazed his uncle Laban's sheep –
This Jacob from our holy Abram was
(As his wise mother wrought in his behalf)   65
The third possessor; ay, he was the third –
ANTONIO And what of him, did he take interest?
SHYLOCK No, not take interest, not as you would say
Directly interest. Mark what Jacob did:
When Laban and himself were compromised   70
That all the eanlings which were streaked and pied
Should fall as Jacob's hire, the ewes being rank
In end of autumn turnèd to the rams,
And when the work of generation was
Between these woolly breeders in the act,   75
The skilful shepherd pilled me certain wands

63–82 Rudolf Schildkraut, playing Shylock in New York, counted to three on his fingers before saying 'Jacob', as if silently counting off all three patriarchs (Berkowitz, 'A True Jewish Jew', p. 86). Fritz Kortner recited the story 'as if to teach a naughty boy' (Sehrt, 'Der Shylock', p. 85); Robert Helpmann 'poured all the pride and beliefs of his race' into the speech (Clarke, *Shakespeare at the Old Vic*, np).
　　The last of over twenty Shylocks Gordon Crosse saw, and 'one of the very best', was Paul Rogers. He 'was very Jewish, e.g. in his pronunciation of "Jacob" – something like "Yakkobh" ' (*Diaries*, vol. xx, p. 135). David Calder and Philip Voss gave the same pronunciation; Donald Davis and Hal Holbrook said 'Yakov' (see 83 for the response of some Antonios).

67 Nunn's Antonio, David Bamber, said this testily, showing his irritation.

72b–5 The Bell text shows that Macklin spoke these lines, but they were too coarse for the nineteenth century – some modern productions make use of the passage to bring out a vulgar side to Shylock. Philip Voss placed his posterior against Bassanio at 'turned to the rams'; both Warren Mitchell and Antony Sher made coital sounds by rhythmically slapping a fist against their palm. In Sellars's 'Venice Beach', a woman and an office worker (who later turned out to be Jessica and Lancelot Gobbo) were seen having sexual intercourse at this point (Graham-White, 'Critical Responses', p. 153).

76 Olivier inserted 'his stick with a corkscrew movement through his outstretched left hand, brilliantly summoning up both the peeling-process and animalistic copulation' (Billington, *The Modern Actor*, p. 84).

> And in the doing of the deed of kind
> He stuck them up before the fulsome ewes,
> Who then conceiving, did in eaning time
> Fall parti-coloured lambs, and those were Jacob's.   80
> This was a way to thrive, and he was blest;
> And thrift is blessing if men steal it not.
>
> ANTONIO This was a venture, sir, that Jacob served for,
> A thing not in his power to bring to pass,
> But swayed and fashioned by the hand of heaven.   85
> Was this inserted to make interest good?
> Or is your gold and silver ewes and rams?
>
> SHYLOCK I cannot tell, I make it breed as fast.
> But note me, signor –
>
> ANTONIO   Mark you this, Bassanio,
> The devil can cite Scripture for his purpose.   90
> An evil soul producing holy witness
> Is like a villain with a smiling cheek,
> A goodly apple rotten at the heart.
> O what a goodly outside falsehood hath!
>
> SHYLOCK Three thousand ducats, 'tis a good round sum.   95
> Three months from twelve, then let me see, the rate –

79 Peter O'Toole unleashed a sudden snarl here (Brown, *SS* 1961).

83 Leo Ciceri (Gascon), Clifford Rose (Thacker) and Julian Curry (Doran) responded to Shylock's 'Yakov' or 'Yakob' with an English 'Jacob'. Keith Baxter (Kahn) paused before saying 'Yakov', as if trying hard to impress Shylock with the correct pronunciation.

88 Both Olivier and Mitchell laughed heartily at their own joke; Forbes-Robertson was content 'with a little smile of pride, with excellent effect' (*pmt* Ames[1]).

89b–94 Schenk's Antonio, Max Eckard, spoke with furious anger; Anthony Nicholls was openly insulting in Miller's production, speaking only to Bassanio but being sure Shylock heard him. Ian McDiarmid visibly flinched when hearing himself called a devil, 'this elicits a tiny but important sympathy from the audience' (Baker, *TES* 20 April 1984). Both Mitchell and Goodman shook their heads in disappointment, as if to say 'here we go again'.

95–6 Booth: 'Shylock shows his true feeling in his face as he turns from them; then, just loud enough for them to hear, calculates the rate, &c.' (Furness, *A New Variorum Edition*, p. 45). Sothern has Shylock speak this to himself, and 'after the two lines are spoken his face lights up as he conceives his plan . . . full of malignant hatred . . . grim determination settles on his face as he brings down his left hand upon the right which clasps his cane' (*pmt* Sothern[1]). Olivier hid his face behind *Il Tempo*, apparently looking for current interest rates; Stewart calculated the rate in a pocket book (Warren, *SS* 1979); Leibman sang 'Three

ANTONIO Well, Shylock, shall we be beholding to you?
SHYLOCK Signor Antonio, many a time and oft
      In the Rialto you have rated me
      About my monies and my usances.   100
      Still have I borne it with a patient shrug
      For suff'rance is the badge of all our tribe.
      You call me misbeliever, cut-throat dog,
      And spit upon my Jewish gaberdine,
      And all for use of that which is mine own.   105
      Well then, it now appears you need my help.

thousand ducats, 'tis a good round sum' mockingly; Holbrook spoke to the other Jewish men present.

98–121 Patrick Stewart regards this speech as 'a masterly piece of controlled and brilliant irony' (Barton, *Playing Shakespeare*, p. 78). Booth delivered it as a 'vehement summary of past slights' – Winter heard 'suppressed passion [that] burned and glowed beneath a glitter of sarcasm' (Porter, 'The Drama', p. 122; Winter, *Shakespeare on the Stage*, p. 157). Irving began quietly, his intensity increasing gradually (Irving, *Henry Irving*, p. 340).

Helpmann 'stated his feelings strongly enough, but there was a suggestion that his mind was elsewhere – seeking and seeking some way in which he might use this opportunity for revenge' (Clarke, *Shakespeare at the Old Vic*, np); Goodman raised his voice in sharp, but restrained anger; Leibman exploded into a violent accusation; Dustin Hoffman was the opposite, showing little observable emotion.

Several celebrated Shylocks raised the intensity of the scene by pausing before speaking. Tree simply sat, recording entries in his book (Lelyveld, *Shylock on the Stage*, p. 99); Rain waited several seconds, as did Kortner – when he spoke it was in 'a very tired voice, and rather resignedly' (Sehrt, 'Der Shylock', p. 85). In one of the finest moments of his performance, Olivier began calmly, with his face behind his newspaper, lowering it at 'rated me'. Suchet paused after 'many a time', so that 'and oft in the Rialto' took on added importance, as if to say 'and even in my place of business!'.

102 Barrett spoke 'with bitter weariness, significantly laying one hand upon his sleeve to show the red cross he wore there' ('The Drama', p. 525). Booth's promptbook has 'I prefer the yellow cap to the cross upon the shoulder which other actors have worn, my Father among them. Cooke used the cap, and said Macklin also used it' (Furness, *A New Variorum Edition*, p. 46).

103 In a brilliant reading, Orson Welles said '*You* call *me* misbeliever', as if expressing his astonishment that anyone could take such an attitude to an observant Jew. He then paused between 'cut-throat' and 'dog', making them two different terms of abuse, rather than the one 'cut-throat dog' as is usually spoken.

Go to, then, you come to me, and you say,
'Shylock, we would have monies' – you say so,
You that did void your rheum upon my beard,
And foot me as you spurn a stranger cur   110
Over your threshold: monies is your suit.
What should I say to you? Should I not say
'Hath a dog money? Is it possible
A cur can lend three thousand ducats?' Or
Shall I bend low, and in a bondman's key,   115
With bated breath and whisp'ring humbleness,
Say this:
'Fair sir, you spat on me on Wednesday last,
You spurned me such a day, another time
You called me dog: and for these courtesies   120
I'll lend you thus much monies.'
ANTONIO I am as like to call thee so again,

107–9 What Ellen Terry refers to as Irving's 'ejaculations, the interjections and grunts with which Henry interlarded the text' were parodied by an American critic as 'ou com'n say Ah! Silok, um! ouch! we wode heve moanies' (Terry, *Story*, pp. 273–4). Bob Peck, sitting across a table from Antonio and Bassanio, spoke softly, but levelled a pointed finger at Antonio with each 'you'; the speech was backed with ominous music. In Olivier's reading also, 'the element of icy racial fury under the bland exterior only emerges in the speech to Antonio about the insults he has repeatedly borne – and he highlights this fury simply through a [repeated] sharp emphasis on the word "You" ' (Billington, *The Modern Actor*, p. 84). Suchet laughed through these lines, even amusing Antonio with 'the ludicrousness of the situation' (Cushman, *Obs* 26 April 1981); LeBow made fun of Antonio by saying 'Shylock, we would have monies' in a deep stentorian voice.

112 Kortner sarcastically cupped his hand behind his ear at 'What should I say', waiting for Antonio to prompt him.

118–21 John Woodvine and David Calder indulged in a high level of mockery, by rendering the lines in a heavy, stereotypical 'stage-Jewish' accent; LeBow said all four lines in an extraordinary high-pitched squeal. Kortner kissed the tips of his fingers and gave a mock bow (Sehrt, 'Der Shylock', p. 86), and Mitchell brought his face very close to Antonio's here, so that the plosives in 'spat' and 'spurned' caused Antonio to flinch.

120 Kean paused before saying 'dog': Furness writes 'its effectiveness still remains vivid in my father's memory' (*A New Variorum Edition*, p. 48).

122 Hall's Antonio, Leigh Lawson, spat directly in Shylock's face, but Hoffman 'smiles patiently and silkily retaliates by brushing imaginary specks of dust off Antonio's velvet coat' (Billington, *Gdn* 2 June 1989). John Carlisle roughed Antony Sher up physically, 'brusquely

To spit on thee again, to spurn thee too.
If thou wilt lend this money, lend it not
As to thy friends, for when did friendship take   125
A breed for barren metal of his friend?
But lend it rather to thine enemy,
Who if he break, thou mayst with better face
Exact the penalty.
SHYLOCK Why look you how you storm!   130
I would be friends with you, and have your love,
Forget the shames that you have stained me with,
Supply your present wants, and take no doit
Of usance for my monies, and you'll not hear me.
This is kind I offer.
BASSANIO   This were kindness.   135
SHYLOCK This kindness will I show.

---

raising him up with both hands and . . . shoving him centre stage' (Bulman, *Shakespeare in Performance*, p. 122); Serban's Antonio, Jonathan Epstein, also hit and manhandled Shylock.

123   In an interview, Irving said of Antonio's promise to spit on Shylock again, 'From that moment I imagine Shylock resolving to propose his pound of flesh' (*qtd* Sprague, *Shakespearian Players*, p. 113).

133–5 David Bamber was so convinced that Henry Goodman could not be serious that he picked up his briefcase and, to the dismay of Bassanio, began to walk out – only when Alexander Hanson said 'this were kindness' did he stop to hear Goodman out.

136–44 'Thespis' admires Cooke's 'affected levity and apparent carelessness in obtaining from Antonio the conditions of the bond', and his 'subsequent smile of triumph and anticipated revenge' (*Annals. II*, p. 359). John Ranken Towse, who thought Booth 'was seen at his best' as Shylock, notes that 'the ultimate purpose' of the bond 'was deftly concealed beneath a veil of slightly transparent banter . . . his emphasis was grimly jocose, not malicious, though the smile on his face was crafty' (*Sixty Years*, p. 189).

Irving introduced some stage business at this point that was remarked upon by most critics: 'the Jew touches Antonio on the heart, and, seeing the merchant recoil from him, apologises for his error by a bow in which we can perceive all the bitterness induced by the hard distinction drawn between Christian and Jew' (*Theatre* 1 December 1879). *Blackwood's* remarks:

> This has been praised as a fine stroke of truth. But is it so? Antonio has just told Shylock that he is 'as like to spit on him again, to spurn him too'. Would Shylock with these words fresh in his ears, forget himself so far as to lay a finger on the haughty merchant, never haughtier than at that moment, when asking a loan from a man he despised?

Go with me to a notary, seal me there
Your single bond, and, in a merry sport,
If you repay me not on such a day,
In such a place, such sum or sums as are   140
Expressed in the condition, let the forfeit
Be nominated for an equal pound
Of your fair flesh, to be cut off and taken
In what part of your body pleaseth me.
ANTONIO Content, in faith! I'll seal to such a bond,   145
And say there is much kindness in the Jew.
BASSANIO You shall not seal to such a bond for me;
I'll rather dwell in my necessity.

Again, is such an action conceivable in one who feels the pride of race so strongly as Shylock? For one of 'the sacred nation' like himself to touch the Christian merchant would in his mind be viewed as nothing less than contamination and defilement. The momentary stage effect, which Mr Irving gains by the introduction of this novelty, is surely dearly purchased at the sacrifice of all probability. (December 1879)

Judging by these and other descriptions, Cooke, Booth and Irving appear to have wanted Shylock's resentment, although hidden from Antonio, to be apparent to the audience.

Early in the twentieth century, the dominant interpretation shifted to one of Shylock's sincere amusement in proposing a bond he does not expect to enforce. Jacob Adler's offer was 'rather a merry quip – one almost imagines that he intends showing the unique bond to his colleagues on the Rialto for a laugh' (*JE qtd* Berkowitz, 'A True Jewish Jew', p. 78); Novelli 'even made the Christians laugh with him at the thought of so ridiculous a bargain' (*pmt* Ames[1]). Closer to our time, Olivier, Cronyn, Mitchell, Rain and Goodman all seemed to enjoy telling a far-fetched joke, as did Frederick Valk in Guthrie's 1955 Ontario production, although Griffin noted 'a brief flashing of the eyes that warned us that the "pound of flesh" proposal was not just a jest' (Griffin, *TA* 1955). Hoffman, 'a shy and halting, hesitant figure . . . seems embarrassed by his first-act demand for a pound of the merchant's flesh' (Morley, *IHT* 7 June 1989).

142 In Zhang Qi-hong's production, the setting was a marketplace, and at this moment Shylock cast 'a momentary glance to the left at a shopkeeper serving a customer – he is a butcher and his scales are poised' (Brockbank, 'Shakespeare Renaissance', p. 197).

144 Philip Voss made a point of facetiously putting his hands on Antonio here, as if choosing which vital organ to remove (Billington, *Gdn* 11 December 1997).

ANTONIO Why, fear not, man, I will not forfeit it.
        Within these two months, that's a month before   150
        This bond expires, I do expect return
        Of thrice three times the value of this bond.
SHYLOCK O father Abram, what these Christians are,
        Whose own hard dealings teaches them suspect
        The thoughts of others! Pray you tell me this: 155
        If he should break his day what should I gain
        By the exaction of the forfeiture?
        A pound of man's flesh, taken from a man,
        Is not so estimable, profitable neither,
        As flesh of muttons, beefs, or goats. I say   160
        To buy his favour, I extend this friendship.
        If he will take it, so; if not, adieu,
        And for my love, I pray you wrong me not.
ANTONIO Yes, Shylock, I will seal unto this bond.
SHYLOCK Then meet me forthwith at the notary's.   165
        Give him direction for this merry bond,
        And I will go and purse the ducats straight,
        See to my house left in the fearful guard
        Of an unthrifty knave, and presently
        I'll be with you.   *Exit*
ANTONIO   Hie thee, gentle Jew.   170
        The Hebrew will turn Christian, he grows kind.

153–5a At Drury Lane in 1815, William Dowton said this as an aside, as did Junius Brutus Booth. Edwin Booth approved of his father's idea, 'but in that case the tone and look should express disgust' (Furness, *A New Variorum Edition*, p. 52).

163 Having raged through the scene, Leibman stopped suddenly and said 'I pray you, wrong me not' with quiet sincerity, making a potent connection with 'And if you wrong us, shall we not revenge?' (3.1.52).

165 Goodman nicely added the realistic business of writing the notary's address on the back of a business card and handing it to Antonio.

170b Clifford Rose exuded false *bonhomie* towards David Calder: changing 'Hie thee' to 'Farewell', and embracing Shylock awkwardly before making an even more awkward pun on 'gentle' and 'gentile'. Calder laughed politely, making a face to the audience and 'asking for complicity in his mockery of these odd things gentiles found funny' (Jackson, *SQ* 1994; Holland, *English Shakespeares*, p. 164).

> BASSANIO I like not fair terms and a villain's mind.
> ANTONIO Come on, in this there can be no dismay,
>   My ships come home a month before the day.

Exeunt

174sd The Folio text shows separate exits for Shylock at 170 and Antonio and Bassanio at 174, but the actor-managers of the nineteenth and early twentieth centuries always closed the scene with themselves alone on stage. This practice became so universal that Gordon Crosse expressed his astonishment with Hay Petrie at the Old Vic in 1924: 'He alone of all the Shylocks I have seen left the stage before Bassanio and Antonio, and with no demonstration of hatred' (*Diaries*, vol. VIII, p. 138).

Crosse's *Diaries* have these (and other) several examples of what was customary: Irving 'walks slowly in the opposite direction until they are out of sight when he turns and raising aloft with a threatening gesture the hand that grasps his staff, sends after them a terrible look of concentrated malice'. Ten years later Crosse saw Tree 'turning and spitting vehemently after the departing friends – this was not an improvement on the leer of malicious triumph which marked the exit of Sir Henry Irving at this point' (vol. I, p. 174; vol. IV, p. 100).

A reviewer at Jacob Adler's performance in 1905 notes, 'round and round his hands he twists his great purple handkerchief, as though he were twisting Antonio tighter and tighter still, his grave face has turned all vindictive cunning' (Berkowitz, 'A True Jewish Jew', p. 79) Winthrop Ames's promptbook has Antonio (Leonard Willey) raising his arm 'in a gesture of farewell' and giving 'two short laughs'; George Arliss 'looks after him, raises his arm as Antonio did, and laughs mockingly – two short laughs' (*pmt* Ames[2]). Booth interpolated material from elsewhere in the play: with the departure of Antonio and Bassanio, he moved off in the other direction, and then paused 'to turn and gaze after them, with a look of horrible hate and a gesture of menace, as he spoke the lines "Thou called'st me dog before thou hadst a cause / But since I am a dog, beware my fangs" '. Winter approved of this and everything else Booth did; his view of Novelli was less favourable: 'After he had agreed to lend the money he departed, arm-in-arm, with Bassanio and Antonio, as though, in amity and social equality, they were going to "the notary's"; in Shakespeare's text, it is expressly appointed that they shall meet there' (Winter, *Shakespeare on the Stage*, pp. 157, 165).

In Nunn's production, Henry Goodman paid for his tea and scrupulously left a tip before leaving, in pointed contrast to Bassanio and his friends having left Antonio with the bill at the end of 1.1. Horrox's scene closes with a close-up of the bond being signed and sealed; Elizabeth Swados's lively *klezmer* music covered the scene change to 2.1 in Serban's version.

ACT 2, SCENE 1

2.[1] [*A flourish of cornets.*] *Enter* [*the Prince of*] MOROCCO, *a tawny Moor all in white, and three or four followers accordingly; with* PORTIA, NERISSA, *and their train*

MOROCCO Mislike me not for my complexion,
　　　　　The shadowed livery of the burnished sun,

When Lewis Hallam, the son of the actor Macklin killed in a duel in 1735, brought his company to Virginia in 1752 and selected the *Merchant* for the first-ever professional Shakespeare in America, neither Morocco nor Arragon was listed in the playbill. However, as we learn from C. Effingham's review,

> Beatrice Hallam surveyed the audience while the Prince of Morocco was uttering his speech with perfect simplicity, but her eyes did not rest for a single moment on the young men collected at the corners of the stage. Portia advanced graciously toward the Prince again. Her carelessness was gone; she no longer displayed coldness or indifference. She commenced in a voice of noble and queen-like courtesy – a voice of pure music, and clear utterance, such as few lips possess the power of giving forth. It was not an actress delivering a set speech, but the noble Portia doing the honors at her beautiful palace at Belmont. The scene ended with great applause. (*qtd* Scheff, *TA* December 1952)

In London, a hundred years had passed between Morocco's last appearance on the stage (see p. 18) and Charles Kean's Princess's production of 1858. As Kean notes in his edition, 'The introduction of the Princes of Morocco and Arragon at Belmont, hitherto omitted, is restored, for the purpose of more strictly adhering to the author's text, and of heightening the interest attached to the episode of the caskets.'

Kean's restoration of the suitor scenes was only partial – he combined 2.1 and 2.7 into one scene of only fifty-four lines, bringing the 2.7 material forward – nor was it universally adopted. Booth did without either suitor, as did Jacob Adler in 1903; Irving kept some of 2.7, but 2.1 was cut, as it was in Schenk's television adaptation; Greet delayed 2.1 until after 2.6,

To whom I am a neighbour and near bred.
Bring me the fairest creature northward born,
Where Phoebus' fire scarce thaws the icicles,   5
And let us make incision for your love
To prove whose blood is reddest, his or mine.
I tell thee, lady, this aspèct of mine
Hath feared the valiant; by my love I swear
The best-regarded virgins of our clime   10

and Benson had an even later combined scene, after 3.1 (*pmt* Benson) – Portia did not
appear at all until Act III.

　　More recently, 2.1 and 2.7 have often been played as one scene, and placed in any
number of spots. Doran and Kahn kept 2.1 in its proper position, bringing 2.7 forward;
Thacker did the opposite. In his television version, Miller had a straight sequence of suitors:
2.1, 2.7, 2.9; Nunn, whose treatment of Morocco was strikingly original, delayed this scene
until after 2.3, but kept it separate from 2.7.

osd　Before Komisarjevsky, Morocco was traditionally 'a sexy, dusky, sheik-of-Araby who spoke
poetry beautifully', but as Komisarjevsky's Belmont rose on its lift, the audience first saw a
red umbrella, then a Mexican sombrero upon the head of Stanley Howlett, made up in Al
Jolson blackface (Mennen, 'Theodore Komisarjevsky's Production', p. 392). In Guthrie's
1955 production, Lorne Greene was a 'thorough-going blackamoor who brought more than
a faint whiff of Valentino's Sheik of Araby in with him – his eyes rolled, his scimitar flashed,
and he played the part for all he was worth' (Edinborough, 'Shakespeare Confirmed',
p. 438); Evroy Deer engaged in 'crude stereotyping' as an 'Eddie Murphy-like' Prince for
Doran (Smith, 'The Merchant', p. 120), and in the 1998 Globe production, Nicholas Monu
was 'a caricature of the oversexed black man' (Potter, 'Shakespeare Performed', p. 75).

　　Probably the greatest actor ever to play Morocco was James Earl Jones (then at the start
of his career) in the Papp/Vaughan production of 1962. He was 'spectacularly funny . . .
without falling into the trap of caricaturing his own race – he keeps it personal' (Hatch,
Nation 14 July 1962).

　1　Since a farcical Morocco has come to be expected, Nunn's dashing Chu Omambala, while
not without his comic moments, came as a welcome surprise. Nunn began the scene by
having Derbhle Crotty enter speaking lines from the end of 1.2: 'If he have the condition
of a saint, and the complexion of a devil, I had rather he should shrive me than wive me'
(1.2.106–8). She was embarrassed when Omambala overheard her and said 'Mislike me not'
in response. Barton, in both his 1978 and 1981 productions, had Morocco caress Portia while
he spoke, something she endured with difficulty.

10–11a　Omambala's *dashiki*-wearing servant smilingly nodded confirmation of his master's claim
for Nerissa's benefit; Miller's TV Morocco, Stephen Greif, pronounced 'hue' as 'hoo' – his
make-up, like Howlett's, was 'Al Jolson minstrel' (Ansorge, *PP* 1970), but his dark red

Have loved it too. I would not change this hue,
Except to steal your thoughts, my gentle queen.
PORTIA In terms of choice I am not solely led
By nice direction of a maiden's eyes.
Besides, the lottery of my destiny   15
Bars me the right of voluntary choosing.
But if my father had not scanted me,
And hedged me by his wit to yield myself
His wife who wins me by that means I told you,
Yourself, renownèd prince, then stood as fair   20
As any comer I have looked on yet
For my affection.
MOROCCO   Even for that I thank you.
Therefore I pray you lead me to the caskets
To try my fortune. By this scimitar,
That slew the Sophy and a Persian prince   25
That won three fields of Sultan Solyman,
I would o'er-stare the sternest eyes that look,
Outbrave the heart most daring on the earth,
Pluck the young sucking cubs from the she-bear,
Yea, mock the lion when a roars for prey,   30
To win thee, lady. But alas the while,
If Hercules and Lichas play at dice
Which is the better man, the greater throw
May turn by fortune from the weaker hand.
So is Alcides beaten by his rage,   35
And so may I, blind Fortune leading me,
Miss that which one unworthier may attain,
And die with grieving.
PORTIA   You must take your chance,
And either not attempt to choose at all

uniform with epaulettes made him look more Spanish than Moroccan, indeed more Spanish than Arragon in this production.

24b Marc Zuber, a very pale Morocco for the BBC (1980), said 'try my fortune' and then gave a loud (and meaningless) scream – the screams usually come from Portia and Nerissa, should Morocco draw his scimitar, as in Doran's and Kahn's productions. Omambala, attired in 'a wonderful pale grey pinstriped suit, complete with plus-tours and spats', gave 'a demonstration of scimitar-twirling' that Portia found 'mesmerizingly sexy' (Smallwood, *SS* 2000).

31a Maraden's Morocco, Roy Lewis, picked Portia up in his arms.

> Or swear before you choose, if you choose wrong,   40
> Never to speak to lady afterward
> In way of marriage: therefore be advised.
> MOROCCO Nor will not. Come, bring me unto my chance.
> PORTIA First forward to the temple; after dinner
> Your hazard shall be made.
> MOROCCO   Good fortune then,   45
> To make me blest – or cursèd'st among men!
>
> *Cornets. Exeunt*

43a Keith Glover, Lamos's 'dominating, wooden Morocco' of 1993, was attended by six women,
'swathed in gold gauze, with blue gloves and eye masks, [who] cowered as they crouched
about their master; this traveling harem undercut Morocco's petition and stirred further
laughter at his vow to remain unmarried' (Cook, *SB* 1994).

42–6 Productions that combine 2.1 and 2.7 make the transition at various points: Charles Kean
went to 2.7.12 after 43b, Miller to 2.7.3 after 42, Alexander after 43a.

ACT 2, SCENE 2

[2.2] *Enter* [LANCELOT GOBBO,] *the Clown, alone*

LANCELOT Certainly, my conscience will serve me to run from this
Jew my master. The fiend is at mine elbow and tempts me, saying

This scene began Act II in Charles Kean's version, giving the stagehands interval time to arrange a new set, the 'Exterior of Shylock's House'. It was, notes Cole, 'a general view of Venice, taken from one of its most picturesque points, containing the canals, bridges, and gondolas, with all the peculiar localities and distinctive palaces that mark this strange city as a gem without a parallel' (*Life of Charles Kean*, p. 265).

When Barrett and Booth commissioned new scenery for their 1888 revival, this part of the play 'took place in the street before Shylock's house . . . its mouldy and crumbling walls attesting to the stinginess of its owner' (*Amer. II*, p. 48). Ben Greet's limited resources allowed for a single 'Venice' set at the Olympic in 1897, provoking a complaint from William Archer, 'it appears that Shylock is the Doge's next-door neighbour!' (Archer, *Theatrical World*, p. 152).

Augustin Daly, in his last and most sumptuous Shakespearean revival (1898), played this scene after 1.1 (Felheim, *Theater of Augustin Daly*, p. 267). Although the action remains in Venice, and Lancelot need not be near Shylock's house, this rearrangement radically alters the play, as it provides a great deal of 'information' about Shylock before he appears. But wherever the actor-managers placed the scene, it would begin with a tableau of Venetian street life, just as in 1.1 and 1.3.

Tree's second act, entitled 'The Ghetto', is afforded a detailed description in Crosse's *Diaries*:

When the curtain rose we saw Shylock in his strong room (which was rather dangerously close to the street & separated from it only by a barred window), gloating over his money & jewels, while the faithful Tubal sat waiting on a bench outside the door. Meanwhile other Jews were passing into the Synagogue, presently Shylock & Jessica came out of the house and joined Tubal & all three entered the

to me 'Gobbo, Lancelot Gobbo, good Lancelot', or 'Good
Gobbo', or 'Good Lancelot Gobbo, use your legs, take the start,
run away.' My conscience says 'No: take heed, honest Lancelot,   5
take heed, honest Gobbo' – or (as aforesaid) – 'honest Lancelot
Gobbo; do not run, scorn running with thy heels.' Well, the most
courageous fiend bids me pack. 'Fia!' says the fiend, 'Away!' says
the fiend. 'Fore the heavens, rouse up a brave mind', says the fiend,
'and run.' Well, my conscience, hanging about the neck of my   10

Synagogue. They were apparently the last arrivals for the door was then shut &
sounds of solemn music were heard from within. Shylock's house was so arranged
that we saw a good deal of the interior, the strong room below, & also the upper part
where Jessica appeared to speak to Lorenzo . . . After the preliminaries I have
mentioned which was of Mr Tree's contribution, Shakespeare was allowed a turn and
we had ii.ii with the usual stock business, most of which is legitimate and good.
(vol. IV, pp. 102–3)

osd Crosse liked Norman Forbes, Irving's Lancelot, and thought it was 'a happy idea to allow
Lancelot to be discovered asleep on a bench in the street when the curtain rises on his first
scene' (*Diaries*, vol. II, p. 3). Schenk also had Lancelot lying down, but in a gondola, eating
an apple; Piscator placed him at a precise dividing line between the Ghetto on one side and
the Rialto on the other – each created with projections (Kennedy, *Looking at Shakespeare*,
pp. 201–2). A Sothern promptbook has Shylock crying, off-stage, 'Drones hive not with me'
(2.5.46), followed by Lancelot's 'cry of pain' and his entrance (Sothern[4]).

1–24 This speech is more often endured than enjoyed – Lancelot Gobbo is surely the least
popular of Shakespeare's clowns, and one can understand why John Gielgud, directing the
Merchant for the 1938 Queen's season, 'used to stand at the back of the pit and shout to
George Devine, who was playing Lancelot, "For God's sake make me laugh" ' (Hayman,
John Gielgud, p. 113). Jonathan Miller included 2.1 in 1970, but when he removed Old Gobbo
completely and cut Lancelot's part to a bare minimum for his television version, no critic
complained. Thacker had this scene follow on directly from 1.3; no one in the audience had
any reason to think that the young man who served Shylock and his visitors coffee was
actually Lancelot, a point which pleased Christopher Luscombe:

I hope the audience assumed I was an extra, and were then taken aback to find me
talking to them . . . I decided to treat my first scene as elevenses, an opportunity to take
a break with a KitKat . . . it seemed that there was something inherently comic about an
intimate coffee break in a Shakespeare play, especially sharing it with fifteen hundred
people. (Luscombe, 'Launcelot Gobbo', p. 23).

heart, says very wisely to me, 'My honest friend Lancelot, being
an honest man's son, or rather an honest woman's son' (for indeed
my father did something smack, something grow to; he had a kind
of taste): well, my conscience says 'Lancelot, budge not!' 'Budge!'
says the fiend. 'Budge not!' says my conscience. 'Conscience', say   15
I, 'you counsel well.' 'Fiend', say I, 'you counsel well.' To be ruled
by my conscience, I should stay with the Jew my master who –
God bless the mark! – is a kind of devil; and to run away from the
Jew, I should be ruled by the fiend who – saving your reverence – is
the devil himself. Certainly the Jew is the very devil incarnation,   20
and, in my conscience, my conscience is but a kind of hard conscience to offer to counsel me to stay with the Jew. The fiend gives
the more friendly counsel: I will run, fiend, my heels are at your
commandment, I will run.

12–15 Daly's promptbook offers examples of standard Lancelot business: he is 'stretching forth his
hand to indicate stealing' when saying 'my father did something smack', and at 'budge not',
Lancelot should be 'standing with one leg, and remaining balanced on the other' (*pmt*
Moore/Daly).

16b Nunn began the scene at 'To be ruled', transferring 1–16a to 2.6 (see p. 150). Andrew French,
like Luscombe, transformed Lancelot from stock clown to individual character, lazily
mopping the floor as he spoke.

23 In Messina's television production, Bunny May walked through the marketplace, buying and
then eating a piece of watermelon, while his thoughts were given in voice-over. His decision
having been made, 'I will run, fiend' was spoken aloud.

24sd Leo Leyden, Old Gobbo in Hall's New York production, *ran* on to the stage, even though
he appeared to playing the part as totally blind; more subtle was Maraden's Douglas
Chamberlain, who entered peering through a magnifying glass at a map of the Ghetto. Two
productions of the 1990s featured notably Beckettian Old Gobbos: Sellars had Del Close
carrying a white cane and wearing dark glasses and sandwich boards – their long 'message
running from "Babylon the great" to "In one hour thy judgment is come" ' (Graham-White,
'Critical Responses', p. 153); wearing a bowler hat over a fringe of white hair, Serban's Alvin
Epstein (Tabori's Shylock in 1966) evoked memories of his Lucky in the first American
production of *Waiting for Godot*, as he wandered about the stage, 'keeping his present in a
domed silver dish aloft, in a suppliant posture' (Cook, *SB* 1999). Schenk's Lancelot, Heinz
Petters, made faces at his father for most of the scene; Doran omitted the character of Old
Gobbo completely.

Enter OLD GOBBO *with a basket*

GOBBO Master young-man, you, I pray you, which is the way to   25
    Master Jew's?

LANCELOT [*Aside*] O heavens! This is my true-begotten father who
    being more than sand-blind, high gravel-blind, knows me not. I
    will try confusions with him.

GOBBO Master young-gentleman, I pray you, which is the way to   30
    Master Jew's?

LANCELOT Turn upon your right hand at the next turning, but at the
    next turning of all on your left. Marry, at the very next turning
    turn of no hand but turn down indirectly to the Jew's house.

GOBBO Be God's sonties, 'twill be a hard way to hit! Can you tell me   35
    whether one Lancelot that dwells with him, dwell with him or no?

LANCELOT Talk you of young Master Lancelot? [*Aside*] Mark me
    now, now will I raise the waters. Talk you of young Master
    Lancelot?

GOBBO No 'master', sir, but a poor man's son. His father, though I   40
    say't, is an honest, exceeding poor man and, God be thanked,
    well to live.

LANCELOT Well, let his father be what a will, we talk of young
    Master Lancelot.

GOBBO Your worship's friend and Lancelot, sir.   45

LANCELOT But I pray you, *ergo* old man, *ergo* I beseech you, talk you
    of young Master Lancelot?

GOBBO Of Lancelot, an't please your mastership.

LANCELOT *Ergo* Master Lancelot. Talk not of Master Lancelot,
    father, for the young gentleman, according to fates and destinies,   50
    and such odd sayings, the sisters three, and such branches of

---

25–9 Jim Dale, Miller's Lancelot, added an 'Hullo' at the end of the speech (*pmt*).

35 'By God's sonties' was altered to 'Heaven's sonties', or simply omitted, in the eighteenth
and nineteenth centuries. 'God be thanked' at 41 was handled the same way.

45–7 The Bell text retains these lines, but they were omitted in nineteenth-century performances.

49–59 'Purely for the sake of clarity', Christopher Luscombe changed 'father' to 'old man'. During
this speech he indulged in a display of keyboard wizardry on Shylock's computer: it all 'went
horribly wrong for him when the screen scrambled before his very eyes'. Luscombe
acknowledges, 'there's no denying the pain that Gobbo inflicts on his blind father . . . It
seemed important to face up to this unattractive trait in the character and not smooth it out
to suit our '90s sensibilities' (Luscombe, 'Launcelot Gobbo', p. 23).

learning, is indeed deceased, or as you would say in plain terms, gone to heaven.

GOBBO Marry, God forbid! The boy was the very staff of my age, my very prop. 55

LANCELOT Do I look like a cudgel or a hovel-post, a staff or a prop? Do you know me, father?

GOBBO Alack the day, I know you not, young gentleman, but I pray you tell me, is my boy – God rest his soul! – alive or dead?

LANCELOT Do you not know me, father? 60

GOBBO Alack, sir, I am sand-blind, I know you not.

LANCELOT Nay indeed, if you had your eyes you might fail of the knowing me: it is a wise father that knows his own child. Well, old man, I will tell you news of your son. [*Kneels*] Give me your blessing; truth will come to light, murder cannot be hid long, a 65 man's son may, but in the end truth will out.

GOBBO Pray you, sir, stand up; I am sure you are not Lancelot my boy.

LANCELOT Pray you, let's have no more fooling about it, but give me your blessing; I am Lancelot your boy that was, your son that is, 70 your child that shall be.

GOBBO I cannot think you are my son.

LANCELOT I know not what I shall think of that; but I am Lancelot the Jew's man, and I am sure Margery your wife is my mother.

GOBBO Her name is Margery indeed. I'll be sworn if thou be 75 Lancelot thou art mine own flesh and blood. Lord worshipped might he be, what a beard hast thou got! Thou hast got more hair on thy chin than Dobbin my fill-horse has on his tail.

LANCELOT It should seem then that Dobbin's tail grows backward. I am sure he had more hair of his tail than I have of my face when 80 I last saw him.

---

54 'In Forbes-Robertson's production, Old Gobbo wept, his hand over his eyes' (*pmt* Ames[1]).

66 Gold's Lancelot, Enn Reitel, smelled something 'off' in his father's basket – a good example of the desperate lengths some will go to in order to extract laughs from this scene.

72 Nunn's Old Gobbo, Oscar James, showed some anger here, as if to say 'My son would not play such a cruel joke.'

77–81 Productions from the eighteenth century to the end of the twentieth have had Lancelot kneel with his back to his father, so that Old Gobbo thinks his son's hair is a beard. Nunn was a welcome exception, with James putting his hands on the shaven-headed French's mop.

GOBBO Lord, how art thou changed! How dost thou and thy master agree? I have brought him a present. How 'gree you now?

LANCELOT Well, well; but for mine own part, as I have set up my rest to run away, so I will not rest till I have run some ground. 85 My master's a very Jew. Give him a present? Give him a halter! I am famished in his service; you may tell every finger I have with my ribs. Father, I am glad you are come; give me your present to one Master Bassanio, who indeed gives rare new liveries: if I serve not him, I will run as far as God has any ground. O rare 90 fortune, here comes the man! To him, father, for I am a Jew if I serve the Jew any longer.

Enter BASSANIO *with* [LEONARDO *and*] *a follower or two*

BASSANIO You may do so, but let it be so hasted that supper be ready at the farthest by five of the clock. See these letters delivered, put the liveries to making, and desire Gratiano to come anon to 95 my lodging.

[Exit one of his men]

LANCELOT To him, father.

GOBBO God bless your worship!

BASSANIO Gramercy; wouldst thou aught with me?

GOBBO Here's my son, sir, a poor boy – 100

LANCELOT Not a poor boy, sir, but the rich Jew's man that would, sir, as my father shall specify –

GOBBO He hath a great infection, sir, as one would say, to serve –

LANCELOT Indeed, the short and the long is, I serve the Jew, and have a desire, as my father shall specify – 105

GOBBO His master and he, saving your worship's reverence, are scarce cater-cousins –

LANCELOT To be brief, the very truth is that the Jew having done me wrong doth cause me – as my father being I hope an old man shall frutify unto you – 110

87–8 'The traditional stage business [is] Lancelot placing his father's hand on the fingers of his own hand, which he has spread out to represent ribs' (Mahood, *Merchant*, p. 86).

93–6 In Thacker's office tower, Owen Teale alternated between speaking to his cell phone and to his secretary. Serban cut Bassanio's speech; his instructions for delivering the letters were mimed.

GOBBO I have here a dish of doves that I would bestow upon your
    worship, and my suit is –

LANCELOT In very brief, the suit is impertinent to myself, as your
    worship shall know by this honest old man, and though I say it,
    though old man, yet poor man, my father –   115

BASSANIO One speak for both. What would you?

LANCELOT Serve you, sir.

GOBBO That is the very defect of the matter, sir.

BASSANIO I know thee well, thou hast obtained thy suit.
        Shylock thy master spoke with me this day,   120
        And hath preferred thee, if it be preferment
        To leave a rich Jew's service to become
        The follower of so poor a gentleman.

LANCELOT The old proverb is very well parted between my master
    Shylock and you, sir: you have the grace of God, sir, and he hath   125
    enough.

BASSANIO Thou speak'st it well; go, father, with thy son;
        Take leave of thy old master, and enquire
        My lodging out. [*To a follower*] Give him a livery
        More guarded than his fellows'; see it done.   130

LANCELOT Father, in. I cannot get a service, no, I have ne'er a
    tongue in my head! [*Looks at palm of his hand*] Well, if any man
    in Italy have a fairer table which doth offer to swear upon a book!
    – I shall have good fortune. Go to, here's a simple line of life,
    here's a small trifle of wives: alas, fifteen wives is nothing, eleven   135
    widows and nine maids is a simple coming-in for one man. And
    then to 'scape drowning thrice, and to be in peril of my life with
    the edge of a featherbed: here are simple 'scapes. Well, if
    Fortune be a woman, she's a good wench for this gear. Father,
    come, I'll take my leave of the Jew in the twinkling.   140
                         Exeunt Lancelot [and Gobbo]

BASSANIO I pray thee, good Leonardo, think on this.
        These things being bought and orderly bestowed,

135–6 In Forbes-Robertson's production, at 'eleven widows and nine maids' Lancelot 'kissed his
    palm in gratitude for so much good fortune, with good effect' (*pmt* Ames[1]).

139b-40 Kahn's Teagle F. Bougere ended the speech at 'Father, come', following with 'here Father,
    here Father' as if calling a dog.

141-4 Macready: 'Bassanio has been occasionally writing on tables during Launce's speech and
    speaking to Leonardo' (*pmt*).

Return in haste, for I do feast tonight
My best esteemed acquaintance. Hie thee, go.
LEONARDO My best endeavours shall be done herein.   145

Enter GRATIANO

GRATIANO Where's your master?
LEONARDO   Yonder, sir, he walks.   *Exit*
GRATIANO Signor Bassanio!
BASSANIO Gratiano?
GRATIANO I have a suit to you.
BASSANIO   You have obtained it.
GRATIANO You must not deny me, I must go with you to Belmont.   150
BASSANIO Why then, you must. But hear thee, Gratiano:
          Thou art too wild, too rude, and bold of voice –
          Parts that become thee happily enough,
          And in such eyes as ours appear not faults;
          But where thou art not known, why there they show   155
          Something too liberal. Pray thee take pain
          To allay with some cold drops of modesty
          Thy skipping spirit, lest through thy wild behaviour
          I be misconstered in the place I go to,
          And lose my hopes.
GRATIANO   Signor Bassanio, hear me: 160
          If I do not put on a sober habit,
          Talk with respect, and swear but now and then,
          Wear prayer books in my pocket, look demurely,
          Nay more, while grace is saying, hood mine eyes
          Thus with my hat, and sigh and say 'amen',   165
          Use all the observance of civility
          Like one well studied in a sad ostent
          To please his grandam, never trust me more.
BASSANIO Well, we shall see your bearing.
GRATIANO Nay, but I bar tonight, you shall not gauge me   170
          By what we do tonight.
BASSANIO   No, that were pity.

---

151 Thacker had Mark Lockyer, 'a swaggering office joker', burst in on Bassanio, who was at
   his desk, at 146. He 'celebrated the decision to visit Belmont by spraying champagne over
   Bassanio' (Jackson, *SQ* 1994).

166–8 Omitted in the Bell text, and by Kemble.

        I would entreat you rather to put on
        Your boldest suit of mirth, for we have friends
        That purpose merriment. But fare you well,
        I have some business.   175
GRATIANO And I must to Lorenzo and the rest;
        But we will visit you at supper time.
                               Exeunt

ACT 2, SCENE 3

[2.3] *Enter* JESSICA *and* [LANCELOT] *the Clown*

JESSICA I am sorry thou wilt leave my father so.
          Our house is hell, and thou a merry devil
          Didst rob it of some taste of tediousness.
          But fare thee well: there is a ducat for thee.
          And, Lancelot, soon at supper shalt thou see   5
          Lorenzo, who is thy new master's guest;
          Give him this letter, do it secretly.
          And so farewell: I would not have my father
          See me in talk with thee.
LANCELOT Adieu; tears exhibit my tongue. Most beautiful pagan,   10
    most sweet Jew, if a Christian do not play the knave and get thee,

---

Irving omitted this scene, although the other actor-managers retained it, keeping the action on the street outside Shylock's house – Tree's Jessica 'stole out of the synagogue alone, presumably before the sermon' (Crosse, *Diaries*, vol. IV, p. 106). Crosse, 'shocked' by Arthur Phillips's placing of 1.1 in Antonio's house, was also surprised to see 2.3 set in ' "A Room in Shylock's House", apparently in order that after Jessica's exit Shylock should enter gloating over the bond which he proceeds to lock up in his cash box'. He adds, 'I have seen the play 24 times and have never been inside either of these houses before' (vol. XV, p. 83).

    Nunn began the scene with an exchange in Yiddish between Jessica (Gabrielle Jourdan) and Shylock, in which Goodman scolded her for not scrubbing a pot as well as her mother would have done; hence Jessica was already in tears when Lancelot entered, carrying a suitcase.

4b Denis Lawson, most of his part cut from Miller's television version, added an 'eh, wot!' when Jessica stuffed a ducat into his pocket. The Lancelots of Sothern and Serban bit the coin (*pmt* Sothern[1]).

5–7 Transferred to 2.5 by Nunn.

  7 Not content with 'eh, wot!', Lawson gave a cockney 'o-o-w' here.

I am much deceived. But adieu; these foolish drops do
something drown my manly spirit. Adieu!   [*Exit*]
JESSICA Farewell, good Lancelot.
        Alack, what heinous sin is it in me   15
        To be ashamed to be my father's child!
        But though I am a daughter to his blood
        I am not to his manners. O Lorenzo,
        If thou keep promise, I shall end this strife,
        Become a Christian and thy loving wife.   *Exit*   20

13 Very surprisingly, Luscombe uttered the painful pun of 'adieu' and 'a Jew'. He explains that
it was done 'to suggest both a lapse of taste and an instinctive verbal dexterity – he knew he
shouldn't have said it, but he just couldn't resist it' (Luscombe, 'Launcelot Gobbo', p. 24).
Doran's Lancelot, Jimmy Chisholm, resisted that 'lapse of taste', but made up for it by
walking into a wall as he exited.

15–20 Gold had Leslee Udwin speak directly into the camera – 'we do not doubt the sincerity of
her question' (Bulman, *Shakespeare in Performance*, pp. 106–7). Aysan Celik retrieved
some paper money from under the carpet in Serban's production, and took a long pause
before 'Become a Christian', while *klezmer* music played in the background.

18b-20 These lines were transferred to 2.5 by Nunn (see p. 147).

20 Bell's 1774 edition has a song for Jessica here, although it was usually placed at the end of
2.5 (see pp. 147–8).

ACT 2, SCENE 4

[2.4] *Enter* GRATIANO, LORENZO, SALARINO, *and* SOLANIO

LORENZO Nay, we will slink away in supper time,
    Disguise us at my lodging, and return
    All in an hour.
GRATIANO We have not made good preparation.
SALARINO We have not spoke us yet of torchbearers.   5
SOLANIO 'Tis vile unless it may be quaintly ordered,
    And better in my mind not undertook.
LORENZO 'Tis now but four of clock; we have two hours
    To furnish us.

             Enter LANCELOT [*with a letter*]

            Friend Lancelot! What's the news?
LANCELOT And it shall please you to break up this, it shall seem to   10
    signify.
LORENZO I know the hand; in faith, 'tis a fair hand,
    And whiter than the paper it writ on
    Is the fair hand that writ.
GRATIANO   Love news, in faith!
LANCELOT By your leave, sir.   15
LORENZO Whither goest thou?
LANCELOT Marry, sir, to bid my old master the Jew to sup tonight
    with my new master the Christian.

1–9a Cut by Thacker, the scene commencing with Lorenzo, a young merchant banker, at his desk.
  9b In Kahn's production, 'Friend Lancelot' was spoken with whistles and other mock-admiration of Lancelot's new livery. Nunn began the scene here, continuing to 19, before going back to 1–8.
14bff. Schenk's Lorenzo, Klaus Höring, admired a passing girl while reading Jessica's letter.

LORENZO Hold here, take this. Tell gentle Jessica
           I will not fail her; speak it privately.   20

Exit Lancelot

           Go, gentlemen:
           Will you prepare you for this masque tonight?
           I am provided of a torchbearer.
SALARINO Ay marry, I'll be gone about it straight.
SOLANIO And so will I.
LORENZO   Meet me and Gratiano   25
           At Gratiano's lodging some hour hence.
SALARINO 'Tis good we do so.

Exeunt [Salarino and Solanio]

GRATIANO Was not that letter from fair Jessica?

19 'Take this' is obviously meant as a direction for Lorenzo to give Lancelot a coin, but
    Alexander's Lorenzo handed Lancelot a crucifix – a present for Jessica (Bulman,
    Shakespeare in Performance, p. 133). Nunn changed the line to 'take this to Jessica', as
    Lorenzo hastily scribbled a note.
20 The cue for the old stage business of 'bumping'. Its origins are obscure, but go back at least
    to the mid nineteenth century and Booth. The promptbook for Henry Jewett's Boston Opera
    House production of 1915 gives complete instructions:

> Launcelot bows to Lorenzo and in so doing bumps into Gratiano, who is behind him. He
> backs around in front of him, bowing humbly and in a wheedling way, as if suggesting a
> tip, which Gratiano gives him. In bowing himself back to L. from Gratiano he bumps into
> Solanio, with whom he has the same business. Meanwhile Gratiano runs round behind
> and stands back to Launcelot as he backs away from Salanio, so that he bumps him
> again. This may be repeated *ad libitum*, introducing also Salarino and Lorenzo if
> desired, until Launcelot begins to suspect the trick. Then, instead of bumping into
> Gratiano, who should recur for this business, he suddenly turns upon him, thrusts his
> tongue in his cheek, throws his cap upon his head impudently, and exits L. into house.
> All laugh.

The actors 'all' may have laughed, but it is hard to understand why anyone in the audience
did. Nevertheless Benson and Forbes-Robertson maintained the tradition, as Crosse notes.
'with pathetic fidelity' (*Diaries*, vol. v, p. 149).

21 Daniel Evans said 'So', not 'Go, gentlemen' in Nunn's production, and his friends turned out
    their empty pockets to show that once again, someone else would have to pay their café bill;
    the scene ended at 26.

LORENZO I must needs tell thee all. She hath directed
How I shall take her from her father's house,   30
What gold and jewels she is furnished with,
What page's suit she hath in readiness.
If e'er the Jew her father come to heaven,
It will be for his gentle daughter's sake;
And never dare misfortune cross her foot,   35
Unless she do it under this excuse
That she is issue to a faithless Jew.
Come, go with me; peruse this as thou goest.
Fair Jessica shall be my torchbearer.

                                                    Exeunt

32 Cut by Thacker: Jessica and Lorenzo were eloping via a disco.

ACT 2, SCENE 5

[**2.5**] *Enter* [SHYLOCK] *the Jew and* [LANCELOT] *his man that was,*
the Clown

SHYLOCK Well, thou shalt see, thy eyes shall be thy judge,
　　　　The difference of old Shylock and Bassanio –

This scene of only fifty-five lines has an importance well out of proportion to its length, for barring interpolations such as Nunn's at the start of 2.3, this is our only opportunity to see Shylock and Jessica together. More than any scene in the play, it benefits from being acted in an intimate theatre – it could not have fulfilled its potential in the nineteenth century, as it was always played in the street outside Shylock's house, and therefore was not the 'private scene' that Patrick Stewart, acting in The Other Place, found the most satisfying in his performance (Barton, *Playing Shakespeare*, p. 175). Indeed, 2.5 was little more than a bridging scene in Maraden's 1996 production, as it was played 'outside Shylock's', with Jessica entering from the house when called (*pmt*).

　　The *Spectator* (12 October 1839) was very critical of Macready in 1.3, but found that his

> performance in the second act was excellent: his grave and thoughtful reserve, tempered with kindness to his daughter, but assuming a tone of severity mixed with contempt towards the 'unthrifty knave' Lancelot, expressed the character of a man in whose estimation thrift and wariness were the two cardinal virtues, and to whose abused condition the sound of gayety was a mockery.

Working with the new gas lighting, Macready added some atmosphere by having the lights progressively lowered during the scene (*pmt*). Daly's promptbooks call for the same effect.
　　Ellen Terry's memoirs contain an anecdote about Irving's costume for 2.5: 'He asked my daughter – whose cleverness in such things he fully recognised – to put some stage jewels on to the scarf that he wore round his head when he supped with the Christians. I have an idea that, when he went to that supper, he'd like to flaunt his wealth in the Christian dogs' faces' (Terry, *Story*, pp. 187–8). Crosse notes that Irving appeared 'good humoured in the opening dialogue with Lancelot, but full of suspicion throughout the scene with him and

143

What, Jessica! – Thou shalt not gourmandise
As thou hast done with me – What, Jessica! –
And sleep, and snore, and rend apparel out.   5
Why, Jessica, I say!
LANCELOT   Why, Jessica!
SHYLOCK Who bids thee call? I do not bid thee call.

Jessica' (*Diaries*, vol. I, p. 174); another Shylock whom Crosse greatly admired, Ernest
Milton, was 'discovered, squatting sailor-fashion outside his house, patching his cloak' –
Crosse cites this as Milton emphasizing that 'he was not playing Shylock in the grand style'
(vol. XIII, p. 94).

Thacker provided an opening that added greatly to the characterisations of Shylock and
Jessica:

> Seen at home . . . listening to Schubert on his compact-disc player, and hugging a
> photograph of Leah, this cultured man did not deserve his treatment. It made of
> Jessica's betrayal both something difficult to make sense of and something far more
> culpable, a commitment to the triviality of the yuppie culture, all champagne and
> portable telephones, of the production's view of Venice as modern stock-exchange.
> (Holland, *English Shakespeares*, p. 165)

Christopher Luscombe conveyed the impression that he rented a room from Shylock while
in his employ, entering here 'with a voluminous anorak and a suitcase tightly strapped onto
a trolley' (Luscombe, 'Launcelot Gobbo', p. 25), the anorak showing 'how far he was from
being a fashion victim' (Jackson, *SQ* 1994).

No recent production derived as much value from 2.5 as did Nunn's, in which a simple
table, with Sabbath candles flickering beside a photograph of Leah, gave us a place where
Shylock, 'the lonely widower, desperate and demanding, over-protectively clinging to his
treasured child's love, was vulnerability on view' (Smallwood, *SS* 2000).

3 Sellars's Jessica (Portia Johnson) was the quintessential 1990s adolescent, ignoring her
   father while watching TV: a Japanese animated cartoon of a little witch girl, flying away
   from home (M. Shapiro, *SB* 1994).

6b Sothern: 'Shylock raises his stick as if to strike Launcelot. Launcelot falls on his knees,
   crossing himself' (*pmt* Sothern[2]). In Benthall's 1956 production, when Lancelot aped Robert
   Helpmann's cry of ' "Vy, Jessica!", [he] was thrown to the ground' (Clarke, *Shakespeare at
   the Old Vic*, np).

7 Olivier, 'decked out in white tie, tails and with a watch-chain across a spreading corporation
   . . . [introduced] a note of menace by asking of Gobbo "Who bids thee call?" and then
   dropping his voice to a whisper on "I do not bid thee call" ' (Billington, *The Modern Actor*,
   p. 85).

LANCELOT Your worship was wont to tell me I could do nothing
　　　　　without bidding.

Enter JESSICA

JESSICA Call you? What is your will?　　　　　　　　　　　　10
SHYLOCK I am bid forth to supper, Jessica.
　　　　　There are my keys. But wherefore should I go?
　　　　　I am not bid for love, they flatter me;
　　　　　But yet I'll go in hate, to feed upon
　　　　　The prodigal Christian. Jessica my girl,　　　　　　　15
　　　　　Look to my house. I am right loath to go;
　　　　　There is some ill a-brewing towards my rest,
　　　　　For I did dream of money bags tonight.
LANCELOT I beseech you, sir, go; my young master doth expect your
　　　　　reproach.　　　　　　　　　　　　　　　　　　　20
SHYLOCK So do I his.
LANCELOT And they have conspired together – I will not say you
　　　　　shall see a masque; but if you do, then it was not for nothing that

---

8　Sothern: 'Shylock raises his stick again and Launcelot falls flat on his stomach' (*pmt*
　　Sothern[2]).

10　'In Signior Novelli's business, Jessica appears on balcony and lets down a cord to Shylock to
　　which he ties the keys as she draws them up. It gives the effect as though Jessica were, in
　　oriental fashion, locked in . . . Jessica never appears at stage level 'til she elopes' (*pmt*
　　Ames[1]).

11　Sher spoke 'in the amazed tone of one who has never been asked out before' (Billington,
　　Gdn 1 May 1987).

12　This was the most controversial moment of John Barton's 1978 production, when Stewart
　　suddenly slapped Avril Carson hard across the face. Stewart explained at a conference that
　　the action grew out of a rehearsal improvisation, when he saw a look of rebellion in
　　Jessica's eyes, but as Ernest Colman observes, Jessica's position on The Other Place stage
　　meant that half of the audience could not see what Shylock saw (Colman, 'Autumn Leaves',
　　p. 148). Stewart notes, 'after the blow I made some attempt at a reconciliation: "Perhaps I
　　will return immediately", but by then the damage had been done and she was bound to
　　reject him' (Barton, *Playing Shakespeare*, p. 175).

15b　Barton (p. 175) says of Shylock that 'there's hardly any word of endearment to his daughter'
　　in this scene, but Henry Goodman in Nunn's production expressed an overpowering love
　　for Jessica in these three words, as he began singing *Eshet Chayil*, or 'A Woman of Virtue'
　　(see Appendix 2).

my nose fell a-bleeding on Black Monday last, at six a clock i'the
morning, falling out that year on Ash Wednesday was four year   25
in th'afternoon.

SHYLOCK   What, are there masques? Hear you me, Jessica,
   Lock up my doors, and when you hear the drum
   And the vile squealing of the wry-necked fife,
   Clamber not you up to the casements then   30
   Nor thrust your head into the public street
   To gaze on Christian fools with varnished faces;
   But stop my house's ears – I mean my casements –
   Let not the sound of shallow foppery enter
   My sober house. By Jacob's staff I swear   35
   I have no mind of feasting forth tonight:
   But I will go. Go you before me, sirrah;
   Say I will come.
LANCELOT   I will go before, sir.
   [*Aside to Jessica*] Mistress, look out at window for all this:
   There will come a Christian by   40
   Will be worth a Jewès eye   [*Exit*]
SHYLOCK   What says that fool of Hagar's offspring, ha?
JESSICA   His words were 'Farewell, mistress', nothing else.

27–35a Samuel Phelps's 'injunction to Jessica, when he entrusts her with his keys, was full of quiet
  force' (Rice, *The London Theatre*, p. 65).

 28 Tree removed his ear-rings and handed them to Jessica along with Leah's ring,
  'because that night the Christian hooligans are painting the ghetto red' (*Times* 6 April
  1908).

30–3 As Stewart did earlier in the scene, Goodman slapped Jessica at this point. He then seemed
  to check himself and said 'I mean my casements' in a tone of self-reproach.

34–5 This was the first moment where Dustin Hoffman made a true connection with his role,
  touching Francesca Buller on the face and gazing at her with deep tenderness.

40–1 Alexander had Lancelot hand Jessica, behind Shylock's back, the crucifix given to him by
  Lorenzo (Bulman, *Shakespeare in Performance*, p. 133); Nunn, inserting 2.3.5–7 here, had
  Shylock pray over Leah's picture while Jessica and Lancelot whispered to one another.

38–43 Irving exited into his house at 'Say I will come', and reappeared, carrying a lantern and staff.
  Overhearing Lancelot, 'he swiftly advanced to his daughter, as Launcelot sped away, seized
  her by the wrist, looked suspiciously upon her face and harshly put the question to her –
  pointing with his stick after the departed servant –"*What says* that fool of Hagar's offspring
  – ha?" ' (Winter, *Shakespeare on the Stage*, pp. 185–6).

SHYLOCK The patch is kind enough, but a huge feeder,
      Snail-slow in profit, and he sleeps by day   45
      More than the wildcat. Drones hive not with me,
      Therefore I part with him, and part with him
      To one that I would have him help to waste
      His borrowed purse. Well, Jessica, go in;
      Perhaps I will return immediately.   50
      Do as I bid you, shut doors after you.
      Fast bind, fast find:
      A proverb never stale in thrifty mind.   *Exit*
JESSICA Farewell, and if my fortune be not crossed,
      I have a father, you a daughter, lost.   *Exit*   55

44–9a Calder 'did not seem miserly: he gave the departing Gobbo a large envelope (his wages, perhaps, or at least a reference), and his remarks about the servant's behavior . . . came across as a self-conscious joke to cover what may have been a real sense of loss' (Jackson, *SQ* 1994). Morris Carnovsky's farewell to Lancelot also 'had a genuine strain of regret – he was fond of the boy' (Beckerman, 'The Season', p. 405). Will LeBow spoke these lines to the audience.

49b McDiarmid folded his prayer-shawl and gave Leah's ring to Jessica as he was leaving. He notes, 'with a surge of melancholy, he embraces his daughter, unwittingly for the last time . . . soon Jessica will no longer exist for him, except – like Leah – as a memory to burn his heart' (McDiarmid, 'Shylock' p. 52).

52–3 In the BBC production (1980), Leslee Udwin mouthed the proverb mockingly behind Shylock's back; Kate Duchêne completed it 'with the weariness of one who has heard it every week for years' in Thacker's version (Jackson, *SQ* 1994); Francesca Buller also recited along with Hoffman. Goodman exited, then called out 'Fast bind', with Gabrielle Jourdan replying 'fast find'.

54–5 Jourdan addressed the couplet to the audience, then ended by saying the closing lines from Jessica's previous scene (2.3.15–20), and kissing her mother's picture; Schenk also finished with 2.3.15–20. In Langham's 1989 production, hunchbacked masquers in black costumes entered from the corners of the stage and chased a frightened Jessica back into her house (Ward, *SB* November/December 1989).

    Most managers of the eighteenth and nineteenth centuries inserted Jessica's song here. The lyrics in Inchbald's edition are

    Haste, Lorenzo, haste away,
    To my longing arms repair,
    With impatience I shall die;
    Come, and ease thy Jessy's care:

> Let me then in wanton play,
> Sigh and gaze my soul away.

Kemble has slightly different words, in which Jessica's yearning is less explicitly sexual:

> Haste, Lorenzo, haste away,
> To thy watchful love repair
> Hither come without delay
> Come, and ease thy Jessy's care
> Let me, free from tyrant sway,
> Give my doting soul away.

The Bell text, with the same words as Inchbald's, places the song at the end of 2.3. Charles Kean omitted it.

ACT 2, SCENE 6

[**2.6**] *Enter the masquers,* GRATIANO *and* SALARINO

GRATIANO This is the penthouse under which Lorenzo
　　　　　Desired us to make stand.
SALARINO His hour is almost past.
GRATIANO And it is marvel he outdwells his hour,
　　　　　For lovers ever run before the clock.　　　　　　　5
SALARINO O, ten times faster Venus' pigeons fly
　　　　　To seal love's bonds new made than they are wont
　　　　　To keep obligèd faith unforfeited!

Macready had 2.6 follow on directly from 2.5: 'stage dark . . . a slight pause should occur here, before the entrance of Grat. and Sal' (*pmt*). Irving also had a combined scene, set at 'Shylock's house, by a bridge' (*pmt* Irving[2]). The Meininger company, famous for its staging, made excellent use of gas lighting, as a description from the *Düsseldorfer Volksblatt* (10 June 1886) shows:

> It is twilight: night draws on; soon it falls on the stage, while only a few small circles are illuminated by the green or red lights of signal lanterns. A more powerful lantern is seen far in the background, in another arm of the canal, through an opening in the wall. Its light is reflected in the transparent green water and shatters the thick darkness in the foreground as the gondolas break through it under the high Rialto bridge. The gondoliers, standing high in each bow, steer their crafts with powerful movements while a torch in each vessel shows the steersman his way, its ruddy light on his face deepening the darkness which surrounds him. (*qtd* Carlson, *The German Stage*, p. 178)

osd The Papp/Vaughan Central Park production was during the period of major civil rights demonstrations: Gratiano, Salarino and assorted supernumeraries wore hooded white robes, intended to 'evoke the garb of the Ku Klux Klan' (Gelb, *NYT* 22 June 1962). Nunn began 2.6 in the cabaret, the waitresses taking the stage to sing the old Rudy Vallee hit, 'Everything I Have Is Yours', its lyrics presenting an interesting counterpoint to the inscription on the leaden casket, 'Who chooseth me must give and hazard all he hath.'

GRATIANO   That ever holds: who riseth from a feast
                With that keen appetite that he sits down?   10
                Where is the horse that doth untread again
                His tedious measures with the unbated fire
                That he did pace them first? All things that are
                Are with more spirit chasèd than enjoyed.
                How like a younger or a prodigal   15
                The scarfèd bark puts from her native bay,
                Hugged and embracèd by the strumpet wind!
                How like the prodigal doth she return
                With overweathered ribs and ragged sails,
                Lean, rents and beggared by the strumpet wind!   20

                              Enter LORENZO

SALARINO   Here comes Lorenzo; more of this hereafter.
LORENZO   Sweet friends, your patience for my long abode.
                Not I but my affairs have made you wait.
                When you shall please to play the thieves for wives,
                I'll watch as long for you then. Approach –   25
                Here dwells my father Jew. Ho! Who's within?

9–20 Gratiano's speech on desire and its fulfilment contains some of the finest verse in the play, but
         with the notable exception of Macready (*pmt*), 15–20 were always cut in the eighteenth and
         nineteenth centuries. Schenk created a moving soliloquy, by having Gratiano, Peter Vogel,
         begin with Salarino's three lines (6–9), as he mused over the letter Lorenzo received from
         Jessica in 2.4. Until 14, he spoke over the sounds of carnival gaiety, but the mood became
         more quiet and sombre at 'How like a younger or a prodigal'; after line 20 he spoke Antonio's
         ' 'Tis nine o'clock / Bassanio presently will go aboard / The wind is come about' (64,66,65), as
         the camera followed him to Shylock's house, where Lorenzo and friends were waiting.
22   Booth has Lorenzo entering 'in a gondola, gondolier in boat with oar, pushing it on. Lorenzo
         jumps out of boat coming c.' (*pmt* Booth[3]).
25   Nunn, keeping the action in the cabaret, cut the final word, 'approach', and inserted
         2.2.1–16, which Lancelot did as a stand-up comic routine, to raucous laughter from the
         patrons. Shylock entered at 'the Jew my master', and was shown to Bassanio's table (I sat
         in the first row of the Cottesloe, very close to them, and heard Bassanio make an *ad lib*
         comment about Lancelot to Shylock: 'This is a new vocation for him'). Then 2.4.28–32 was
         given, with Shylock half-overhearing 'Was not that letter from fair Jessica' (Gratiano was
         immediately 'shushed' by the others). Shylock left the cabaret, and a rumba line served as
         segue to 2.6.25b and the remainder of the scene, at the new locale of Shylock's house.
26   From the eighteenth until the mid nineteenth century, Lorenzo's song was customarily
         inserted here:

[*Enter*] JESSICA *above*[*, in boy's clothes*]

JESSICA Who are you? Tell me, for more certainty,
        Albeit I'll swear that I do know your tongue.
LORENZO Lorenzo, and thy love.
JESSICA Lorenzo certain, and my love indeed,   30
        For who love I so much? And now who knows
        But you, Lorenzo, whether I am yours?
LORENZO Heaven and thy thoughts are witness that thou art.
JESSICA Here, catch this casket, it is worth the pains.
        I am glad 'tis night, you do not look on me,   35
        For I am much ashamed of my exchange.
        But love is blind, and lovers cannot see
        The pretty follies that themselves commit;
        For if they could, Cupid himself would blush
        To see me thus transformèd to a boy.   40

My bliss too long my bride denies,
Apace the wasting summer flies;
Nor yet the wint'ry blasts I fear,
Nor storms nor night shall keep me here.

What may for strength with steel compare?
O love has fetters stronger far!
By bolts of steel are limbs confin'd,
But cruel love enchains the mind.

No longer then perplex thy breast,
When thoughts torment, the first are best;
'Tis mad to go, 'tis death to stay,
Away my Jesse, haste away.

While Irving's production is often seen as a transition from the older style to something more modern, he did retain this and other songs. Charles Kean inserted his own 'Glee', setting 'O happy fair / Your eyes are lode-stars' from *A Midsummer Night's Dream* (1.1.182–5) to music, while Booth's and Daly's Jessicas were offered an alternative selection of serenade: 'My lady sweet arise' from *Cymbeline* (*pmt* Booth[2]; *Amer. II*, p. 92). Guthrie's Lorenzo 'meowed' at 'who's within', followed by an exchange of 'meows' between the lovers at 31 (*pmt*).

34 Klaus Höring, Schenk's Lorenzo, eagerly fondled and kissed the money when Jessica was not on screen. One of the treasures she threw down was a large *menorah*.

36 Serban had Jessica lower a ridiculously large money bag, emblazoned with a $ sign.

LORENZO Descend, for you must be my torchbearer.

JESSICA What, must I hold a candle to my shames?
　　　　They in themselves, good sooth, are too too light.
　　　　Why, 'tis an office of discovery, love,
　　　　And I should be obscured.

LORENZO　　　　　　　　　　　So are you, sweet,　　　　45
　　　　Even in the lovely garnish of a boy.
　　　　But come at once,
　　　　For the close night doth play the runaway,
　　　　And we are stayed for at Bassanio's feast.

JESSICA I will make fast the doors, and gild myself　　　50
　　　　With some moe ducats, and be with you straight.

　　　　　　　　　　　　　　[*Exit Jessica above*]

GRATIANO Now by my hood, a gentile and no Jew!

LORENZO Beshrew me but I love her heartily.
　　　　For she is wise, if I can judge of her,
　　　　And fair she is, if that mine eyes be true,　　　55
　　　　And true she is, as she bath proved herself;
　　　　And therefore like herself, wise, fair, and true,
　　　　Shall she be placèd in my constant soul.

　　　　　　　　　Enter JESSICA

　　　　What, art thou come? On, gentleman, away!
　　　　Our masquing mates by this time for us stay.　　　60

　　　　　　　　　　　　Exit [*with Jessica*]

52　Nearly a hundred years apart, and with many others in between, Sothern's and Nunn's
　　actors punned on 'gentle' and 'gentile'.

53–8　Hall's Lorenzo, Richard Garnett, said ' "Beshrew me, but I love her heartily" while groping
　　the casket of jewels' (Hiley, *Lst* 15 June 1989).

58sd　Macready's business, 'Enter Jessica with two bags of money' (*pmt*), was adopted by Charles
　　Kean (*pmt* C. Kean[1]).

60sd　From the nineteenth century until the present day, directors have chosen to cut, or simply
　　ignore, Antonio's announcement of 'No masque tonight' (65), and accompany the
　　elopement of Jessica and Lorenzo with music, dancing or other celebrations (it is most
　　unlikely that any such activities took place in the 1590s). Consistent with his emphasis on
　　spectacle, Charles Kean had the lovers leave by gondola as a street carnival began, to Henry
　　Morley's approval: 'the music and dance of masqued revellers in the street under Jessica's
　　window, against which Shylock had warned her to lock up his doors and shut his house's

Enter ANTONIO

ANTONIO Who's there?
GRATIANO Signor Antonio?
ANTONIO Fie, fie, Gratiano, where are all the rest?
      'Tis nine a clock, our friends all stay for you.
      No masque tonight: the wind is come about,   65
      Bassanio presently will go aboard.
      I have sent twenty out to seek for you.

ears, is such a show as Shakespeare might have been content to see appended to his text' (Morley, *Journal*, p. 174).

Irving's 'masked revelers, merrily singing, passed in the cold moonlight across the bridge over the canal, while a lighted gondola, with throbbing guitars and blended voices, glided below' (*Harper's New Monthly*, *qtd Irv.Amer*, p. 9). Both Sothern and Daly outdid him, in what must have seemed an interminable procession of dancers, singers, musicians, child acrobats and all the supernumeraries they could dredge up from previous scenes – Winter called Daly's effort 'ludicrous and incredible' (*qtd Amer. II*, p. 92).

Tree's staging was 'interspersed with carnival business, crowds of masquers in gondolas and on land who at one point met the Jews coming out of the Synagogue and set upon them, a riot ensuing, which had to be quelled by the guard' (Crosse, *Diaries*, vol. IV, p. 106); Baldridge offered something of the same quality, although it took place in the world of Fellini, with drunken *vitelloni* running through the streets; Rabb turned Baldridge's revels into a 'sacrilegious orgy. A large cross is prominently displayed; Jessica approaches it and the revelers leap at her and tear off her blouse – presumably to show her, and us, what it is she has really converted to' (Novick, *NYT* 11 March 1973).

In 1993, two directors made use of their own 'local culture': Claudio Torres Gonzaga's Brazilian production included 'a raucous, delightful masquerade, reminiscent of Rio's carnival *blocos de rua*, [with] groups of neighborhood musicians, samba dancers, and other revelers' (De Sousa, '*Merchant*', p. 472); Thacker's yuppies emerged from a disco.

Hall's masquers presented an ominous aspect with death's-head costumes, wielding bloody scythes (Wills, *NYRB* 18 January 1990); Doran pointed to Jessica's rejection of her faith by having his masquers wear pig's heads and carry (presumably pork) sausages on poles (Jackson, *SQ* 1999). Tim Luscombe offered perhaps the darkest version in his fascist Italy setting, with an elderly Jew being beaten up by blackshirts (Holland, *English Shakespeares*, p. 95).

61–9 Usually cut in the eighteenth and nineteenth centuries, and cut by Miller; Thacker had Gratiano and Antonio converse by cell phone.

GRATIANO I am glad on't; I desire no more delight
Than to be under sail and gone tonight.

Exeunt

69 Nunn's original approach to this dialogue was to have Antonio and Gratiano unexpectedly encounter Shylock as he returned home. Their stiff, awkward greeting pointed to Antonio's complicity in the elopement of Jessica and Lorenzo.

69sd Irving's famous staging of the end of 2.6 is described by his grandson:

> The last scene of this act was Shylock's house by the bridge. After the elopement of Jessica and Lorenzo, the curtain fell slowly as the maskers, sweeping across the stage, swallowed them up. After a second or two it rose again upon an empty stage. Shylock was seen returning over the bridge. He crossed to his house and, unsuspecting, knocked upon the door. A second and a third knock echoed through the empty house. The curtain fell again as, without word or outward sign, Irving conveyed to the audience Shylock's crushing realization of his daughter's perfidy. (Irving, *Henry Irving*, p. 341)

It has been suggested that Irving got the idea from a similar sequence in Verdi's *Rigoletto*. Whatever its origins, the 'return' was adopted, with variations, by every Shylock of the late nineteenth and early twentieth centuries. Robert Atkins, in Tree's company for a time, describes how his employer outdid anyone before or after him:

> He knocked upon the door, no reply, he tried the handle, the door was unlocked. He went inside, the audience saw him looking round the dining room with apprehension, they heard him run upstairs, saw him in the bedroom, heard him call Jessica and again Jessica as he came downstairs, back in the dining room he was frantically calling Jessica. His cries caught the attention of Jews in the synagogue who poured out and added their lamentations, including sounds of a shofa [*sic*] being sounded. As Tree in his agony turned to look Grand Canalwards a passing gondola was seen upon the skyline and with another agonising cry of 'Jessica', he turned to his door, to find a handy heap of ashes and prostrating himself, poured the ashes over his head accompanied by a song of lamentation from the sorrowing crowd. (Atkins, *Robert Atkins*, p. 64)

Surprisingly, only a few years previously, New York's Yiddish theatre (known for its histrionics), saw Jacob Adler take what seems a more restrained approach:

> Adler unlocked the door of his house, entered, and called his daughter – first with a low, sure call, certain of a response, again with mounting fear, and at last in powerful, vibrating cries of biblical wrath. Following a pause, he came out of the house, seated himself on a low bench. Nothing was heard as the curtain fell but the rasping sound of tearing cloth. (Rosenfeld, *Bright Star*, p. 305)

Maurice Moscovitch was also relatively low-key in his return. The *New Witness* critic said of his 1919 performance, 'Mr Moscovitch cries out neither for his daughter nor his ducats, he suddenly collapses, broken to silence by his loss' (*qtd LD* 13 December 1919).

Rudolf Schildkraut's New York performance is described in the Yiddish newspaper *Der Morgen Zhurnal* (17 November 1920):

> All that he says is 'Jessica,' and that is natural. He runs around the house and looks for his daughter; we hear this by the rapid steps on the boards and by the quickness with which the doors slam. He is not on the stage at all during this, but the audience can picture it as if it were played before their eyes.

This critic approved of Schildkraut then emerging from the house and again calling for Jessica, with 'heartbreak in his voice and such desperation in his tone', but added 'if Schildkraut were satisfied with that call and did not collapse on the bench in front of the house, the impression might have been much stronger' (*qtd* Berkowitz, 'True Jewish Jew', p. 87).

Sothern, like Irving, ended the return with Shylock realising Jessica was not at home, but without any further reaction. As his carnival (see p. 153) was concluding, he entered

> on the stroke of four . . . pushing aside with his big stick a scarf left by a fruit seller, then a mask left by a Satyr. Shylock sneers at the evidence of frivolity, secure in his confidence of his house's freedom from Christian follies. Crossing to his door, he knocks. The only answer is a distant shout and the strains of a serenade afar off. Rising from having placed his lantern beside him, his face gradually shows his realisation of his daughter's flight as the curtain falls. (*pmt* Sothern[2])

The action of Shylock pushing aside a mask with his stick was revived in 1957 by Morris Carnovsky (Cooper, *American Shakespeare Theatre*, p. 47).

George Arliss was very economical: Ames's promptbook shows him simply knocking, knocking again, waiting and standing 'patiently, as the curtain falls slowly' (*pmt* Ames[2]). Crosse observed other variations: at the Old Vic in 1924, Hay Petrie 'returned carrying a lantern, but he did not knock at the door, because there was no door to knock at. The curtain fell as he was slowly walking across the stage' (*Diaries*, vol. VIII, p. 138). In 1932 Ernest Milton arrived 'finding that Jessica had left the door open, then rushing in, and reappearing with gestures of despair' (*Diaries*, vol. XIII, p. 6).

Schenk used television to take us with Shylock as he entered the house, and Fritz Kortner's 'return' took a full two minutes: 'Shylock arrives at his house, tired, feet dragging, silent. He has trouble opening the door, then entering the house, he walks through its rooms, calling out Jessica's name nine times, for the last time by leaning out of the window' (Sehrt, 'Der Shylock', p. 87). During this action we see a quick shot of Jessica and Lorenzo scrambling into a gondola.

What Jackson calls 'another collector's item in the history of the scene since Irving's famous embellishment' was provided by Thacker: David Calder walked past the disguised Jessica, who was just leaving a disco, carrying the casket filled with Shylock's treasure. After being jostled by the revellers, he stood centre stage and called for Jessica as the lights dimmed (*SQ* 1994). Doran also had Shylock come face to face with his daughter, but unlike Calder, Philip Voss recognised her 'and called out her name in astonishment. As she was whisked away, Shylock staggered to his door. Once he had entered, the revelers spun the house around so that the scene closed with an image of the taunted and imprisoned Jew shut up in his bleak prison' (Jackson, *SQ* 1999).

Kahn re-lit Irving's lantern for Hal Holbrook, who knocked on his door and called for Jessica twice; in Serban's version, Will LeBow saw a black dress on the stage floor, and picked it up while uttering a single, soft 'Jessica'; Nunn added a very Chekhovian touch: Henry Goodman knocked, and while he waited as the lights dimmed, a dog was heard barking in the distance.

The Shylock return must be illegal in Canada – from Guthrie onwards, no Ontario production has included it.

ACT 2, SCENE 7

[**2.7**]   *Enter* PORTIA *with* [*the Prince of*] MOROCCO *and both their trains*

PORTIA Go, draw aside the curtains and discover
           The several caskets to this noble prince.
           Now make your choice.
MOROCCO This first of gold, who this inscription bears,
           'Who chooseth me, shall gain what many men desire.'   5

---

osd This scene is frequently combined with 2.1 (see pp. 125–6).

1–2 In the Elizabethan theatre, the caskets would probably have been in the discovery area of the tiring house – these lines are unnecessary when 2.7 follows on from 2.1, or when the caskets are already in view, and are often omitted.

  The most elaborate casket entrance was in Caird's production (see p. 69); Serban's caskets were large spheres wheeled about on platforms; behind each sphere was a warped mirror, giving the suitors comically distorted views of themselves while they contemplated their choice. More conventionally, servants hold the caskets: Guthrie had each servingwoman dressed in the colour of her casket (Edinborough, 'Shakespeare Confirmed', p. 438); Messina had three black boys in Moorish garb place the caskets on a marble table; for Zhang Qi-hong, 'the lead casket was held in the wooing scenes by a simply dressed peasant girl first seen as a silent spectator on the Rialto', while 'the gold casket, in steep and vulgar contrast, was borne by levantine/oriental belly dancers' (Brockbank, 'Shakespeare Renaissance', p. 197).

3 Crosse praises Ellen Terry's Portia for 'the dignity of her bearing towards Morocco, and in her nervous anxiety while he is making his choice; the latter of course repeated during the scene with Bassanio' (*Diaries*, vol. II, p. 2). Komisarjevsky placed Portia on a level eight feet above the downstage area where Morocco stood, to accentuate the distance between the world of Morocco and that of Belmont (Mennen, 'Theodore Komisarjevsky's Production', p. 390). Barton chose to have a symbolic rope of silver, gold and lead placed over Sinead Cusack's lap – she 'managed to lose the rope somewhere between Stratford and London' (Cusack, 'Portia', p. 34).

5 Schenk's Morocco polished the casket's lid with his sleeve before reading.

> The second silver, which this promise carries,
> 'Who chooseth me, shall get as much as he deserves.'
> This third dull lead, with warning all as blunt,
> 'Who chooseth me, must give and hazard all he hath.'
> How shall I know if I do choose the right?   10
> PORTIA The one of them contains my picture, prince.
> If you choose that, then I am yours withal.
> MOROCCO Some god direct my judgement! Let me see:
> I will survey th'inscriptions back again.
> What says this leaden casket?   15
> 'Who chooseth me, must give and hazard all he hath.'
> Must give – for what? For lead? Hazard for lead!
> This casket threatens: men that hazard all
> Do it in hope of fair advantages.
> A golden mind stoops not to shows of dross;   20
> I'll then nor give nor hazard aught for lead.
> What says the silver with her virgin hue?
> 'Who chooseth me, shall get as much as he deserves.'
> As much as he deserves – pause there, Morocco,
> And weigh thy value with an even hand.   25

12 To Crosse, Florence Saunders, 'was beautiful, gracious, strong, and humorous . . . she was more anxious over Morocco's choice than Arragon's – there was much fear of *his* choosing right' (*Diaries*, vol. VIII, p. 141). Benedict Nightingale said of Lisa Harrow, Barton's Portia when the 1978 production transferred to London, she 'is the first Portia I've seen who is actually breathless with fear that someone other than Bassanio may plump for the correct casket . . . in fact, she looks as if she might throw up' (*NS* 4 May 1979). In Nunn's production, Derbhle Crotty spoke with genuine hope that Morocco would choose wisely; she kneeled on a hassock during the three casket scenes.

13–60 Morocco's choosing speech is the longest in the play, packed with rhetorical complexities and dealing with important themes. Yet it is usually abbreviated, sent up, or both. Charles Kean, although boasting of Morocco's return, omitted all but seven of forty-eight lines. Music has played a part in this sequence – Guthrie had the soft singing of a choir assist Lorne Greene's musings; Portia and Nerissa sang the inscriptions, with Morocco listening silently, in Serban's production.

13 Thacker's Ray Fearon, with 'a perfect Oxford accent . . . has all the comic poise of the mock-Anglicized Englishman, [but] this civilized appearance soon disappears when he fears he might lose Portia' (Cheyette, *TLS* 11 June 1993). At the Globe in 1998, Kathryn Pogson entered the annals of coarse acting by crossing herself as Morocco began to speak.

21 Joan Plowright smiled here, making clear that she knew which casket had her picture.

If thou be'st rated by thy estimation
Thou dost deserve enough; and yet enough
May not extend so far as to the lady;
And yet to be afeared of my deserving
Were but a weak disabling of myself.   30
As much as I deserve: why, that's the lady.
I do in birth deserve her, and in fortunes,
In graces, and in qualities of breeding:
But more than these, in love I do deserve.
What if I strayed no farther, but chose here?   35
Let's see once more this saying graved in gold:
'Who chooseth me, shall gain what many men desire.'
Why, that's the lady; all the world desires her.
From the four corners of the earth they come
To kiss this shrine, this mortal breathing saint.   40
The Hyrcanian deserts and the vasty wilds
Of wide Arabia are as throughfares now
For princes to come view fair Portia.
The watery kingdom, whose ambitious head
Spits in the face of heaven, is no bar   45
To stop the foreign spirits, but they come
As o'er a brook to see fair Portia.
One of these three contains her heavenly picture.
Is't like that lead contains her? 'Twere damnation
To think so base a thought; it were too gross   50
To rib her cerecloth in the òbscure grave.
Or shall I think in silver she's immured,
Being ten times undervalued to tried gold?
O sinful thought! Never so rich a gem
Was set in worse than gold. They have in England   55

34 Omambala said this to Crotty with such genuine feeling that it was easy to see why she was
    infatuated.
38–59 Cut by Miller, reinforcing his parodic approach to the scene.
39–40 Hakeem Kae-Kazim kissed Deborah Findlay's hand; he then started working his way up her
    arm (Bulman, *Shakespeare in Performance*, p. 136). Findlay remarks that the scene is less
    about racial than sexual politics: 'We felt that Morocco would treat a wife as his property,
    appropriate her physically, so there was a bit of manhandling in the scene which Portia
    reacted against. This may have been seen as reacting against his colour but it is much more
    to do with being treated as a sexual object' (Findlay, 'Portia', p. 58).

A coin that bears the figure of an angel
Stampèd in gold; but that's insculped upon:
But here an angel in a golden bed
Lies all within. Deliver me the key:
Here do I choose, and thrive I as I may.   60
PORTIA There take it, prince, and if my form lie there,
Then I am yours.
                        [*Morocco unlocks the gold casket*]
MOROCCO   O hell! What have we here?
A carrion death, within whose empty eye
There is a written scroll. I'll read the writing.
            'All that glisters is not gold;   65
            Often have you heard that told.
            Many a man his life hath sold
            But my outside to behold.
            Gilded tombs do worms infold.
            Had you been as wise as bold,   70
            Young in limbs, in judgement old,
            Your answer had not been inscrolled.
            Fare you well, your suit is cold.'
Cold indeed, and labour lost;
Then farewell heat, and welcome frost.   75
Portia, adieu; I have too grieved a heart
To take a tedious leave: thus losers part.
                        Exit [*Morocco with his train*]
PORTIA A gentle riddance! Draw the curtains, go.
Let all of his complexion choose me so.
                        Exeunt. [*A flourish of cornets*]

---

62 Komisarjevsky's Morocco 'said "O hell, what have we here" as though he were a motorist who
   had just discovered a flat tire' (Mennen, 'Theodore Komisarjevsky's Production', p. 391).

63 Terry Hands's 1971 production had 'large and imaginatively furnished' caskets, the golden
   one containing, 'beneath a golden effigy of a recumbent girl, a complete skeleton, as though
   it was Tutankhamen's sarcophagus' (Esslin, *PP* 1972). John Caird's crane-borne gold casket
   also had a life-size skeleton, 'suggesting [Portia's] father was a singularly malign practical
   joker' (Billington, *Gdn* 11 April 1984).

74 'Novelli's Morocco shut down the lid of the casket with an audible sound before beginning
   "cold indeed", etc.' (*pmt* Ames[1]).

78–9 We do not know how the Elizabethans would have reacted to Portia's comment, and for
   much of the eighteenth and nineteenth centuries, Morocco was not in the play at all, but

today this couplet is a pointer to how a production does or does not confront the question of racial and religious prejudice. Lois Harvey was 'never more sincere than when she dismisses the Prince of Morocco, her failed wooer, with a sneer about his "complexion" ' (Nightingale, *Times* 2 August 1991); Nichola McAuliffe made the 'unthinkingly spiteful remark of a heroine who gradually goes on to learn, among other things, racial sensitivity as the play proceeds' (Macaulay, *FT* 10 July 1999).

   With the contemporary theatre's greater use of interracial casting, this remark can take on extra resonance if Nerissa or another member of Portia's household is black. Irving Wardle noted Caird's lack of consistency in having Portia 'triumphantly' declare her feelings, only to exit 'affectionately, arm in arm, with [Josette Simon,] her black maid Nerissa' (*Times* 11 April 1984). In the same year, Lamos also had a black Nerissa, but Caroline Clay 'glared in disapproval' at Portia (Brantley, *NYT* 29 October 1989). Kahn had another of Portia's maids played by a black actress; she was clearly offended by Portia's jibe (Mahon, 'Holbrook Triumphs', p. 15), as was Alexander's black Stephano (Billington, *Gdn* 1 May 1987).

   Thacker 'neatly sanitized' Portia 'by the cutting of her vicious final comment on Morocco' (Holland, *English Shakespeares*, p. 166); Crotty spoke the couplet through tears, trying to convince herself that she did not really want the handsome Omambala for a husband.

79sd Miller had no exit, the action going directly to 2.9. As Serban's Morocco exited, an absurdly chubby Arragon, wearing a red and yellow matador costume, made his entrance to loud Spanish music. Winthrop Ames omitted Arragon, and inserted 2.9.83–94, announcing Bassanio's arrival: Nerissa said 'Bassanio?', and 'Portia, who has been looking off right, turns suddenly with a look of happy understanding as the curtain falls' (*pmt* Ames[2]).

ACT 2, SCENE 8

[2.8] *Enter* SALARINO *and* SOLANIO

SALARINO Why, man, I saw Bassanio under sail,
    With him is Gratiano gone along;
    And in their ship I am sure Lorenzo is not.
SOLANIO The villain Jew with outcries raised the Duke,
    Who went with him to search Bassanio's ship.   5
SALARINO He came too late, the ship was under sail.
    But there the Duke was given to understand
    That in a gondola were seen together
    Lorenzo and his amorous Jessica.
    Besides, Antonio certified the Duke   10
    They were not with Bassanio in his ship.

The nineteenth-century actor-managers, even when including Arragon's scene, shortened
2.8 and combined it with 3.1, placing the action in one of their street locations. For
modern-dress productions, a café or bar is a common locale: Maraden placed the scene at
the same restaurant used for 1.3, but this time there were blackshirts sitting at another table,
who laughed and applauded when Solanio imitated Shylock at 2.8.15–22.
 Crosse enjoyed the Croydon Repertory's modern-dress production of 1935: 'the happiest
application of modernity was the appearance of the Sallies in 2.8 (played straight on from
2.6) in evening dress and comic noses, as coming home drunk from the Carnival. This was
comically done, and reminded me of the similar scene . . . in *Trilby*' (*Diaries*, vol. XV, p. 109).
Over sixty years later, Kahn's Salerio/Salarino, Sean Arbuckle, remained in his 'drag' outfit
from the 2.6 carnival, and Serban's Salads were also in their masquerade costumes for a
combined 2.8 and 3.1. Thacker placed 2.8 in a wine bar, where the Salads were joined by
secretaries and other office workers. Miller omitted the scene entirely.

8–9 In Nunn's production, Peter de Jersey read this information from the gossip column of a
newspaper.

SOLANIO I never heard a passion so confused,
So strange, outrageous, and so variable,
As the dog Jew did utter in the streets:
'My daughter! O my ducats! O my daughter!   15
Fled with a Christian! O my Christian ducats!
Justice! The law! My ducats and my daughter!
A sealèd bag, two sealèd bags of ducats,
Of double ducats, stolen from me by my daughter!
And jewels – two stones, two rich and precious stones,   20
Stolen by my daughter! Justice! Find the girl!
She hath the stones upon her and the ducats!'
SALARINO Why, all the boys in Venice follow him,
Crying his stones, his daughter, and his ducats.
SOLANIO Let good Antonio look he keep his day,   25
Or he shall pay for this.
SALARINO Marry, well remembered:
I reasoned with a Frenchman yesterday

12–22 While Maraden limited Solanio's audience to a couple of blackshirts, Schenk, also placing the scene outdoors at an inn, gave him a large crowd of listeners who added much loud comment. Many Solanios mock Shylock's accent: Crosse saw Atkins's Old Vic *Merchant* in 1924 and wrote in his diary, 'I was amused to hear Solanio, when imitating [Shylock] in 2.8, say "mit" for "with" ' (*Diaries*, vol. VIII, p. 137). Years later, Ian Lavender, Hall's London Solanio, spoke in the manner of 'lousy comedians [who] tell Cohen jokes' (Nathan, *JC* 9 June 1989).

Gregory Doran, who played Solanio for Bill Alexander in 1987 before directing the play himself ten years later, notes that 'Solanio takes enormous pleasure in the terrible suffering of Shylock, raging through the streets, bereft both of his daughter and a large portion of his wealth. He launches into his cruel diatribe with gleeful relish'. Doran worked to imitate Antony Sher's Turkish accent and his 'rude Turkish gestures, supplied by Jondon Gourkan, one of the RSC stage managers' (G. Doran, 'Solanio', p. 73).

Thacker's Solanio, Tim Hudson, used a broad Yiddish accent, although David Calder spoke perfect 'City' English – a telling reminder that Solanio is hardly a reliable source of what Shylock might have actually said or done.

18–24 Retained in the Bell text, but omitted in the nineteenth century.

23 Serban went to 3.1.18 here. Most productions with a combined 2.8/3.1 make the transfer at 29.

25 As Schenk's Solanio and Salarino leave the inn and walk along the street, we hear the sound of breaking glass – surely an allusion to the horrors of Hitler's *Kristallnacht*. At the scene's end, ruffians carrying sticks run past them to the sound of more shattering glass.

Who told me, in the Narrow Seas that part
The French and English, there miscarri èd   30
A vessel of our country richly fraught.
I thought upon Antonio when he told me,
And wished in silence that it were not his.
SOLANIO You were best to tell Antonio what you hear.
Yet do not suddenly, for it may grieve him,   35
SALARINO A kinder gentleman treads not the earth.
I saw Bassanio and Antonio part:
Bassanio told him he would make some speed
Of his return: he answered, 'Do not so.
Slubber not business for my sake, Bassanio,   40
But stay the very riping of the time;
And for the Jew's bond which he hath of me,
Let it not enter in your mind of love.
Be merry, and employ your chiefest thoughts
To courtship, and such fair ostents of love   45
As shall conveniently become you there.'
And even there, his eye being big with tears,
Turning his face, he put his hand behind him,
And with affection wondrous sensible
He wrung Bassanio's hand, and so they parted.   50

29–54 From Kemble to Irving, the absence of Arragon led to a combined 2.8 and 3.1, the transition
made by cutting these lines (see p. 172). Even when Arragon was included, as in Charles
Kean's version, a combined 2.8/3.1 minimised scene changes, and 29–54 were omitted.

36 Thacker gave the line, 'A kinder gentleman treads not the earth' to a yuppie at the wine bar,
who happened to be black. He was 'very pointedly ignored' by the others, adding to the
picture of Thacker's Venice as a place where racism was always present (Holland, *English
Shakespeares*, pp. 165–6).

39–46 In Nunn's production, Mark Umbers did an excellent imitation of Antonio's 'flat northern
vowels' (Smallwood, *SS* 2000).

49–51 Several directors have made use of these lines to suggest or reinforce the homosexual
theme. Lamos, in his Hartford production, had Salerio/Salarino say 'He wrung Bassanio's
. . . hand', the pause (with a knowing look at Solanio) an invitation to substitute another
part of the body. Solanio struck a limp-wristed pose when replying 'I think he only loves the
world for him' (King, 'Shylock', p. 63). Umbers accompanied 51 with similar gestures; in
Thacker's wine bar, the line 'was greeted with mock campy "oohs"' (Jackson, *SQ* 1994);
Alexander had Salerio/Salarino move next to the reclining Solanio and make a sexual
advance during this dialogue (Bulman, *Shakespeare in Performance*, p. 126); Edelstein had
them exchange a very long kiss.

SOLANIO I think he only loves the world for him.
   I pray thee let us go and find him out
   And quicken his embracèd heaviness
   With some delight or other.
SALARINO   Do we so.

                 Exeunt

ACT 2, SCENE 9

[2.9]   *Enter* NERISSA *and a Servitor*

NERISSA   Quick, quick, I pray thee, draw the curtain straight.
The Prince of Arragon hath tane his oath,
And comes to his election presently.

Even after Charles Kean reintroduced Arragon, both Irving and Benson chose to omit him, and there is little performance history of this scene to deal with until the twentieth century (as late as 1928, Winthrop Ames presented a *Merchant* without 2.9).

Nearly always, Arragon has been played for laughs, with some historical justification, since Spaniards are often a figure of fun in the plays of Shakespeare and his contemporaries. Eric House, Guthrie's Arragon, 'was a solemn black-suited figure whose movements were as carefully choreographed as any ballet dancer's might be. He was accompanied by a group of tutors who looked as though they had wandered away from a nearby production of *The Barber of Seville*' (Edinborough, 'Shakespeare Confirmed', p. 438).

In Benthall's Old Vic production, Dudley Jones was a figure whose 'foppish manners, sudden affected laughs, and exaggerated heel-clicking (all echoed studiously by his attendants), was absurdly comic' (Clarke, *Shakespeare at the Old Vic*, np). Gold's Arragon, Peter Gale, entered with a purple-robed priest, who remained at the back and out of close camera range, and a dwarf, who provided much comic byplay. Ian Richardson, Langham's Arragon of 1960, brought his mother along to supervise the choice of caskets (Findlater, *FT* 14 April 1960).

For Edelstein, Walker Jones wore ridiculous platform shoes, while Serban's Prince, Remo Airaldi, 'stole the show. Decorated with medals, holding ball and scepter, he sagged and lolled, strapped in yellow-orange satin tights, with red sash and hose, in absurd competition with a gross dildo bulging from his left trouser leg. A jiggling flamenco toreador, arms up and down, fingers snapping, he spoke riotously in a squeaky Taco-Bell voice' (Cook, *SB* 1999). Raymond Coulthard, Nunn's Arragon, was also a walking catalogue of everything absurdly Spanish, accompanied by his own private flamenco guitarist.

[*A flourish of cornets.*] *Enter* [*the Prince of*] ARRAGON,
his train, and PORTIA

PORTIA Behold, there stand the caskets, noble prince.
　　　　If you choose that wherein I am contained, 5
　　　　Straight shall our nuptial rites be solemnised;
　　　　But if you fail, without more speech, my lord,
　　　　You must be gone from hence immediately.

Dennis Edwards was more a Prussian than a Spanish Prince for Barton in 1978, complete with an Iron Cross; he busily pawed Portia while he contemplated the caskets (Levin, *ST* 21 May 1978). Thacker's Robert Portal was in 'Franco-like' military uniform, 'but was not egregiously vain' (Jackson, *SQ* 1994). Baldridge put Gordon Gould in a wheelchair; Miller's Charles Kay was able to walk about unassisted, but was so old as to border on blindness and senility – he looked (and sounded) more Scottish than Spanish.

While all of these Princes were too ridiculous to be taken seriously as suitors, Hall and Plaza inserted a note of menace. John Simon denounced Hall's idea of dressing Arragon and his attendants in

> the ludicrous garb the Spanish Inquisition inflicted on the heretics it burned at the stake; dunce cap and all, but with the added bizarreness of little red tongues of flame forming an ornamental border around the hems of their white penitential gowns. Not only is this concept disgusting in its decorative cruelty, it is also dumb: Why would a suitor remind Portia of the horrors being perpetrated in his country, as if they were a tourist attraction? (*New York* 8 January 1990)

In Madrid, Plaza's Arragon was 'a macabre specter of Inquisitorial Spain', speaking in an effeminate voice 'much at odds with the sober Gregorian chants that accompany his entourage [and] with his severe and formal garb, cartwheel ruff and black velvet doublet slashed with purple inserts' (Fischer, *SB* 1995).

osd In Max Reinhardt's Berlin production,

> the arrival of the Prince of Arragon involved introductory trumpetcalls, the gathering of the servants, the unrolling of a carpet, the ceremonial placement of Portia and her revenue, the arrival of a magnificently decorated boat, the dignified disembarkation of the prince with his retinue in a replica of full Spanish ceremonial, the exchange of presents, and the formal singing of tenors. After this, Portia began to speak her welcome. (Williams, *Shakespeare on the German Stage*, p. 211)

1–3 Miller had 2.9 follow on from 2.7, so these lines were given to a maid.

4–8 Assuming that Arragon spoke only Spanish, Derbhle Crotty accompanied her remarks with broad sign-language gestures.

ARRAGON I am enjoined by oath to observe three things:
      First, never to unfold to anyone   10
      Which casket 'twas I chose; next, if I fail
      Of the right casket, never in my life
      To woo a maid in way of marriage; lastly,
      If I do fail in fortune of my choice,
      Immediately to leave you and be gone.   15
PORTIA To these injunctions everyone doth swear
      That comes to hazard for my worthless self.
ARRAGON And so have I addressed me. Fortune now
      To my heart's hope! Gold, silver, and base lead.
      'Who chooseth me, must give and hazard all he hath.'   20
      You shall look fairer ere I give or hazard.
      What says the golden chest? Ha, let me see:
      'Who chooseth me, shall gain what many men desire.'
      What many men desire: that 'many' may be meant
      By the fool multitude that choose by show,   25
      Not learning more than the fond eye doth teach,
      Which pries not to th'interior, but like the martlet
      Builds in the weather on the outward wall,
      Even in the force and road of casualty.
      I will not choose what many men desire,   30
      Because I will not jump with common spirits,
      And rank me with the barbarous multitudes.
      Why then, to thee, thou silver treasure house:
      Tell me once more what title thou dost bear.
      'Who chooseth me, shall get as much as he deserves.'   35

19 Gale and Coulthard caricatured the Spanish 'h', as in expressions such as 'To my *khart's khope*'. David Warburton, Maraden's foppish Prince, brought his own portrait with him, and addressed his speech to it (Liston, 'The Merchant', p. 87).

20, 23, 35 Serban had Portia and Nerissa sing the inscriptions, as in 2.7.

23–30 Charles Kay's doddering old Arragon pulled a knotted handkerchief from his pocket, but forgot what he was supposed to remember (Brown, *SS* 1971).

32 Like Kay, Kahn's Arragon, Emery Battis, was nearly blind; to this he added an inability to say 'r' – hence 'And wank me with the babawous multitudes'.

34–48 Kay took his tea from Plowright here, and proceeded to add lump after lump of sugar. He eventually handed the cup back to her without having drunk any.

35 Coulthard made a big show of saying 'chooseth' properly.

And well said too, for who shall go about
To cozen Fortune and be honourable
Without the stamp of merit? Let none presume
To wear an undeservèd dignity.
O, that estates, degrees, and offices, 40
Were not derived corruptly, and that clear honour
Were purchased by the merit of the wearer!
How many then should cover that stand bare!
How many be commanded that command!
How much low peasantry would then be gleaned 45
From the true seed of honour, and how much honour
Picked from the chaff and ruin of the times
To be new varnished! Well, but to my choice.
'Who chooseth me, shall get as much as he deserves.'
I will assume desert. Give me a key for this, 50
And instantly unlock my fortunes here.
      [*Arragon unlocks the silver casket*]
PORTIA Too long a pause for that which you find there.
ARRAGON What's here? The portrait of a blinking idiot
Presenting me a schedule! I will read it.
How much unlike art thou to Portia! 55
How much unlike my hopes and my deservings.
'Who chooseth me, shall have as much as he deserves.'
Did I deserve no more than a fool's head?
Is that my prize? Are my deserts no better?
PORTIA To offend and judge are distinct offices, 60
And of opposèd natures.
ARRAGON   What is here?

36 In Williams's production, Donald Burton took a long pause before 'And well said too'; the audience was 'reminded of the danger incurred by daring to respond to the riddle that protects Portia' (Brown, *SS* 1966).

53 Kay said 'what's this?' – the blinking idiot's portrait was a mirror in which the near-sighted Arragon saw himself. Serban also used a mirror, but this was a large warped one behind the spherical casket. Hands's elaborate silver casket held 'a huge jack-in-the-box fool's head' (Esslin, *PP* 1972).

59 Battis uttered a delightful 'Is that my pwize?'

60–1 Barton's 1978 Portia, Marjorie Bland, delivered these lines as a 'tart rebuke' to Arragon after he 'complained with furious wounded pride and no trace of humour, "Did I deserve no more than a fool's head?" ' (Warren, *SS* 1979).

[He reads]

'The fire seven times tried this;
Seven times tried that judgement is
That did never choose amiss.
Some there be that shadows kiss;   65
Such have but a shadow's bliss.
There be fools alive iwis
Silvered o'er, and so was this.
Take what wife you will to bed,
I will ever be your head.   70
So be gone, you are sped.'
Still more fool I shall appear
By the time I linger here.
With one fool's head I came to woo,
But I go away with two.   75
Sweet, adieu; I'll keep my oath,
Patiently to bear my wroth.

              [Exit Arragon with his train]

PORTIA Thus hath the candle singed the moth.
O, these deliberate fools! When they do choose
They have the wisdom by their wit to lose.   80
NERISSA The ancient saying is no heresy:
'Hanging and wiving goes by destiny.'
PORTIA Come draw the curtain, Nerissa.

Enter a MESSENGER

MESSENGER Where is my lady?
PORTIA   Here. What would my lord?
MESSENGER Madam, there is alighted at your gate   85

62–71 Eric House's 'deadpan zombie-like Prince of Arragon' for Guthrie read the 'schedule' from 'a
piece of ticker tape coming from the mouth of a miniature statue' (Hewes, *SR* 23 July 1955).
The lines were alternately spoken by Arragon, and sung by Portia and Nerissa, in Serban's
production.

62 Lazaro Perez, Lamos's very Latino Prince, opened the silver casket with a loud 'What *i-i-i-s*
this' (Cook, *SB* 1994).

76–7 In both Gold's and Nunn's productions, Portia made fun of Arragon's *español* 'wroth' by
mispronouncing 'moth' in the next line.

85–94 Charles Kean made Balthazar the messenger; many directors since have done the same,
although Nunn gave the line to one of Portia's maids. Komisarjevsky had Portia on a raised

        A young Venetian, one that comes before
        To signify th'approaching of his lord,
        From whom he bringeth sensible regreets:
        To wit, besides commends and courteous breath,
        Gifts of rich value. Yet I have not seen   90
        So likely an ambassador of love.
        A day in April never came so sweet
        To show how costly summer was at hand
        As this forespurrer comes before his lord.
PORTIA No more I pray thee, I am half afeared   95
        Thou wilt say anon he is some kin to thee,
        Thou spend'st such highday wit in praising him.
        Come, come, Nerissa, for I long to see
        Quick Cupid's post that comes so mannerly.
NERISSA Bassanio, Lord Love, if thy will it be!   100
                                   Exeunt

upper stage during 2.7 and 2.9; as the Messenger described the 'ambassador of love', the upper stage came down to stage level –'love literally lowering Portia from her pedestal' (Mennen, 'Theodore Komisarjevsky's Production', p. 391). As Langham's Messenger made his announcement, others brought in many gifts from Bassanio, including a music box that played under the ensuing dialogue.

100 Miller's butler stared down at the leaden casket as the scene ended in the TV version, reinforcing (not very subtly) that everyone knew which was the right casket.

ACT 3, SCENE 1

3.[1] *Enter* SOLANIO *and* SALARINO

SOLANIO Now, what news on the Rialto?
SALARINO Why, yet it lives there unchecked that Antonio hath a

Michael Billington regards this as 'the key scene where you really know what a Shylock is made of' (*The Modern Actor*, p. 85). Since his last appearance in 2.5, we have seen Jessica's elopement, and have heard from the Salads of Shylock's reaction. There has also been bad news concerning some Venetian shipping (2.8.27–33), and when we hear in this scene that Antonio's ships have foundered, the Jessica–Lorenzo plot and the bond plot merge into Shylock's determination to have his revenge.

    Miller cut 2.8 completely, so Shylock's running through the streets, as reported, never occurred in that production. Thacker cut most of lines 1–18, retaining only enough to establish Antonio's losses, and then moved with a lighting change to Shylock's office for the Tubal sequence, before returning to 19–57.

1–18 The pace of these passages can depend on whether or not this is a separate scene, or is combined with 2.8 (see p. 162). When Arragon intervenes, or there is some other rearrangement, 3.1 takes on the quality of new and urgent developments – this was evident in Langham's 1989 production, when the leisurely gossip of 2.8 was replaced by the quick pace of important news being delivered. Barry James, in Miller's television version, read 2–6 as a newspaper report; Thacker placed his Salads on an upper gallery, in their office, so that news of Antonio's ships could arrive by fax (Taylor, *Ind* 8 June 1993). Kelly had Salarino's announcement preceded by a radio weather report (Hopkins, *SB* 1994), and Peter Sellars turned 1–18 into a 'duet scene [with] a creepy pair of breakfast TV hosts', Sellars pointing to 'the terrible way in which modern living is indeed being geared for perpetual broadcast' (Macaulay, *FT* 18 November 1994). Nunn put the scene in dim light, with the Salads dressed in overcoats, as Solanio scanned the lagoon with binoculars.

2 The most common way of joining 2.8 to 3.1 was to go from 2.8.28 to here: 'I reasoned with a Frenchman yesterday / that Antonio hath a ship . . .'.

ship of rich lading wrecked on the Narrow Seas; the Goodwins I
think they call the place – a very dangerous flat, and fatal, where
the carcases of many a tall ship lie buried, as they say, if my   5
gossip Report be an honest woman of her word.

SOLANIO I would she were as lying a gossip in that as ever knapped
ginger or made her neighbours believe she wept for the death of
a third husband. But it is true, without any slips of prolixity, or
crossing the plain highway of talk, that the good Antonio, the   10
honest Antonio – O that I had a title good enough to keep his
name company! –

SALARINO Come, the full stop.

SOLANIO Ha, what sayest thou? Why, the end is, he hath lost a
ship.   15

SALARINO I would it might prove the end of his losses.

SOLANIO Let me say 'amen' betimes, lest the devil cross my prayer,
for here he comes in the likeness of a Jew.

18   Schenk's Salarino and Solanio quickly removed the rings from their fingers and put them in
      their pockets – obviously they were stolen from Shylock.

18sd Lichtenberg describes Macklin's entrance:

> In the scene where he first misses his daughter, he comes on hatless, with disordered
> hair, some locks a finger long standing on end, as if raised by a breath of wind from
> the gallows, so distracted was his demeanour. Both his hands are clenched and his
> movements abrupt and convulsive. To see a deceiver, who is usually calm and resolute,
> in such a state of agitation is terrible. (*Visits*, p. 40)

Irving entered 'hurriedly and distractedly, his hair streaming, without a cap, his shirt torn
open, he gesticulated wildly at them and was evidently frantic with grief, of which the first
outburst was hardly over' (Irving, *Henry Irving*, p. 341). Helpmann 'put aside his great black
cloak and his golden rings and chains, and wore old and tattered garments of mourning'
(Clarke, *Shakespeare at the Old Vic*, np). Olivier 'begins the scene on the balcony of his
house, eavesdropping on Solanio's news of Antonio's misfortunes and feverishly searching
for his daughter. He comes down to street level visibly distracted and confused. He rests for
support on a side rail with his back to us and is obviously more obsessed by news of his
daughter's flight than anything else' (Billington, *The Modern Actor*, pp. 85–6).

Ian McDiarmid describes his interpretation: 'He enters in the first scene of act three,
dragging his gown, hair unkempt, half crazed with grief, fury, and exhaustion and
encounters the two Christian sycophants. "You knew". Suddenly it all becomes clear.
Something in Solanio's tone brings everything into focus. The Christian plot to steal his
daughter was a premeditated act' (McDiarmid, 'Shylock', p. 52).

Enter SHYLOCK

How now, Shylock, what news among the merchants?

SHYLOCK You knew, none so well, none so well as you, of my   20
daughter's flight.

SALARINO That's certain; I for my part knew the tailor that made
the wings she flew withal.

SOLANIO And Shylock for his own part knew the bird was fledged,
and then it is the complexion of them all to leave the dam.   25

SHYLOCK She is damned for it.

SALARINO That's certain – if the devil may be her judge.

SHYLOCK My own flesh and blood to rebel!

SOLANIO Out upon it, old carrion! Rebels it at these years?

SHYLOCK I say my daughter is my flesh and my blood.   30

SALARINO There is more difference between thy flesh and hers than
between jet and ivory; more between your bloods than there is

---

It is not a given, however, that Shylock should enter in a distracted or disordered state.
Discussing the scene with fellow Shylock David Suchet in *Playing Shakespeare*, Patrick
Stewart notes that Shakespeare 'describes Shylock at the height of his passion off-stage.
We never see it. It's all reported by someone else. So the man that we see is someone who
. . . has been over that hill and is now down on the other side.'

Suchet agrees, 'Yes: I'm on my way home, I'm finished, if [Salarino] and Solanio didn't
speak, I'd go straight off the other side of the stage' (Barton, *Playing Shakespeare*,
p. 177).

A common approach taken in recent years is for a tumultuous entrance, with Shylock
followed by a crowd that taunts, or even physically molests him. The first to do this was
Augustin Daly in 1898, when Sidney Herbert entered 'pursued and jeered at by a mob of
children' (Sprague, *Shakespeare and the Actors*, p. 23). Gregory Doran, Alexander's
Solanio, recalls that Antony Sher 'arrived on stage like a whirlwind, bruised and bloodied
from the street boys' catapults, dazed with grief. The Salads, bored with each other, and
tetchy, fall upon this new distraction like vultures on a rattlesnake. We taunted and sneered
at the Jew, shoving him between us, and knocked him to the ground' (Doran, 'Solanio', pp.
73–4). In Doran's own production, Philip Voss arrived in the same condition, although the
assault took place off-stage. David Calder, having already played the latter half of the scene
in Thacker's production, was already intent on revenge before he confronted the Salads.

29 This is one of several indecent puns retained in the eighteenth-century Bell text, but omitted
in the more prudish nineteenth century – the same is true of 31–3a. In Gold's BBC
production, John Rhys-Davies lunged for Shylock's genitals, 'as though Shylock had spoken
of sexual desire' (Perret, 'Shakespeare and Anti-Semitism', p. 156).

between red wine and Rhenish. But tell us, do you hear whether
Antonio have had any loss at sea or no?

SHYLOCK There I have another bad match: a bankrupt, a prodigal,   35
who dare scarce show his head on the Rialto, a beggar that was
used to come so smug upon the mart. Let him look to his bond. He
was wont to call me usurer; let him look to his bond. He was wont
to lend money for a Christian courtesy; let him look to his bond.

SALARINO Why, I am sure if he forfeit thou wilt not take his flesh.   40
What's that good for?

SHYLOCK To bait fish withal; if it will feed nothing else, it will feed my

---

35–9 Booth's 'ferocious element . . . was not revealed until the street scene, in which his
exhibition of mixed emotions – wounded avarice, rage, scorn, revengeful hate, and
domestic grief – was masterful. His "Let him look to his bond!" was pregnant with
concentrated fury and savage anticipation' (Towse, *Sixty Years*, p. 189). Irving delivered
'the repeated phrase . . . through the teeth with a concentrated venom that has the
effect commonly called "making one's blood run cold" ' (*Chicago Times*, qtd *Irv.Amer*,
p. 27).

    So it was with Olivier. In one of his great moments, he interrupted Salerio/Salarino with a
roar: pausing for breath after 'mart', a bell tolling in the distance, he then turned around,
and his facial expression (a head–shoulders shot in the television version) was one of Dr
Jekyll becoming Mr Hyde. As he slowly said 'let him look to his bond' with a madman-like
passion, Olivier showed that he had made his decision to exact the penalty at that moment.

38–9 In Philip Voss's reading, 'not until the second time that he delivers the warning to Antonio,
"let him look to his bond", does [Shylock] realise what this might mean, and not until the
third time does a plan begin to form in his mind' (Nightingale, *Times* 12 December 1997).
Peter O'Toole 'waited for the third "to his bond" before fully realizing and uttering his
hatred, slowly and quietly' (Brown, *SS* 1961).

42 Winter records that at 'To bait fish', Mansfield, 'for a time, pointed toward the canal, by way
of illustration' (Sprague, *Shakespeare and the Actors*, p. 23). Miller omitted 'if it will feed
nothing else it will feed my revenge' (*pmt*).

42–57 As many commentators have noted, this famous passage is more a denunciation of Antonio
and justification of revenge than a plea for religious tolerance, although Stewart's view that
'it is a calculating, coldblooded justification' (Barton, *Playing Shakespeare*, p. 177) is surely
an overstatement (in *Playing Shakespeare*, Stewart took the speech at a fast and nervous
pace).

    Macready delivered 'the beautiful expostulation . . . with a passionate earnestness that
was touching, notwithstanding the fierce spirit of vengeance that breathed through it'
(*Spectator* 12 October 1839). Gordon Crosse was disappointed with Irving, who commenced

revenge. He hath disgraced me, and hindered me half a million,
laughed at my losses, mocked at my gains, scorned my nation,
thwarted my bargains, cooled my friends, heated mine enemies –   45
and what's his reason? I am a Jew. Hath not a Jew eyes? Hath not a
Jew hands, organs, dimensions, senses, affections, passions? Fed

in 'too high and passionate' a manner, and therefore could not build on his beginning
(*Diaries*, vol. I, p. 174).

   Frederick Valk's delivery was 'the logical working of a keen mind, not as a plea for pity,
for he never stooped to the Venetians . . . resembling a bearded Old Testament prophet, he
roared for revenge and justice' (Griffin, *TA* 1955). Valk once fell on his entrance, and the
stage manager noted in the promptbook that it was his 'best job on the speech yet'.

   In *Playing Shakespeare*, when Salarino laughs on 'To bait fish withal', an infuriated David
Suchet slams his walking stick down on the table in front of him, and delivers the speech
with fierce anger; Avner Hyskiahu, in Yzraeli's production, snarled at 'the two *goyim* . . .
practically spitting in their faces' (Oz, 'Transformations', p. 68); Ron Leibman was no
different, offering 'machine-gun fire, spat out with blistering force that only years of pentup
rage could conjure' (Gerrard, *Variety* 7 February 1995).

   Not all Shylocks address the Salads. Brian Bedford spoke to 'the mocking ragamuffins
who've been taunting him in the streets . . . grabbing one of them by the lapels' (Richards,
WP 4 May 1988); Tree had 'a party of Jews on the stage . . . to give Shylock their moral
support (Crosse, *Diaries*, vol. IV, p. 108).

   In Sellars's production, Paul Butler's delivery was 'straight to a video-camera, and relayed
on the fifteen screens dotted around the stage and auditorium; very measured, it sounds
like something Shylock had said a million times before' (Macaulay, *FT* 18 November 1994).
Hall's direction was for Solanio to spit at Dustin Hoffman just before this speech. Gordon
Gould, who played Solanio in New York, told me that one evening he dined on spicy
Chinese food, and was unable to raise any saliva at the key moment – Hoffman, who was
also co-producer, instructed cast members to refrain from Chinese cuisine for the
remainder of the run.

46 Olivier changed 'what's' to 'what is his reason'. At 'I am a Jew', Sher 'erupted . . . he blasted
   his anger, white hot, into the air. He seemed to tower with ferocity, fuelled with all the
   suffering of the Jewish nation' (Doran, 'Solanio', p. 75). Hal Holbrook was knocked over by
   the mob; helped to his feet by two Jewish children, he gave the remainder of the speech
   with his arms around their shoulders. Gold's no less strange staging for the BBC was to have
   the Salads laughing at Shylock, making obscene gestures and manhandling him as he
   spoke.

47 Will LeBow, doing the entire scene as a mad comic routine, pointed to his genitals at

with the same food, hurt with the same weapons, subject to the same diseases, healed by the same means, warmed and cooled by the same winter and summer as a Christian is? If you prick us, do   50
we not bleed? If you tickle us, do we not laugh? If you poison us, do we not die? And if you wrong us, shall we not revenge? If we are like you in the rest, we will resemble you in that. If a Jew wrong a Christian, what is his humility? Revenge. If a Christian wrong a Jew, what should his sufferance be by Christian example? Why,   55
revenge! The villainy you teach me I will execute, and it shall go hard but I will better the instruction.

'organs'. George Frederick Cooke, 'the avowed disciple of Macklin . . . dwelt pathetically on the word "affections" ' (Winter, *Shakespeare on the Stage*, pp. 138–9).

47b–50 'Fed with the same food . . . winter and summer as a Christian is' was deleted by Miller (of course, strictly speaking, Jews are *not* 'fed with the same food'). Eric Porter, in Williams's production, 'gains a measure of effectiveness by increasing tempo progressively in the last half of [the] speech' (Brown, *SS* 1966).

52 At 'if you wrong us' Sher suddenly grabbed Solanio's stick, and 'with a terrible howl', demanded 'shall we not revenge!' (Doran, 'Solanio' p. 74). LeBow, mocking himself mercilessly up until now, raised his voice 'in sudden anguish and fury'. For the repeated word 'revenge', Olivier devised 'an extraordinary gesture that consists of slapping the right hand into the palm of the left and shooting the thumb of the left hand outwards: it suggests a butcher slapping a piece of meat on to a weighing machine' (Billington, *The Modern Actor*, p. 86).

53b Kortner spoke reflectively, until he flew into a 'roaring rage' at 'If a Jew wrong a Christian', giving each individual word heavy stress (Sehrt, 'Der Shylock', pp. 88–9).

54 Olivier inserted a 'why,' between 'humility' and 'revenge'. LeBow sang 'If a Christian wrong a Jew' as if celebrating Mass.

55 Leibman pointed to the yellow badge on his chest on 'sufferance'.

56–7 Charles Cowden Clarke recalls Edmund Kean's

wonderful eyes flashing out their red sparkles, the body writhing from head to foot, the arms thrown up as witness to the recorded oath of vengeance. The attitude, as the voice, rose to a sublime climax when these words were uttered; then there was a drop, both of person and tone, as he hissed out the closing sentence of deep concentrated malignity. (Furness, *A New Variorum Edition*, p. 128)

Thacker ended the scene with Shylock alone on stage after 'better the instruction'.

Enter a [SERVING]MAN *from Antonio*

SERVINGMAN Gentlemen, my master Antonio is at his house, and
    desires to speak with you both.
SALARINO We have been up and down to seek him.   60

Enter TUBAL

SOLANIO Here comes another of the tribe; a third cannot be
    matched, unless the devil himself turn Jew.
                        Exeunt [*Salarino and Solanio with the Servingman*]
SHYLOCK How now, Tubal, what news from Genoa? Hast thou
    found my daughter?

58–60   The Servingman is often omitted, although he is retained in the Inchbald and Kemble
        editions, under the name of 'Pietro'. Miller shifted the scene 'into a darkened room of
        Shylock's house' for the meeting with Tubal (Sullivan, 'Strumpet Wind', p. 36). As did
        Belasco (see p. 108), he placed a *mezuzah* (the encapsuled parchment scroll of
        Deuteronomy 6.4–9 and 11.13–21), on Shylock's doorpost, and Olivier performed the ritual
        of placing his hand on it as he entered. In what John Gielgud considers a 'brilliant touch',
        Olivier re-entered carrying Jessica's dress (Gielgud, *Acting Shakespeare*, p. 72), though the
        business was dropped for the television version.

60sd   Although he is a 'wealthy Hebrew' who can advance Shylock three thousand ducats,
        Ferdinand Fleck's Tubal in 1788 'was played as a low-caste, peddling Jew', one critic noting
        the 'subtle realism exhibited by Fleck in vulgarising his tone and manner down to Tubal's
        level during his scene with that abased and cringing broker' (Beatty-Kingston, 'Shylock',
        pp. 86–7); Schenk adopted this idea, making Karl Paryla a shabby itinerant peddler,
        carrying a large sack. Tony Church's Tubal, in contrast to Patrick Stewart's seedy Shylock,
        'dressed impeccably and smoked cigars, like the smart Venetians-about-town' (Warren, *SS*
        1979); for Miller, Lewis Jones was 'another top-hatted banker all in black . . . come to offer
        condolences to a grieving friend' (Bulman, *Shakespeare in Performance*, p. 90) – Jones,
        unlike Olivier, did not wear a yarmulke. Thacker made the opposite distinction by giving
        Nick Simons a yarmulke, but having Calder bare-headed in the first half of the play.

61–2   Doran's Salads spat on Tubal as he entered; Maraden's much subtler business of having
        some blackshirts tip up the chairs at the café to keep Tubal from being seated was a
        more effective statement. These same blackshirts later 'laugh at Shylock as he reacts
        excruciatingly to a report from Tubal about Jessica's betrayal' (Newell, *SB* 1997).

63ff.   Some Shylocks are remembered most for their playing of this part of the play. Kean is said
        to have been so powerful that the trial was an anti-climax (Lelyveld, *Shylock on the Stage*,
        p. 44), but Irving was 'too restless . . . the violent shaking of the head and one or two similar

TUBAL I often came where I did hear of her, but cannot find her.   65
SHYLOCK Why there, there, there, there! A diamond gone cost me
two thousand ducats in Frankfurt! The curse never fell upon
our nation till now, I never felt it till now. Two thousand ducats
in that, and other precious, precious jewels! I would my

things suggesting snappishness rather than passion' (Knight, *Theatrical Notes*, p. 305).
Jacob Adler was 'all a fury of rage and revenge . . . Shylock's dignity and self-mastery are
gone. He shakes his staff at the jeering bystanders. He clutches at Tubal. He barely totters off
the stage' (*GCA, qtd* Berkowitz, 'A True Jewish Jew', p. 79). John Gielgud remembers Ernest
Milton, 'clutching his head in his hands in the Tubal scene of the Merchant at the Old Vic in
the early 1920s, with clouds of white powder floating like a snowstorm against the black
velvet curtains behind him' (*ST* 17 March 1996).

Komisarjevsky played 'the meeting of Shylock and Tubal on a windy night with the sky
behind them an ominous coppery green' (Harris, *qtd* Mennen, 'Theodore Komisarjevsky's
Production', p. 394), the sound of thunder counterpointing the dialogue. Fabia Drake
commented that Randle Ayrton, who as Shylock was uncertain about Komisarjevsky's
staging, was so pleased with this effect during rehearsals that he became much more
amenable to his director's ideas (Mennen, 'Theodore Komisarjevsky's Production',
p. 394).

Peter O'Toole did the scene 'brilliantly . . . allowing the desire for revenge to increase in
direct proportion to his disgust with his daughter's behaviour' (Billington, *The Modern
Actor*, p. 85). Gregory Doran, after his exit as Solanio, 'would always stay to watch the rest of
the scene in the wings', as Sher 'wiped the spittle from Tubal's gabardine, screamed with
fury at his daughter's loss, gasped and panted with disbelief at news of Antonio's
misfortunes, and then beat the air with his fists, hurling his righteous thanks to God' (Doran,
'Solanio', p. 75).

65 Alvin Epstein played Tubal as well as Old Gobbo for Serban. Here he showed a large
'wanted' poster with Jessica's picture.

66 Amongst Crosse's impressions of Hay Petrie in 1924 was that he 'had his "moments"'
though he did not depend on them; one was his grovelling in the dust as Tubal enumerates
Jessica's excesses and springing up with new life when he speaks of Antonio's losses'
(*Diaries*, vol. VIII, p. 139). Leibman chanted 'there, there, there' with powerful effect.

67–8 Irving 'beat his breast slowly with his clenched fist' (Irving, *Henry Irving*, p. 341); Hoffman
and Suchet strongly emphasized the first-person singular: '*I* never felt it till now' (Nathan,
JC 9 June 1989; Cushman, *Obs* 26 April 1981).

69–71 At 'I would my daughter', Kean 'started back, as with a revulsion of paternal feeling from the
horrible image his avarice had conjured up, and borrowing a negative from the next inquiry
("no news of them") gasped an agonizing "No, no, no"' (Fox, *qtd* Lelyveld, *Shylock on the*

daughter were dead at my foot, and the jewels in her ear: would   70
she were hearsed at my foot, and the ducats in her coffin. No
news of them, why so? And I know not what's spent in the
search. Why thou loss upon loss – the thief gone with so much,
and so much to find the thief, and no satisfaction, no revenge,
nor no ill luck stirring but what lights o'my shoulders, no sighs   75
but o'my breathing, no tears but o'my shedding!

Stage, p. 44). Irving also interjected a series of 'no's here', his face hidden in his hands (Irving, *Henry Irving*, p. 341). Schildkraut 'made a small movement of the hand', placing it over his mouth before the curse of 'dead at my foot' could 'tear itself from his throat' (*Morgen Zhurnal, qtd* Berkowitz, 'A True Jewish Jew', p. 87).

This was a shattering moment in Baldridge's production, as Tubal, played by Will Geer, tried to comfort Shylock, and Paul Sparer pounded his fists against his friend's chest. In Miller's stage version, Olivier hurled Jessica's dress to the ground, 'as if the folds of cloth did indeed contain Jessica, and tramples on it as if to exorcise her spirit for ever' (Billington, *The Modern Actor*, p. 85); for television, he threw Jessica's photograph to the floor, smashing it. Kortner 'sounded angry, stubborn and lastly weeping' (Sehrt, 'Der Shylock', p. 89), but the lines were undercut by the weary Tubal taking off his shoes to massage his feet.

Thacker placed the speech at the beginning of the scene: Calder tore open his shirt, 'revealing a Star of David on a chain. The exclamations about the lost ducats seemed an attempt to hide the force of his grief for a lost daughter. After this, Shylock's carefully cultivated urbanity left him; the assimilation had been revoked' (Jackson, *SQ* 1994). After 'ducats in her coffin', Holbrook began chanting the *Kaddish*; the rest of the speech was omitted.

71 Macready's promptbook shows 'Tubal signifies "No" ' in response to 'No news of them?'.

72 Irving: 'thumping breast' at 'I know not what's spent in the search' (*pmt* Irving[1]). In Barton's 1978 production, 'Tubal presented his bill of expenses which included, in writing just too small for the audience to read, a huge bar and restaurant bill for two nights at the Genoa Hilton' (Stewart, 'Shylock', p. 23). Serban's Tubal did a tally on his calculator and showed it to Shylock, who yelled.

74 Crosse thought that Irving overplayed much of 3.1, but liked 'the pathetic calmness of the passage "no satisfaction, no revenge, etc." ' (*Diaries*, vol. I, p. 174).

75–6 In O'Toole's performance ' "no tears but o" my shedding' was not said for sympathy, but with ritualistic beating on his breast. He expressed pain here and at the memory of Leah by showing his effort to bear it himself, with clenched control' (Brown, *SS* 1961). Stewart 'scrupulously paid out there and then with soiled notes from a pocket book in which he had calculated the "rate" of Bassanio's loan' (Warren, *SS* 1979); LeBow simply checked the date on his watch and wrote out a cheque for Tubal's expenses.

TUBAL Yes, other men have ill luck too. Antonio as I heard in
    Genoa –
SHYLOCK What, what, what? Ill luck, ill luck?
TUBAL – hath an argosy cast away coming from Tripolis.   80
SHYLOCK I thank God, I thank God. Is it true, is it true?
TUBAL I spoke with some of the sailors that escaped the wreck.
SHYLOCK I thank thee, good Tubal: good news, good news! Ha, ha,
    heard in Genoa!
TUBAL Your daughter spent in Genoa, as I heard, one night four   85
    score ducats.
SHYLOCK Thou stick'st a dagger in me; I shall never see my gold
    again. Four score ducats at a sitting! Four score ducats!

---

77 Tubal interpolated three extra 'yes's' in Guthrie's production (*pmt*).

79 Edmund Kean said 'Ill luck, ill luck' with 'a horrid expression of savage joy' (*pmt* E. Kean).
    Goodman was incredulous at first – 'What? *Ill* luck? *Ill* luck?'.

80 Schenk inserted an oddly comic moment here with Tubal blowing his nose, and the
    exasperated Shylock grabbing Tubal's handkerchief and throwing it to the ground.

81a 'Sr. Novelli spoke these words with the Oriental gesture of carrying dust to the lips and then
    the forehead, and then raising his hands to heaven' (*pmt* Ames[1]).

81–4 The Philadelphia *Mirror* admired how Cooke, as he heard of Antonio's losses at sea, showed
    'the impatience of a ravening appetite for the blood of the merchant' with 'the significant
    eagerness of his ghastly looks and the clawing of his fingers' (*qtd* Sprague, *Shakespeare
    and the Actors*, pp. 23–4); Charles Kemble suddenly fell to his knees (Sprague, *Shakespeare
    and the Actors*, 24). Booth 'flings his arms over his head, he comes staggering down in
    mighty strides to the footlights and sobbing in a delirium of revengeful joy, he flings himself
    into Tubal's arms, crying all the while, "I thank God. I thank God. Is it true? Is it true?" '
    (Winter, *qtd* Sprague, *Shakespeare and the Actors*, p. 24) Irving's 'rendering of this line was
    like a flash of lightning in its naturalness' (*CT*, *qtd* Irv.Amer., p. 29).
        Every reviewer commented on Olivier's dance of joy at 'Is it true, is it true?', a piece of
    business that goes at least as far back as Novelli in 1907, who began 'to dance, infirmly,
    with senile joy' (Winter, *Shakespeare on the Stage*, p. 166). In 1919, Maurice Moscovitch
    'positively dance[d] with joy, round and round' (*Times* 10 October 1919), and Carnovsky's
    'mad caper of joy' earned the approval of Harold Clurman (*Nation* 3 August 1957).
    At 'I thank thee, good Tubal' George Arliss threw his arms around his friend (*pmt* Ames[2]);
    Zadek's Shylock, Gert Voss, whirled around 'with his friend Tubal in glee in the prospect of
    revenge' (Nightingale, *Times* 31 August 1995).

87–8 'Here, Novelli, seated, rocked to and fro in the Oriental fashion, giving an excellent exotic
    touch' (*pmt* Ames[2]). Philip Voss paused before 'gold' as if to say 'daughter' instead, making

TUBAL There came divers of Antonio's creditors in my company to
Venice that swear he cannot choose but break.   90
SHYLOCK I am very glad of it. I'll plague him, I'll torture him. I am
glad of it.
TUBAL One of them showed me a ring that he had of your daughter
for a monkey.
SHYLOCK Out upon her! Thou torturest me, Tubal: it was my   95
turquoise, I had it of Leah when I was a bachelor. I would not
have given it for a wilderness of monkeys.

'a pathetic attempt to put a brave face on the effective bereavement he had suffered' (Smith, 'The Merchant', p. 120).

91–2 In *Playing Shakespeare*, Suchet spoke while lighting his cigar.

95–7 A key moment for any Shylock. To Patrick Stewart,

> a simple gift, possibly a betrothal ring, from a woman to her lover: 'I had it of Leah
> when I was a bachelor.' That word shatters our image of this man Shylock and we see
> the man that once was, a bachelor, with all the association of youth, innocence and love
> that is to come. Shakespeare doesn't need to write a pre-history of Shylock. Those two
> lines say it all. (Stewart, 'Shylock', p. 23)

Given the eloquence of this analysis, it is hardly surprising that in Stewart's performance, the lowering of his head into his arms at the mention of Leah's ring was 'the only time he threatened to engage us sympathetically' in a generally unsympathetic portrayal (M. Shapiro, *Shofar* 1986).

A reviewer of Booth's opening at New York's Winter Garden recalled, and preferred, the reading of Edmund Kean, who would pause before 'speaking of the turquoise . . . and then, full of memories that belong to the Jewish as to every human heart, pronounce with a depth of softness that brought down showers of Hebrew tears, [the words] Mr Booth passed over in the ordinary tone' (review pasted into *pmt* Moore/Daly). At 'my turquoise', Forbes-Robertson 'made an affecting little pause . . . and tapped the third finger of his left hand, as though the turquoise was his wedding or engagement ring' (*pmt* Ames[1]). For Irving, 'there was a whole life's history of love and devotion in his expression "I had it of Leah when I was a bachelor" ' (*BDET*, qtd *Irv.Amer*, p. 15).

Peter O'Toole rent his 'gown of watered silk' on 'wilderness', having ordered the costume department to construct something that would tear with a loud sound (Billington, *The Modern Actor*, p. 85; Freedland, *Peter O'Toole*, pp. 64–5). Olivier elongated 'all the vowel sounds on the word . . . as if to suggest an eternity of pain and anguish' (Billington, *The Modern Actor*, p. 86); 'Out upon her! Thou torturest me, Tubal' was cut.

TUBAL But Antonio is certainly undone.

SHYLOCK Nay, that's true, that very true. Go, Tubal, fee me an
officer, bespeak him a fortnight before. I will have the heart of   100
him if he forfeit, for were he out of Venice I can make what
merchandise I will. Go, Tubal, and meet me at our synagogue,
go, good Tubal, at our synagogue, Tubal.

Exeunt

Luther Adler's delivery 'was slowly paced and voiced with singing clarity and touching
pathos; in the audience there were damp eyes and lumps in throats, just as Mr Adler
intended there should be' (Barbour, 'Theatre Chronicle', pp. 284–5). Valk 'gave a quietly
sad reading of the lines' (Griffin, *TA* 1955); Sher 'sank to the floor, as if mortally wounded'
(Doran, 'Solanio', pp. 75–6); Rain 'launched a cry that seemed to come from a wounded
animal' (Leggatt, *SB* 1997). But Leibman was very quiet, after the fury of his previous
speech, and Hoffman also spoke quietly, with tears in his eyes – one of his most effective
moments.

99–103 'One can never forget', writes Winter, 'Irving's dark eyes, blazing with wrath, the jaws
champing, the left hand turning the sleeve up on the right arm as far back as the elbow, and
the fingers of the right hand stretched forth and quivering, as if already they were tearing
out the heart of his hated enemy' (*Shakespeare on the Stage*, pp. 191–2).

Kortner exploded with a wrathful *vierzehn Tage vorher* – 'a fortnight before'. Olivier
paused before 'Go, Tubal', and placed his *tallith* over his shoulders at 'I will have the heart of
him'. To Billington 'the veneer of bourgeois amiability has now been torn aside to expose
the naked racial hostility underneath' (*The Modern Actor*, p. 86). 'After a pause to light the
inevitable drooping cigarette', Stewart arrived at the idea of enforcing the bond (Warren,
SS 1979). Suchet and Goodman, also, did not make a firm decision until this late moment in
the scene. Calder put his hand on an open prayer-book on his desk, and 'Tubal registered
horror at this abuse of religion' (Holland, *English Shakespeares*, p. 164).

101–2 This expression of a commercial motive for exacting the penalty was cut by Webster,
Schenk, Miller and in the Globe production.

103sd George Arliss embellished Shylock's exit, but in a characteristically understated way:

Shylock is left standing by door step, arm upraised in final religious signal. His hand
turns as if swearing an oath to heaven. Gradually his arm comes down, and his eyes rest
on his left hand. He rubs his hand across the empty finger, then turns sadly to the house.
He raises his hand as if to knock, then realizing the futility, he sighs audibly, wipes his
eyes and goes into the house, as the curtain falls. (*pmt* Ames[2])

Tim Luscombe closed the scene with 'the actual meeting in the synagogue that the text
promises: a group of Jews don prayer-shawls and begin a service' (Biggs, *SB* 1991).

Holbrook resumed chanting the *Kaddish*, and was joined by four elderly Jews standing on an upper gallery.

Most modern productions end the scene (and go to an interval) with Shylock alone on stage as the lights dim. Sher 'sat at the corner of the stage, prayed in Hebrew, and rocked backwards and forwards muttering obsessively of revenge as the house lights went up. From being a representative of a wronged race he had become a vindictive individual' (Wells, *SS* 1988). Leibman sat silently, and Philip Voss 'stood alone downstage in a stark cross-beam howling his grief to the heavens' (Smith, 'The Merchant', p. 120); Eric Porter gave 'a passionate cry in unintelligible Hebrew' (Brown, *SS* 1966); Nunn closed the act with Goodman speaking lines transferred from 1.3:

If I can catch him once upon the hip . . .
Cursed be my tribe. If I forgive him.

ACT 3, SCENE 2

[3.2] *Enter* BASSANIO, PORTIA, GRATIANO, [NERISSA,] *and all their trains*

PORTIA I pray you tarry, pause a day or two
                    Before you hazard, for in choosing wrong

Throughout the play's performance history, 3.2 has undergone some heavy cutting and alteration. Before Charles Kean restored Morocco and Arragon, Bassanio's choosing speech had to be rewritten to include deliberation of the gold and silver caskets (see Appendix 1). But with or without the other two suitors in the cast, the actor-managers of the nineteenth century were quite happy to remove as much of the play as possible that did not directly concern Shylock. Even Irving, with a famous and popular Portia, omitted large sections of 3.2.

Portia and Bassanio are not seen together until now: having appeared in four scenes, Portia must suddenly show a completely new aspect to her character – 'Portia in Love'. Fabia Drake was having great difficulties with this until Komisarjevsky murmured to her 'in his laconic, under-the-eyelids, almost sleepy way of speaking . . . "This scene not sentimental – physical" '. Drake recalls, 'that one phrase lifted me right over what was becoming a stumbling block. My mood, voice, pace, actions, everything was indicated. The whole conception of the scene became charged with a new vibrancy' (*qtd* Mennen, 'Theodore Komisarjevsky's Production', p. 393).

osd Early promptbooks offer no detail of costuming, and do not reveal how, if at all, Bassanio may have spent Antonio's three thousand ducats. Nathaniel Parker, shabbily dressed in 1.1 of Hall's production, entered with perhaps a dozen attendants. Sinead Cusack remarks that her Bassanio, Jonathan Hyde, 'persuaded the designer Christopher Morley to make a swinging Byronic cloak for [him] in Venice; but there is no justification whatever for him turning up at Portia's in the same coat – what did he do with the three thousand ducats he got to furnish him for Belmont?' (Cusack, 'Portia', p. 40). Similarly, a reviewer of Sellars's production remarks, 'Why Bassanio's wooing would need the large loan Antonio obtains from Shylock . . . is a mystery, since he turns up at Belmont in the same old jeans and jacket he had previously worn' (Graham-White, 'Critical Responses', p. 153).

I lose your company; therefore forbear a while.
There's something tells me, but it is not love,
I would not lose you; and you know yourself   5
Hate counsels not in such a quality.
But lest you should not understand me well –
And yet a maiden hath no tongue but thought –
I would detain you here some month or two
Before you venture for me. I could teach you   10
How to choose right, but then I am forsworn.
So will I never be. So may you miss me;
But if you do, you'll make me wish a sin,
That I had been forsworn. Beshrew your eyes!
They have o'erlooked me and divided me: 15
One half of me is yours, the other half yours –
Mine own, I would say: but if mine then yours,
And so all yours. O these naughty times
Puts bars between the owners and their rights!
And so though yours, not yours. Prove it so,   20
Let Fortune go to hell for it, not I.
I speak too long, but 'tis to peize the time,
To eche it, and to draw it out in length,
To stay you from election.
BASSANIO   Let me choose,
For as I am, I live upon the rack.   25

In his television version, Miller began the scene in his first non-studio exterior, with Portia and Bassanio returning from a horseback ride. This created an interesting costume problem for Joan Plowright (see p. 188).

1 At Stratford, Ontario, Langham had Bassanio and Portia enter to a welcoming choir singing John Wilbye's madrigal, 'Adieu Sweet Amaryllis', the words changed to 'Welcome Sweet Amaryllis'. Ward notes that Bassanio 'gets more than a little help in choosing his casket . . . when he begins to walk toward the gold one, Portia jumps from her seat and stops him with "I pray you, tarry" ' (*SB* 1989).

3b–10b Cut by Charles Kean, along with 14b–21 and 22–4, reducing Portia's speech from twenty-four to eight lines (*pmt* C. Kean[2]).

5 Marjorie Bland 'pinpointed her anxieties and ecstasies in the casket scenes: "I / would / not / lose / you" was intensely emphatic' (Warren, *SS* 1979).

14b–21 Omitted in the Bell text, and nineteenth-century managers always followed suit.

24 On one occasion at Stratford in 1971, Judi Dench said 'To stay you from erection'. The musicians, on stage and ready for 'Where is fancy bred', were laughing too hard to play and walked off, so Nerissa (Polly James) did the song unaccompanied (Dench, 'A Career', p. 204).

PORTIA Upon the rack, Bassanio? Then confess
　　　　What treason there is mingled with your love.
BASSANIO None but that ugly treason of mistrust
　　　　Which makes me fear th'enjoying of my love.
　　　　There may as well be amity and life   30
　　　　'Tween snow and fire, as treason and my love.
PORTIA Ay, but I fear you speak upon the rack
　　　　Where men enforcèd do speak anything.
BASSANIO Promise me life and I'll confess the truth.
PORTIA Well then, confess and live.
BASSANIO   'Confess and love'   35
　　　　Had been the very sum of my confession.
　　　　O happy torment, when my torturer
　　　　Doth teach me answers for deliverance!
　　　　But let me to my fortune and the caskets.
PORTIA Away then! I am locked in one of them: 40
　　　　If you do love me, you will find me out.
　　　　Nerissa and the rest, stand all aloof.
　　　　Let music sound while he doth make his choice;
　　　　Then if he lose he makes a swan-like end,
　　　　Fading in music. That the comparison   45
　　　　May stand more proper, my eye shall be the stream
　　　　And watery deathbed for him. He may win,
　　　　And what is music then? Then music is
　　　　Even as the flourish when true subjects bow
　　　　To a new-crownèd monarch. Such it is   50
　　　　As are those dulcet sounds in break of day,
　　　　That creep into the dreaming bridegroom's ear
　　　　And summon him to marriage. Now he goes
　　　　With no less presence, but with much more love,
　　　　Than young Alcides when he did redeem   55

26–38 Usually omitted in eighteenth and nineteenth centuries, but included by Booth/Barrett.

45b–62 Macready had Portia begin the speech at 53b, his promptbook showing 'Symphony of the Duet, Tell me &c. begins here, pianissimo . . . the curtains in C. are drawn by Nerissa, on R., and the caskets are disclosed behind in an elegant cabinet, Bassanio goes slowly up towards them, as Portia speaks "Now he goes" &c. through the music.' Thacker's very effective treatment was to have Penny Downie speak these lines as a soliloquy.

47b–62 Omitted in the eighteenth and nineteenth centuries, except for Macready, and Booth/Barrett, who retained 53b–62.

53b–60a Done loudly, with broad gestures, by Laila Robins in Edelstein's production.

> The virgin tribute paid by howling Troy
> To the sea-monster. I stand for sacrifice.
> The rest aloof are the Dardanian wives,
> With bleared visages come forth to view
> The issue of th'exploit. Go, Hercules!   60
> Live thou, I live. With much much more dismay
> I view the fight than thou that mak'st the fray.
> *[Here music.] A song the whilst Bassanio comments on the*
> *caskets to himself*
> Tell me where is fancy bred,
> Or in the heart, or in the head?

62   As noted, in Miller's television version Portia began the scene in riding costume. At this critical moment of the play, when Bassanio is about to make the decision upon which her happiness supposedly depends, Plowright left the room to change her dress. She remained absent for close to three minutes, missing nearly all of Bassanio's deliberations, and did not re-enter until 'Hard food for Midas'. One is hard-pressed to see any reasoning behind such absurd direction, unless absurdity was intended.

63–72   The song does not appear in the Bell text, so was probably omitted in most eighteenth-century productions. Macready included it, but Kemble and Booth did not; nor, at times, did Irving (some promptbooks show him retaining it).

What has now become a strong performance tradition was suggested in the *Times Literary Supplement* of 12 July 1923, and first seen in Komisarjevsky's production. Bassanio was about to choose gold when Nerissa intervened with the song, emphasizing 'bred', 'head' and 'nourishèd', each rhyming with 'lead': W. A. Darlington called this idea 'an uncommonly dirty trick' (*DT*, *qtd* Mennen, 'Theodore Komisarjevsky's Production', p. 393). Harold Hobson's comment is typical of the critical response to Miller's staging, with 'Fancy Bred' being 'inconceivably sung by two smirking Victorian harridans, like a cod music-hall turn down the Old Kent Road. If this really is Portia's idea of a musical evening, then she is very different from the clever, well-bred lady we have always thought her' (*ST* 3 May 1970).

Katharine Hepburn repeated all the words that rhymed with 'lead' in the song (Hewes, *SR* 27 July 1957); Langham had his choir perform the same service (Ward, *SB* 1989), and Kahn went for laughs as eagerly as did Miller by having Portia (Enid Graham) direct her three singers, moving to the gold casket at 'ding', the silver at 'dong' and upon reaching the lead for 'bell', she indicated a *fortissimo* with gestures worthy of Leonard Bernstein conducting the New York Philharmonic. Peter Holland notes of Sellars's production, 'Expecting something ostentatiously brash, I could hardly complain when Portia's dresses for the casket scenes were colour-coded and when she so subtly suggested which casket Bassanio should choose by standing on it' (*TLS* 2 December 1994). What many directors,

How begot, how nourishèd?   65
     Reply, reply.
It is engend'red in the eye,
With gazing fed, and fancy dies
In the cradle where it lies.
Let us all ring fancy's knell.   70
I'll begin it – Ding, dong, bell.
ALL   Ding, dong, bell.
BASSANIO So may the outward shows be least themselves:

John Barton a worthy exception, seem unwilling to accept is that 'Fancy Bred' is indeed a hint, but a serious one that depends on Bassanio giving careful attention to all its words, not just the rhymes. Barton had Portia do the singing, and although this prospect terrified Cusack, she agreed with her director that 'Portia is telling Bassanio that appearance is not everything', while discounting the idea of a rhyming hint 'as too cheap or trite on either Shakespeare's or Portia's part' (Cusack, 'Portia', p. 36). Maraden, Edelstein and Nunn all gave the song to Nerissa: Maraden, staging the entire scene as a cocktail party, also provided three ladies as a backing chorus, and in Edelstein's version Gratiano moved towards Nerissa during the song as an indication of his feelings towards her. Benthall had Portia speak (not sing) the lines softly (Clarke, *Shakespeare at the Old Vic*, np).

Guthrie exploited Ontario's large thrust stage with an elaborate show of circling figures, weaving patterns in the air with pennants above Bassanio's head, while 'court beauties danced between him and his fate, and the choir sang full voice above' (Edinborough, 'Shakespeare Confirmed', p. 438). Alexander also assembled a choir comprising his entire cast in disguise: 'the full resources of the Belmont Choral Society' (Wells, *SS* 1988).

73 The 1774 Bell text, making no concession for the lack of Morocco and Arragon, allows the audience no opportunity to hear the inscriptions on the three caskets – Bassanio's choosing speech is much reduced, with 87–101a omitted, but is otherwise unchanged. By about 1800, a conflated speech was adopted, taking lines from Morocco and Arragon (see Appendix 1), so that the riddle of the caskets remained in the play. Macready's simpler emendation was to have Bassanio read the inscription on each casket before speaking 73–86.

In productions where the game is given away by the song, Bassanio's meditation on the caskets has no real meaning, and one wonders why Miller included it at all, instead of omitting half the lines and transposing others as he did. Serban also cut many lines, and his staging emphasised the cynicism with which the whole business was being treated, as attendants rolled about the mirror-backed spheres, 'in the manner of a shell game', while Bassanio spoke – 'he had only to turn and select the lead casket, with Portia's reflection in its mirror' (Cook, *SB* 1999).

The world is still deceived with ornament.
In law, what plea so tainted and corrupt   75
But, being seasoned with a gracious voice,
Obscures the show of evil? In religion,
What damnèd error but some sober brow
Will bless it and approve it with a text,
Hiding the grossness with fair ornament?   80
There is no vice so simple but assumes
Some mark of virtue on his outward parts.
How many cowards whose hearts are all as false
As stayers of sand, wear yet upon their chins
The beards of Hercules and frowning Mars,   85
Who inward searched have livers white as milk,
And these assume but valour's excrement
To render them redoubted. Look on beauty,
And you shall see 'tis purchased by the weight,
Which therein works a miracle in nature,   90
Making them lightest that wear most of it.
So are those crispèd snaky golden locks
Which maketh such wanton gambols with the wind
Upon supposèd fairness, often known
To be the dowry of a second head,   95
The skull that bred them in the sepulchre.
Thus ornament is but the guilèd shore
To a most dangerous sea; the beauteous scarf

In Schenk's staging, Sabine Sinjen nodded enthusiastically to Folker Bohnet as he rejected gold and silver at 3.2.101–4, and she spoke 3.2.108ff. to Bassanio *before* he opened the leaden casket; Zadek had Bassanio assisted by 'his business cronies who offered shrewd market advice about which casket to plump for' (Billington, *Gdn* 18 April 1991). Nicholas Farrell, Alexander's 'charmingly vapid Bassanio . . . limbers up before the casket test as though he were about to enter a try-your-strength contest rather than a moral trial' (Taylor, *Ind* 28 April 1988).

Other directors take seriously Portia's, 'If you do love me, you will find me out', allowing Bassanio (and the audience) to engage with the rhetorical nuances of the speech. Barton, working in the round at The Other Place, had John Nettles circle the caskets in deliberate, formal patterns as he spoke, and his correct choice was 'an electric moment' (Warren, *SS* 1979). Edelstein's Bassanio, Jay Goede, injected real tension into his soliloquy, as did Scott Handy for Doran.

81 From here onwards nineteenth-century managers made large excisions, in various places.

Veiling an Indian beauty; in a word,
The seeming truth which cunning times put on   100
To entrap the wisest. Therefore thou gaudy gold,
Hard food for Midas, I will none of thee,
Nor none of thee, thou pale and common drudge
'Tween man and man. But thou, thou meagre lead
Which rather threaten'st than dost promise aught,   105
Thy paleness moves me more than eloquence:
And here choose I. Joy be the consequence!
PORTIA [*Aside*] How all the other passions fleet to air:
As doubtful thoughts, and rash-embraced despair,
And shudd'ring fear, and green-eyed jealousy!   110
O love, be moderate, allay thy ecstasy,
In measure rain thy joy, scant this excess!
I feel too much thy blessing: make it less
For fear I surfeit.
     [Bassanio opens the leaden casket]
BASSANIO   What find I here?
Fair Portia's counterfeit! What demi-god   115
Hath come so near creation? Move these eyes?
Or whether riding on the balls of mine
Seem they in motion? Here are severed lips
Parted with sugar breath; so sweet a bar
Should sunder such sweet friends. Here in her hairs   120
The painter plays the spider, and hath woven

---

101 Billington remarks of Caird's production that 'it is a little odd for Bassanio to piously inveigh
against "gaudy gold" whilst wearing a glittering Spanish toreador's outfit whose spangles
glisten in the light' (*Gdn* 11 April 1984).

108–14a Deborah Findlay remembers this speech as 'a wonderful moment when time stands still,
a moment of sheer joy quietly expressed before the great cheer from the household on . . .
"Fair Portia's counterfeit" ' (Findlay, 'Portia', p. 60) Miller cut the speech, hence Portia was
not required to express any passionate sentiment.

114b–48 The *Referee* approved of Ellen Terry openly showing her desire for Bassanio: 'the eager
surging love that ever and anon would vent itself in ejaculations more eloquent than words,
was exquisitely expressed' (Foulkes, 'Helen Faucit', p. 30; see above, p. 25). Serban omitted
all of Bassanio's speech; the scroll was sung by Portia and Nerissa. Maraden had Portia and
Nerissa embrace while Bassanio opened the casket. Hands's leaden casket contained
'a complete Madam Tussaud's waxworks' of Portia (Esslin, *PP* 1972).

115b–29a Cut by Macready.

A golden mesh t'entrap the hearts of men
Faster than gnats in cobwebs. But her eyes –
How could he see to do them? Having made one,
Methinks it should have power to steal both his   125
And leave itself unfurnished. Yet look how far
The substance of my praise doth wrong this shadow
In underprizing it, so far this shadow
Doth limp behind the substance. Here's the scroll,
The continent and summary of my fortune.   130
                    [*He reads*]
        'You that choose not by the view
        Chance as fair, and choose as true.
        Since this fortune falls to you,
        Be content and seek no new.
        If you be well pleased with this,   135
        And hold your fortune for your bliss,
        Turn you where your lady is,
        And claim her with a loving kiss.'
A gentle scroll! Fair lady, by your leave,

131–8   In one of Hall's odder pieces of direction, Nathaniel Parker read the scroll quickly to a
        steady drumbeat, in what sounded strangely like Shakespeare's attempt at rap lyrics.
139ff. Details of Helen Faucit's Portia are few. *Blackwood's* reviewer of Faucit's book *On Some of
        Shakespeare's Female Characters*, remembers when, as a young girl, she

> first saw Helen Faucit on the Dublin stage . . . we seem still to see the upward gaze as of
> a St Cecilia, with which, in silent prayer, and with one knee scarce perceptibly drooped
> upon the cushioned footstool, she awaited the issue, and all the subsequent changes of
> expression that passed across her face during the caskets, to the final gleam of joy that
> lighted her countenance as her lover chose rightly. We felt how the too tumultuous
> passion had been chastened by that prayer. Subdued, yet intensely happy, she rose
> from her seat and awaited the approach of him who was now 'her lord, her governor,
> her king'. (December 1885)

William Winter approves of Terry's actions upon Bassanio opening the leaden casket: 'she
crumbled some roses and allowed the leaves to flutter down into the leaden casket from
which the happy lover had taken her picture, and then, bending over it, seemed to
consecrate it with a kiss' (Winter, *Shakespeare on the Stage*, p. 218). Walter Kerr provides
this splendid description of Katharine Hepburn: 'When Bassanio selected the right casket –
the caskets were little gingerbread mountains held up to view by cross-legged menials

I come by note to give, and to receive.   140
Like one of two contending in a prize
That thinks he hath done well in people's eyes,
Hearing applause and universal shout,
Giddy in spirit, still gazing in a doubt
Whether those peals of praise be his or no –   145
So, thrice-fair lady, stand I even so,
As doubtful whether what I see be true,
Until confirmed, signed, ratified by you.
PORTIA You see me, Lord Bassanio, where I stand,
Such as I am. Though for myself alone   150
I would not be ambitious in my wish
To wish myself much better, yet for you
I would be trebled twenty times myself,
A thousand times more fair, ten thousand times
More rich, that only to stand high in your account   155
I might in virtues, beauties, livings, friends,
Exceed account. But the full sum of me

sitting side by side – and then turned to Portia as though he might kiss her, Miss Hepburn jiggled up and down with the impatient ecstasy of a woman of six' (*Theater in Spite of Itself*, p. 278).

149–74 This speech is Portia's longest (four lines longer than 'The quality of mercy'), but commentary on how different actresses have approached it is rare, perhaps because substantial sections of it have so often been omitted in performance – its sentiments presumably would have appealed to Victorian ideals, but little of it was heard from the stage. Sinead Cusack violently threw her ceremonial cloak, the caskets and the table they rested on across the stage. She considers it 'an unashamedly theatrical moment, but it serves as a release of tension both for the audience and for the actress playing Portia. It provides too a springboard for the speech "You see me, Lord Bassanio, where I stand" which has as much to do with release as with commitment' (Cusack, 'Portia', p. 37). At the opposite extreme, Michael Feingold had 'never seen a Portia greet the choice of the right casket so unenthusiastically' as did Geraldine James in Hall's production: 'Her subtext for the scene . . . seems to be "Close your eyes and think of Belmont" ' (*VV* 26 December 1989).

Sprague notes that 'it was usual, after Bassanio's choosing, for Gratiano and Nerissa to act out in pantomime a little courtship scene of their own', but when this byplay was introduced is not known (Sprague, *Shakespeare and the Actors*, p. 25).

157b–67a Retained in the Bell text, except for the syntactically obscure 158, and retained by Irving for Ellen Terry; otherwise usually omitted in the nineteenth century. Removing this section

Is sum of something: which to term in gross
Is an unlessoned girl, unschooled, unpractised;
Happy in this, she is not yet so old   160
But she may learn; happier than this,
She is not bred so dull but she can learn;
Happiest of all, is that her gentle spirit
Commits itself to yours to be directed
As from her lord, her governor, her king.   165
Myself, and what is mine, to you and yours
Is now converted. But now I was the lord
Of this fair mansion, master of my servants,
Queen o'er myself; and even now, but now,
This house, these servants, and this same myself   170
Are yours, my lord's. I give them with this ring,
Which when you part from, lose, or give away,
Let it presage the ruin of your love,
And be my vantage to exclaim on you.
BASSANIO Madam, you have bereft me of all words.   175

relieves Portia of having to refer to herself as an 'unlessoned girl . . . not yet so old / But she may learn', a good thing given the age of many a Portia.

165 In Winthrop Ames's staging, Bassanio was kneeling, and the promptbook direction for Peggy Wood is 'She raises him and he takes her in his arms in a long embrace. She draws gently away' (*pmt* Ames[2]). Traditionally, near or at this line, depending on how much of the speech was retained, Portia kneeled before Bassanio – Ellen Terry remained standing, and Lady Pollock (see p. 23) expressed her approval: 'I used to feel that too much like worship from any girl to her affianced, and Portia's position being one of command, I should doubt the possibility of such an action' (Terry, *Story*, pp. 185–6). Just how old-fashioned Benthall's 1956 Old Vic production was is shown by his restoration of the old business: 'Portia's reply . . . was spoken to him from a distance of half the stage, but she gradually approached until at the end she knelt at his feet' (Clarke, *Shakespeare at the Old Vic*, np). The line was cut by Thacker, and in the 1998 Globe production.

166–74 Cut by Booth, but of course Booth usually omitted Act v and its ring business.

170 In Nunn's production, Portia and Bassanio knelt 'side by side to exchange vows and rings with a degree of solemnity that had a touch of foreboding about it, a mood deepened rather than dissipated by Gratiano's coarse, noisy laughter as the champagne flowed, and the jokes too, about getting sons and "stakes down" ' (Smallwood, *SS* 2000).

175 Eighteenth- and nineteenth-century managers always took Bassanio's comment at face value and cut 176–83a.

Only my blood speaks to you in my veins,
And there is such confusion in my powers
As after some oration fairly spoke
By a belovèd prince there doth appear
Among the buzzing, pleasèd multitude,   180
Where every something being blent together
Turns to a wild of nothing, save of joy
Expressed, and not expressed. But when this ring
Parts from this finger, then parts life from hence:
O then be bold to say Bassanio's dead!   185
NERISSA My lord and lady, it is now our time,
That have stood by and seen our wishes prosper,
To cry 'good joy'. Good joy, my lord and lady!
GRATIANO My lord Bassanio, and my gentle lady,
I wish you all the joy that you can wish;   190
For I am sure you can wish none from me.
And when your honours mean to solemnise
The bargain of your faith, I do beseech you
Even at that time I may be married too.
BASSANIO With all my heart, so thou canst get a wife. 195
GRATIANO I thank your lordship, you have got me one.
My eyes, my lord, can look as swift as yours:
You saw the mistress, I beheld the maid.
You loved, I loved; for intermission
No more pertains to me, my lord, than you.   200
Your fortune stood upon the caskets there,
And so did mine too as the matter falls.
For wooing here until I sweat again,
And swearing till my very roof was dry
With oaths of love, at last – if promise last –   205
I got a promise of this fair one here

188 Macready: 'All bow/curtsy to Bassanio and Portia' (*pmt*).

198–208a Nunn inserted some very clever business here, implying that Gratiano had been having an
excellent time at Belmont. As Richard Henders revealed that he, too, had fallen in love –
'You saw the mistress, I beheld the maid' – it became clear that one of Portia's other maids
thought that he was referring to her; she was deflated when Henders looked right past her
to Nerissa.

203b–4a 'Sweat' being an indelicate word, this was usually omitted in Victorian productions. Miller,
with his Victorian setting, also made the deletion.

>   To have her love, provided that your fortune
>   Achieved her mistress.
> PORTIA   Is this true, Nerissa?
> NERISSA Madam, it is, so you stand pleased withal.
> BASSANIO And do you, Gratiano, mean good faith?   210
> GRATIANO Yes 'faith, my lord.
> BASSANIO Our feast shall be much honoured in your marriage.
> GRATIANO We'll play with them the first boy for a thousand
>   ducats.
> NERISSA What, and stake down?   215
> GRATIANO No, we shall ne'er win at that sport and stake down.
>   But who comes here? Lorenzo and his infidel!
>   What, and my old Venetian friend Salerio!
>
> *Enter* LORENZO, JESSICA, *and* SALERIO, *a messenger from Venice*
>
> BASSANIO Lorenzo and Salerio, welcome hither –
>   If that the youth of my new interest here   220
>   Have power to bid you welcome. By your leave
>   I bid my very friends and countrymen,
>   Sweet Portia, welcome.
> PORTIA   So do I, my lord.
>   They are entirely welcome.
> LORENZO I thank your honour. For my part, my lord,   225
>   My purpose was not to have seen you here,
>   But meeting with Salerio by the way

210 Spoken privately to Gratiano in Thacker's production.

213–15 Bell and Inchbald retained these lines, Kemble and the Victorians omitted them.

217 Hall's Jessica (Francesca Buller) was visibly hurt by 'infidel'.

218sd Schenk is one of the few directors to provide three Salads, bringing Salerio on here. In Serban's production, Portia was given a warning about her new husband's other relationships, as Salerio/Salarino entered wearing his *carnevale* outfit from 2.6, 'eye-shadow and all'. Portia 'was compelled to wonder, as she looked askance, whether she had made a terrible mistake, after she read Antonio's letter' (Cook, *SB* 1999).

219 Bassanio welcomes his friends, but does not mention Jessica. Miller, Alexander and Hall placed Jessica in an isolated position, ignored by Portia, who did nothing to make her feel welcome. Gabrielle Jourdan, in Nunn's production, was shy and ill at ease, but was not snubbed. Interestingly, Charles Kean's 1858 edition has a direction for Bassanio to bow to Jessica.

He did entreat me past all saying nay
To come with him along.
SALERIO   I did, my lord,
And I have reason for it. [*Giving letter*] Signor Antonio   230
Commends him to you.
BASSANIO   Ere I ope his letter,
I pray you tell me how my good friend doth.
SALERIO   Not sick, my lord, unless it be in mind,
Nor well, unless in mind: his letter there
Will show you his estate.   235

      [*Bassanio*] *opens the letter*

GRATIANO   Nerissa, cheer yond stranger, bid her welcome.
Your hand, Salerio; what's the news from Venice?
How doth that royal merchant, good Antonio?
I know he will be glad of our success;
We are the Jasons, we have won the fleece.   240
SALERIO   I would you had won the fleece that he hath lost.
PORTIA   There are some shrewd contents in yond same paper
That steals the colour from Bassanio's cheek:
Some dear friend dead, else nothing in the world
Could turn so much the constitution   245
Of any constant man. What, worse and worse?
With leave, Bassanio, I am half yourself
And I must freely have the half of anything
That this same paper brings you.
BASSANIO   O sweet Portia,
Here are a few of the unpleasant'st words   250
That ever blotted paper. Gentle lady,
When I did first impart my love to you,
I freely told you all the wealth I had
Ran in my veins: I was a gentleman.
And then I told you true; and yet, dear lady,   255
Rating myself at nothing, you shall see
How much I was a braggart. When I told you

235sd Kemble: 'Lords and Ladies converse'.

 236 Alexander's and Luscombe's Nerissas both ignored Gratiano's request. In Miller's television version, Michael Jayston said 'Go, Nerissa'; at 249, Jeremy Brett omitted the 'O' in 'O . . . Portia', and at 267 he omitted the 'from' before 'Mexico': all three lines were made unmetrical. At 262 Brett said 'It is a letter', not 'Here is a letter'. One cannot say if these and similar line changes were intentional, or simply due to sloppiness.

> My state was nothing, I should then have told you
> That I was worse than nothing; for indeed
> I have engaged myself to a dear friend,   260
> Engaged my friend to his mere enemy,
> To feed my means. Here is a letter, lady,
> The paper as the body of my friend,
> And every word in it a gaping wound
> Issuing lifeblood. But is it true, Salerio?   265
> Hath all his ventures failed? What, not one hit?
> From Tripolis, from Mexico, and England,
> From Lisbon, Barbary, and India,
> And not one vessel 'scape the dreadful touch
> Of merchant-marring rocks?

SALERIO   Not one, my lord.   270
> Besides, it should appear that if he had
> The present money to discharge the Jew,
> He would not take it. Never did I know
> A creature that did bear the shape of man
> So keen and greedy to confound a man.   275
> He plies the Duke at morning and at night,
> And doth impeach the freedom of the state
> If they deny him justice. Twenty merchants,
> The Duke himself, and the magnificoes
> Of greatest port have all persuaded with him,   280
> But none can drive him from the envious plea
> Of forfeiture, of justice, and his bond.

JESSICA When I was with him, I have heard him swear
> To Tubal and to Chus, his countrymen,
> That he would rather have Antonio's flesh   285
> Than twenty times the value of the sum
> That he did owe him; and I know, my lord,
> If law, authority, and power deny not
> It will go hard with poor Antonio.

PORTIA Is it your dear friend that is thus in trouble?   290
BASSANIO The dearest friend to me, the kindest man,
> The best conditioned and unwearied spirit
> In doing courtesies; and one in whom

283–9 Retained in the Bell text, but often omitted in the nineteenth century; Macready deleted only
287b–89, and Irving retained the entire passage. Kelly's Christians were especially boorish
to Jessica – Bassanio spat at her when she spoke of her father's feelings about Antonio
(Hopkins, *SB* 1994). Cut by Thacker.

The ancient Roman honour more appears
Than any that draws breath in Italy.   295
PORTIA What sums owes he the Jew?
BASSANIO For me, three thousand ducats.
PORTIA   What, no more?
Pay him six thousand, and deface the bond.
Double six thousand, and then treble that,
Before a friend of this description   300
Shall lose a hair through Bassanio's fault.
First go with me to church, and call me wife,
And then away to Venice to your friend!
For never shall you lie by Portia's side
With an unquiet soul. You shall have gold   305
To pay the petty debt twenty times over.
When it is paid, bring your true friend along.
My maid Nerissa and myself meantime
Will live as maids and widows. Come away,
For you shall hence upon your wedding day.   310
Bid your friends welcome, show a merry cheer;
Since you are dear bought, I will love you dear.
But let me hear the letter of your friend.
BASSANIO [*Reads*] 'Sweet Bassanio, my ships have all miscarried, my
creditors grow cruel, my estate is very low; my bond to the Jew   315
is forfeit, and since in paying it, it is impossible I should live, all
debts are cleared between you and I if I might but see you at my
death. Notwithstanding, use your pleasure; if your love do not
persuade you to come, let not my letter.'
PORTIA O love! Dispatch all business and be gone.   320
BASSANIO Since I have your good leave to go away,
I will make haste. But till I come again
No bed shall e'er be guilty of my stay
Nor rest be interposer 'twixt us twain.
                                                                Exeunt

305b–13 Cut by Ben Greet.
  311–12 The second couplet was often omitted in the nineteenth century.
  314–19 The letter does not need to be read aloud, and Miller, Thacker and Nunn omitted it.
           Belasco's Bassanio, Philip Merivale, 'achieved one of the finest moments of the play. While
           reading the letter from Antonio, telling of the ruin of his fortunes his voice choked and he
           was obliged to give over the reading to Portia. The effect was of an emotion most poignantly
           masculine and true' (Corbin, *NYT* 22 December 1922).
  321–4   Thacker replaced these lines, ending the scene with 302–5a, then 308–10.

ACT 3, SCENE 3

[**3.3**] *Enter* [SHYLOCK] *the Jew, and* [SOLANIO,] *and* ANTONIO, *and the Jailer*

SHYLOCK Jailer, look to him. Tell not me of mercy.
       This is the fool that lent out money gratis.
       Jailer, look to him.
ANTONIO   Hear me yet, good Shylock –
SHYLOCK I'll have my bond, speak not against my bond;
       I have sworn an oath that I will have my bond.   5
       Thou call'dst me dog before thou hadst a cause,
       But since I am a dog, beware my fangs.

Charles Kean notes in his 1858 edition that 'this scene is generally omitted'. Kemble and Macready did play it, and given the brevity of Shylock's part when compared with the other great Shakespearean roles, it is surprising that later actor-managers did without it, but they would not have wanted to return to Venice for a very short scene between two Belmont episodes, something to which the pictorial theatre of that era was not suited. Even Booth, who usually left out Act V, passed 3.3 by, and when Gordon Crosse saw Forbes-Robertson in 1913, he noted that 3.3. was 'restored, its effect being to emphasize the odious light in which Antonio appears, pleading to Shylock after having in 1.3 challenged the Jew to treat him as an enemy' (*Diaries*, vol. V, pp. 149–50).

1–5 Gold set the action at night, the actors carrying torches. In Thacker's production, with the scene placed in Shylock's office, Antonio was accompanied by Solanio, not a jailer. 'Jailer, look to him' was cut, and Calder said 'Tell me not of mercy' to Tubal, who was standing by his side. He then 'emphasized the "oath" by laying his hand on what appeared to be an open Bible . . . Tubal, who clearly supported Antonio, noticed this; from that point on, Shylock had no allies' (Jackson, *SQ* 1994). Nunn placed the scene outdoors – Goodman, returning from synagogue, was carrying his *tallith* in a velvet case, and a prayer-book which he held up at 'I have sworn an oath'.

The Duke shall grant me justice. I do wonder,
Thou naughty jailer, that thou art so fond
To come abroad with him at his request.   10
ANTONIO I pray thee hear me speak –
SHYLOCK I'll have my bond; I will not hear thee speak;
I'll have my bond, and therefore speak no more.
I'll not be made a soft and dull-eyed fool,
To shake the head, relent, and sigh, and yield   15
To Christian intercessors. Follow not!
I'll have no speaking, I will have my bond.   *Exit*
SOLANIO It is the most impenetrable cur
That ever kept with men.
ANTONIO   Let him alone.
I'll follow him no more with bootless prayers.   20
He seeks my life, his reason well I know:
I oft delivered from his forfeitures
Many that have at times made moan to me;
Therefore he hates me.
SOLANIO   I am sure the Duke
Will never grant this forfeiture to hold.   25
ANTONIO The Duke cannot deny the course of law;
For the commodity that strangers have
With us in Venice, if it be denied,
Will much impeach the justice of the state,
Since that the trade and profit of the city   30
Consisteth of all nations. Therefore go.
These griefs and losses have so bated me
That I shall hardly spare a pound of flesh
Tomorrow to my bloody creditor.

---

9 Calder said 'Signor Solanio' instead of 'naughty jailer'.

13 LeBow brandished a knife here.

17 Douglas Rain slammed and bolted his door after he exited: 'The sound of the bolt – loud, hard, final – was the sound of Shylock's mind closing' (Leggatt, *SB* 1997). There was also an audible locking of the door in Nunn's production.

18 In trying to make sense of the two-or-three Salad situation, the Inchbald, Irving and Charles Kean texts have Salarino here, not Solanio, as in Mahood's edition. Modern productions always have Solanio.

> Well, jailer, on. Pray God Bassanio come   35
> To see me pay his debt, and then I care not.

Exeunt

35b–6 Clifford Rose spoke these last words as a soliloquy in Thacker's production.

36sd Alexander heightened the vituperation in this scene: Shylock spat several times at Antonio – 'the gaoler and Solanio draw swords, but Shylock, confident of the law's protection, exits laughing; the scene concludes with Solanio spitting in the direction of Shylock's exit, just as Antonio has done' (Bulman, *Shakespeare in Performance*, p. 124).

ACT 3, SCENE 4

[3.4] *Enter* PORTIA, NERISSA, LORENZO, JESSICA, *and* [BALTHAZAR] *a man of Portia's*

LORENZO Madam, although I speak it in your presence,
        You have a noble and a true conceit
        Of god-like amity, which appears most strongly
        In bearing thus the absence of your lord.
        But if you knew to whom you show this honour,   5
        How true a gentleman you send relief,
        How dear a lover of my lord your husband,
        I know you would be prouder of the work
        Than customary bounty can enforce you.
PORTIA I never did repent for doing good,   10
        Nor shall not now; for in companions
        That do converse and waste the time together,
        Whose souls do bear an equal yoke of love,
        There must be needs a like proportion
        Of lineaments, of manners, and of spirit;   15
        Which makes me think that this Antonio,
        Being the bosom lover of my lord,
        Must needs be like my lord. If it be so,

The previous scene being frequently omitted in the eighteenth and nineteenth centuries, an abbreviated 3.4 would follow on from 3.2. Booth began at line 45, as did Thacker, and while not all cuts were so drastic, this sequence was, and is, rarely played in full. In his only reordering of scenes, Komisarjevsky played a combined 3.2/3.4.

osd Most productions have an interval at the end of 3.1, or less commonly, after 3.2, but Hall's interval was after 3.3; Portia (for no apparent reason) ran on to begin the act.

11b–21 Gentleman's note in the Bell edition, 'these lines should be retained', went unheeded in the eighteenth and nineteenth centuries.

> How little is the cost I have bestowed
> In purchasing the semblance of my soul   20
> From out the state of hellish cruelty!
> This comes too near the praising of myself,
> Therefore no more of it: hear other things.
> Lorenzo, I commit into your hands
> The husbandry and manage of my house   25
> Until my lord's return; for mine own part
> I have toward heaven breathed a secret vow
> To live in prayer and contemplation,
> Only attended by Nerissa here,
> Until her husband and my lord's return.   30
> There is a monastery two miles off,
> And there we will abide. I do desire you
> Not to deny this imposition,
> The which my love and some necessity
> Now lays upon you.

LORENZO   Madam, with all my heart   35
> I shall obey you in all fair commands.

PORTIA My people do already know my mind,
> And will acknowledge you and Jessica
> In place of Lord Bassanio and myself.
> So fare you well till we shall meet again.   40

LORENZO Fair thoughts and happy hours attend on you.

JESSICA I wish your ladyship all heart's content.

PORTIA I thank you for your wish, and am well pleased
> To wish it back on you: fare you well, Jessica.

Exeunt [Jessica and Lorenzo]

---

24 Several Portias forget Jessica's name later in the scene; Sabine Sinjen could not remember Lorenzo's here.

26b–32a Marked for cut, Irving edition.

38 Like Joan Plowright, Lois Harvey treated Jessica 'with icy politeness, while pointedly forgetting her name' in Luscombe's production (Billington, *Gdn* 9 February 1991). In Nunn's production Jessica, looking very uncomfortable, had trouble swallowing her first taste of champagne.

43–4 Deborah Findlay spoke to Jessica 'in the kind of patronising singsong that one might use when speaking to a child' (Bulman, *Shakespeare in Performance*, p. 137). Geraldine James also adopted a formal tone that she did not use with anyone else (Kliman, *SB* 1990).

Now, Balthazar –   45
As I have ever found thee honest-true,
So let me find thee still; take this same letter,
And use thou all th'endeavour of a man
In speed to Padua. See thou render this
Into my cousin's hand, Doctor Bellario;   50
And look, what notes and garments he doth give thee
Bring them, I pray thee, with imagined speed
Unto the traject, to the common ferry
Which trades to Venice. Waste no time in words
But get thee gone; I shall be there before thee.   55
BALTHAZAR Madam, I go with all convenient speed.   [*Exit*]
PORTIA Come on, Nerissa; I have work in hand
That you yet know not of. We'll see our husbands
Before they think of us.
NERISSA   Shall they see us?
PORTIA They shall, Nerissa, but in such a habit   60
That they shall think we are accomplishèd
With that we lack. I'll hold thee any wager,
When we are both accoutred like young men
I'll prove the prettier fellow of the two,
And wear my dagger with the braver grace,   65
And speak between the change of man and boy
With a reed voice, and turn two mincing steps
Into a manly stride; and speak of 'frays
Like a fine bragging youth; and tell quaint lies
How honourable ladies sought my love,   70
Which I denying, they fell sick and died –

53 Enid Graham paused after 'traject' in Kahn's production, then said 'to the common ferry' as
    if explaining to her servant what a traject is.
56 In the Croydon Repertory's 1935 production, 'Balthasar was habited as an airman, and we
    heard his aeroplane starting' (Crosse, *Diaries*, vol. xv, p. 109).
60b–80 Retained in Bell's edition, but cut in the nineteenth century, with only 74–80 marked for
    omission in Irving's edition. Sellars's Portia, Elaine Tse, had a fine comic moment here:
    'When she tells Nerissa they will follow their husbands dressed as men, she turns her shoe
    into a phallus to represent what she lacks, falling into rap rhythms and "strutting her stuff"
    to mock male folly by parodying black ghetto expressions of machismo' (M. Shapiro, *SB*
    1994). Susan Coyne led Nerissa in a tango in Maraden's version.
66–78, 80 Cut by Macready (*pmt*).

I could not do withal. Then I'll repent,
And wish for all that that I had not killed them;
And twenty of these puny lies I'll tell,
That men shall swear I have discontinued school   75
Above a twelvemonth. I have within my mind
A thousand raw tricks of these bragging jacks,
Which I will practise.

NERISSA   Why, shall we turn to men?

PORTIA   Fie, what a question's that,
    If thou wert near a lewd interpreter!   80
    But come, I'll tell thee all my whole device
    When I am in my coach, which stays for us
    At the park gate; and therefore haste away,
    For we must measure twenty miles today.

Exeunt

81–3 Cut by Serban, therefore ending the scene without a couplet.

84 Irving had servants enter and tidy up the room after Portia and Nerissa exited (Sprague, *Shakespeare and the Actors*, p. 26).

ACT 3, SCENE 5

[3.5] *Enter* [LANCELOT *the*] *Clown and* JESSICA

LANCELOT Yes truly, for look you, the sins of the father are to be laid
  upon the children. Therefore I promise you I fear you. I was
  always plain with you, and so now I speak my agitation of the
  matter. Therefore be o'good cheer, for truly I think you are
  damned. There is but one hope in it that can do you any good,   5
  and that is but a kind of bastard hope neither.
JESSICA And what hope is that, I pray thee?
LANCELOT Marry, you may partly hope that your father got you not,
  that you are not the Jew's daughter.
JESSICA That were a kind of bastard hope indeed; so the sins of my   10
  mother should be visited upon me.

This scene with Jessica, Lorenzo and Lancelot at home in Belmont is the most expendable in
the play. Kemble played an abbreviated version, as did Macready, with no break from the
previous scene, but the list of productions to omit it includes those of Charles Kean, Booth,
Irving, Sothern, Benson, Jewett, Tree, Ames, Benthall, Landau, Schenk, Miller (1973) and
Langham (1988/9). Baldridge began at 31, and in an unusual but quite effective
transposition, Serban moved 1–25 to the start of 5.1 (26–78 were deleted).

osd Hall had Jessica and Lancelot run on, just as Portia did at the start of 3.4. John Simon
    wondered if all were not preparing for an Olympic relay (*New Yorker* 8 January 1990).

1–6 Nunn began the scene with Lancelot skimming Portia's swimming pool, while Jessica,
    dressed in a bathing suit, lay on a deck chair. Thacker's opening sequence was played as
    'a heavily ironic Bible class', with Christopher Luscombe 'preaching palpable nonsense for
    comic effect'. He paused after 'for look you', searching the large Bible for the reference,
    before finding 'the sins of the father'. Next to the Bible on the table was a photograph of
    Leah (Luscombe, 'Launcelot Gobbo', pp. 24–5; Geckle, *SB* 1994).

8 Macready and Kemble deleted 'that your father got you not'.

LANCELOT Truly, then, I fear you are damned both by father and
mother; thus when I shun Scylla your father, I fall into
Charybdis your mother. Well, you are gone both ways.

JESSICA I shall be saved by my husband; he hath made me a Christian.   15

LANCELOT Truly, the more to blame he; we were Christians enow
before, e'en as many as could well live one by another. This
making of Christians will raise the price of hogs; if we grow all
to be pork eaters, we shall not shortly have a rasher on the coals
for money.   20

Enter LORENZO

JESSICA I'll tell my husband, Lancelot, what you say: here he
comes.

LORENZO I shall grow jealous of you shortly, Lancelot, if you thus
get my wife into corners.

JESSICA Nay, you need not fear us, Lorenzo: Lancelot and I are out.   25
He tells me flatly there's no mercy for me in heaven, because I
am a Jew's daughter; and he says you are no good member of the
commonwealth, for in converting Jews to Christians you raise
the price of pork.

LORENZO I shall answer that better to the commonwealth than you   30
can the getting up of the Negro's belly: the Moor is with child
by you, Lancelot.

LANCELOT It is much that the Moor should be more than reason;
but if she be less than an honest woman, she is indeed more than
I took her for.   35

16–20 Lancelot's joke about the price of pork 'sounded quaint rather than threatening' in
Thacker's production (Jackson, *SQ* 1994).

21 In Tim Luscombe's production, Jessica slapped Lancelot's face (Biggs, *SB* 1991).

30–8a This passage about Lancelot's affair with a Moorish woman is retained in the Bell text. The
nineteenth-century managers, if they played the scene at all, omitted it, as did Thacker,
where it would have been incongruous with Christopher Luscombe's characterisation.
Edney Giovenazzi, who played Shylock in Gonzaga's Brazilian production, said that with
Brazil's large black population, *'ficaria gratuito e agressivo'* (it would have been gratuitous
and aggressive) to retain passages such as this one (De Sousa, *'The Merchant'*, p. 472).
Sellars's Shylock and Jessica were played by black actors, so 'the Negro' was Jessica:
Michael Shapiro disliked the inconsistency of such racial statements, offering confusion
rather than insight, in the casting (*SB* 1994).

LORENZO How every fool can play upon the word! I think the best
grace of wit will shortly turn into silence, and discourse grow
commendable in none only but parrots. Go in, sirrah, bid them
prepare for dinner.

LANCELOT That is done, sir; they have all stomachs.   40

LORENZO Goodly Lord, what a witsnapper are you! Then bid them
prepare dinner.

LANCELOT That is done too, sir; only 'cover' is the word.

LORENZO Will you cover then, sir?

LANCELOT Not so, sir, neither; I know my duty.   45

LORENZO Yet more quarrelling with occasion! Wilt thou show the
whole wealth of thy wit in an instant? I pray thee understand a
plain man in his plain meaning: go to thy fellows, bid them cover
the table, serve in the meat, and we will come in to dinner.

LANCELOT For the table, sir, it shall be served in; for the meat, sir, it   50
shall be covered; for your coming in to dinner, sir, why, let it be
as humours and conceits shall govern.   *Exit*

LORENZO O dear discretion, how his words are suited!
　　　　The fool hath planted in his memory
　　　　An army of good words; and I do know   55
　　　　A many fools that stand in better place,
　　　　Garnished like him, that for a tricksy word
　　　　Defy the matter. How cheer'st thou, Jessica?
　　　　And now, good sweet, say thy opinion:
　　　　How dost thou like the Lord Bassanio's wife?   60

JESSICA Past all expressing. It is very meet
　　　　The Lord Bassanio live an upright life,
　　　　For having such a blessing in his lady
　　　　He finds the joys of heaven here on earth,
　　　　And if on earth he do not merit it,   65
　　　　In reason he should never come to heaven.
　　　　Why, if two gods should play some heavenly match,
　　　　And on the wager lay two earthly women,
　　　　And Portia one, there must be something else

61b–71 Jessica's praise of Portia appears in the Bell text, but was always omitted in the nineteenth
century. In Tim Luscombe's production, Jessica said only 'Past all expressing . . . the poor
rude world / Hath not her fellow' with heavy irony, Portia having snubbed her earlier (Biggs,
SB 1991).

Pawned with the other, for the poor rude world   70
Hath not her fellow.
LORENZO   Even such a husband
Hast thou of me, as she is for a wife.
JESSICA Nay, but ask my opinion too of that.
LORENZO I will anon; first let us go to dinner.
JESSICA Nay, let me praise you while I have a stomach.   75
LORENZO No, pray thee, let it serve for table talk;
Then howsome'er thou speak'st, 'mong other things
I shall digest it.
JESSICA   Well, I'll set you forth.

Exeunt

78 The traditional place for Jessica and Lorenzo to sing a duet, as shown in Kemble's edition:

JESS   With vows of everlasting truth
You've won my captive heart
But, parted once, might I not find
That 'Out of sight were out of mind'?

LOR   Ah, do thyself no wrong, my dear!
Away with every jealous fear;
For each fair object, I might see,
Could but inspire a thought of thee.

BOTH   Thus absence fans to stronger flame
The love that fires the constant soul:
As distance points with surer aim
The faithful needle to its darling pole.

ACT 4, SCENE 1

4.[1] *Enter the* DUKE, *the Magnificoes,* ANTONIO, BASSANIO, [SALERIO,] *and* GRATIANO [*with others*]

DUKE What, is Antonio here?
ANTONIO Ready, so please your grace.

The word 'trial' is heard only once in 4.1, in Bellario's letter, but with such expressions as 'court', 'judge', 'judgment' and 'sentence' sprinkled throughout, the traditional label of 'trial scene' is not inappropriate. Any attempt to reconstruct the original staging is 99 per cent supposition – since the entering stage direction includes magnificoes, none of whom speaks, we may assume that Shakespeare's company would have used this scene, the only truly public one in the play, as an opportunity for some visual display.

The great actor-managers, just as they did with the earlier Venice scenes, competed to provide the most genuine reproduction of a known Renaissance interior. Charles Kean's scenic artists, Thomas Grieve and William Telbin, based their design on Odoardo Fialetti's painting of the Doge receiving Sir Henry Wootton, James I's ambassador to Venice (Furness, *A New Variorum Edition*, p. 189); Barrett and Booth's version of the Doge's council chamber included a reproduction of Tintoretto's fresco, *The Glory of Paradise*, on the back wall (*Amer. II*, p. 50).

osd One of the few details we have of Granville's *Jew of Venice* shows a desire to make the court as English as possible: Antonio enters '*as a Prisoner*', attended by 'Officers of the Court', while Nerissa enters with a '*Bagg and Papers*'.

Komisarjevsky, believing that this scene represents 'the crash of justice in the face of prejudice', had a crowd with sheeps' faces painted on the backdrop, 'and the magnificoes, identically costumed in scarlet robes with ruffs at the neck, had faces made up a nearly pure white' (Mennen, 'Theodore Komisarjevsky's Production', p. 395). In many respects, Serban's trial was strikingly similar to Komisarjevsky's: seated on benches, the magnificoes wore red robes and white masks, but Serban went a step further by having Portia and Nerissa costumed and masked the same way when they entered the court. The set 'featured an enormous red Bible upstage, open to *1 Corinthians* 13 written in gold, the words on charity being ironically salient' (Cook, *SB* 1999).

Piscator's courtroom was 'a square platform raised above the mirrored floor . . . as brightly lit as a boxing-ring, the dark walls of the Ghetto enclosing it' (Kennedy, *Looking at Shakespeare*, p. 202).

In all of the productions mentioned so far, Shylock was isolated against a large assembly of gentiles. Irving's court, 'a fine medieval chamber, with portraits of Venetian dignitaries of times gone by on the walls', also had 'a crowd of deeply-interested spectators, including Tubal and other Jews at the back' (*Theatre* 1 December 1879). Tree followed Irving's lead in providing Jewish spectators, to the disapproval of *The Times* (6 April 1908): 'As he makes each successive point he seems to glance in the direction of the little crowd of Jewish sympathizers, as though seeking their applause.' The *Times* critic did say, however, that Tree's 'staging of the trial scene is a great improvement' on Irving's, 'which squeezed the judicial bench into a corner: the Doge . . . and his crimson-robed councillors sit fairly and squarely facing the audience, and look as imposing as a Doge and his council should look'.

Guthrie used all of the large Ontario stage, and 'opened with a processional entry from all aisles of the auditorium – by clerks, red-robed justices and the retinue of the presiding Duke' (Griffin, *TA* 1955). He also included Tubal, played by Bruno Gerussi, who earned a stage manager's note of praise in the promptbook for a 'beautiful little performance in [the] court scene'.

Kahn made further use of Shylock's four bearded friends, and Kelly added 'a very large group of local, non-professional women performers, who appeared to be praying constantly, especially during the trial scene' (Schafer, *Ms-Directing Shakespeare*, p. 120). While an ostensibly Renaissance setting can more easily justify a large crowd of extras at the trial, Kelly's staging was unusual for her 1930s version – modern-dress productions usually strive for a greater sense of verisimilitude with a more intimate court, and of course few companies can afford too many extras (Kelly's were 'non-professional').

Jonathan Miller notes that his entire production concept for the *Merchant* grew out an idea of 'a rather boyish figure leaning forward over a table on one elbow' and giving the 'quality of mercy' speech in a 'rather irritable, explanatory tone of voice' (Berry, *On Directing Shakespeare*, pp. 29–30). Harold Hobson's assessment was, 'in the long history of *The Merchant of Venice* the trial scene can never have generated so little excitement; it is as flat as a puncture' (*ST* 3 May 1970).

Working in The Other Place, John Barton placed chairs around a 'central debating-area which became a combat-area' for what was 'essentially a duel between Shylock and Portia' (Warren, *SS* 1979) – Bernard Levin did not like 'such foolishness as a Ducal courtroom where the defendant is allowed to smoke' (*ST* 21 May 1978). On Stratford's main stage, Thacker provided a large boardroom table, and this was a court where 'Antonio was backed

DUKE I am sorry for thee. Thou art come to answer
　　　　　A stony adversary, an inhuman wretch,
　　　　　Uncapable of pity, void and empty　　　　　　　　　　5
　　　　　From any dram of mercy.
　　ANTONIO　　　　　　　　　　　I have heard
　　　　　Your grace hath tane great pains to qualify
　　　　　His rigorous course; but since he stands obdùrate
　　　　　And that no lawful means can carry me
　　　　　Out of his envy's reach, I do oppose　　　　　　　10
　　　　　My patience to his fury, and am armed
　　　　　To suffer with a quietness of spirit
　　　　　The very tyranny and rage of his.
DUKE Go one and call the Jew into the court.
SALERIO He is ready at the door; he comes, my lord.　　　15

by his friends, Shylock was conspicuously alone, the seats behind him empty' (Holland, *English Shakespeares*, p. 164). Nunn's traverse staging at the Cottesloe accommodated a judge's table at one end, and a spectators' gallery at the other.

1　Appearing with Macklin at Covent Garden on 10 October 1788, 'Mr [James] Fearon comported himself perfectly in the Duke – his taking Notes, &c. was good' (*World*, *qtd* Sprague, *Shakespeare and the Actors*, p. 26). Both Tree and Fagan dressed and made up the Duke to look like Doge Leonardo Loredani, as in the famous portrait by Giovanni Bellini; Tim Luscombe's crowd shouted 'Duce!' before Hugh Sullivan spoke (Biggs, *SB* 1991).

2　Antonio had to repeat this for a very deaf Duke in Schenk's production.

3　Miller's and Thacker's Duke made a point of not shaking hands with Antonio.

13　Nunn's Tubal (John Nolan) entered the courtroom here.

15sd　Reinhardt's stage direction is for Shylock to enter 'with a slow step, as perfectly in control of himself as at the beginning of the play, richly dressed and almost stonelike in his hate, armed with a sinister calm' (Styan, *Max Reinhardt*, p. 63). Arliss entered as 'the cultured and well-mannered broker' (Lelyveld, *Shylock on the Stage*, p. 110); Olivier walked in with two secretaries, 'jauntily, swinging a black briefcase, as if off for a day at the races' (Billington, *The Modern Actor*, p. 88). There was much murmuring from the extras as Warren Mitchell entered, placing scales and a knife on the table; Will LeBow also carried scales and knife – both he and Xia Zhiqing, in Kang Ansheng's Shanghai production, placed the scales on the floor centre stage while the Duke spoke.

　　David Calder caused some consternation when he entered wearing a yarmulke and a 'Jewish gaberdine' over a collarless shirt, a stark change from what he wore earlier in the play. In Barton's production, the 'mood of calm politeness and restraint was emphasized by the Duke himself serving Shylock with coffee' (Stewart, 'Shylock', p. 24).

Enter SHYLOCK

DUKE Make room and let him stand before our face.
　　　　Shylock, the world thinks, and I think so too,
　　　　That thou but leadest this fashion of thy malice
　　　　To the last hour of act, and then 'tis thought
　　　　Thou'lt show thy mercy and remorse more strange　　　20
　　　　Than is thy strange apparent cruelty.
　　　　And where thou now exacts the penalty,
　　　　Which is a pound of this poor merchant's flesh,
　　　　Thou wilt not only loose the forfeiture
　　　　But, touched with human gentleness and love,　　　25
　　　　Forgive a moiety of the principal,
　　　　Glancing an eye of pity on his losses
　　　　That have of late so huddled on his back,
　　　　Enow to press a royal merchant down
　　　　And pluck commiseration of his state　　　30
　　　　From brassy bosoms and rough hearts of flint,
　　　　From stubborn Turks, and Tartars never trained
　　　　To offices of tender courtesy.
　　　　We all expect a gentle answer, Jew.
SHYLOCK I have possessed your grace of what I purpose,　　　35
　　　　And by our holy Sabbath have I sworn
　　　　To have the due and forfeit of my bond.
　　　　If you deny it, let the danger light
　　　　Upon your charter and your city's freedom!
　　　　You'll ask me why I rather choose to have　　　40
　　　　A weight of carrion flesh than to receive

35–62 The *Spectator* (12 October 1839) says that with Macready, 'as in the first scene, the absence
　　　of personal malice towards Antonio was sensibly felt; it seemed as if a hard creditor were
　　　doggedly insisting upon an abstract legal right, and no more'. Gordon Crosse notes that
　　　Irving 'is absolutely sure of success as he stands up in the middle of the court, solitary but
　　　confident; he bows low to the Duke but to all others his attitude is one of scorn' (*Diaries*,
　　　vol. I, p. 175). Olivier, all business, took the bond from his briefcase as he spoke, sounding
　　　like 'a professor patiently trying various ways of explaining an idea to a slightly dull class'
　　　(Perret, 'Shakespeare and Anti-Semitism', p. 150).
38–9 Junius Brutus Booth gave these lines 'with an outreaching and arching motion of the arm
　　　and hand, palm downward, like the stoop of a bird of prey' (Gould, in Furness, *A New
　　　Variorum Edition*, p. 192).

Three thousand ducats. I'll not answer that –
But say it is my humour: is it answered?
What if my house be troubled with a rat,
And I be pleased to give ten thousand ducats   45
To have it baned? What, are you answered yet?
Some men there are love not a gaping pig;
Some that are mad if they behold a cat;
And others when the bagpipe sings i'the nose
Cannot contain their urine: for affection   50
Masters oft passion, sways it to the mood
Of what it likes or loathes. Now for your answer:
As there is no firm reason to be rendered
Why he cannot abide a gaping pig,
Why he a harmless necessary cat,   55
Why he a woollen bagpipe, but of force
Must yield to such inevitable shame
As to offend, himself being offended:
So can I give no reason, nor I will not,
More than a lodged hate and a certain loathing   60
I bear Antonio, that I follow thus
A losing suit against him. Are you answered?
BASSANIO This is no answer, thou unfeeling man,
　　To excuse the current of thy cruelty.
SHYLOCK I am not bound to please thee with my answers.   65
BASSANIO Do all men kill the things they do not love?
SHYLOCK Hates any man the thing he would not kill?
BASSANIO Every offence is not a hate at first.

47–9　LeBow pointed to Gratiano and the two Salads as he began his 'Some men there are'
　　discourse; they obligingly stood as examples, going along with what they thought was a
　　joke.
49–52a, 56a　Shylock's earthy comments about bagpipes and urine were always omitted in the
　　nineteenth century; also cut by Komisarjevsky and in the Globe production. Olivier's
　　delivery was staccato, pronouncing 'urine' with a long 'i'.
58b–62　Ron Leibman gave this speech a furious start, but suddenly changed his demeanour here
　　and spoke with quiet and sincere power.
63–9　Douglas Rain's 'careful unfolding of the cloths that hold his knives (while all around him, the
　　other characters are noisily arguing) shows a quietly chilling attachment to decorum and his
　　belief in his own rightness' (Bemrose, *MacI* 17 June 1996).

SHYLOCK What, wouldst thou have a serpent sting thee twice?
ANTONIO I pray you think you question with the Jew.   70
       You may as well go stand upon the beach
       And bid the main flood bate his usual height;
       You may as well use question with the wolf
       Why he hath made the ewe bleat for the lamb;
       You may as well forbid the mountain pines   75
       To wag their high tops and to make no noise
       When they are fretten with the gusts of heaven;
       You may as well do anything most hard
       As seek to soften that – than which what's harder? –
       His Jewish heart. Therefore I do beseech you   80
       Make no moe offers, use no farther means,
       But with all brief and plain conveniency
       Let me have judgement, and the Jew his will.
BASSANIO For thy three thousand ducats here is six.
SHYLOCK If every ducat in six thousand ducats   85
       Were in six parts, and every part a ducat,
       I would not draw them; I would have my bond.
DUKE How shalt thou hope for mercy, rendering none?
SHYLOCK What judgement shall I dread, doing no wrong?
       You have among you many a purchased slave,   90

69 Edmund Kean spoke with a 'horrid expression' (*pmt* E. Kean)

70 Charles Kean: 'Not to move or speak 'til Shy still' (*pmt* C. Kean[2]). Spoken as two sentences in Miller's television version: 'I pray you think! You question with the Jew?'.

84 Macready changed this line to 'here are six', his direction reading 'Takes a bag of money from Leonardo and advances to Shylock' (*pmt* C. Kean[1]). Ames's promptbook notes of Forbes-Robertson: '[He] picks up a few ducats from the open bag and lets them drop contemptuously with good effect' (*pmt* Ames[1]). Alexander's production had 'a good moment when both [Shylock] and Antonio laugh jointly at the offer of six thousand ducats' (Billington, *Gdn* 1 May 1987).

85–7 Macready: 'Goes up to Bassanio before he speaks' (*pmt*). Peter O'Toole spoke with a 'quiet voice and almost closed eyes' (Brown, *SS* 1961).

88 David Burt spoke this very angrily in Nunn's production.

90–7 Antony Sher seized 'an abject, shivering black slave and [shook] him in front of the Venetian nobility as they seek to lecture him on Christian love and compassion' (Nathan, *JC* 8 May 1987). In Kelly's modern setting, Gary Waldhorn pointed to a black court usher with the same effect (Hopkins, *SB* 1994). Sellars used the television cameras and monitors he placed about the stage, focussing on a black police guard, Paul Butler saying 'Let them be free'

Which, like your asses and your dogs and mules,
You use in abject and in slavish parts
Because you bought them. Shall I say to you,
'Let them be free! Marry them to your heirs!
Why sweat they under burdens? Let their beds   95
Be made as soft as yours, and let their palates
Be seasoned with such viands'? You will answer,
'The slaves are ours.' So do I answer you.
The pound of flesh which I demand of him
Is dearly bought; 'tis mine, and I will have it.   100
If you deny me, fie upon your law:
There is no force in the decrees of Venice.
I stand for judgement. Answer: shall I have it?
DUKE Upon my power I may dismiss this court,
Unless Bellario, a learned doctor   105
Whom I have sent for to determine this,
Come here today.
SALERIO   My lord, here stays without
A messenger with letters from the doctor,
New come from Padua.
DUKE Bring us the letters. Call the messenger.   110
BASSANIO Good cheer, Antonio! What, man, courage yet!
The Jew shall have my flesh, blood, bones, and all,
Ere thou shalt lose for me one drop of blood.

three times as the monitors showed President Bush (Sr) 'apparently urging on the cops to
smash Black Power demonstrations' (Macaulay, *FT* 18 November 1994). Thacker, in an effort
to avoid an obvious anachronism, changed 'purchased slave' to 'purchased man' (*pmt*). In
Olivier's performance this line was 'driven in like a series of hammer-blows' (Billington,
The Modern Actor, p. 83).

103a O'Toole's strong 'I stand for judgement' suddenly 'stilled an angry court' (Brown, *SS* 1961);
Frederick Valk created the opposite effect, provoking a 'big reaction' from the onlookers
(*pmt* Guthrie). Dustin Hoffman went for 'Chaplinesque vulgarity' by rasping 'I stand for
judgement' and then squatting down on a portmanteau (Hiley, *Lst* June 1989); similarly
Chaplinesque was LeBow's choosing this moment to pop a peanut into his mouth.

107b–9 Schenk had Salarino enter and whisper to Salerio, who, after much mutual winking,
announced the arrival of the messenger from Padua. Their secret (obviously the real
identity of Balthazar and the Clerk) was then passed amongst the other spectators.

112–13 Booth: 'Shylock smiles scornfully, and slowly drawing his knife, at [119], kneels to whet it'
(Furness, *A New Variorum Edition*, p. 204).

ANTONIO I am a tainted wether of the flock,
        Meetest for death; the weakest kind of fruit   115
        Drops earliest to the ground, and so let me.
        You cannot better be employed, Bassanio,
        Than to live still and write mine epitaph.

Enter NERISSA [*disguised as a lawyer's clerk*]

DUKE Came you from Padua, from Bellario?
NERISSA From both, my lord: [*Presenting letter*] Bellario greets your
        grace.   120
BASSANIO Why dost thou whet thy knife so earnestly?

114–18 Alexander's Antonio cast Bassanio 'violently aside, in the fierce intensity of his wish to sustain his role of a "tainted wether of the flock" to the point of martyrdom' (Wells, *SS* 1988). Olivier 'chuckled knowingly . . . which instantly tells us that the Merchant's homosexuality was a common secret' (Billington, *The Modern Actor*, p. 80).

119 Macready: 'Shylock comm. sharpening his knife on the stage, and afterwards, on the sole of his shoe' (*pmt*).

120 Charles Kean: 'Herald points to Nerissa to take her seat. Shylock whets his knife. All shudder and look intently' (*pmt* C. Kean[2]). Schenk's Nerissa, Anna Tardi, disguised her voice by pretending to have a cold.

121 Early Shylocks were known for the wicked gusto with which they sharpened their knives. In 1781 Macklin was reported to have been so terrifying that 'a young man who was in the pit fainted away', while Cooke impressed with his 'savage and determined method of whetting his knife on the floor, and the fiend-like look that accompanied it' (Sprague, *Shakespeare and the Actors*, p. 27). A clergyman named Alfred Gatty saw Edmund Kean in his youth: 'I remember him in Shylock giving, with savage glee, a few strokes of his knife on the floor of the stage, in anticipation of the pound of flesh, and the whole house felt the flash of his look' (*NQ* 30 Dec 1893).

    Jacob Adler was at pains to show that his sole aim was to terrify Antonio, and that he did not intend to exact the penalty: 'When he sharpened the knife to cut the pound of flesh from the bankrupt . . . Shylock slyly noted whether the proud merchant quailed' (*American Hebrew*, qtd Berkowitz, 'A True Jewish Jew', p. 80).

    Stewart, Suchet, Hoffman and Leibman all used their shoe, as the text requires; when a favourable verdict was slow in coming Stewart 'pounded the chair with it impatiently and angrily' (Velz, 'The Merchant', p. 101); Suchet turned the whetting of his blade 'into a moment of utter, aching solitude for Shylock' (Maguin, 'The Merchant', p. 114). The most frightening knife-sharpening was in Miller's production, as one of Olivier's silent secretaries calmly worked the blade against a small stone; Bassanio addressed the question to him.

SHYLOCK To cut the forfeiture from that bankrupt there.
GRATIANO Not on thy sole, but on thy soul, harsh Jew,
          Thou mak'st thy knife keen. But no metal can,
          No, not the hangman's axe, bear half the keenness   125
          Of thy sharp envy. Can no prayers pierce thee?
SHYLOCK No, none that thou hast wit enough to make.
GRATIANO O be thou damned, inexecrable dog,
          And for thy life let justice be accused!
          Thou almost mak'st me waver in my faith,   130
          To hold opinion with Pythagoras
          That souls of animals infuse themselves
          Into the trunks of men. Thy currish spirit
          Governed a wolf, who – hanged for human slaughter –
          Even from the gallows did his fell soul fleet,   135
          And whilst thou layest in thy unhallowed dam
          Infused itself in thee; for thy desires
          Are wolfish, bloody, starved, and ravenous.
SHYLOCK Till thou canst rail the seal from off my bond
          Thou but offend'st thy lungs to speak so loud.   140
          Repair thy wit, good youth, or it will fall
          To cureless ruin. I stand here for law.

123–6a Omitted Inchbald edition, Kemble, Charles Kean and other early promptbooks, since Shylock did not use his shoe to whet the knife. Line 123 only cut by Miller, Thacker and Maraden for the same reason.

127 The origins of Shylock pulling a hair from his head or beard in order to test the blade are not clear – Booth and Novelli both did it, and the *New York Times* (4 February 1867) called Booth's action 'an absurdity'. Mitchell revived the absurdity for the BBC as he spoke this line; O'Toole performed the test on a piece of cloth held by Tubal (Findlater, *FT* 14 April 1960).

139–40 Edmund Kean pointed 'to the seal on his bond with a savage expression' (*pmt*); Furness notes that his father remembered the actor's 'prolonged, grating, guttural tone of utter contempt' (Furness, *A New Variorum Edition*, p. 207). Booth spoke with 'imperturbable and assured insolence' (Towse, *Sixty Years*, p. 189); Olivier nicely beckoned Gratiano with his finger before giving his retort; Hoffman made a broader 'come on, keep going' gesture with his hand.

142b Alexander's Gratiano, Geoffrey Freshwater, spat in Shylock's face. Charles Kean's drier direction is 'All turn enquiring to the Duke' (*pmt* C. Kean[2]).

DUKE This letter from Bellario doth commend
          A young and learned doctor to our court:
          Where is he?
NERISSA   He attendeth here hard by   145
          To know your answer whether you'll admit him.
DUKE With all my heart. Some three or four of you
          Go give him courteous conduct to this place.

                                        [*Exeunt officials*]
          Meantime the court shall hear Bellario's letter.
[*Reads*] 'Your grace shall understand, that at the receipt of your   150
          letter I am very sick; but in the instant that your messenger
          came, in loving visitation was with me a young doctor of Rome:
          his name is Balthazar. I acquainted him with the cause in
          controversy between the Jew and Antonio the merchant. We
          turned o'er many books together; he is furnished with my   155
          opinion which, bettered with his own learning, the greatness
          whereof I cannot enough commend, comes with him at my
          importunity, to fill up your grace's request in my stead. I
          beseech you let his lack of years be no impediment to let him
          lack a reverend estimation, for I never knew so young a body   160
          with so old a head. I leave him to your gracious acceptance,
          whose trial shall better publish his commendation.'

144 Being aware of who the 'young and learned doctor' is, Antonio's friends in Schenk's
     production grinned at this announcement.
150–62 Ames's Duke used a magnifying glass (*pmt* Ames[2]). Irving had a court clerk read the letter,
     as did Komisarjevsky, whose Duke nodded off, while the clerk shouted a few times in an
     attempt to awaken him, and Antonio 'preened himself in a little mirror that hung around his
     neck, totally unconcerned about losing his flesh' (Mennen, 'Theodore Komisarjevsky's
     Production', p. 396). Gascon's Nerissa began to read in her disguised voice, and heaved a
     sigh of relief when a court official took over (Barnes, *NYT* 10 June 1970).
160 Miller's Duke said 'I never knew so young a body' as a complete sentence, then turned the
     page over and added 'with so old a head'. This ranks alongside Lancelot's 'adieu/a Jew' (see
     p. 139) as the worst-ever *Merchant* joke.
162sd Ellen Terry and her predecessors customarily wore a scarlet lawyer's gown; Helena
     Modjeska was noteworthy in that she 'wore, instead of the red robes of recent Portias,
     a black cloak with black velvet trunks and black silk tights' (*NYT* 29 October 1889). The
     Birmingham Repertory received praise for Portia's yellow and white robes in 1915, 'which
     contrasted with Antonio's gold-coloured costume as he stood on the opposite side of

Enter PORTIA [*disguised as Doctor Balthazar, followed by officials*]

> You hear the learn'd Bellario what he writes,
> And here I take it is the doctor come.
> Give me your hand. Come you from old Bellario?   165

PORTIA I did, my lord.

DUKE   You are welcome; take your place.
> Are you acquainted with the difference
> That holds this present question in the court?

the stage' (Cochrane, *Shakespeare and the Birmingham Repertory Theatre*, p. 63). Komisarjevsky did away with the gown, and dressed Fabia Drake 'in the clothes of a modern young lawyer, with "a Henry Lyttonish wig and bicycle-wheel spectacles" ' (*The Stage, qtd* Mennen, 'Theodore Komisarjevsky's Production', p. 396). At the Old Vic in 1953, Kenneth Tynan was impressed with Roger Furse's Restoration 'knee-breeches and full-bottomed wig' for Irene Worth, transforming her 'into a dazzling coffeehouse spark' (*Curtains*, p. 36).

   Ellen Terry notes in her memoirs that 'the German actress plays Portia as a low comedy part: she wears an eighteenth-century law wig, horn spectacles, a cravat (this last anachronism is not confined to Germany), and often a moustache!' (Terry, *Story*, p. 185). One wonders what Terry would have thought of Schenk's 1969 television production, where, except for the wig, Sabine Sinjen was faithful to German tradition.

   In modern-dress productions, Portia is able to wear a business suit: Billington observes that Penny Downie resembled 'a sober-suited Sir Norman Fowler', then chairman of Britain's Conservative Party (*Gdn* 4 April 1994). In Nunn's 1930s setting, Derbhle Crotty looked 'eerily like an overworked young male barrister' (Spencer, *DT* 21 June 1999), somehow appearing with a short, masculine haircut.

   Serban's very unusual staging had Portia and Nerissa don the same white masks worn by the magnificoes: their amplified voices were thin and disembodied. In Shanghai, Kang Ansheng's Portia and Nerissa 'played their transformation strongly: both women appeared dressed in black lawyers' gowns, with dark pageboy hair in place of their curly blond wigs' (Stanley, '1994 Shanghai', p. 77).

165 In Langham's 1960 production, Dorothy Tutin looked 'so slight a figure' as Balthazar that 'one sympathises with this Duke's astonished "Come *you* from old Bellario?" ' (Roberts, *PP* 1960).

166 For Benthall, Barbara Jefford 'came face to face with Bassanio and for a second halted in confusion but then, turning aside her face, went bravely on' (Clarke, *Shakespeare at the Old Vic*, np). Macready and Booth had Portia sit after replying (*pmt* Macready, Booth[1]).

PORTIA I am informèd thoroughly of the cause.
            Which is the merchant here and which the Jew?   170
DUKE Antonio and old Shylock, both stand forth.
PORTIA Is your name Shylock?
SHYLOCK   Shylock is my name.
PORTIA Of a strange nature is the suit you follow,
            Yet in such rule that the Venetian law
            Cannot impugn you as you do proceed.   175
            – You stand within his danger, do you not?
ANTONIO Ay, so he says.
PORTIA   Do you confess the bond?
ANTONIO I do.
PORTIA   Then must the Jew be merciful.
SHYLOCK On what compulsion must I? Tell me that.
PORTIA The quality of mercy is not strained,   180

170 In the Globe production, Bassanio and Gratiano were angry 'to learn that an inexperienced youngster was taking the place of the distinguished lawyer they had been expecting' (Potter, 'Shakespeare Performed', p. 76); for Edelstein it was Shylock who was annoyed.

172 In Zadek's Berliner Ensemble production, Eva Mattess mistook Ignaz Kirchner's Antonio, 'a small, dark, unprepossessing figure, myopically blinking behind his specs', for Shylock, and addressed '*Ist Ihr Name Shylock?*' to him. Gert Voss curtly answered for Antonio: '*Shylock ist mein Name*' (Nightingale, *Times* 31 August 1995).

179 At the Globe, Norbert Kentrup spoke 'like a teacher politely pointing out a pupil's failure in logic' (Potter, 'Shakespeare Performed', p. 76).

180–201 When Sarah Siddons did Portia at Drury Lane for her brother John Philip Kemble's benefit on 6 April 1786, the *Morning Chronicle* noted 'Mrs Siddons spoke the speech on mercy as it certainly should be spoken – but as in truth we never heard it spoken – as a reply to "On what compulsion must I?". From every other Portia it has always appeared as a *recitation*, prepared for the occasion' (*qtd London Stage*, pt. 5, p. 876).

Clearly, by this time the 'Mercy' speech had become a 'Treasure from Shakespeare', in large part due to the ease with which it can be anthologised. The first fourteen lines, until 'Therefore, Jew', are without indication of context, and hence we have Shakespeare's, not Portia's, encomium to mercy. Ellen Terry had less success than Mrs Siddons: the London *Truth* (6 November 1879) was delighted with her Portia in the first half of the play, but the 'famous appeal for mercy . . . [was] the recitation of a speech learnt by heart by a school-girl tricked out in her brother's clothes'.

Every Portia faces the challenge of avoiding the 'set piece', exacerbated here because the message is a religious one – the combination of 'set piece and sermon' is enough to drive many an actress and her director to desperate measures, or, as Geraldine James appeared to do in Hall's production, just get through it as quickly as possible. When reading the play, we tend to think only about the speaker, but if the trial is to be exciting drama rather than recitation, then our concern is not just with Portia's appeal, but whether or not Shylock is listening to it. Television directors have not helped us a great deal on this point: both Miller and Gold announced 'here it comes' by going to a medium-shot of Portia before she spoke, and then (somewhat shakily in Gold's case) moving closer over the first few lines. Messina, although he did not zoom in on Maggie Smith, kept the camera on her throughout – Smith's classroom elocution was also unfortunate. Miller did not show Shylock's face until 'see salvation', Messina and Gold not at all. Alan Horrox, by changing his camera angle several times during the speech, putting both Haydn Gwynne and Bob Peck on screen in a single shot, and giving Peck reaction shots, succeeded in retrieving the passage from the high school auditorium and returning it to the drama.

Helena Modjeska made a quiet and private appeal, meant for Shylock's ears only, not a lawyer's argument in open court. She said in an interview, 'It was not addressed to judge or jury; it was a woman talking to the Jew: a woman pleading with the man' (*qtd* Coleman, *Fair Rosalind*, pp. 644–5). Ethel Barrymore had great success with the same approach:

> Instead of making a speech I merely answered his question very quietly, 'The quality of mercy is not strained', and then proceeded, still very quietly as the speech went on, becoming more and more legal and developing the plea that Portia was going to make. It had a curious, overwhelming effect on the audience. I never heard such silence, and then a sort of gasp, much as to say, 'Why, that was the speech!' (Barrymore, *Memories*, p. 186).

At the Old Vic in 1932, Peggy Ashcroft spoke 'naturally, her hands behind her back', and at Stratford in 1978, Marjorie Bland's appeal for mercy 'is spoken without heaviness or artifice, and falls on the ear as if we have never heard it before' (Billington, *Peggy Ashcroft*, p. 63; Levin, *ST* 21 May 1978).

Two German Portias spoke quietly to Fritz Kortner: in 1927, Monty Jacobs heard Elisabeth Bergner appealing to 'Shylock's gentler instincts', showing 'heartfelt sadness' when receiving no response (*qtd* Sehrt, 'Der Shylock', p. 91); Alfred Kerr notes that Kortner 'looked at her in awe for a moment, as if looking upon a granddaughter' (*qtd* Sehrt, 'Der Shylock', p. 91). In 1969, Sabine Sinjen sat down next to Kortner and attempted to reason with him, although in a patronising manner, speaking very slowly as if to a child; he was abrupt and dismissive.

An alternative to the 'gentle approach' is to lecture Shylock rather sternly. Fabia Drake, 'leaning over her desk, snaps the poor old Jew's head off with the retort – the effect is electrical' (*Obs*, *qtd* Mennen, 'Theodore Komisarjevsky's Production', p. 396). Plowright, also leaning across the table (see p. 212), 'in a flat voice, develops the argument

It droppeth as the gentle rain from heaven
Upon the place beneath. It is twice blest:
It blesseth him that gives, and him that takes.
'Tis mightiest in the mightiest, it becomes
The thronèd monarch better than his crown.   185
His sceptre shows the force of temporal power,
The attribute to awe and majesty,
Wherein doth sit the dread and fear of kings;
But mercy is above this sceptred sway.
It is enthronèd in the hearts of kings,   190
It is an attribute to God himself,
And earthly power doth then show likest God's
When mercy seasons justice. Therefore, Jew,

exactly in the manner used by Mrs Barbara Castle when, as Minister for Transport, she defended the merits of the breathalyser on television' (Weightman, *Enc* 1970). Other less than successful attempts were made by Margaret Phillips for Marre, who set 'back the cause of women lawyers twenty years' by speaking 'as if she were delivering a chemical abstract' (Hewes, *SR* 21 March 1953), and Katharine Hepburn, who 'so broke up the passage that she seemed literally to have forgotten it; in the end it sounded as though she were dictating a letter to a not terribly efficient secretary' (Kerr, *Theater in Spite of Itself*, p. 278).

Derbhle Crotty, several lines into the speech, took a chair and sat down directly opposite Henry Goodman, 'delivering the rest of it straight to him with an earnest intensity that rivetted his attention. Never before, one felt, had a member of the Christian community spoken to him with this degree of immediacy, and it was curiously welcome' (Smallwood, *SS* 2000).

184 'Charles Macklin and his daughter are said to have been estranged for years by a quarrel as to the correct way of speaking one phrase in the address on Mercy. Miss Macklin insisted on saying, "Tis mightiest in the *mightiest*"; her father maintained that it should be, "Tis mightiest *in* the mightiest" ' (Archer, *Theatrical World*, p. 155).

191 Modjeska describes how she surprised Booth by touching him on the shoulder at this point: 'He started back, and in a whisper cried to me, "that is all wrong, all wrong"; and his horror of my innovation quite distorted his face.' But the 'starting back' got Booth a round of applause, and after commending Modjeska later that evening, he incorporated the business into his production (Coleman, *Fair Rosalind*, p. 645).

192 Booth: 'At the mention of the sacred name, Shylock bows reverently, which none of the Christians do. Cooke, when commended for this, said it was Macklin's business' (Furness, *A New Variorum Edition*, p. 213).

Though justice be thy plea, consider this:
That in the course of justice, none of us   195
Should see salvation. We do pray for mercy,
And that same prayer doth teach us all to render
The deeds of mercy. I have spoke thus much
To mitigate the justice of thy plea,
Which if thou follow, this strict court of Venice   200
Must needs give sentence 'gainst the merchant there.
SHYLOCK My deeds upon my head! I crave the law,
The penalty and forfeit of my bond.

197–8a Here Cooke 'made a movement of head and hand to signify his rejection of the sentiment as
something completely irrelevant to himself and his race' (Dunlap, *ctd* Winter, *Shakespeare
on the Stage*, p. 146). Kortner also made a firm gesture of dismissal, and Sinjen addressed
the court for 198b–201.

198–9   Charles Kean: 'All speak to each other of Portia's speech' (*pmt* C. Kean[2]).

202–3   Charlotte Porter provides a vivid description of how Booth responded to Portia's appeal (the
Portia is likely to have been Minna Gale):

> he stands, stolid, his eyes closed, every muscle still, in a quietude fixed as stone and
> as impenetrable. He does not attend, except to know the end, it seems at first, when
> suddenly it is borne in upon you that after all he is listening intently, as one would listen
> to a half-remembered refrain of music calling from a long way off . . . The voice stops.
> There is a pause. Then Shylock stirs, shakes his head free from the spell, and in the same
> breath, decides – 'My deeds upon my head! I crave the *Law*'. (Porter, 'The Drama',
> pp. 123–4)

This is an important moment for any Shylock. Is he at all persuaded by Portia's plea, so
that he pauses, as Booth did, or is he as adamant as Irving, who spoke 'with stubborn
monotony – he was perfectly unruffled and stood with head erect' (Irving, *Henry Irving*,
p. 342). In recent times, Leibman, Rain, Peck and Holbrook showed no hesitation at all;
Olivier did not speak at once, but slammed his hand down on the table before an emphatic
'I crave the LAW!', and did so twice again, at 'forfeit' and 'bond' in the following line. Bedford
paused only momentarily, but Suchet, after hearing Sinead Cusack's 'strictly forensic
argument', took a 'tremendously prolonged pause' (Wardle, *Times* 22 April 1981).

Henry Goodman created 'almost unbearable suspense, before a returning awareness of
the Gratiano mob rekindled his resolve, and he just managed to find the strength to say
"my deeds upon my head" ' (Smallwood, *SS* 2000). In the 17 August 1999 performance,
videotaped for the Royal National Theatre's archives, Goodman's pause lasted an
astonishing twenty-eight seconds.

PORTIA Is he not able to discharge the money?
BASSANIO Yes, here I tender it for him in the court,   205
          Yea, twice the sum; if that will not suffice,
          I will be bound to pay it ten times o'er
          On forfeit of my hands, my head, my heart.
          If this will not suffice, it must appear
          That malice bears down truth. And I beseech you   210
          Wrest once the law to your authority;
          To do a great right, do a little wrong,
          And curb this cruel devil of his will.
PORTIA It must not be; there is no power in Venice
          Can alter a decree establishèd.   215
          'Twill be recorded for a precedent,
          And many an error by the same example
          Will rush into the state: it cannot be.
SHYLOCK A Daniel come to judgement; yea a Daniel!
          O wise young judge, how I do honour thee!   220
PORTIA I pray you let me look upon the bond.
SHYLOCK Here 'tis, most reverend doctor, here it is.
PORTIA Shylock, there's thrice thy money offered thee.

205–6 Mansfield had Shylock's friends make pleading gestures for him to accept the ducats, but after 'a grim pause . . . [he] finally dashes the gold upon the ground and claims his bond' (Sprague, *Shakespeare and the Actors*, p. 26). Doran, in 'the most spectacular visual effect of the production', had Bassanio open a large chest of golden coins and spill them across the floor (Jackson, *SQ* 1999). Serban's Bassanio, Andrew Garman, placed a packet of bank notes on Shylock's scales.

206 'Twice' often changed to 'thrice' in the eighteenth and nineteenth centuries, to create consistency with 223, but see 84.

219 Edmund Kean displayed 'savage exultation and joy' at this moment (*pmt* E. Kean); Paul Sparer had all of Kean's 'exultation and joy', but none of the savagery; his happy astonishment at the young advocate's reply to Bassanio was electrifying. Valk kissed the hem of Portia's gown (*pmt* Guthrie), a 'point' extending back through Sothern and Irving to Booth, and possibly further (Furness, *A New Variorum Edition*, p. 214). Luther Adler, who 'throughout the trial . . . kept up an air of amused detachment, smiling condescendingly at Antonio's slow-witted stoicism', complimented Portia 'in the same patronizing and sarcastic vein' (Barbour, 'Theatre Chronicle', p. 284). Kahn's Jewish spectators on the gallery shouted 'a Daniel!'.

221 Kortner fumbled for the bond, momentarily unable to find it.

223 Goodman tore up the cheque Bassanio handed him: 'mercy he might have been moved by, money never' (Smallwood, *SS* 2000).

SHYLOCK An oath, an oath. I have an oath in heaven!
           Shall I lay perjury upon my soul?   225
           No, not for Venice.
PORTIA   Why, this bond is forfeit,
           And lawfully by this the Jew may claim
           A pound of flesh, to be by him cut off
           Nearest the merchant's heart. Be merciful:
           Take thrice thy money; bid me tear the bond.   230
SHYLOCK When it is paid, according to the tenour.
           It doth appear you are a worthy judge,
           You know the law, your exposition
           Hath been most sound. I charge you by the law,
           Whereof you are a well-deserving pillar,   235
           Proceed to judgement. By my soul I swear
           There is no power in the tongue of man
           To alter me. I stay here on my bond.
ANTONIO Most heartily I do beseech the court
           To give the judgement.
PORTIA   Why then, thus it is: 240
           You must prepare your bosom for his knife.
SHYLOCK O noble judge, O excellent young man!
PORTIA For the intent and purpose of the law
           Hath full relation to the penalty
           Which here appeareth due upon the bond.   245

---

225 Charles Kemble once said 'Shall I lay surgery upon my pole?' (Murdoch, *The Stage*, p. 394).

226a Guthrie: 'Shylock raises arms, Tubal turns away' (*pmt*).

229a In an original touch, Maggie Smith said 'Nearest the merchant's heart' as if this provision in the bond took her by surprise.

229b–30 Urged privately, 'in intimate tones' by Gemma Jones (Bulman, *Shakespeare in Performance*, p. 114).

231 Cooke's audience was 'surprised and delighted by the abruptness of his reply to Portia's request that he would permit the bond to be torn . . . indicating a degree of apprehension lest she *should* tear it, and at the same time, a malignant recognition of the penalty due' (Dunlap, *qtd* Furness, *A New Variorum Edition*, pp. 215–16).

236b–8 Calder was loud and forceful; Goodman kissed the fringe of his *tallith*.

240–8 Miller did some liberal rearranging of the text here.

242 Moscovitch 'carefully takes off his rings that they shall not get soiled with his victim's blood – a very grim touch. He seizes Antonio and forces him to his knees' (*Times* 10 October 1919).

SHYLOCK 'Tis very true. O wise and upright judge,
How much more elder art thou than thy looks!
PORTIA Therefore lay bare your bosom.
SHYLOCK   Ay, his breast.
So says the bond, doth it not, noble judge?
'Nearest his heart': those are the very words.   250
PORTIA It is so. Are there balance here to weigh
The flesh?
SHYLOCK   I have them ready.
PORTIA Have by some surgeon, Shylock, on your charge,
To stop his wounds, lest he do bleed to death.
SHYLOCK Is it so nominated in the bond?   255
PORTIA It is not so expressed, but what of that?
'Twere good you do so much for charity.
SHYLOCK I cannot find it, 'tis not in the bond.

248b–50 'Thespis' describes Cooke's rendering of 'the shocking depravity and fiend-like revenge of this subtle and malignant Israelite . . . from the moment Shylock whets his knife . . . to the favorable decision of the judge, his rising expressions of demoniac joy and exultation at the prospect of obtaining unqualified revenge, were strikingly expressive, and executed with the most masterly skill' (*Annals*. II, pp. 359–60).

251 'Kean hardly allowed time to utter the words "Are there balances [*sic*] here" before their clink jarred on the ear, and they glittered in his hand; Macready had to dive down into a deep pocket for, and then to adjust, them' (*Spectator* 12 October 1839). Norbert Kentrup's 'those are the very words' caused Kathryn Pogson to 'look again at the bond, realizing, that its precise wording would be the key to the case' (Potter, 'Shakespeare Performed', p. 76).

251 Katharine Hepburn's question was 'purely rhetorical, as the most prominent property on the stage [was] an oversize pair of scales' (Wyatt, *CW* 1957).

252b 'Mr Forbes-Robertson does not produce scales, but merely says "I have them ready" with a quiet look to Tubal for affirmation' (*pmt* Ames[1]). Guthrie's direction is 'Shylock motions to Tubal, who produces scales.' Charles Kean, with his characteristic attention to the supernumeraries, demands a 'slight movement of disgust' (*pmt* C. Kean[2]).

255 Gert Voss 'became less an heroic victim than a cool capitalist: advised to have a surgeon standing by, he spent a good couple of minutes scanning the contract' (Billington, *Gdn* 18 April 1991).

258 Cooke said this 'with a savage sneer' (Findlater, *Player Kings*, p. 73); Edmund Kean, while 'looking on the bond', offered 'a transported chuckle' (*pmt* E. Kean; Hillebrand, *Edmund Kean*, p. 110). Olivier said 'I cannot find it' quietly, then shouted ' 'tis not in the bond!'; Calder held up the bond for Antonio to see.

PORTIA You, merchant: have you anything to say?

ANTONIO But little; I am armed and well prepared.   260

        Give me your hand, Bassanio. Fare you well.

        Grieve not that I am fall'n to this for you.

        For herein Fortune shows herself more kind

        Than is her custom: it is still her use

        To let the wretched man outlive his wealth,   265

        To view with hollow eye and wrinkled brow

        An age of poverty; from which ling'ring penance

        Of such misery doth she cut me off.

        Commend me to your honourable wife.

        Tell her the process of Antonio's end,   270

        Say how I loved you, speak me fair in death,

        And when the tale is told, bid her be judge

        Whether Bassanio had not once a love.

        Repent but you that you shall lose your friend

        And he repents not that he pays your debt.   275

        For if the Jew do cut but deep enough

        I'll pay it instantly with all my heart.

BASSANIO Antonio, I am married to a wife

        Which is as dear to me as life itself;

        But life itself, my wife, and all the world,   280

        Are not with me esteemed above thy life.

        I would lose all, ay, sacrifice them all

        Here to this devil, to deliver you.

PORTIA Your wife would give you little thanks for that

        If she were by to hear you make the offer.   285

260 Helen Faucit introduced the business of Portia quietly conferring with the Duke while Antonio speaks (Sprague, *Shakespeare and the Actors*, p. 16).

267 Guthrie: 'Portia motions to Nerissa to cross to Portia with book' (*pmt*).

269–73 Moved to the end of Antonio's speech by Miller and by Hands.

273 For Alexander, John Carlisle stroked 'the hair and neck of his young friend'; for Nunn, David Bamber 'fondled his friend's face and kissed him' (Bulman, *Shakespeare in Performance*, p. 130; Smallwood, *SS* 2000).

274–7 Guthrie had Portia turn the page of a law book, mark it with a red ribbon and give it to Nerissa (*pmt*).

284–5, 289–90 Portia and Nerissa making somewhat risqué remarks was unacceptable in the nineteenth century, and these lines were deleted, although they are not marked for omission in Irving's edition.

GRATIANO I have a wife who I protest I love;
                    I would she were in heaven, so she could
                    Entreat some power to change this currish Jew.
NERISSA 'Tis well you offer it behind her back;
                    The wish would make else an unquiet house.   290
SHYLOCK These be the Christian husbands! I have a daughter:
                    Would any of the stock of Barabbas
                    Had been her husband, rather than a Christian!
                    We trifle time; I pray thee pursue sentence.
PORTIA A pound of that same merchant's flesh is thine,   295
                    The court awards it, and the law doth give it.
SHYLOCK Most rightful judge!
PORTIA And you must cut this flesh from off his breast;
                    The law allows it, and the court awards it.
SHYLOCK Most learned judge! A sentence: come, prepare.   300

291–3 Hoffman, 'in his one cheap touch, nudges the audience to milk a laugh . . . with a Henny Youngman shrug on "These be the Christian husbands" ' (Rich, *NYT* 20 December 1989). Holbrook spoke while Gratiano, Antonio and Bassanio loudly prayed; Calder sobbed as he recalled Jessica, while Downie regarded him with an anguished expression, 'but then he recollects himself and, in full view, his face becomes marble once more' (Geckle, *SB* 1994; Macaulay, *FT* 5 June 1993).

294 Daly: 'Gratiano attitude of alarm. Nerissa her face buried in her hands . . . Bassanio staying Antonio who is about to bare his breast. Senators and Clerks half rise in various attitudes' (*pmt* Moore/Daly). Guthrie had a bell rung here, and three more times, at 296, 299, 300. Schenk's courtroom became a madhouse, as Nerissa clanged a cymbal and the Salads exchanged alarmed whispers, concerned that something had gone wrong with the rigging of the trial.

296, 299 Nunn gave these lines to the Duke.

300 Edmund Kean was seen 'hastening to Antonio, the knife ready in his hand' (*pmt* E. Kean). Macready was too 'tame and deliberate' throughout the scene, so 'when he stepped forward, knife in hand, to enforce sentence, the unlikelihood of the scene struck one – not the terrible nature of the deed' (*Spectator* 12 October 1839).
         Irving, as Crosse witnessed, 'takes a step towards Antonio with the knife and scales in his hands, at the same moment the spectators headed by Gratiano are about to dash forward, when Portia, interposing, checks both Shylock & them with the words "tarry a little" ' (*Diaries*, vol. I, p. 175). More theatrical was Moscovitch's 'shrill, acrid cry' and his 'leap upon the victim' (*NYT* 16 November 1930). When Louis Bouwmeester took over the part (see p. 43),

he took three or four diabolical minutes to sharpen an evil little knife on his shoes; then he tested the scales for weighing the flesh with his thin fingers in a peculiarly sickening way. Just before he was to sink the knife into Antonio's flesh, he was seized with a paroxysm of excitement – it was like watching a maniac shaken by some profane orgasm. It was so scarifying that a woman in the audience at the first performance let out a terrified shriek and fainted. (Denham, *Stars in My Hair*, p. 93)

Margaret Webster included a monk bearing a white cross in the scene. 'When Antonio prepared himself for the knife, the monk lowered the cross over him' and administered the Sacrament of Absolution (Matthews, *TW* 1956; *pmt* Webster).

Marre's staging had Luther Adler approach Antonio 'in a long, slow cross, taking the full stage left to right, plainly relishing the panic calculated by his delay; and, having reached him, he held out his hand, palm outward and fingers extended down, in a gesture that made no sense if it was not intended as a signal of reprieve'. When Antonio 'uncharitably spat into the forgiving hand, Shylock, crying out in disgust, might have been ready then to draw out his knife . . . but he was too late' (Barbour, 'Theatre Chronicle', p. 284.) Kortner screamed '*Kommt, macht Euch fertig!*', and, during a long silence, 'walked toward Antonio, as if he were in a state of hypnosis' (Sehrt, 'Der Shylock', p. 94). Max Eckard fainted as he approached.

Alexander aroused a good deal of controversy by having Sher don a *tallith* when preparing to take Antonio's pound of flesh, and begin what purported to be 'an old Hebraic song of sacrifice' (Pitcher, *TLS* 15 May 1987), although no such ritual exists in Hebrew scripture (Nathan, *JC* 8 May 1987). According to Deborah Findlay, Alexander 'suggested that this would be a marvellous way for Portia to get the idea of "no drop [*sic*] of blood" ' (Findlay, 'Portia', p. 63).

Nunn's staging bore some superficial resemblance to Alexander's, but was laden with suspense in that it was far more subdued: both Antonio and Shylock prayed – the Lord's Prayer and *Shemah Yisroel* ('Hear O Israel') – as 'Shylock stood, fixated and hesitant, in front of Antonio, the knife raised, his hand trembling, his eyes filling with tears, patently incapable of doing it. He stepped back to collect himself, covering his trousers with a protective white cloth' (Smallwood, *SS* 2000).

Leibman, LeBow and Calder all marked out the area on Antonio's chest for cutting. Jonathan Epstein willingly prostrated himself before LeBow, but in Thacker's version, Clifford Rose 'shook uncontrollably and needed guards to hold him down' (Holland, *English Shakespeares*, p. 165). Michael Cashman, Kelly's 'daringly unsympathetic' Antonio, also showed 'undignified panic in the face of his impending death', which Portia, his rival for Bassanio's love, seemed to enjoy (Macaulay, *FT* 26 March 1994). Dustin Hoffman spat on Antonio before raising his knife.

PORTIA Tarry a little, there is something else.
         This bond doth give thee here no jot of blood.
         The words expressly are 'a pound of flesh'.
         Take then thy bond, take thou thy pound of flesh,
         But in the cutting it, if thou dost shed   305
         One drop of Christian blood, thy lands and goods
         Are by the laws of Venice confiscate
         Unto the state of Venice.
GRATIANO   O upright judge!
         Mark, Jew – O learned judge!
SHYLOCK Is that the law?
PORTIA   Thyself shall see the Act.   310

301–8a In Granville's adaptation, Shylock '*starts surpriz'd*' and says 'Humph'. Cooke's 'countenance
         in an instant lost its wonted glow of malicious satisfaction, and became horribly convulsed
         with disappointed rage, [and] his manner of dropping the scales at the annihilation of his
         hopes, was strongly indicative of the writhing tortures of a despairing soul' ('Thespis', *qtd*
         Annals. II, p. 359). Daly's promptbook has 'General start and gesture of joy and surprise,
         Shylock gasps with eagerness and grasping at the bond, falls on his knees' (*pmt* Moore/Daly).
             An observer at Charles Kean's production was more concerned with the reaction of
         Antonio: 'Sinking back in a swoon, and held by his friends at the approach of the Jew to take
         his forfeit, he gradually awoke as from a terrible dream, opening his eyes in surprise at his
         safety' (*Athenaeum*, qtd Sprague, *Shakespeare and the Actors*, p. 28).
             Ellen Terry writes that in the trial, 'Portia is acting on a preconceived plan up to moment
         of pronouncing sentence, then she has an inspiration . . . hence her "tarry a little" '; Terry
         concedes that this is not wholly consistent with her actions at 343–59 (Foulkes, 'Helen
         Faucit', pp. 32–3). Margaret Webster once got her inspiration from another source: she
         recalls a Ben Greet 'Pastoral Tour' performance (see p. 36), where 'Venice was on a
         driveway, and the Trial Scene was enlivened by a postman on a bicycle, riding
         phlegmatically up to the front door just as I was saying: "Tarry a little: there is something
         else" ' (Webster, *The Same*, p. 321).
310a   Edmund Kean dropped his knife and scales 'with a horrid look of disappointment' (*pmt* E.
         Kean); Booth 'carried the very essence of amazed horror and incredulity . . . he spoke in
         broken murmurs like a man in a bad dream' (Towse, *Sixty Years*, pp. 189–90). Valk 'fell
         across the rail of the dock where Antonio had been seated' (Griffin, *TA* 1955), and Olivier
         revived memories of his 'upon Saint Crispin's d-a-a-a-y' in *Henry V* with his scream of 'Is
         that the l-a-a-a-w?'.
310b–12 Daly's Portia, Ada Rehan, consulted her law book before answering (Sprague, *Shakespeare
         and the Actors*, p. 16), as did Enid Graham in Kahn's production. The lines were yelled by

               For as thou urgest justice, be assured
               Thou shalt have justice more than thou desirest.
GRATIANO O learned judge! Mark, Jew: a learned judge.
SHYLOCK I take this offer then. Pay the bond thrice
               And let the Christian go.
BASSANIO   Here is the money.   315
PORTIA Soft.
               The Jew shall have all justice; soft, no haste;
               He shall have nothing but the penalty.
GRATIANO O Jew, an upright judge, a learned judge!
PORTIA Therefore prepare thee to cut off the flesh.   320
               Shed thou no blood, nor cut thou less nor more
               But just a pound of flesh. If thou tak'st more
               Or less than a just pound, be it but so much
               As makes it light or heavy in the substance
               Or the division of the twentieth part   325
               Of one poor scruple – nay, if the scale do turn
               But in the estimation of a hair,
               Thou diest, and all thy goods are confiscate.
GRATIANO A second Daniel; a Daniel, Jew!
               Now, infidel, I have you on the hip.   330

Edelstein's Laila Robins, 'a one-woman chamber of theatrical horrors, mannered and shrieky, who . . . plays the courtroom scene, from "Tarry a little", as one long, frantic screech' (Feingold, *VV* 8 February 1995).

314–15a Some argue that if Shylock were genuinely a tragic figure, he would kill Antonio even if it meant his own death. Valk seemed to have been ready to act in this manner: Guthrie's promptbook reads 'Shylock makes to stab Antonio, Guards grab him amongst screams, Guards release Shylock when he says "Let the Christian go." ' Sothern picked up his knife slightly later in the scene and advanced toward Antonio, as did Morris Carnovsky in Allen Fletcher's San Diego production, but in these instances Shylock's own resolve weakened. LeBow had no hesitation in taking the bank notes resting on the scales and attempting to leave.

315b Daly: 'Eagerly' (*pmt* Moore/Daly).

319 Two of Schenk's soldiers roughly shoved Shylock back into the courtroom; coins spilled on to the table and floor, and while Antonio and the Salads eyed them greedily, a soldier furtively pocketed some.

320 In Kelly's production, Nichola McAuliffe, 'after trumping Shylock with her superior command of the law .. still urges him "prepare thee to cut off the flesh", not without a spasm of malice against Antonio' (Macaulay *FT* 26 March 1994).

328 Charles Kean: 'Shout of Senators – delight' (*pmt* C. Kean[2]).

PORTIA Why doth the Jew pause? Take thy forfeiture.
SHYLOCK Give me my principal, and let me go.
BASSANIO I have it ready for thee; here it is.
PORTIA He hath refused it in the open court.
    He shall have merely justice and his bond.   335
GRATIANO A Daniel, still say I, a second Daniel!
    I thank thee, Jew, for teaching me that word.
SHYLOCK Shall I not have barely my principal?
PORTIA Thou shalt have nothing but the forfeiture,
    To be so taken at thy peril, Jew.   340
SHYLOCK Why then, the devil give him good of it!
    I'll stay no longer question.
PORTIA   Tarry, Jew:
    The law hath yet another hold on you.
    It is enacted in the laws of Venice,
    If it be proved against an alien   345

332 Booth: 'After a brief struggle, Bassanio offers the bag of money; Shylock takes it, but Gratiano seizes it from him' (Furness, *A New Variorum Edition*, p. 224).

341–2 Schenk's courtroom spectators riotously manhandled Shylock and scrambled for coins on the floor. The Duke eventually restored order with his bell.

342b 'Mrs Kean gave a long pause here' (*pmt* C. Kean[1]).

343–59 The 'unkind *Blackwood's* article', as Ellen Terry referred to it, observes that

> Miss Terry, following the reading for the first time given upon the stage by Miss Helen Faucit, turns to the volume of the Venetian statutes, and reads from the passage, beginning 'It is enacted in the laws'. . . But this was only one of many touches of genius by which this great actress used to make the whole of the scene a living reality. (December 1789)

> An obvious objection to reading the law *verbatim* is that few law books are written in verse, although there is some justification: letters are not normally written in verse either, but Aufidius reads one aloud in *Coriolanus* (1.2.9–17). Julia Marlowe adopted Faucit's business, and more recent law-book readers are Joan Plowright, Gemma Jones, Haydn Gwynne and Kelly McGillis, whose Portia 'is so tender-hearted that she cries as she reads aloud and . . . realizes its impact on Shylock' (Tocci, *SB* 1988). Sabine Sinjen was the opposite of McGillis, 'icy, catlike, and cruel, and [at 359] finally abrupt, with the tone of a lion tamer' (Sehrt, 'Der Shylock', pp. 91–2).

345 Goodman immediately recognised the statute and spoke along with Crotty 'with weary, contemptuous familiarity' (Smallwood, *SS* 2000). Suchet was close to choking 'in bitter, silent laughter' (Maguin, 'The Merchant', p. 114).

That by direct or indirect attempts
He seek the life of any citizen,
The party 'gainst the which he doth contrive
Shall seize one half his goods, the other half
Comes to the privy coffer of the state,   350
And the offender's life lies in the mercy
Of the Duke only, 'gainst all other voice.
In which predicament I say thou stand'st;
For it appears by manifest proceeding
That indirectly, and directly too,   355
Thou hast contrived against the very life
Of the defendant, and thou hast incurred
The danger formerly by me rehearsed.
Down, therefore, and beg mercy of the Duke.
GRATIANO Beg that thou mayst have leave to hang thyself –   360
And yet, thy wealth being forfeit to the state,
Thou hast not left the value of a cord;
Therefore thou must be hanged at the state's charge.

351 Terry 'laid a significant emphasis on "mercy" as if to remind the Jew how he had but lately treated that word' (Crosse, *Diaries*, vol. II, pp. 2–3).

353 Charles Kean: 'slight movement among judges' (*pmt* C. Kean[1]).

359 Stella Adler recalls her father Jacob at the moment Portia (Sara Adler) commanded him to beg for mercy: 'When the verdict was pronounced, taking from him everything, taking even his religion, his strength left him. He crumbled and broke. The Venetians, exulting at his defeat, now laid hands on him, brutally forcing him down to the earth. Chattering with fear, bent, stooped, he was an image of defenseless terror' (Adler, *A Life on the Stage*, p. xiv).

Like Adler, Ayrton, Philip Voss and Mitchell were forced to their knees; Leibman was thrown violently to the floor. Suchet knelt for mercy 'with a wearily smiling sense of habit, as though it were an old game, this, of bearing the ancient curse' (Hankey, *TLS* 15 May 1981). Alexander was somewhat unusual in having his Bassanio join in abusing Shylock; in Miller's production, Jeremy Brett was troubled by Shylock's humiliation.

360 Sothern's Gratiano, seeing Shylock 'faint with emotion', and pretending to assist him, pushed him to the floor; 361–3 were cut (*pmt* Sothern[3]). LeBow desperately tried to cover his head with his hands after Gratiano knocked his hat off. Kortner was jeered at and beaten as Schenk's courtroom descended into chaos (Sehrt, 'Der Shylock', p. 92); fights also broke out in Kahn's courtroom.

363 Guthrie: 'General laughter' (pmt).

DUKE That thou shalt see the difference of our spirit,
  I pardon thee thy life before thou ask it.   365
  For half thy wealth, it is Antonio's;
  The other half comes to the general state,
  Which humbleness may drive unto a fine.
PORTIA Ay, for the state, not for Antonio.
SHYLOCK Nay, take my life and all, pardon not that: 370
  You take my house when you do take the prop
  That doth sustain my house; you take my life
  When you do take the means whereby I live.
PORTIA What mercy can you render him, Antonio?
GRATIANO A halter gratis – nothing else, for God's sake. 375
ANTONIO So please my lord the Duke and all the court
  To quit the fine for one half of his goods,
  I am content, so he will let me have
  The other half in use, to render it
  Upon his death unto the gentleman   380
  That lately stole his daughter.
  Two things provided more: that for this favour
  He presently become a Christian;

370–4 Edmund Kean had 'a look of sorrow and despair' (*pmt* E. Kean). His son's reading was marred, though, by persistent bronchial problems, that gave him trouble with his consonants: 'you take my life / When you do take the *beans* whereby I live' (*Punch*, *qtd Amer. 1*, p. 104). Calder remained on his knees for this speech; Philip Voss, attempting to rise, repeatedly slipped on the gold coins Bassanio earlier scattered across the stage – while the effect was theatrical, it was hard to see its logic, implying as it did that Shylock was being punished for his pursuit of money. Olivier substituted 'if' for 'when' at 371 and 373.

374 Asked 'almost in desperation' by Deborah Findlay: 'I was rewarded with cold comfort from my Antonio (whom John Carlisle played as a vengeful, fanatical Christian) as he spat out his conditions' (Findlay, 'Portia', pp. 64–5).

383 When Cooke heard Antonio's demand, his 'groan of convulsive agony, that seemed to burst from the very innermost recesses of his soul, was electric in its effects' (*Annals.II*, p. 359). Irving turned 'a haggard look of anxiety on the speaker, as if to see what further humiliation is in store for him' (Crosse, *Diaries*, vol. I, p. 175). Sothern's directions call for 'a cry like that of a hunted animal' (*pmt* Sothern[3]); Crosse thought Moscovitch's 'collapse at the catastrophe of the Trial was as undignified as anything well could be' (*Diaries*, vol. VII, p. 14).

  Rudolf Schildkraut, for Reinhardt in 1905, is the earliest Shylock I know of to intone *Shemah Yisroel* at this point (see Sehrt, 'Der Shylock', p. 94). In 1993, Mike Nussbaum did

The other, that he do record a gift,
Here in the court, of all he dies possessed   385
Unto his son Lorenzo and his daughter.

so, not only in reaction to Antonio's words, but to Antonio's removing the crucifix from around his own neck and placing it around Shylock's (Cook, *SB* 1994). Holbrook also said the *Shemah*, joined by the other Jews Kahn placed in the court, while Antonio's friends shouted gleeful taunts.

Kortner did not speak, but his placing a *tallith* over his face was perhaps more eloquent in its silence: as Kortner reveals in his memoirs, he passed through Nuremberg in 1932, riding in an open car, and inadvertently stumbled upon a Nazi parade. Wishing to remain unseen, he began to raise the canvas top: 'When I extended my arms and cast my eyes skywards and pulled the canvas over my head, I remembered that the Jews use the same gesture when pulling the prayer shawl over their head in order to be alone with God in prayer' (*qtd* Sehrt, 'Der Shylock', p. 95).

Guthrie's promptbook direction for Valk is 'Shy[lock] begins heart attack bus[iness]'; in a very different and unusual approach, Luther Adler appeared 'not overly dismayed', and when Tubal rushed to comfort him, he 'whispered some consolation in his companion's ear and dispatched him upon some urgent matter. Just what this secret business was, the audience never knew; but it was reasonable to conclude that Shylock had a plan to mitigate the harshness of his sentence' (Barbour, 'Theatre Chronicle', p. 284). Understandably, commentators and reviewers have generally focussed on Shylock's reaction to forced conversion, but Antonio's motivation is also important. If we accept that in the world of the play, saving one's soul through baptism is an act of mercy, even when the baptism is coerced, then Antonio motives are genuine, but some actors have chosen to show that Antonio has little interest in Shylock's soul, and cares only for his own revenge. Miller's Antonio, Anthony Nicholls, 'eyes gleaming, all but sneers the words', while Bassanio, 'raising a hand in futile protest . . . looks around at each of the others, then drops his hand, disheartened' (Perret, 'Shakespeare and Anti-Semitism', pp. 151–2). Leigh Lawson swiped the yarmulke from Dustin Hoffman's head; David Bamber paused after 'provided more', and then flaunted the scales in Henry Goodman's face, 'looking like a Nazi prototype' (Fischer, *SB* 2000).

Maraden's and Nunn's Portias, Susan Coyne and Derbhle Crotty, were visibly shocked by Antonio's version of 'mercy'. Some directors give special attention to the reaction of supernumeraries: the Duke's judgment hit Irving's 'eager and interested Jews . . . like a thunderbolt' (Brereton, *Life of Henry Irving*, vol. I, p. 307). Many years later, Kelly's Jewish spectators had the same reaction (Hopkins, *SB* 1994).

384–6 Antonio's demand that Shylock make Lorenzo and Jessica his heirs seems like an afterthought following a demand for conversion. Deborah Findlay notes, 'we swapped the lines round here so that "He presently become a Christian" concluded the speech, as the

DUKE He shall do this, or else I do recant
　　　　The pardon that I late pronouncèd here.
PORTIA Art thou contented, Jew? What dost thou say?
SHYLOCK I am content.
PORTIA　　　　　　　　　Clerk, draw a deed of gift.　　　　390

last and most shocking of Antonio's conditions, rather than being less conspicuous in the middle of it' (Findlay, 'Portia', p. 65). The *Spectator*'s review (12 October 1839) of Macready's performance has no mention at all of baptism:

> Macready was dejected too soon after his discomfiture. The vexation of Shylock first breaks forth, and he is going out in a fit of a angry disappointment, when Portia stops him with the sentence of confiscation; it is only then that his fierce spirit gives way under the loss of all his money, and he said 'content' to the forfeiture of half his wealth, with reversion of the other to his daughter: he submits perforce, but although baffled, he is still stubborn.

389　Geraldine James emerged 'by her hesitant and soft question . . . as the only person sympathetic to Shylock' (Kliman, *SB* 1990); Crotty knelt beside Goodman and spoke in the same manner.

390a　With the daring theatricality for which he is famous, Olivier's 'I am content' was 'delivered with rigid, poker-stiff back, eyeballs bulging and hands clapped firmly to the sides like a carefully welded toy soldier: clearly the man is undergoing some kind of fit' (Billington, *The Modern Actor*, p. 83).

O'Toole was 'happy with a very little ironical laugh and an unemotional but whispered "I am content"' (Roberts, *PP* 1960). Ernst Deutsch spoke 'with a trembling voice' (Verch, '*The Merchant*', p. 87); in Paul Sparer's performance, the three words seemed to tear themselves from somewhere deep within him, as he momentarily staggered. Rabb's Shylock, Sydney Walker (a brilliant Antonio for Baldridge) first said, in Yiddish, 'Am I satisfied? No, I am not satisfied', before saying 'I am content' (Clurman, *Nation* 19 March 73). While Cusack knelt beside Suchet, he responded 'quietly, still smiling – he has learnt the old lesson once again' (Wardle, *Times* 22 April 1981). LeBow made a choking motion with the crucifix that Antonio had placed around his neck; Goodman removed his yarmulke and *tallith* and, 'glaring pointedly at Antonio while muttering a palpably jolting "I am content"' (Fischer, *SB* 2000), put them on the scales, showing that something far weightier than a pound of flesh had just been taken.

390b　Gold's burly Salerio/Salarino took a cross from his neck and placed it around Shylock's, making Mitchell kiss it in a powerful close-up – 'the brutality of the conversion at the end of the trial scene could be felt' (M. Shapiro, *Shofar* 1986).

SHYLOCK I pray you give me leave to go from hence;
          I am not well. Send the deed after me
          And I will sign it.
DUKE   Get thee gone, but do it.
GRATIANO In christening shalt thou have two godfathers:
          Had I been judge, thou shouldst have had ten more, 395
          To bring thee to the gallows, not to the font.

                                        Exit [*Shylock*]

391–3a In a famously bad piece of acting, Mansfield

> made Shylock place the point of his curved knife, inside his dress, at the throat,
> intimating the purpose or act of suicide, and he spoke the words, 'I am not well' in a
> weak, thin voice, as though to signify that the Jew was bleeding to death from a stoically
> self-inflicted wound, a piece of business not merely unwarranted but preposterous.
> (Winter, *Shakespeare on the Stage*, p. 199)

> Jacob Adler spoke 'in the tone of a man near death' (Rosenfeld, *Bright Star*, p. 305),
> Kortner 'quietly and with long pauses' (Sehrt, 'Der Shylock', p. 94). O'Toole, surrounded by
> jeering Christians, stumbled to the ground; when Tutin moved to help him, the crowd fell
> back, and Shylock found himself 'face to face with the boy-like lawyer who has spoken of
> mercy and of fines. There were no words for them to speak, but the point of the moment
> was to show that all had been done, that the two were irreconcilable' (Brown, *SS* 1961).
> LeBow said 'I am not well', and vomited into his ever-present bag of peanuts.

394–6 Thacker ended the scene here, with Mark Lockyer, the last to leave the courtroom, speaking
        to Shylock with a quiet viciousness. The lights dimmed on Shylock as he struggled into a
        chair, turning to face the audience as he did so. The remainder of 4.1 was played on an
        upper gallery.

396sd Shylock's exit, unlike the 'return' invented by Irving, is not an interpolation: unless the lights
        are to dim out, as in Thacker's production, he must walk off the stage, and the manner in
        which he does so is the culminating point of an actor's characterisation. Edmund Kean was
        notably stoical – *The Theatrical Observer* understood his intention, but was less than
        enthusiastic:

> We are aware of Mr Kean's idea, he considers the Jew so completely overwhelmed
> . . . that he ought to represent the mind in calm though bitter anguish. This style loses
> all effect on the stage, by the circumstance of the only power of expression to indicate
> this state of feeling, lying in the features . . . the perfect stillness of the frame, the
> clenched hands, and downcast eyes. (*qtd* Sprague, *Shakespeare and the Actors*,
> pp. 29–30)

Kean gave Gratiano a look of contempt as he walked by him, but the *Dramatic Magazine* argued that Kean's Shylock would not 'bestow a thought on Gratiano, or even be supposed to have heard the jest' (*qtd* Sprague, *Shakespeare and the Actors*, p. 30).

Phelps 'groped his way out, leaning against the wall of the courtroom to keep himself from falling' (Sprague, *Shakespeare and the Actors*, p. 30). In Irving's version, as reported in the *Baltimore Herald*, 'a hand is laid on his shoulder, and turning he sees the jeering face of Gratiano. He draws himself up to his full height, and back in his eyes comes the look of hate and defiance. Then he goes out of sight forever' (*qtd Irv.Amer*, p. 18). Jacob Adler's prideful exit was hailed by Alter Epstein in the Yiddish press: 'how we thrilled, how fierce the beating of our hearts as, arms folded on his breast, with a burning glance of scorn, he slowly left the hall!' (*qtd* Rosenfeld, *Bright Star*, p. 305)

Albert Basserman made a defiant exit for Reinhardt, 'with clenched fists, still dangerously threatening, in the manner of one, who remains undefeated' (Sehrt, 'Der Shylock', p. 94); Ernst Deutsch 'resembled an accusing Job', as he left the stage 'erect, covering his head and face with his black cloak, in the Old Testament manner' (Verch, '*The Merchant*', p. 87).

At the Old Vic in 1924, Hay Petrie ignored Tubal's proffered arm, 'walking out with firm step and head erect' (Crosse, *Diaries*, vol. VIII, p. 139); on the same stage in 1956, Robert Helpmann first turned to Gratiano and friends 'with a majesty that cowed them and caused them to turn away. Then, his face broken with despair, he made his slow exit down the front of the stage, his rich mantle seeming to crush him to the ground as he dragged it wearily after him down the steps' (Clarke, *Shakespeare at the Old Vic*, np).

Existing side by side with the dignity of an Irving or a Petrie was the tumultuous exit of Forbes-Robertson, 'a figure of dismay and despair, of frenzied fear and frenzied abasement, fleeing he knew not whither or how, his garments flying, his eyes raving, his arms beating vainly' (*BET, qtd Amer.II*, p. 206).

Novelli chose not to leave silently; he 'vanishes from the scene after spitting out the word "Christian" – squirted like vitriol from a syringe – at those in the courtroom' (De Caseres, *Theatre Magazine* 1907). Like the Italian star, several American Shylocks of the 1990s showed their contempt for this brand of Christian 'justice': Nussbaum 'made his final exit from front to back stage, he made a full turn as he looked back in near contempt at his tormenters' (King, 'Shylock after Auschwitz', p. 62); Holbrook held up the scales high for all to see, then slammed them down on to the Duke's table and left after a mocking bow. Most telling was Leibman, who claimed victory of a sort by choosing this moment to tear the yellow badge from his gaberdine, as if to ask, 'What will you do when there are no Jews left to hate?'.

Leibman's question was also implicit in Goodman's dropping his *tallith* and yarmulke on the scales. He, too, achieved something of a victory, when Peter de Jersey's Salerio/Salarino showed that at least one Venetian had learned something from the events he had witnessed, indeed had taken part in, by following Shylock from the court.

DUKE Sir, I entreat you home with me to dinner.
PORTIA I humbly do desire your grace of pardon.

George Arliss, as he crossed the stage, stumbled and fell to the floor: 'a pause, then Antonio steps forward, raising him gently. Shylock, dazed, slowly regains some vitality, looks up and his "Samaritan" is Antonio. Slowly with his left hand he takes off Antonio's hand from his arm. Drawing himself up to his full height, he goes slowly to the door' (*pmt* Ames[2]). In Luscombe's 1991 production, John Woodvine was offered no such help – keeling over with what appeared to be a stroke, he was left to crawl off unaided (Holland, *TLS* 22 February 1991).

Some Shylocks have shown neither dejection, nor contempt, nor illness as they left the court. Stewart laughed as he walked off (Greenwald, *Directions by Indirections*, p. 111), and Barton's second Shylock, David Suchet, 'stumbles a little getting up, but with a quick self-deprecating laugh refuses Portia's hand . . . he removes the skull-cap and simply takes himself off' (Hankey, *TLS* 15 May 1981). The most unperturbed of all was Gert Voss: in Zadek's Wall Street world, he provided 'a telling image of his shacklement to the time-bound, cash-bound city' by checking the date on his wrist watch, quietly writing the required cheques for the Duke and Antonio, and making 'a dignified exit, presumably to ring up his Swiss bank manager' (Savage, *TLS* 8 September 1995; Billington, *Gdn* 18 April 1991). Less dignified was Xia Zhiqing in Shanghai, who kicked over the scales 'like a petulant child' at his exit (Stanley, '1994 Shanghai', p. 76).

Others were, in a sense, denied the opportunity to make a final statement in the way they left the stage. Valk was roughly 'jeered off' by the Christians: 'here director Guthrie pointed up the irony that they too have not learned that mercy should temper justice' (Griffin, *TA* 1955). Sher was also 'ejected from the court', and at the end of the scene, Solanio 'seized upon Shylock's knife, and pocketed it as a souvenir' (Doran, 'Solanio', p. 76). Hoffman was 'literally kicked off the stage' (Wills, *NYRB* 18 January 1990).

One of the hallmarks of Olivier's career was the terrifying off-stage scream he gave as Oedipus at the Old Vic. Twenty-five years later, he was helped off the stage by his secretaries, and 'we hear an anguished crescendo of a wail, as if Shylock's wretched soul had died within him' (Hewes, *SR* 11 July 1970). In the television version, four close-ups followed, showing the reaction of Portia, Bassanio, Antonio and finally the Duke.

Schenk's camera followed Kortner as he walked slowly from the courtroom, with his *tallith* over his face, and then down a long corridor. This silence, lasting forty-five seconds, was as heart-rending as Olivier's scream.

397 Macready: 'The Duke descends, as he speaks, and advances, leaning on the shoulder of his Knight' (*pmt*). Booth's four-act version for the Winter Garden revival of 1867 went from Shylock's exit to Portia speaking Bassanio's line, 'Most worthy gentleman' (404a) and then directly to 5.1.267 (*pmt* Booth[2]).

I must away this night toward Padua,
And it is meet I presently set forth.   400
DUKE I am sorry that your leisure serves you not.
Antonio, gratify this gentleman,
For in my mind you are much bound to him.

Exit Duke and his train

BASSANIO Most worthy gentleman, I and my friend
Have by your wisdom been this day acquitted   405
Of grievous penalties, in lieu whereof
Three thousand ducats due unto the Jew
We freely cope your courteous pains withal.
ANTONIO And stand indebted over and above
In love and service to you evermore.   410
PORTIA He is well paid that is well satisfied;
And I delivering you am satisfied
And therein do account myself well paid;
My mind was never yet more mercenary.
I pray you know me when we meet again.   415
I wish you well, and so I take my leave.
BASSANIO Dear sir, of force I must attempt you further.
Take some remembrance of us as a tribute,
Not as a fee. Grant me two things, I pray you:
Not to deny me, and to pardon me.   420
PORTIA You press me far, and therefore I will yield.
Give me your gloves, I'll wear them for your sake;
And for your love I'll take this ring from you.

404–12 Kelly's Antonio and Bassanio began to treat 'Balthazar' as a possible member of 'their gay
mafia . . . so when Bassanio finally gives up the ring he had from his wife as a present to this
wonderboy lawyer, [Portia] is aghast – and teeters right back into full despair' (Macaulay, *FT*
26 March 1994). This idea was also a factor in Alexander's production, as Deborah Findlay
remarks, 'Portia will not tolerate the martyrdom of a former lover hanging over her
marriage to Bassanio, so she condemns Antonio to life . . . "I delivering you am satisfied"'
(Findlay, 'Portia', p. 65).

421ff. It was the rare reviewer who failed to go into effusive praise of Ellen Terry's playing of
the end of 4.1. The *Baltimore Herald*'s critic is typical in saying 'the by-play about the ring
was the cleverest and most sparkling bit of acting that we have ever seen' (*qtd Irv.Amer*,
p. 17).

        Do not draw back your hand; I'll take no more,
        And you in love shall not deny me this.   425
BASSANIO This ring, good sir? Alas, it is a trifle;
        I will not shame myself to give you this.
PORTIA I will have nothing else but only this;
        And now methinks I have a mind to it.
BASSANIO There's more depends on this than on the value.   430
        The dearest ring in Venice will I give you,
        And find it out by proclamation.
        Only for this I pray you pardon me.
PORTIA I see, sir, you are liberal in offers.
        You taught me first to beg, and now methinks   435
        You teach me how a beggar should be answered.
BASSANIO Good sir, this ring was given me by my wife,
        And when she put it on, she made me vow
        That I should neither sell, nor give, nor lose it.
PORTIA That 'scuse serves many men to save their gifts;   440
        And if your wife be not a mad woman,
        And know how well I have deserved this ring,
        She would not hold out enemy for ever
        For giving it to me. Well, peace be with you.
                             Exeunt [*Portia and Nerissa*]
ANTONIO My lord Bassanio, let him have the ring.   445
        Let his deservings and my love withal
        Be valued 'gainst your wife's commandement.
BASSANIO Go, Gratiano, run and overtake him;
        Give him the ring, and bring him if thou canst
        Unto Antonio's house. Away, make haste.   450
                             Exit Gratiano

444sd *Blackwood's* notes that Ellen Tree (Mrs Charles Kean) was the last of a long line of Portias to exit 'tucking her arms under the back of her doctor's gown, and tripping with the affected gait of the Old Bailey barrister off the stage' (December 1879). Of Terry, the *Chicago Tribune* asked, 'What is finer than the swagger with which Portia leaves the court room?', and the *Philadelphia Press* recorded that 'she stepped jauntily off the stage amid a storm of applause which only ceased after three recalls' (*Irv.Amer*, pp. 29, 12).

    Charles Kean's 1858 promptbook has, 'when finished in four acts go to [5.1.266]' (C. Kean[1]). Jacob Adler's Yiddish version ended with Shylock's exit, but Booth was the only 'mainstream' actor-manager who customarily omitted the fifth act (see p. 26).

> Come, you and I will thither presently,
> And in the morning early will we both
> Fly toward Belmont. Come, Antonio.

Exeunt

453sd Guthrie's Ontario production was in the third year of the Stratford Festival, when the stage was housed in a gigantic tent. On 15 August 1955, the stage manager duly noted a unique end to the trial scene: 'Chipmunk, looked like a ferret, ran across stage and up aisle.'

ACT 4, SCENE 2

[4.2] *Enter* [PORTIA *and*] NERISSA

PORTIA Enquire the Jew's house out, give him this deed,
        And let him sign it. We'll away tonight
        And be a day before our husbands home.
        This deed will be well welcome to Lorenzo.

                    Enter GRATIANO

GRATIANO Fair sir, you are well o'ertane.   5
        My lord Bassanio upon more advice

This scene was omitted by a number of managers and directors of the late nineteenth and early twentieth centuries, including Irving, Greet, Tree, Mantell, Sothern, Jewett, Belasco, Hampden and, in more recent times, Schenk. As Bassanio's decision to give Portia's ring away is taken at the end of 4.1, we need not witness it, although Nerissa's possession of Gratiano's ring then just 'happens'. In the modern theatre, when the ring plot is treated as something more than Portia's practical joke, but as a further interrogation of the value and quality of her relationship with Bassanio, the sequence is an important one, especially in productions where Bassanio and Antonio are shown or implied to have been lovers.

osd Charles Kean's setting is 'Venice, The Foscari Gate of the Ducal Palace, Leading to the Giant's Staircase'. Baldridge inserted a violent sequence between 4.1 and 4.2, with young toughs searching the streets for Shylock. In Kelly's production, Portia had gravel thrown at her by Jewish children while she sought Shylock's house in the Ghetto; she showed 'a saddened comprehension of their resentment' (Hopkins, *SB* 1994). Maraden had some blackshirts recognise 'Balthazar' and applaud; Susan Coyne showed her distress.

1–2 Said reluctantly by Derbhle Crotty. Deborah Findlay, while waiting for the ferry back to Belmont, suddenly realised that she had forgotten to send Shylock the deed of gift for signature (Findlay, 'Portia', p. 65).

  5 Serban's Portia and Nerissa put on their masks, and returned to their disembodied court voices, when talking to Gratiano.

Hath sent you here this ring, and doth entreat
Your company at dinner.
PORTIA   That cannot be.
His ring I do accept most thankfully,
And so I pray you tell him. Furthermore,   10
I pray you show my youth old Shylock's house.
GRATIANO That will I do.
NERISSA   [*To Portia*] Sir, I would speak with you.
[*Aside*] I'll see if I can get my husband's ring
Which I did make him swear to keep for ever.
PORTIA Thou mayst, I warrant. We shall have old swearing   15
That they did give the rings away to men;
But we'll outface them, and outswear them too.
– Away, make haste, thou know'st where I will tarry.
NERISSA Come, good sir, will you show me to this house?
                                          [*Exeunt*]

7 Derbhle Crotty, Geraldine James and Penny Downie were clearly upset at being presented
with the ring. Joan Plowright seemed no more troubled than if she were being handed a
forgotten umbrella.

ACT 5, SCENE 1

5.[1] *Enter* LORENZO *and* JESSICA

LORENZO The moon shines bright. In such a night as this,
      When the sweet wind did gently kiss the trees,

In praising 'the repose and harmony of the moonlight garden' in Charles Kean's staging of Act V at the Princess's in 1858, John William Cole notes that 'some sapient commentators, who persuade themselves that they could dictate improvements to Shakespeare, have denounced the last act as trifling and unnecessary' (*Life of Charles Kean*, p. 266). Kean himself did have a four-act version of the play ready for use (see p. 243), but the actor-managers, with the exception of Booth, usually included 5.1 – Irving omitted it as an experiment on one or two occasions but no more than that.

    Daly and Sothern were particularly wise to continue beyond the trial scene, since their Portias, Ada Rehan and Julia Marlowe, were far greater attractions than their Shylocks. A good deal of the text was always absent, however – Daly provided a magnificent Belmont set for his 1898 revival, but it took longer to change the scenery than it did to play the act, and John Corbin wrote in *Harper's Weekly* that 'any sensible man would have put on his coat at the end of the fourth act and go home and read [the rest] unhampered in his study' (*qtd Amer.II*, p. 92).

    The unsensible ones who did remain for Act V, from the eighteenth to the early twentieth century, saw only a much-shortened version.

osd In the modern theatre, with no interval between Acts IV and V to change the scenery, the scene begins within minutes of Shylock's forced conversion. Deborah Findlay notes that in Alexander's production, 'having concentrated so much on the racism . . . it was difficult to place this scene. Here are the men who spat at Shylock and knocked him to the ground; here is the ruling class at play. Are we expected to forget their atrocities and be charmed by them?' (Findlay, 'Portia', p. 66). Alexander ignored the references to moonlight, placing Jessica and Lorenzo in a harsh light (Kingston, *Times* 27 April 1988), and on opposite sides of the stage, as if 'looking out to sea, showing that their relationship had soured by this time' (Wells, *SS* 1988).

And they did make no noise, in such a night
Troilus methinks mounted the Troyan walls
And sighed his soul toward the Grecian tents,   5
Where Cressid lay that night.

JESSICA   In such a night
Did Thisbe fearfully o'ertrip the dew,
And saw the lion's shadow ere himself,
And ran dismayed away.

LORENZO   In such a night
Stood Dido with a willow in her hand   10
Upon the wild sea banks, and waft her love
To come again to Carthage.

JESSICA   In such a night
Medea gathered the enchanted herbs
That did renew old Aeson.

LORENZO   In such a night
Did Jessica steal from the wealthy Jew   15
And with an unthrift love did run from Venice
As far as Belmont.

JESSICA   In such a night
Did young Lorenzo swear he loved her well,
Stealing her soul with many vows of faith,
And ne'er a true one.

LORENZO   In such a night   20
Did pretty Jessica (like a little shrew)
Slander her love, and he forgave it her.

Rabb's Jessica 'met Lorenzo's playful endearments with accusation and scorn' (Hirsch, 'The Merchant', p. 512); in Serban's disquieting beginning, Jessica knelt alone on stage, praying in Latin – she and Lancelot played 3.5.1–20, with the jokes about pork prices, before Lorenzo entered.

1–24   In 1900, Gordon Crosse saw Benson's troupe at Oxford, and admired Lily Brayton's 'oriental voluptuousness, suggested by her get-up . . . It was a pity the "on such a night" speeches were so cruelly cut' (*Diaries*, vol. II, p. 147). Gold, who saw the sequence as a 'sexual' rather than a 'poetry contest', treated the opening dialogue as 'foreplay' (Bulman, *Shakespeare in Performance*, p. 107); Miller's production was the opposite: the opening lines were 'brilliantly ruined by Lorenzo being made to pace up and down with a pipe in his mouth, like an enthusiastic but slightly crass Eng. Lit. don, quoting Shakespeare rather than acting him' (Weightman, *Enc* 1970). Schenk (in the year of Woodstock) began with Lorenzo strumming a lute, as he and Jessica tried to sing their lines.

JESSICA I would outnight you, did nobody come:
   But hark, I hear the footing of a man.

Enter [STEPHANO,] *a messenger*

LORENZO Who comes so fast in silence of the night?   25
STEPHANO A friend.
LORENZO A friend? What friend? Your name, I pray you, friend?
STEPHANO Stephano is my name, and I bring word
   My mistress will before the break of day
   Be here at Belmont. She doth stray about   30
   By holy crosses where she kneels and prays
   For happy wedlock hours.
LORENZO   Who comes with her?
STEPHANO None but a holy hermit and her maid.
   I pray you, is my master yet returned?
LORENZO He is not, nor we have not heard from him.   35
   But go we in, I pray thee, Jessica,
   And ceremoniously let us prepare
   Some welcome for the mistress of the house.

Enter [LANCELOT,] *the Clown*

LANCELOT Sola, sola! Wo ha, ho! Sola, sola!
LORENZO Who calls?   40
LANCELOT Sola! Did you see Master Lorenzo? Master Lorenzo,
  sola, sola!
LORENZO Leave holloaing, man! Here!
LANCELOT Sola! Where, where?
LORENZO Here!   45
LANCELOT Tell him there's a post come from my master, with his
  horn full of good news: my master will be here ere morning,
  sweet soul.

30b–2a Kelly gave special weight to these lines, implying that Portia, having realised at the trial 'that her lover is actually in love with another man . . . was desperately praying that she might salvage something from the wreckage of her marriage' (Schafer, *Ms-Directing Shakespeare*, pp. 121–2).

39 Christopher Luscombe entered, hilariously, while 'out for an early-morning jog with his walkman' (Holland, *SS* 1994). Luscombe had originally planned to ride a bicycle, but the steel columns of the set proved too difficult to negotiate (Luscombe, 'Launcelot Gobbo', p. 25).

LORENZO Let's in and there expect their coming.
                  And yet no matter: why should we go in?   50
                  My friend Stephano, signify I pray you,
                  Within the house, your mistress is at hand,
                  And bring your music forth into the air.

                                                    [*Exit Stephano*]

                  How sweet the moonlight sleeps upon this bank!
                  Here will we sit, and let the sounds of music   55
                  Creep in our ears; soft stillness and the night
                  Become the touches of sweet harmony.
                  Sit, Jessica. Look how the floor of heaven
                  Is thick inlaid with patens of bright gold.
                  There's not the smallest orb which thou behold'st   60
                  But in his motion like an angel sings,
                  Still choiring to the young-eyed cherubins.
                  Such harmony is in immortal souls,
                  But whilst this muddy vesture of decay
                  Doth grossly close it in, we cannot hear it.   65

                  [*Enter* STEPHANO *with musicians*]

                  Come, ho! and wake Diana with a hymn.
                  With sweetest touches pierce your mistress' ear,
                  And draw her home with music.

53–88 Omitted, Inchbald edition.

   54 In 1916 the Birmingham Repertory went for a functional fountain to supply some
         atmosphere. A stagehand would lie under the stage and blow water through a piece of iron
         tubing for fifteen minutes, while Jessica and Lorenzo 'had to combat the noise of plops and
         gurgles'. One night the fountain began to flood the stage, and Lorenzo (played by Felix
         Aylmer) got his dagger caught in the grass matting covering 'this bank', to reveal 'the
         indispensable collection of ginger-beer boxes which formed its foundation' (Cochrane,
         Shakespeare and the Birmingham Repertory Theatre, p. 66).

   57 In Hall's production, 'while the characters speak of "sweet harmony", the musicians play
         something almost indistinguishable from the dimly heard sounds of car horns bleating on
         46th Street' (Kissel, *NYDN* 20 December 1989).

   59 Often changed to 'patterns', as in the second Folio; pronounced 'pa*teens*' by Malcolm Reid
         in Miller's television version.

66–8 Kemble's promptbook has, in place of these lines, 'Come, with some strain let's pierce fair
         Portia's ear / And draw her home with musick.' Lorenzo and Jessica then sing a duet:

Music plays

JESSICA I am never merry when I hear sweet music.
LORENZO The reason is your spirits are attentive.   70
          For do but note a wild and wanton herd
          Or race of youthful and unhandled colts
          Fetching mad bounds, bellowing and neighing loud –
          Which is the hot condition of their blood –
          If they but hear perchance a trumpet sound,   75
          Or any air of music touch their ears,
          You shall perceive them make a mutual stand,
          Their savage eyes turned to a modest gaze
          By the sweet power of music. Therefore the poet
          Did feign that Orpheus drew trees, stones, and floods;   80
          Since naught so stockish, hard, and full of rage,
          But music for the time doth change his nature.
          The man that hath no music in himself,
          Nor is not moved with concord of sweet sounds,
          Is fit for treasons, stratagems, and spoils;   85
          The motions of his spirit are dull as night
          And his affections dark as Erebus.
          Let no such man be trusted. Mark the music.

      LOR.   For thee, my gentle Jessy,
              What labour would seem hard!

      JES.   For thee, each task how easy
              Thy love the sweet reward!

      BOTH.   The bee thus, uncomplaining
              Esteems no toil severe
              The sweet reward obtaining
              Of honey all the year.

Bell's edition gives Lorenzo a solo, with slightly different words; Charles Kean used 'It Was a Lover and his Lass' from *As You Like It*.
69 This is the last time Jessica speaks in the play.
70–88 Lorenzo competed with a choir singing Ben Jonson's 'Hymn to Diana' in Langham's 1989 production. At the Croydon Repertory in 1935, the modern-dress Jessica and Lorenzo 'danced to the music from the house' (Crosse, *Diaries*, vol. XV, p. 113).
83–8 As Lorenzo spoke, Yossi Yzraeli's puppets (see p. 65) 'enacted a symbolic ritual in which Shylock was baptized by the Christians' (Oz, 'Transformations', p. 67).

Enter PORTIA *and* NERISSA

PORTIA That light we see is burning in my hall.
How far that little candle throws his beams!   90
So shines a good deed in a naughty world.
NERISSA When the moon shone we did not see the candle.
PORTIA So doth the greater glory dim the less:
A substitute shines brightly as a king
Until a king be by, and then his state   95
Empties itself, as doth an inland brook
Into the main of waters. Music, hark!
NERISSA It is your music, madam, of the house.
PORTIA Nothing is good, I see, without respect;
Methinks it sounds much sweeter than by day.   100
NERISSA Silence bestows that virtue on it, madam.
PORTIA The crow doth sing as sweetly as the lark
When neither is attended; and I think
The nightingale, if she should sing by day
When every goose is cackling, would be thought   105
No better a musician than the wren.
How many things by season seasoned are
To their right praise and true perfection.
Peace, ho! The moon sleeps with Endymion
And would not be awaked!
[*Music ceases*]
LORENZO   That is the voice,   110
Or I am much deceived, of Portia!
PORTIA He knows me as the blind man knows the cuckoo
By the bad voice.
LORENZO   Dear lady, welcome home!
PORTIA We have been praying for our husbands' welfare,
Which speed we hope the better for our words.   115
Are they returned?
LORENZO   Madam, they are not yet.
But there is come a messenger before
To signify their coming.

92–108 Omitted, Bell, Inchbald, Kemble, Charles Kean, and Irving editions.
   109 Crosse, at Stratford in 1935, noted, 'it has now become accepted practice to make 'the moon
        sleeps with Endymion' refer to Lorenzo and Jessica – a rather silly joke' (*Diaries*, vol. xv,
        p. 62).

PORTIA   Go in, Nerissa:
          Give order to my servants that they take
          No note at all of our being absent hence –   120
          Nor you Lorenzo, Jessica nor you.
                    [*A tucket sounds*]
LORENZO Your husband is at hand, I hear his trumpet.
          We are no telltales, madam; fear you not.
PORTIA This night methinks is but the daylight sick,
          It looks a little paler; 'tis a day   125
          Such as the day is when the sun is hid.

          Enter BASSANIO, ANTONIO, GRATIANO, *and their followers*

BASSANIO We should hold day with the Antipodes,
          If you would walk in absence of the sun.
PORTIA Let me give light, but let me not be light,
          For a light wife doth make a heavy husband,   130
          And never be Bassanio so for me –
          But God sort all! You are welcome home, my lord.
BASSANIO I thank you, madam. Give welcome to my friend.
          This is the man, this is Antonio,
          To whom I am so infinitely bound.   135
PORTIA You should in all sense be much bound to him,
          For as I hear he was much bound for you.

121sd A car horn provided the tucket in Luscombe's production (Biggs, *SB* 1991).

123–32a Usually cut in the eighteenth and nineteenth centuries.

124–6 Moved to the end of the play by Nunn (see pp. 261–2).

124 Penny Downie took Jessica by the hand.

126sd With the entrance of Bassanio, Gratiano and Antonio, the play moves into its final phase. Barton, in 1978, had his cast 'sitting in a circle for *al fresco* drinks, a ring of harmony broken by argument and re-formed again' (Warren, *SS* 1979). Barton's 1981 Portia, Sinead Cusack, recalls saying to him that the scene 'should not be played as a mischievous little game, it was not comic. John in his wisdom said, "You can combine the two . . . there is room for the important issues of love and the betrayal of love within a comedic framework"' (Cusack, 'Portia', p. 30).

127–32a Usually omitted in the eighteenth and nineteenth centuries.

136–7 Nichola McAuliffe was cold to Antonio in Kelly's production, showing 'that she was taking possession of Bassanio, physically separating him from Antonio, and wrapping Bassanio's arms around herself' (Schafer, *Ms-Directing Shakespeare*, pp. 122–3).

ANTONIO No more than I am well acquitted of.

PORTIA Sir, you are very welcome to our house.
    It must appear in other ways than words: 140
    Therefore I scant this breathing courtesy.

GRATIANO [*To Nerissa*] By yonder moon I swear you do me wrong!
    In faith, I gave it to the judge's clerk,
    Would he were gelt that had it, for my part,
    Since you do take it, love, so much at heart.   145

PORTIA A quarrel ho, already! What's the matter?

GRATIANO About a hoop of gold, a paltry ring
    That she did give me, whose poesy was
    For all the world like cutler's poetry
    Upon a knife: 'Love me, and leave me not.'   150

NERISSA What talk you of the poesy or the value?
    You swore to me when I did give it you.
    That you would wear it till your hour of death,
    And that it should lie with you in your grave.
    Though not for me, yet for your vehement oaths   155
    You should have been respective and have kept it.
    Gave it a judge's clerk! No, God's my judge
    The clerk will ne'er wear hair on's face that had it.

GRATIANO He will, and if he live to be a man.

NERISSA Ay, if a woman live to be a man.   160

GRATIANO Now by this hand, I gave it to a youth,
    A kind of boy, a little scrubbèd boy
    No higher than thyself, the judge's clerk,
    A prating boy that begged it as a fee;
    I could not for my heart deny it him.   165

PORTIA You were to blame, I must be plain with you,
    To part so slightly with your wife's first gift,
    A thing stuck on with oaths upon your finger
    And so riveted with faith unto your flesh.

---

138 Schenk's Antonio, Max Eckard, was obviously tipsy.

144–5 Marked for cut, Irving edition. 'Gelt' changed to 'hanged' in Bell, Inchbald, Kemble, Charles Kean editions.

166ff. Ellen Terry and the other members of Irving's troupe delighted Crosse by playing 'the ring episode' with 'much vivacity', although Crosse felt it was 'a little spoilt by a rather ponderous Nerissa, whose vivacity suggested the gambollings of an elephant' (*Diaries*, vol. II, p. 4).

I gave my love a ring, and made him swear   170
Never to part with it, and here he stands.
I dare be sworn for him he would not leave it
Nor pluck it from his finger for the wealth
That the world masters. Now in faith, Gratiano,
You give your wife too unkind a cause of grief;   175
And 'twere to me, I should be mad at it.

BASSANIO [*Aside*] Why, I were best to cut my left hand off
And swear I lost the ring defending it.

GRATIANO My lord Bassanio gave his ring away
Unto the judge that begged it, and indeed   180
Deserved it too; and then the boy his clerk
That took some pains in writing, he begged mine,
And neither man nor master would take aught
But the two rings.

PORTIA   What ring gave you, my lord?
Not that, I hope, which you received of me?   185

BASSANIO If I could add a lie unto a fault,
I would deny it; but you see my finger
Hath not the ring upon it, it is gone.

PORTIA Even so void is your false heart of truth.
By heaven, I will ne'er come in your bed   190
Until I see the ring.

NERISSA   Nor I in yours
Till I again see mine.

BASSANIO   Sweet Portia,
If you did know to whom I gave the ring,
If you did know for whom I gave the ring,
And would conceive for what I gave the ring,   195
And how unwillingly I left the ring,
When naught would be accepted but the ring,
You would abate the strength of your displeasure.

PORTIA If you had known the virtue of the ring,
Or half her worthiness that gave the ring,   200
Or your own honour to contain the ring,
You would not then have parted with the ring.
What man is there so much unreasonable,
If you had pleased to have defended it

190–2a 'Bed' changed to 'sight', Inchbald and Charles Kean editions.

With any terms of zeal, wanted the modesty   205
To urge the thing held as a ceremony?
Nerissa teaches me what to believe:
I'll die for't, but some woman had the ring!
BASSANIO No by my honour, madam, by my soul
No woman had it, but a civil doctor,   210
Which did refuse three thousand ducats of me,
And begged the ring, the which I did deny him,
And suffered him to go displeased away,
Even he that had held up the very life
Of my dear friend. What should I say, sweet lady?   215
I was enforced to send it after him;
I was beset with shame and courtesy;
My honour would not let ingratitude
So much besmear it. Pardon me, good lady,
For by these blessèd candles of the night,   220
Had you been there I think you would have begged
The ring of me to give the worthy doctor.
PORTIA Let not that doctor e'er come near my house.
Since he hath got the jewel that I loved
And that which you did swear to keep for me,   225
I will become as liberal as you;
I'll not deny him anything I have,
No, not my body, nor my husband's bed:
Know him I shall, I am well sure of it.
Lie not a night from home. Watch me like Argus.   230
If you do not, if I be left alone,
Now by mine honour which is yet mine own,
I'll have that doctor for my bedfellow.
NERISSA And I his clerk; therefore be well advised
How you do leave me to mine own protection.   235
GRATIANO Well, do you so. Let not me take him then,
For if I do, I'll mar the young clerk's pen.

227–8 Retained in the Bell text, but normally cut in the nineteenth century. However, Inchbald and
Macready delete only 'my body nor' – what else Portia might do in bed with 'that doctor'
remains a mystery.

233–4a Guthrie had Bassanio and Gratiano exclaim 'Portia!' and 'Nerissa!' in turn (*pmt*).

236–7 Retained in Inchbald, but too risqué from Kemble onwards. Macready leaves it unmarked,
however (*pmt*).

ANTONIO I am th'unhappy subject of these quarrels.

PORTIA Sir, grieve not you; you are welcome notwithstanding.

BASSANIO Portia, forgive me this enforcèd wrong;   240
    And in the hearing of these many friends
    I swear to thee, even by thine own fair eyes
    Wherein I see myself –

PORTIA   Mark you but that?
    In both my eyes he doubly sees himself:
    In each eye one. Swear by your double self,   245
    And there's an oath of credit!

BASSANIO   Nay, but hear me.
    Pardon this fault, and by my soul I swear
    I nevermore will break an oath with thee.

ANTONIO I once did lend my body for his wealth,
    Which but for him that had your husband's ring   250
    Had quite miscarried. I dare be bound again,
    My soul upon the forfeit, that your lord
    Will nevermore break faith advisedly.

PORTIA Then you shall be his surety. Give him this,
    And bid him keep it better than the other.   255

ANTONIO Here, Lord Bassanio, swear to keep this ring.

BASSANIO By heaven, it is the same I gave the doctor!

PORTIA I had it of him; pardon me, Bassanio,
    For by this ring the doctor lay with me.

NERISSA And pardon me, my gentle Gratiano,   260
    For that same scrubbèd boy the doctor's clerk,
    In lieu of this, last night did lie with me.

GRATIANO Why, this is like the mending of highways

---

256 'In Forbes-Robertson's version, Nerissa has at the same time given Gratiano a ring.
    They start to swear over the rings simultaneously – and as their eyes fall on the rings,
    [they] start, both at once. A good comedy point, if done quickly and lightly'
    (*pmt* Ames[1]).

259–65 As with 227–8, different managers handled the references to cuckoldry in some very
    curious ways. From the era of Macklin through to Cooke, if the Bell and Inchbald texts are
    any guide, these lines were spoken unaltered, but Kemble's promptbook shows a change
    from 'lay' and 'lie' to 'sleep' in 259 and 262. Whether these changes are by Kemble or a later
    hand, they do not seem to accomplish much, especially since 265 ('What, are we cuckolds')
    is left alone (see also 281–5).

                    In summer where the ways are fair enough!
                    What, are we cuckolds ere we have deserved it?   265
    PORTIA   Speak not so grossly; you are all amazed.
                    Here is a letter, read it at your leisure;
                    It comes from Padua, from Bellario.
                    There you shall find that Portia was the doctor,
                    Nerissa there her clerk. Lorenzo here   270
                    Shall witness I set forth as soon as you,
                    And even but now returned; I have not yet
                    Entered my house. Antonio, you are welcome;
                    And I have better news in store for you
                    Than you expect. Unseal this letter soon;   275
                    There you shall find three of your argosies
                    Are richly come to harbour suddenly.
                    You shall not know by what strange accident
                    I chancèd on this letter.
    ANTONIO   I am dumb.
    BASSANIO   Were you the doctor and I knew you not?   280
    GRATIANO   Were you the clerk that is to make me cuckold?
    NERISSA   Ay, but the clerk that never means to do it,
                    Unless he live until he be a man.

266a   Macready replaced 'Speak not so grossly' with the single admonition 'Patience!' (*pmt*).
       Nunn had Bassanio, not Portia, reprove Gratiano; in Miller's television version, Plowright
       uttered a shocked 'oh!' before a true Victorian 'we-are-not-amused' reading.

274–9 In Benthall's production, 'all the explanations and papers which came out of Portia's pocket
       (the letter from Bellario, and the letter to Antonio) were treated with similar gaiety, as if all
       this world of bonds and caskets was no more than make-believe' (Clarke, *Shakespeare at
       the Old Vic*, np). Sellars presented a very different world: Gratiano threw his ring at Nerissa
       and walked off, while Antonio presented Portia's ring to Bassanio 'with prolonged
       solemnity'. Portia gave Antonio no letter with news of his ships' safe return, but instead
       wrote 'a large cheque to buy him off from posing a demand on Bassanio's bisexuality'
       (M. Shapiro, *SB* 1994; Holland, *English Shakespeares*, p. 257).

281–5 Gratiano's line was usually changed in the nineteenth century to a repeat of Bassanio's 'and
       I knew you not'. Macready substitutes, 'Were you the clerk that is to wrong my bed?' (*pmt*),
       rendering Gratiano, and perhaps the audience, as confused as Portia apparently was at 228
       about just what it is, other than sleep, that men and women do in bed. Kemble's
       promptbook, having emended 259 and 262, is even stranger in that it leaves Gratiano's
       'Were you the clerk that is to make me cuckold?' unchanged.

BASSANIO Sweet doctor, you shall be my bedfellow;
          When I am absent, then lie with my wife.   285
ANTONIO Sweet lady, you have given me life and living;
          For here I read for certain that my ships
          Are safely come to road.
PORTIA   How now, Lorenzo?
          My clerk hath some good comforts too for you.
NERISSA Ay, and I'll give them him without a fee.   290
          There do I give to you and Jessica
          From the rich Jew, a special deed of gift
          After his death of all he dies possessed of.
LORENZO Fair ladies, you drop manna in the way
          Of starvèd people.
PORTIA   It is almost morning;   295

291-3 One of the factors that makes Jessica such a difficult part is that Shakespeare gives her
       nothing to say when told of the deed of gift, and yet we expect her to say or do something:
       Jackson thought Emma Handy, in Doran's production, 'undercharacterized, with no sense
       that she was a wastrel and father-betrayer, or romantically attractive, or (most interesting
       possibility) both . . . she did not react to the deed of gift and the news of her father' (*SQ*
       1999). Yet the under-characterisation might be Shakespeare's, not the actress's.
          Some Jessicas do react overtly, but this can seem inconsistent with the Jessica we see
       earlier, even moments earlier. Serban's Jessica, Aysan Celik, whose 'scene with her lover is
       directed as one of innocent joy . . . weeps for her father, which comes out of nowhere and
       seems tacked on because it's the "right" thing to do – in an otherwise bold production,
       it rings utterly false' (Hartigan, *BG* 19 December 1998).
          One point, easily overlooked, is that Jessica has no knowledge of the events of 4.1,
       beyond the fact that the pound of flesh, for some reason, was not taken from Antonio. She is
       not aware of the forced baptism, nor that Shylock was *compelled* to make her and Lorenzo
       his beneficiaries. Jessica's guilt, if that is what the actress chooses to emphasise, may derive
       from what she believes to be an undeserved act of forgiveness by her father, which, in many
       ways, is what it is. 'I am content' (4.1.390) has as much to do with the deed of gift as it does
       with forced baptism. To show any of this without any lines is a daunting prospect, and Trevor
       Nunn helped Gabrielle Jourdan tremendously in his unusual close to the play (see pp. 261–2).
294-5a Kahn's Lorenzo, Mark H. Dold, 'remains a cad in all of his appearances . . . when Portia
       hands him Shylock's deed of gift, [he] dances for joy, pointedly ignoring his wife, as he
       prances off in self-satisfied glee' (Mahon, *SN* 1999).
  295b Sothern's *Merchant* had technical difficulties on opening night in New York, and the
       performance did not finish until after midnight. When Julia Marlowe said 'it is almost
       morning', someone in the balcony shouted 'You bet it is!' (Russell, *Julia Marlowe*, p. 338).

And yet I am sure you are not satisfied
Of these events at full. Let us go in,
And charge us there upon inter'gatories,
And we will answer all things faithfully.

GRATIANO Let it be so. The first inter'gatory   300

300–7 Gratiano ends the play with a bawdy speech of two unrhymed lines and three couplets.
Kemble and Macready cut all but the final couplet, and from Charles Kean through to
Beerbohm Tree and Ben Greet, Portia's 'all things faithfully' were the last words to be heard.
This ending was revived by Hall, with Geraldine James coming downstage and addressing
the audience.

Crosse attended Oswald's Stoll's revival of the *Merchant* in 1934 and thought that Basil
Gill was 'a very good Antonio . . . by an odd arrangement he was made unusually
prominent in the last scene and at the end was left alone on the stage rejoicing over the
recovery of his ships' (*Diaries*, vol. XIV, p. 115). Stoll's 'odd arrangement', of course, was in a
production that would have been without any suggestion of Antonio's homosexuality –
hence Gill was 'musing happily'. Antonio's demeanour has usually been much less cheerful
since Tyrone Guthrie's production, when Robert Goodier's 'lone figure occupied the stage
as, brooding, he let slip away the letter containing the good news of the return of his
argosies' (Griffin, *TA* 1955). Guthrie's staging was so influential that when Rabb's Antonio
stood 'abandoned on the darkened stage, the lover left behind but not scorned . . . ever
brooding, slowly, stylishly, [he] extinguished his last cigarette' (Hirsch, 'The Merchant',
p. 512), Julius Novick said in the *New York Times* that this was 'practically a stage tradition
by now' (11 March 1973).

Gascon had Jessica 'staring wonderingly at Antonio, before running in to join her
Christian husband' (Barnes, *NYT* 10 June 1970), and Terry Hands also left Antonio alone,
'pale and serious, in his black suit, his unanswered, undeclared love for Bassanio thwarted'.
As the lights dimmed, a *shofar*, the ram's horn traditionally used to call Jews to prayer,
was heard in the distance (Smallwood, 'Director's Shakespeare', p. 193).

Barton's 1978 production closed much more happily, untroubled by any darker
feelings: as everyone celebrated with champagne, Nerissa and Gratiano, and Jessica and
Lorenzo went off first – then Antonio refilled his, Portia's and Bassanio's glasses, 'drank a
final toast to Portia and Bassanio, and walked briskly from the stage, leaving them to
make their departure slowly, hand in hand, as the sound of the dawn chorus of birds
began' (Smallwood, 'Director's Shakespeare', p. 193). Michael Langham, in three
productions from 1960 to 1989, ended with a sad and solitary Antonio, but with a slight
amendment each time: Patrick Allen (1960) 'was left alone on the stage, seated and idly
playing with the piece of paper which had given him the irrelevant news [of] his argosies';
Jack Ryland (1988) tore the paper in two, and Nicholas Pennell (1989) got to tear it into

several pieces, and then toss it into the air (Brown, *SS* 1961; Richards, *WP* 4 May 1988; Ward, *SB* 1989).

Some directors bring the two 'outsiders' together for a final tableau. In Alexander's production, Lorenzo, already estranged from Jessica, followed the two other couples off, as Jessica, having dropped the crucifix she was given earlier by Lorenzo (see pp. 141, 146), knelt to retrieve it – Antonio grasped it first, and held it just out of her reach as the lights faded (Jackson, *SQ* 1994). Maraden's Jessica, who 'by the end . . . knew she had made a mistake', separated herself from Lorenzo and came back to stand by Antonio (Leggatt, *SB* 1997; Liston, 'The Merchant', p. 87). Kahn's Lorenzo exited laughing, leaving Jessica with Antonio, who looked at her as he let the letter fall.

Edelstein presented an intriguing variation on this theme. Portia, seeing Jessica ignored by everyone, including Lorenzo, addressed 296–9 to her; and all exited but Antonio. But then Portia returned, her rival Antonio went in and Portia stood alone at the close. Piscator 'cut the last verses of Shakespeare's text and left a perplexed Jessica holding her father's deed of gift to close the play' (Verch, '*The Merchant*', p. 87); Schenk followed this lead by having Lorenzo say 'In such a night / Did pretty Jessica . . .' (5.1.20–2) while falling asleep; the play closes with a close-up on a tearful Jessica as a Hebrew lament is heard on the soundtrack. Miller had Jessica decline to join the others as they went into the house, and while she read her father's deed of gift, an off-stage voice sang the *Kaddish*, which in the television version continued over the credits. Kelly ended with Jessica, in tears, standing by a *menorah*, while traditional Jewish music played (Schafer, *Ms-Directing Shakespeare*, p. 121).

No mention has been made of the ending of the play's first performance, since it would not have ended here – although the text shows 'exeunt', there would soon have been a re-entry for a jig. The 1998 Globe production closed with its cast cheerfully singing a madrigal – at least one critic was troubled by not being sure whether the actors were still in character (Potter, 'Shakespeare Performed', p. 76). Komisarjevsky had a jig of sorts, with a return of the carnival that began the play, the Pierrots of the opening sequence doing a final dance, 'followed by Lancelot, yawning and stretching' (Mennen, 'Theodore Komisarjevsky's Production', p. 397).

Serban ended his *Merchant* in as provocative a manner as he started it. After a tableau of a rejected Antonio and a disconsolate Jessica, the others re-entered, sang 'Where is fancy bred' together, and departed with Jessica. Then Shylock entered and 'jigged' around Antonio, LeBow holding out his bag of nuts to Jonathan Epstein as the lights faded. I doubt that I am the only person to wonder if this was the same bag he vomited into at the end of the trial scene.

Nunn finished his *Merchant* in such a distinctive way that it seems fitting to close this commentary with it. While Antonio sat at the piano playing the same tune with which the play began, Lorenzo received the deed of gift with 'Fair ladies, you drop manna in the

That my Nerissa shall be sworn on is:
Whether till the next night she had rather stay,
Or go to bed now, being two hours to day.
But were the day come, I should wish it dark,
Till I were couching with the doctor's clerk.   305
Well, while I live I'll fear no other thing
So sore as keeping safe Nerissa's ring.

Exeunt

way/Of starvèd people (294–5a), and then Portia spoke 296–9 directly to Jessica, in an effort to comfort her. After Gratiano's closing speech, Portia spoke lines taken from earlier in the scene,

> This night methinks is but the daylight sick,
> It looks a little paler; 'tis a day
> Such as the day is when the sun is hid. (124–6)

While the others looked on with concern, Jessica once again sang a verse from *Eshet Chayil*, and as the sound of thunder was heard in the distance, Portia said softly, 'It is almost morning' (295b), and the lights dimmed.

APPENDIX 1

BASSANIO'S CASKET SPEECH IN
THE NINETEENTH CENTURY

When Morocco and Arragon are omitted, the riddle of the three caskets disappears from the play, unless Bassanio's speech in 3.2 is somehow rewritten to restore it. The new version given here is found in Kemble's edition of 1810; from Cooke until Charles Kean, nineteenth-century managers with the exception of Macready (see p. 89) used this speech or something close to it (Inchbald's 1808 edition is only slightly different).

Over half of what Bassanio says belongs to Morocco or Arragon, with a key change to 2.9.50. The result is an intelligent and meaningful meditation on the caskets – a powerful reminder that the common practice of burlesquing Portia's unsuccessful suitors is not necessarily the best approach.

[Morocco]   Some god direct my judgement! Let me see.

(2.7.13)

'Who chooseth me shall gain what many men desire.'
. . . that . . . may be meant
[Of] the fool multitude, that choose by show.

(2.9.23–5)

[Bassanio]   The world is still deceived with ornament.
In law, what plea so tainted and corrupt
But, being seasoned with a gracious voice,
Obscures the show of evil? In religion,
What damnèd error but some sober brow
Will bless it and approve it with a text,
Hiding the grossness with fair ornament?

(3.2.74–80)

Thus ornament is but the guilèd shore
To a most dangerous sea, the beauteous scarf
Veiling an Indian beauty.

(3.2.97–9)

Therefore, thou gaudy gold,
Hard food for Midas, I will none of thee.

(3.2.101–2)

[Arragon]   'Who chooseth me shall get as much as he deserves.'
And well said too, for who shall go about
To cozen fortune, and be honourable
Without the stamp of merit?

(2.9.35–8)

O, that estates, degrees, and offices
Were not derived corruptly, and that clear honour
Were purchased by the merit of the wearer!
How many then should cover that stand bare,
How many be commanded that command!
How much low peasantry would then be gleaned
From the true seed of honour,[1] and how much honour
Picked from the chaff and ruin of the times
To be new varnished! . . .
[*I'll not*] assume desert.

(2.9.40–50)

'Who chooseth me must give and hazard all he hath.'

(2.9.20)

[Bassanio]   [I'll] none of thee . . . thou pale and common drudge
'Tween man and man. But thou, thou meagre lead,
Which rather threaten'st than dost promise aught,
Thy paleness moves me more than eloquence,
And here choose I. Joy be the consequence!

(3.2.102–7)

---

1 2.9.45–46a are not in Inchbald.

APPENDIX 2

ESHET CHAYIL

In Trevor Nunn's production, after Henry Goodman said 'Jessica my girl' to Gabrielle Jourdan (2.5.15), he began to sing a traditional Hebrew melody – most reviewers remarked upon it, and the National Theatre's website received many enquiries asking for more information. Even for those with no knowledge of Hebrew, it was a wistful and poignant moment, but those who recognised the song would have appreciated the wealth of insight it brought to the play's complex character relationships.

Shylock sang *Eshet Chayil*, or 'a woman of virtue',[1] verses taken from Proverbs 31:10–31, in which a husband and children pay tribute to the woman of the house on the Sabbath, praising her as provident and hard-working: 'she possesses optimism, faces life with confidence, and speaks in wisdom and kindness'.[2] This tradition, still observed by many families, goes back to the sixteenth century; a commentary on *Eshet Chayil* by Abraham Jaghel Gallichi was published in that major centre of Jewish scholarship, the Republic of Venice, in 1601.[3]

In their entirety, the twenty-two verses form an acrostic, one verse for each letter of the Hebrew alphabet. To Israel Abrahams, 'nothing in ancient literature equals this remarkable attestation to the dignity and individuality of woman',[4] although many modern Jews object to the depiction of women as 'subservient homemakers'.[5]

In Nunn's *Merchant*, while the Sabbath candles burned beside Leah's photograph, Shylock sang verses 10 and 11:

> Who shall finde a vertuous woman? for her price is farre above the pearles.
> The heart of her husband trusteth in her, so that he shall have no need of spoile.

Jessica then repeated verse 11, and together they sang verse 12: 'She will doe him good, and not evill all the dayes of her life.' Goodman's singing of 'Who shall finde a vertuous woman . . .' brought his grief at the loss of Leah into the play before Jessica's elopement. But the song was directed as much to Jessica as to Leah's memory, for Jessica is now the woman of the house – when Jourdan joined in, one could discern her disquiet, and as she reached verse 12, her sense of betrayal was both visible and audible.

1 *Eshet* is the genitive form of 'woman' or 'wife'. *Chayil* literally means 'strong', but idiomatically it can denote excellence, bravery, virtue or any positive quality: the Bishops' Bible has 'honest, faithful woman'; the Geneva and King James versions have 'virtuous woman'; Geneva text quoted here.
2 *Encyclopaedia Judaica*.
3 Werblowsky and Wigoder, *The Oxford Dictionary of the Jewish Religion*, p. 234; Shulvass, *The Jews*, p. 168.
4 Abrahams, *A Companion*, p. 139.
5 Werblowsky and Wigoder, *The Oxford Dictionary of the Jewish Religion*, p. 234.

Not only is Jessica about to leave her father, she is forsaking her religion, and her duty as given in Proverbs. The high living in Genoa, culminating in the sale of Leah's precious turquoise (3.1.95–7), is more than callous frivolity, but a rejection of what is expressed in the culminating, penultimate verse of *Eshet Chayil*: 'Favour is deceitfull, and beautie is vanitie: but a woman that feareth the Lorde, she shall be praysed.'

Nunn's production ended with Jourdan tearfully singing verse 12: 'She will doe him good, and not evill all the dayes of her life.'

BIBLIOGRAPHY

EDITIONS

Bawcutt, N. W., ed. *The Jew of Malta*. Manchester: Manchester University Press, 1978.

Furness, H. H. *A New Variorum Edition of Shakespeare: The Merchant of Venice*. Philadelphia: J. B. Lippincott, 1888.

Granville, George. *The Jew of Venice*. London: 1701.

Inchbald, Elizabeth. *The Merchant of Venice: A Comedy*. London: 1808.

Irving, Sir Henry and Frank A. Marshall. *The Works of William Shakespeare*. 14 vols. London: Gresham, 1907.

Kean, Charles. *Shakespeare's Play of The Merchant of Venice*. London: 1858.

Kemble, J. P. *Shakspeare's Merchant of Venice*. London, 1810. In John Philip Kemble Promptbooks, vol. VI. Ed. Charles H. Shattuck. Charlottesville: University Press of Virginia, 1974.

Mahood, M. M., ed. *The Merchant of Venice*. Cambridge: Cambridge University Press, 1987.

The Merchant of Venice, A Comedy, by Shakespeare. London: John Bell, 1774.

PROMPTBOOKS

Only promptbooks cited in the introduction or commentary are listed here. The number in the last column is for reference to Charles H. Shattuck's *The Shakespeare Promptbooks: A Descriptive Catalogue* (Urbana: University of Illinois Press, 1965).

Production	Year	Location	Shattuck no.
J. P. Kemble	1810	Kemble edition	
Edmund Kean	1814	Folger	9
Charles Kean[1]	1838	Folger	12
W. C. Macready	c.1841	Folger	17
Edwin Booth[1]	1857	Folger	33
Charles Kean[2]	1858	Folger	34
Edwin Booth[2]	1867	Harvard	48
John Moore/Augustin Daly	c.1875	Folger	53
Henry Irving[1]	1879	Folger	55
Henry Irving[2]	1880s	Harvard	

F. R. Benson	c.1905	Shakespeare Centre, Stratford	88
E. H. Sothern[1]	c.1905	Folger	91
E. H. Sothern[2]	c.1905	Folger	92
E. H. Sothern[3]	c.1905	Folger	93
E. H. Sothern[4]	c.1905	NYPL	95
Edwin Booth[3]/R. B. Mantell	1906	Folger	103
Henry Jewett	1915	Folger	114
Winthrop Ames[*1]	1920s	NYPL	102
Winthrop Ames[2]	1928	NYPL	117
Tyrone Guthrie	1955	Stratford, Ontario	
Margaret Webster	1956	Shakespeare Centre, Stratford	127
Jonathan Miller	1970	Royal National Theatre	
Michael Langham	1989	Stratford, Ontario	
David Thacker	1993	Shakespeare Centre, Stratford	
Marti Maraden	1996	Stratford, Ontario	
Andrei Serban	1998	ART, Massachusetts	

STANDARD REFERENCE WORKS

A Biographical Dictionary of Actors, Actresses, Musicians, Dancers & Other Stage Personnel in London, 1660–1800. Ed. Philip H. Highfill, Jr, Kalman A. Burnim and Edward A. Langhans. Carbondale: Southern Illinois University Press, 1973–8.

Calendar of State Papers, Domestic Series, Of the Reign of Elizabeth, 1591–4. Nendeln: Kraus, 1967.

Encyclopaedia Judaica. Jerusalem: Keter Publishing, 1971.

Genest, John. *Some Account of the English Stage from the Restoration in 1660 to 1830*. 10 vols. [1832]. New York: B. Franklin, 1965.

Halstead, William P. *Shakespeare as Spoken: A Collation of 5000 Acting Editions and Promptbooks*. 12 vols. Ann Arbor, MI: University Microfilm International, 1977–9.

The London Stage, 1660–1800 : A calendar of plays, entertainments & afterpieces, together with casts, box-receipts and contemporary comment / Compiled from the playbills, newspapers and theatrical diaries of the period. 5 pts. Carbondale: Southern Illinois University Press, 1960–8.

* contains notes on earlier productions, including Novelli and Forbes-Robertson.

OTHER WORKS: PRINTED

Abrahams, Israel. *A Companion to the Daily Prayer Book*. New York: Hermon Press, 1966.

Adler, Jacob. *A Life on the Stage*. Ed. Lulla Rosenfeld. New York: Knopf, 1999.

Alter, Iska. 'When the Audience Called "Author! Author!"': Shakespeare on New York's Yiddish Stage'. *Theatre History Studies* 10 (1990): 141–62.

Ansorge, Peter. 'Old Vic: *The Merchant of Venice*'. *Plays and Players* (June 1970): 39–43.

Archer, William. *The Theatrical World of 1897* [1898]. New York: Benjamin Blom, 1969.

Asp, Carolyn. 'The Merchant of Venice'. *Theatre Journal* 42 (1990): 375–7.

Atkins, Robert. *Robert Atkins: An Unfinished Autobiography*. Ed. George Rowell. London: Society for Theatre Research, 1994.

Atkinson, Brooks. *Broadway*. London: Cassell, 1971.

Ball, Robert Hamilton. *Shakespeare on Silent Film*. New York: Theatre Arts Books, 1968.

Bancroft, Marie and Squire. *The Bancrofts: Recollections of Sixty Years*. London: Thomas Nelson & Sons, 1911.

Banham, Martin, ed. *Cambridge Guide to World Theatre*. Cambridge: Cambridge University Press, 1988.

Barbour, Thomas. 'Theatre Chronicle'. *Hudson Review* 6 (1953): 278–86.

Barrymore, Ethel. *Memories*. London: Hulton, 1956.

Barton, John. *Playing Shakespeare*. London: Methuen, 1984.

Bate, Jonathan. *The Romantics on Shakespeare*. Harmondsworth: Penguin, 1992.

'The Romantic Stage'. In *Shakespeare: An Illustrated Stage History*. Ed. Jonathan Bate and Russell Jackson. Oxford: Oxford University Press, 1996.

Baum, Paul Franklinn. 'Judas's Red Hair'. *Journal of English and Germanic Philology* 21 (1922): 520–9.

Beatty-Kingston, William. 'Shylock in Germany'. *The Theatre* 1 (1880): 17–20, 86–90.

Beauman, Sally. *The Royal Shakespeare Company: A History of Ten Decades*. Oxford: Oxford University Press, 1982.

Beckerman, Bernard. 'The Season at Stratford Connecticut, 1967'. *Shakespeare Quarterly* 18 (1967): 405–8.

Berek, Peter. 'The Jew as Renaissance Man'. *Renaissance Quarterly* 51 (1998): 128–62.

Berkowitz, Joel. 'A True Jewish Jew: Three Yiddish Shylocks'. *Theatre Survey* 37 (1996): 75–88.

Berry, Ralph. *On Directing Shakespeare: Interviews with Contemporary Directors.* London: Hamish Hamilton, 1989.

Biggs, Murray. 'A Neurotic Portia'. *Shakespeare Survey* 25 (1972): 153–9.

Billington, Michael. *The Modern Actor.* London: Hamilton, 1973.
Peggy Ashcroft. London: Mandarin, 1989.
One Night Stands. London: Nick Hern Books, 1993.

Bloom, Harold. *Shakespeare: The Invention of the Human.* London: Fourth Estate, 1999.

Booth, Michael R. *Victorian Spectacular Theatre: 1850–1910.* London: Routledge, 1981.

Bordman, Gerald Martin. *The Oxford Companion to American Theatre.* New York: Oxford University Press, 1984.

Braun, Edward. *The Director and the Stage.* London: Methuen, 1982.

Brereton, Austin. *The Life of Henry Irving.* 2 vols. London: Longmans, Green, and Co., 1908.

Brockbank, J. Philip. 'Shakespeare Renaissance in China'. *Shakespeare Quarterly* 39 (1988): 195–204.

Brown, Ivor and George Fearon. *Amazing Monument: A Short History of the Shakespeare Industry.* London: Heinemann, 1938.

Brown, John Russell. 'Shakespeare Festivals in Britain'. *Shakespeare Quarterly* 7 (1956): 407–10.
'Three Directors: A Review of Recent Productions'. *Shakespeare Survey* 14 (1961): 129–37.
'The Royal Shakespeare Company 1965'. *Shakespeare Survey* 19 (1966): 111–18.
'Free Shakespeare'. *Shakespeare Survey* 24 (1971): 112–18.

Brownlow, Kevin. *David Lean.* London: Richard Cohen Books, 1996.

Bruford, W. H. *Theatre Drama and Audience in Goethe's Germany.* London: Routledge & Kegan Paul, 1950.

Bulman, James C. *Shakespeare in Performance: The Merchant of Venice.* Manchester: Manchester University Press, 1991.

Carlisle, Carol Jones. *Helen Faucit: Fire and Ice on the Victorian Stage.* London: Society for Theatre Research, 2000.

Carlson, Marvin. *The German Stage in the Nineteenth Century.* Metuchen, NJ: Scarecrow Press, 1972.

Caseres, Benjamin de. 'Ermete Novelli Coming to America', *Theatre Magazine,* March 1907.

Casson, John. *Lewis & Sybil: A Memoir.* London: Collins, 1972.

Chambers, David and Brian Pullan, eds. *Venice: A Documentary History, 1450–1630.* Oxford: Blackwell, 1992.

Clarke, Mary. *Shakespeare at the Old Vic: Fourth Season, 1956–7*. London: Hamish Hamilton, 1957.

Cochrane, Claire. *Shakespeare and the Birmingham Repertory Theatre, 1913–1929*. London: Society for Theatre Research, 1993.

Cole, John William. *The Life and Theatrical Times of Charles Kean, F.S.A.*, vol. II [1859]. New York: Garland, 1986.

Coleman, Marion Moore. *Fair Rosalind: The American Career of Helena Modjeska*. Cheshire, CT: Cherry Hill Books, 1969.

Collier, J. Payne. *Memoirs of the Principal Actors in the Plays of Shakespeare*. London: Shakespeare Society, 1846.

Colman, E. A. M. 'Autumn Leaves on the Avon'. *Literary Half-Yearly* 20 (1979): 146–8.

Cook, Ann Jennalie. '*The Merchant of Venice* at The Other Place'. *Shakespeare Quarterly* 30 (1979): 158–60.

Cook, Dorothy and Wayne. 'The Merchant of Venice'. *Shakespeare Bulletin* 12, no. 2 (1994): 10–11.

'The Merchant of Venice'. *Shakespeare Bulletin* 17, no. 2 (1999): 8–9.

Cooper, Roberta Krensky. *The American Shakespeare Theatre: Stratford, 1955–1985*. Washington, DC: Folger Books, 1986.

[Cornwall, Barry]. *The Life of Edmund Kean*. New York: Harper & Brothers, 1835.

Crosse, Gordon. *Theatrical Diary: 1890–1953*. Unpublished manuscript in 31 vols. City of Birmingham Central Library.

Fifty Years of Shakespearean Playgoing. London: A. R. Mowbray, 1941.

Cunliffe, Marcus. *The Literature of the United States*. Harmondsworth: Penguin, 1967.

Curiel, Roberta and Bernard Dov Cooperman, *The Venetian Ghetto*. New York: Rizzoli, 1990.

Cusack, Sinead. 'Portia in *The Merchant of Venice*'. In *Players of Shakespeare 1*. Ed. Philip Brockbank. Cambridge: Cambridge University Press, 1985.

Danson, Lawrence. 'The Problem of Shylock'. In *Major Literary Characters: Shylock*. Ed. Harold Bloom. New York: Chelsea House, 1991.

Dench, Judi. 'A Career in Shakespeare'. In *Shakespeare: An Illustrated Stage History*. Ed. Jonathan Bate and Russell Jackson. Oxford: Oxford University Press, 1996.

Denham, Reginald. *Stars in My Hair*. New York: Crown, 1958.

De Sousa, Gerald U. '*The Merchant of Venice*: Brazil and Cultural Icons'. *Shakespeare Quarterly* 45 (1994): 469–74.

Devrient, Eduard. *Geschichte der Deutschen Schauspielkunst*, vol. I. Berlin: Henschelverlag, 1967.

Dobson, Michael. 'Improving on the Original: Actresses and Adaptations'. In *Shakespeare: An Illustrated Stage History*. Ed. Jonathan Bate and Russell Jackson. Oxford: Oxford University Press, 1996.

Doran, Gregory. 'Solanio in *The Merchant of Venice*'. In *Players of Shakespeare 3*. Ed. Russell Jackson and Robert Smallwood. Cambridge: Cambridge University Press, 1993.

Doran, John. *Their Majesties' Servants*. 2 vols. London: Allen, 1864.

'The Drama'. *Shakespeariana* 3 (1886): 523–6.

Edelman, Charles. 'Which is the Jew that Shakespeare Knew?: Shylock on the Elizabethan Stage'. *Shakespeare Survey* 52 (1999): 99–106.

Edinborough, Arnold. 'Shakespeare Confirmed: At the Canadian Stratford'. *Shakespeare Quarterly* 6 (1955): 435–46.

Elwood, William R. 'Werner Krauss and the Third Reich'. In *Theatre in the Third Reich: The Prewar Years*. Ed. Glen W. Gadberry. Westport, CT: Greenwood Press, 1995.

Epstein, Helen. *Joe Papp: An American Life*. Boston: Little, Brown and Co., 1994.

Esslin, Martin. 'The Merchant of Venice'. *Plays and Players* (May 1972): 34–5.

Evans, Gareth Lloyd. 'Shakespeare Memorial Theatre 1960'. *International Theatre Annual* 5 (1961): 154–69.

Ewbank, Inga-Stina. 'European Cross Currents: Ibsen and Brech'. In *Shakespeare: An Illustrated Stage History*. Ed. Jonathan Bate and Russell Jackson. Oxford: Oxford University Press, 1996.

Fan Shen. 'Shakespeare in China: *The Merchant of Venice*'. *Asian Theatre Journal* 5 (1988): 23–37.

Feinberg, Anat. *Embodied Memory: The Theatre of Georg Tabori*. Iowa City: University of Iowa Press, 1999.

Felheim, Marvin. *The Theater of Augustin Daly: An Account of the Late Nineteenth-Century American Stage*. New York: Greenwood Press, 1969.

Findlater, Richard. *The Player Kings*. New York: Stein and Day, 1971.

Lilian Baylis: The Lady of the Old Vic. London: Allen Lane, 1975.

Findlay, Deborah. 'Portia in *The Merchant of Venice*'. In *Players of Shakespeare 3*. Ed. Russell Jackson and Robert Smallwood. Cambridge: Cambridge University Press, 1993.

Finlay, Robert. 'The Foundation of the Ghetto: Venice, the Jews, and the War of the League of Cambrai'. *Proceedings of the American Philosophical Society* 126 (1982): 140–54.

Fischer, Susan L. 'The Merchant of Venice'. *Shakespeare Bulletin* 13, no. 1 (1995): 29–30.

'The Merchant of Venice'. *Shakespeare Bulletin* 17, no. 1 (1999): 12–13.

'The Merchant of Venice'. *Shakespeare Bulletin* 18, no. 1 (2000): 25–7.

Fischer-Lichte, Erika. 'Theatre as Festive Play: Max Reinhardt's Production of *The Merchant of Venice*'. In *Venetian Views, Venetian Blinds: English Fantasies of Venice*. Ed. Manfred Pfister and Barbara Schaff. Amsterdam: Rodopi. 1999.

Foakes, R. A. and R. T. Rickert, ed. *Henslowe's Diary*. Cambridge: Cambridge University Press, 1961.

Fortis, Umberto. *The Ghetto on the Lagoon*. Trans. Roberto Matteoda. Venice: Edizioni Storti, 1988.

Foulkes, Richard. "Helen Faucit and Ellen Terry as Portia'. *Theatre Notebook* 31 (1977): 27–36.

Freedland, Michael. *Peter O'Toole*. London: W.H. Allen, 1983.

Gatty, Alfred. 'Kean in 1805'. *Notes and Queries* 4, 8th series (1893): 538.

Gay, Penny, introd. *The Merchant of Venice*. Sydney: Science Press, 1995.

Geckle, George L. 'The Merchant of Venice'. *Plays and Players* (April 1994): 11–12.

Gentleman, Francis. *The Dramatic Censor, or Critical Companion*. 2 vols. London: J. Bell, 1770.

Gielgud, John. *Acting Shakespeare*. London: Pan, 1991.

Golder, John, and Richard Madelaine, ed. *O Brave New World: Two Centuries of Shakespeare on the Australian Stage*. Sydney: Currency Press, 2001.

Goodale, Katherine [Kitty Molony]. *Behind the Scenes with Edwin Booth*. Rprt edn New York: Benjamin Blom, 1969.

Goodman, Godfrey. *The Court of King James the First*, vol. 1. Ed. J. S. Brewer. London: Richard Bentley, 1838.

Graham-White, Anthony. 'Critical Responses to *The Merchant of Venice* and *The Winter's Tale*'. *Text and Performance Quarterly* 15 (1995): 153–7.

Greenwald, Michael L. *Directions by Indirections: John Barton of the Royal Shakespeare Company*. Newark: University of Delaware Press, 1985.

Griffin, Alice. 'Shakespeare and Sophocles at Stratford'. *Theatre Arts* (September 1955): 30, 91–2.

'The New York Season, 1961–2'. *Shakespeare Quarterly* 13 (1962): 553–7.

Gross, John. *Shylock: Four Hundred Years in the Life of a Legend*. New York: Vintage, 1994.

Grunberger, Richard. *A Social History of the Third Reich*. London: Weidenfeld and Nicolson, 1971.

Guthrie, Tyrone. *In Various Directions*. New York: Macmillan, 1955.

Halio, Jay L., introd. *The Merchant of Venice*. Oxford: Oxford University Press, 1993.

Hankey, Julie. 'Victorian Portias: Shakespeare's Borderline Heroine'. *Shakespeare Quarterly* 45 (1994): 426–48.

Hare, Arnold. *George Frederick Cooke: The Actor and the Man*. London: Society for Theatre Research, 1980.

Harwood, Ronald. *Sir Donald Wolfit: His Life and Work in the Unfashionable Theatre*. London: Amber Lane Press, 1983.

Häublein, Renata. 'Ein Stück, gemacht, um, den Charakter des Juden in's Licht zu setzen': Die Mannheimer *Kauffmann von Venedig*–Bearbeitung von 1783'. *Shakespeare Jahrbuch* 137 (2001): 23–37.

Hawkins, Frederick William. *The Life of Edmund Kean*. 2 vols. London: Tinsley Brothers, 1969.

Hayman, Ronald. *John Gielgud*. New York: Random House, 1971.

Hazlitt, William. *A View of the English Stage*. Ed. W. Spencer Jackson. London: Bell, 1906.

Hillebrand, Harold Newcomb. *Edmund Kean*. New York: Columbia University Press, 1933.

Hirsch, Foster. 'The Merchant of Venice'. *Educational Theatre Journal* 25 (1973): 511–13.

Holland, Peter. 'Shakespeare Performed in England, 1992–1993'. *Shakespeare Survey* 47 (1994): 181–208.

   English Shakespeares: Shakespeare on the English Stage in the 1990s. Cambridge: Cambridge University Press, 1997.

Honigmann, E. A. J. *Shakespeare's Impact on His Contemporaries*. London: Macmillan, 1982.

   '"There is a World Elsewhere", William Shakespeare, Businessman'. In *Images of Shakespeare: Proceedings of the Third Congress of the International Shakespeare Association, 1986*. Ed. Werner Habicht, D. J. Palmer, Roger Pringle. Newark: University of Delaware Press, 1986.

Hopkins, Lisa. 'The Merchant of Venice'. *Shakespeare Bulletin* 12, no. 3 (1994): 33–4.

Hoppit, Julian. *A Land of Liberty?: England 1689–1727*. Oxford: Clarendon Press, 2000.

Hornby, Richard. 'The Other Stratford'. *Hudson Review* 49 (1996): 468–74.

Hortmann, Wilhelm. *Shakespeare on the German Stage: The Twentieth Century*. Cambridge: Cambridge University Press, 1998.

Houseman, John. *Final Dress*. New York: Simon and Schuster, 1983.

Irving, Laurence. *Henry Irving: The Actor and His World*. London: Faber & Faber, 1951.

Isaac, Dan. 'What's Happening With Drama'. *Judaism* 16 (1967):462–74.

Isaac, Winifred. *Ben Greet and the Old Vic*. London (published by author): 1964.

Jackson, Berners A. W. 'Stratford Festival of Canada'. *Shakespeare Quarterly* 28 (1977): 197–206.

Jackson, Russell. 'Shakespeare Performed: Shakespeare at Stratford-upon-Avon, 1993–94'. *Shakespeare Quarterly* 45 (1994): 332–48.

'Actor-Managers and the Spectacular'. In *Shakespeare: An Illustrated Stage History*. Ed. Jonathan Bate and Russell Jackson. Oxford: Oxford University Press, 1996.

'Shakespeare Performed: Shakespeare at Stratford-upon-Avon', 1996–98. *Shakespeare Quarterly* 50 (1999): 185–205.

James, Henry. *The Scenic Art: Notes on Acting and the Drama*. London: Rupert Hart-Davis, 1949.

Jones, Eldred D. *The Elizabethan Image of Africa*. Washington, DC: Folger Shakespeare Library, 1971.

Jones, Norman. *God and the Moneylenders*. London: Blackwell, 1989.

Kahane, A. 'Max Reinhardt's Shakespearezyklus im Deutschen Theater zu Berlin'. *Shakespeare Jahrbuch* 50 (1914): 107–19.

Katz, David S. *The Jews in the History of England 1485–1850*. Oxford: Clarendon Press, 1994.

Katz, Ephraim. *The International Film Encyclopedia*. London: Macmillan, 1982.

Kennedy, Dennis. *Looking at Shakespeare*. Cambridge: Cambridge University Press, 1993.

Kerr, Walter. *The Theater in Spite of Itself*. New York: Simon and Schuster, 1963.

Thirty Plays Hath November. New York: Simon and Schuster, 1969.

King, Robert L. 'Shylock after Auschwitz'. *Chicago Review* 40 (1994): 59–67.

'The Texture of Contemporary Life'. *North American Review* 280 (1995): 43–8.

Kleb, William. 'Shakespeare in Tottenham Street'. *Theatre Survey* 16 (1975): 97–120.

Kliman, Bernice W. 'The Hall–Hoffman Merchant: Which is the Anti-Semite Here?'. *Shakespeare Bulletin* 8, no. 2 (1990): 11–13.

Knight, Joseph. *Theatrical Notes* [1893]. New York: Benjamin Blom, 1972.

Krensky-Cooper, Roberta. *The American Shakespeare Theatre: Stratford, 1955–1985*. Washington: Folger Books, 1986.

Langhoff, Thomas. 'Growing Up with Shakespeare: Furthering the Tradition'. In *Redefining Shakespeare: Literary Theory and Theater Practice in the German Democratic Republic*. Ed. J. Lawrence Guntner and Andrew M. McLean. Newark: University of Delaware Press, 1998.

Leggatt, Alexander. 'The Merchant of Venice'. *Shakespeare Bulletin* 15, no. 1 (1997): 23–5.

Lelyveld, Toby. *Shylock on the Stage*. London: Routledge and Kegan Paul, 1961.

Levy, Emanuel. *The Habima: Israel's National Theatre, 1917–77*. New York: Columbia University Press, 1979.

Lichtenberg, Georg. *Lichtenberg's Visits to England*. Trans. M. Mare and W. H. Quarrell. Oxford: Clarendon Press, 1938.

Lion, Leon M. *The Surprise of My Life*. London: Hutchinson, 1948.

Liston, William T. 'The Merchant of Venice'. *Cahiers élisabéthains* 50 (1996): 87–88.

Luscombe, Christopher. 'Launcelot Gobbo in *The Merchant of Venice* and Moth in *Love's Labour's Lost*'. In *Players of Shakespeare 4*. Ed. Robert Smallwood. Cambridge: Cambridge University Press, 1998.

Macliammóir, Micheál. *All for Hecuba: An Irish Theatrical Autobiography*. London: Methuen, 1946.

Magarshack, David. *Stanislavski, A Life*. Westport, CT: Greenwood Press, 1975.

Maguin, J. M. 'The Merchant of Venice', *Cahiers élisabéthains* 20 (1981): 112–14.

Mahon, John W. 'Holbrook Triumphs as Shylock'. *Shakespeare Newsletter* 49, no. 1 (1999): 15, 24.

Marker, Lise-Lone. *David Belasco: Naturalism in the American Theatre*. Princeton: Princeton University Press, 1975.

Marowitz, Charles. 'Giving Them Hell'. *Plays and Players* (July 1977): 15–17.

   The Marowitz Shakespeare. New York: Drama Book Specialists, 1978.

Matthews, Harold. ' "Hamlet", "Othello", and "The Merchant of Venice" '. *Theatre World* (July 1956): 14–15.

McCarthy, Desmond. *Drama*, London: Putnam, 1940

McDiarmid, Ian. 'Shylock in *The Merchant of Venice*'. In *Players of Shakespeare 2*. Ed. Russell Jackson and Robert Smallwood. Cambridge University Press, 1988.

Mennen, Richard E. 'Theodore Komisarjevsky's Production of *The Merchant of Venice*'. *Theatre Journal* 31 (1979): 386–97.

Moore, Edward M. 'William Poel'. *Shakespeare Quarterly* 23 (1972): 21–36.

   'Henry Irving's Shakespearean Productions'. *Theatre Survey* 17 (1976): 195–216.

Morley, Henry. *The Journal of a London Playgoer* [1866]. Leicester: Leicester University Press, 1974.

Mr Henry Irving and Miss Ellen Terry in America: Opinions of the Press. Chicago: J. Morris, 1884.

'Mr Lawrence Barrett's Shylock'. *Shakespeariana* 3 (1886): 523–6.

Murdoch, James. *The Stage: Or Recollections of Actors and Acting* [1880]. New York: Benjamin Blom, 1969.

Newell, Alex. 'The Stratford, Ontario, Festival 1996: A Canadian's Overview'. *Shakespeare Bulletin* 15, no. 1 (1997): 20–2.

Odell, George C. D. *Annals of the New York Stage*. 15 vols. New York: Columbia University Press, 1927–49.

Shakespeare from Betterton to Irving. 2 vols. New York: Dover, 1966.

Olivier, Laurence. *Confessions of an Actor*. London: Weidenfeld and Nicolson, 1982.

Oz, Avraham. 'Transformations of Authenticity: The Merchant of Venice in Israel'. In *Foreign Shakespeare*. Ed. Dennis Kennedy. Cambridge: Cambridge University Press, 1993.

Pauley, Bruce F. *From Prejudice to Persecution: A History of Austrian Anti-Semitism*. Chapel Hill: University of North Carolina Press, 1992.

Perret, Marion D. 'Shakespeare and Anti-Semitism: Two Television Versions of *The Merchant of Venice*'. *Mosaic* 16 (1983): 145–63.

Porter, Charlotte [C.P.]. 'The Drama'. *Shakespeariana* 4 (1887): 120–4.

Potter, Lois. 'Shakespeare Performed'. *Shakespeare Quarterly* 50 (1999): 74–6.

Prior, Roger. 'A Second Jewish Community in Tudor London'. *Jewish Historical Studies* 31 (1990): 137–52.

Proudfoot, Richard. 'The 1998 Globe Season'. *Shakespeare Survey* 52 (1999): 215–28.

Pullan, Brian. *Rich and Poor in Renaissance Venice*. Oxford: Blackwell, 1971.

'A Ship with Two Rudders: Righetto Marrrano [Nunes] and the Inquisition in Venice'. *Historical Journal* 20 (1977): 25–58.

The Jews of Europe and the Inquisition of Venice 1550–1670. London: Basil Blackwell, 1983.

Quayle, Anthony. *A Time to Speak*. London: Barrie and Jenkins, 1990.

Ranald, M. L. 'The Merchant of Venice'. *Shakespeare Bulletin* 13, no. 2 (1995): 31–2.

Ravid, Benjamin. 'The Establishment of the *Ghetto Vecchio* of Venice, 1541'. *Proceedings of the Sixth World Congress of Jewish Studies* 2 (1973): 153–67.

'The First Charter of the Jewish Merchants of Venice, 1589'. *Association for Jewish Studies Review* 1 (1976): 187–222.

Rentschler, Eric. *The Ministry of Illusion*. Cambridge, MA: Harvard University Press, 1996.

Rice, Charles. *The London Theatre in the Eighteen-Thirties*. Ed. Arthur Colby Sprague and Bertram Shuttleworth. London: Society for Theatre Research, 1950.

Roberts, Peter. 'The Merchant of Venice'. *Plays and Players* (May 1960): 15.

Rosenbaum, Jonathan. 'The Invisible Orson Welles: A First Inventory'. *Sight and Sound* 55, no. 3 (1986): 164–71.

Rosenfeld, Lulla. *Bright Star of Exile: Jacob Adler and the Yiddish Theatre*. New York: Thomas Crowell, 1977.

Roth, Cecil. *Venice*. Philadelphia: Jewish Publication Society of America, 1930.
  A History of the Jews in England. 3rd edn. Oxford: Clarendon Press, 1964.
Rothwell, Kenneth. *Shakespeare on Screen: An International Filmography and
  Videography*. London: Mansell, 1990.
Rowell, George. *The Old Vic Theatre: A History*. Cambridge: Cambridge
  University Press, 1993.
Rozmovits, Linda. 'New Woman Meets Shakespeare Woman: The Struggle
  over the Figure of Portia in the Late Nineteenth and Early Twentieth
  Centuries'. *Women's History Review* 4 (1995): 441–63.
Rubinstein, W. D. *A History of the Jews in the English-Speaking World: Great
  Britain*. Houndmills, Hampshire: Macmillan, 1996.
Russell, Charles Edward. *Julia Marlowe: Her Life and Art*. New York: D.
  Appleton and Co., 1926.
Schafer, Elizabeth. *Ms-Directing Shakespeare: Women Direct Shakespeare*.
  London: Women's Press, 1998.
Scheff, Aimee. 'Oldest and Newest Merchant of Venice'. *Theatre Arts*
  (December 1952): 80–1.
Schildkraut, Joseph. *My Father and I*. New York: Viking, 1953.
Schoenbaum, S. *Shakespeare's Lives*. Oxford: Clarendon Press, 1991.
Scott, Clement. *From 'The Bells' to 'King Arthur'*. London: John Macqueen,
  1896.
  The Drama of Yesterday and Today. Vol. 1 [1899]. New York: Garland, 1986.
Sehrt, Ernst Th. 'Der Shylock Fritz Kortners'. *Shakespeare Jahrbuch West*
  (1973): 78–96.
Shaked, Gershon. 'The Play: Gateway to Cultural Dialogue'. Trans. Jeffrey
  Green. In *The Play out of Context: Transferring Plays from Culture to
  Culture*. Ed. Hannah Scolnicov and Peter Holland. Cambridge:
  Cambridge University Press, 1989.
Shapiro, James. *Shakespeare and the Jews*. New York: Columbia University
  Press, 1996.
Shapiro, Michael J. 'Shylock the Jew Onstage: Past and Present'. *Shofar* 4, no. 2
  (1986): 1–11.
  'The Merchant of Venice'. *Shakespeare Bulletin* 12, no. 4 (1994): 32–3.
Shattuck, Charles H. *Shakespeare on the American Stage: From the Hallams to
  Edwin Booth*. Washington: Folger Shakespeare Library, 1976.
  *Shakespeare on the American Stage: From Booth and Barrett to Sothern and
  Marlowe*. Washington: Folger Shakespeare Library, 1987.
Shulvass, Moses A. *The Jews in the World of the Renaissance*. Trans. Elvin I.
  Kose. Leiden: E. J. Brill, 1973.
Sinsheimer, Hermann. *Shylock, The History of the Character, or The Myth of the
  Jew*. London: Gollancz, 1947.

Smallwood, Robert. 'Director's Shakespeare'. In *Shakespeare: An Illustrated Stage History*. Ed. Jonathan Bate and Russell Jackson. Oxford: Oxford University Press, 1996.

'Shakespeare Performances in England, 1998'. *Shakespeare Survey* 52 (1999): 229–53.

'Shakespeare Performances in England, 1999'. *Shakespeare Survey* 53 (2000): 244–73.

Smith, Peter J. 'The Merchant of Venice'. *Cahiers élisabéthains* 54 (1998): 119–20.

Speaight, Robert. *Shakespeare on the Stage*. Boston: Little, Brown, 1973.

Spedding, James. *Reviews and Discussions, Literary, Political and Historical*. London: C. Kegan Paul, 1879.

Spedding, James and Robert Leslie Ellis, Douglas Denon Smith, eds. *The Works of Francis Bacon*, vol. VI. London: Longmans, 1870.

Sprague, Arthur Colby. *Shakespeare and the Actors: The Stage Business of his Plays (1660–1905)*. New York: Russell & Russell, 1944.

Shakespearian Players and Performances. London: Adam and Charles Black, 1953.

Stanley, Audrey. 'The 1994 Shanghai International Shakespeare Festival'. *Shakespeare Quarterly* 47 (1996): 72–80.

Stevenson, Laura Caroline. *Praise and Paradox: Merchants and Craftsmen in Elizabethan Popular Literature*. Cambridge: Cambridge University Press, 1984.

Stewart, Patrick. 'Shylock in *The Merchant of Venice*'. In *Players of Shakespeare 1*. Ed. Philip Brockbank. Cambridge: Cambridge University Press, 1985.

Stoll, E. E. *Shakespeare Studies*. New York: Stechert, 1942.

Stonex, A. B. 'The Usurer in Elizabethan Drama'. *PMLA* 31 (1919): 190–210.

Styan, J. L. *Max Reinhardt*. Cambridge: Cambridge University Press, 1982.

Sullivan, Patrick J. 'Strumpet Wind – The National Theatre's *Merchant of Venice*'. *Educational Theatre Journal* 26 (1974): 31–44.

Taylor, George. *Players and Performances in the Victorian Theatre*. Manchester: Manchester University Press, 1989.

Terry, Ellen. *The Story of My Life*. London: Hutchinson, 1908.

Four Lectures on Shakespeare. London: Martin Hopkinson, 1932.

Thorndike, Sybil and Russell, *Lilian Baylis*. London: Chapman & Hall, 1938.

Tocci, Margaret M. 'The Merchant of Venice'. *Shakespeare Bulletin* 6, no. 4 (1988): 19–20.

Towse, John Ranken. *Sixty Years of the Theater: An Old Critic's Memories*. New York: Funk & Wagnalls, 1916.

Tree, Herbert Beerbohm. *Thoughts and After-Thoughts*. London: Cassell, 1915.

Trewin, J. C. *Benson and the Bensonians*. London: Barrie and Rockliff, 1960.

Shakespeare on the English Stage: 1900–1964. London: Barrie and Rockliff, 1964.

Tynan, Kenneth. *Curtains*. London: Longmans, 1961.

   A View of the English Stage. London: Granada, 1976.

Valk, Diana. *Shylock for a Summer*. London: Cassell, 1958.

Velz, John W. 'The Merchant of Venice'. *Cahiers élisabéthains* 14 (1978): 100–2.

Verch, Maria. 'The Merchant of Venice on the German Stage Since 1945'. *Theatre History Studies* 5 (1985): 84–94.

Wapshott, Nicholas. *Peter O'Toole*. London: New English Library, 1983.

Ward, Royal. 'The Merchant of Venice'. *Shakespeare Bulletin* 7, no. 6 (1989): 15–16.

Warren, Roger. 'A Year of Comedies: Stratford, 1978'. *Shakespeare Survey* 32 (1979): 201–9.

   'Interpretations of Shakespearian Comedy'. *Shakespeare Survey* 35 (1981): 141–52.

Webster, Margaret. *The Same Only Different: Five Generations of a Great Theatrical Family*. London: Victor Gollancz, 1969.

Weightman, John. 'Dr Miller's Transplant'. *Encounter* 35 (July 1970): 54–6.

Welles, Orson and Peter Bogdanovich. *This is Orson Welles*. Ed. Jonathan Rosenbaum. London: HarperCollins, 1993.

Wells, Stanley. 'Shakespeare Performances in London and Stratford-upon-Avon, 1986–7'. *Shakespeare Survey* 41 (1988): 159–81.

Werblowsky, R. J. and Geoffrey Wigoder, eds. *The Oxford Dictionary of the Jewish Religion*. Oxford: Oxford University Press, 1997.

Wigoder, Geoffrey, ed. *Encyclopedia of Judaism*. New York: Macmillan, 1989.

Wilcocks, Richard. 'The Merchant of Venice'. *Plays and Players* (April 1994): 43.

Williams, Simon. *German Actors of the Eighteenth and Nineteenth Centuries: Idealism, Romanticism, and Realism*. Westport, CT: Greenwood Press, 1985.

   Shakespeare on the German Stage, Volume I: 1586–1914. Cambridge: Cambridge University Press, 1990.

Williamson, Audrey. *The Theatre of Two Decades*. London: Rockliff, 1957.

Wilson, Garff B. *A History of American Acting*. Bloomington: University of Indiana Press, 1966.

Winter, William. *Shakespeare on the Stage: First Series*. New York: Benjamin Blom, 1969.

Wistrich, Robert S. *Anti-Semitism: The Longest Hatred*. London: Thames, 1992.

Wolford, Lisa. 'Critical Responses to *The Merchant of Venice* and *The Winter's Tale*'. *Text and Performance Quarterly* 15 (1995): 157–9.

Worthen, W. B. *Shakespeare and the Authority of Performance*. Cambridge: Cambridge University Press, 1997.

Wyatt, Euphemia Van Rensselaer. 'Theater'. *Catholic World* 185 (1957): 467–9.

Yang Zhang. *Shakespeare in China: A Comparative Study in Two Traditions and Cultures*. Newark: University of Delaware Press, 1996.

Young, Stark. *Immortal Shadows*. New York: Charles Scribner's Sons, 1948.

OTHER WORKS: NON-PRINT MEDIA

Barton, John. *Playing Shakespeare*, vol. VIII. 'Exploring a Character' [video-recording]. London: RM Arts/London Weekend Television, 1983.

Gold, Jack [director]. *The Merchant of Venice* [video-recording]. London: BBC Enterprises, 1980.

Horrox, Alan [director]. *The Merchant of Venice* [video-recording]. Avalon Beach, NSW: Maxwell's Collection, 1996.

Miller, Jonathan [director]. *The Merchant of Venice* [video-recording]. London: PolyGram Video, 1992.

Silent Shakespeare [video-recording]. London: BFI, 1999.

Welles, Orson. *The Merchant of Venice* [compact disc]. Sparrows Green, UK: Pavilion Records, 1998.

INDEX